Dear Irvie, Dear Lucy,

Civil War Letters Of
Capt. Irving A. Buck
General Cleburne's AAG
& Family

Letters From The Army
and
Letters From His Home in the Shenandoah Valley

BUCK PUBLISHING COMPANY
Birmingham, Alabama

Published and distributed throughout the World by
BUCK PUBLISHING COMPANY
2409 VESTAVIA DRIVE
BIRMINGHAM, ALABAMA 35216

Edited by
Dr. William Pettus Buck

ISBN 0-934530-12-2

Library of Congress Control Number: 2002090649
Printed in Republic of Singapore

At 'Buckton' Cemetery

In the shadow of the Massanutten
The ancient Bucks repose
They slumber 'neath bright summer skies
They sleep beneath the snows.

From the waters of the Shenandoah
The Bucks have gone away
They live alas in other lands
They're unknown here today.

From those other lands where Bucks are living
They come back here with pride
To honor well while yet they may
The ancient Bucks who've died.

Walter Hooper Buck
July 20, 1951

Contents

Introduction

"A more patriotic people never lived. Here the two branches of the Shenandoah River converged in this little pocket of the Valley between the Massanutten Mountains and the mighty Blue Ridge.

This land was surveyed by the teenager George Washington, for Lord Fairfax. It was first settled by Germans immigrating from the north out of Pennsylvania. They followed the Shenandoah River south up the Valley. The English entered the Valley from the east through the old buffalo trails in the passes of the great Blue Ridge.

These early settlers, along with their leader, George Washington, fought back the Indians from their homes and small community fortresses when they were enticed by the French. They marched off with George Washington to establish Fort Necissity and Dequesne.

During the Revolutionary War, these Valley folks sent their sons to Fort Pitt while others followed Captain Morgan Alexander, 2nd Virginia Regiment to fight for independence. Others became Minute Men to fight when the alarm arose." So wrote Laura Virginia Hale, the twentieth century historian of Warren County and Front Royal, Virginia.

The first Buck to enter the Valley was Charles Buck who came in 1735, one hundred years after his grandfather, Thomas Buck landed at Jamestown.

Charles and his three sons, John, Charles and Thomas, fought the Indians and then the British. Again they fought in 1812. They named their sons for La Fayette. The Bucks, along with their kinsmen the Helms, Catletts, Blakemores, Ashbys, Baylys, Nevilles, Mauzys and Calmes were all Revolutionary War heroes.

When time came to separate from the Union, they, like the descendents of George Washington, who still lived nearby, wished to remain in the Union, the nation for which they had fought and bled. But when Virginia seceded, their inborn patriotism swelled and all cast their lot for their mother state.

Seventeen Bucks from Warren County plus 30 or more near kinsmen would bear arms for the Confederacy. They again fought for independence and against invading armies and not to perpetuate slavery.

Well before the Revolutionary War, southern colonies protested to England to stop slave trading. Virginia, in 1778, passed a law, "that from and after the passing of this act no slave or slaves shall hereafter be imported into this commonwealth by sea or land."

Other Southern states were active in stopping slave trade. Georgia, whose lands extended through what is now Alabama and Mississippi, closed slave trading in 1798.

By 1824 Tennessee had 27 branches of an abolition society. All over the South people were becoming more hostile to slavery and were making efforts to free themselves from the burden of the sin of slavery. By 1830, ten percent of Southern African Americans were free. Virginia counted 46,729 freed slaves.

While the Southern states were moving slowly toward abolition, many Northern states were terrorizing black people. Illinois passed a law that fined any free Negro $50 if they stayed in the state 10 days. If the fine was not paid, the black man or woman was to be sold! In Philadelphia and New York, Negro churches were burned, the people terrorized and many were slain by violent mobs.

In the middle and late 1800s a different type of abolitionist arose in the North. They were militant, agitators and demanded immediate and unconditional abolition without regard to the welfare of the freed slaves.

These Northern abolitionists encouraged slaves to rise up and kill their masters and families. Joshua Giddings, a great leader in Ohio, said: "I look forward to the day when the black man shall wage a war of extermination against the whites, when the master shall see his dwelling in flames and his hearth polluted; and though I may not mock at their calamity, yet I shall hail it as the dawn of a political millennium."

In October 1859, a known murderer, John Brown, and his followers took over the arsenal at Harper's Ferry, Virginia. Earlier in May 1856 he had led a band of men on a killing spree at several homes in Kansas along the Pottawatomie Creek. The first person killed by Brown's men in Harper's Ferry was a free Negro who was a train baggage master. Brown was captured, tried and hanged.

One Southerner wrote, "What surprised the South was to see his (Brown's) actions endorsed by a large portion of the North — to see requiems over the death of the 'martyred hero,' as they called him, from pulpit, press and rostrum, and bells tolling from steeples in almost every large city in the North the day he (Brown) was hanged. When we reflect what Negro insurrection meant, as Brown wished it to be, we can readily understand the revelation this evidence of feelings in his behalf was to our people in the South. That a large part of our countrymen (in the North) should allow themselves to sympathize with a plot involving the indiscriminate rape of innocent women, the subsequent murder, and murder of all children, before the men of the country could collect to prevent it, is a stain forever upon our country. This," he continued, "is when the South started to arm itself for defense."

The South as well as several New England states believed in a principle guaranteed by the Constitution; vis, that any state had the power to withdraw from the Union if it were denied its rights. Patrick Henry raised this question at the Constitutional Convention. He received the assurance from James Madison that this was the correct interpretation. Otherwise, many states, North and South, would not have adopted the Constitution.

Lincoln, on the other hand, wrote, "No state can, in any way lawfully, get out of the union, without the consent of the others." He felt the right to secede was not open to question, but had been settled by President Andrew Jackson when South Carolina expressed its "States Rights" and nullified an action regarding a tariff passed by the Federal government. But this state later backed down at President Jackson's request.

In the mid 1800s there were all sorts of sectional differences other than slavery that separated North and South. Some of these were tariffs, territorial statehood, personal antagonisms, and many other issues, including religion. The North was becoming more liberal in its religion, many adopting Unitarianism. They resented the Calvinist in the South who clung to the literal interpretation of the Bible.

The election of Lincoln came by a three-way split of the votes. He won with less than forty percent of the popular vote, but a majority of electoral votes. It was ominous that Lincoln did not receive a single vote in ten of the Southern states. Southerners had already announced that if a Republican was elected, they would secede.

Six Southern states seceded in late 1860 and early 1861. Virginia, the keystone state of the South, voted against secession. This would have been a great time to settle peacefully the issues between North and South, using Virginia as mediator. Instead, Lincoln called for 75,000 volunteers to invade the South to quell what he called "the rebellion." The border states, including Virginia, North Carolina, Tennessee and Arkansas, would not supply troops to fight their sister states and were forced to take sides. They joined the Confederacy.

Alexander H. Stephens, the vice-president of the Confederacy, wrote, "The Southern people, were willing to sacrifice property, life, everything for the cause, which was then simply the right of self-government."

Jefferson Davis stated, "We recur to the compact (Union) which binds us together; we recur to the principles upon which our government was founded; and when you deny them, and when you deny us the right to withdraw from a government which, thus perverted threatens to be destructive to our rights." He went on to say that the South would follow in the footsteps of their Revolutionary War Fathers, proclaiming their independence, wherever the cost. He added, "this is done not in hostility to others, not to injure any section of the country, not even for our own pecuniary benefit; but from the high and solemn motive of defending and protecting the rights we inherited, and which it is our sacred duty to transmit unshorn to our children."

The constitution for the Confederate States included the immediate and perpetual prohibition of the African slave trade. This statement was not included anywhere in the United States Constitution!

The term, "Confederacy of States" was first used by the colonies when they freed themselves from England. They formed a confederacy of states. The South had no desire to overthrow the existing United States Government. They desired only to separate. This is why Southerners prefer to call the war, "The War Between the States," rather than "Civil War." A Civil war is when a group overthrows, or tries to overthrow, an existing government. This was not the case in the Confederacy. With a duly elected government, the Confederate States of America established a new nation and prepared to defend themselves from Northern invaders. When war came, like their grandfathers they were fighting "the second war for independence."

The state of Virginia elected delegates to the State Convention on February 4, 1861. Of 152 delegates chosen, only about 30 were in favor of immediate secession.

Abraham Lincoln was inaugurated as the 16th President of the United States on March 4, 1861. Marcus B. Buck of Front Royal, Virginia and uncle of I.A. Buck, wrote on this date, "I apprehend blood shed and a horrible tragedy. God avert it. I still pray for peace, though almost without hope". He was to see one son killed and another severely wounded in the war.

Union forces at Fort Sumter surrendered to South Carolina troops on April 13, 1861. On April 17, 1861 the Virginia Convention passed an ordinance of secession,

103 to 46, after Lincoln issued a proclamation calling on Virginia for troops to help suppress by invasion her sister Southern states.

The various Virginia County volunteer companies were mustered into service on that same date. In Front Royal, Warren County, Virginia the Warren Rifles under the command of Capt. Robert Simpson joined other state troops and captured the armory at Harpers Ferry on April 18, 1861.

The Warren Rifles were on guard duty in Alexandria, Virginia on May 24, 1861 when the Federal Troops invaded Virginia by crossing over the Potomac River and capturing the town. The Rifles retreated to Manassas, Virginia and were mustered into Beauregard's Army of the Potomac on June 10 as Company B of the 17th Regiment Virginia Infantry, Longstreet's Corps.

The Corps headquarters was Camp Pickens near Centerville. The first major battle of the war was fought on July 21, 1861 along Bull Run near Manassas.

Alvin Buck, age 23, had been working in Hopkinsville, Kentucky before Virginia seceded. He returned home on May 22, 1861 and joined the Warren Rifles before the Battle of Bull Run (Manassas).

Irving Buck, age 21, was working in Baltimore, Maryland and had to fulfill a business promise before joining the Warren Rifles. He participated in the Battle of Bull Run as a messenger at General Beauregard's headquarters according to Thomas Robson Hay who was the editor of the republished book, *Cleburne and His Command* by I.A. Buck; McCowat-Mercer Press, Inc., Jackson, Tennessee, 1959. However, Irving's letter of July 25, 1861 and a letter to Colonel Jordon by Irving's uncle written on July 29, 1861 indicates he had not arrived with the army.

Irving A. Buck, his brother, Alvin Buck, George Williams, Benton Roy and George Hope were assigned to Col. Thomas Jordan's staff. Jordan was Chief of Staff to General Beauregard. When Beauregard was ordered west, these Front Royal, Virginia boys went along with Colonel Jordan as clerks.

Alvin and George Hope remained clerks on Beauregard's staff. George Williams became a captain on General Liddell's staff and later General Govin's staff. Benton Roy became a colonel and General Hardee's AAG. Irving Ashby Buck became captain and Gen. Patrick Cleburne's AAG.

After the war, Irving wrote the book, *Cleburne and His Command*, published by the Neale Publishing Company in 1908. This book has become a classic for the study of the Army of Tennessee.

These letters are mainly those written home by Captain Irving Ashby Buck. However, for a complete overview, additional correspondence from his brother, Alvin Duvall Buck, his mother, sisters, and a few others are included.

These letters which are over 100 years old are frail and some words are illegible. When the word is totally indistinguishable, a blank space occurs.

William Pettus Buck

Peace
(Before Virginia Seceded)
February 10, 1860 - April 18, 1861

Bel Air

Feb. 10, 1860

(I.A. Buck's home in Front Royal, Virginia)

It is your time to get a letter now is it not Irvie dear? I will do my best towards writing you one but I fear it will prove a very uninteresting one owing to lack of news.

We received your favor of the 7th instant this morning with the corks for both of which I am desired to thank you. The corks have not been tried yet but I presume they will suit very well. I must tell you what I have been doing since my return. I generally hear the children's lessons in the morning and draw, then I mount on old John with Cary for escort and take a trot somewhere. I rode down to see Eltie the other morning then went around by Uncle Tom's and then called at the Academy. I mean to become a very accomplished horsewoman if possible. I sew and housekeep in the afternoon and play and sing and read aloud to Father during the evenings. I almost wish you were here sometimes to divide the attentions of the children for they overpower me with their condescensions.

The young men held their debating society last evening and as Nellie, Laura and myself *(all sisters)* promised to stay at Uncle Tom's we all went down from there to the Academy to hear them. There was a large audience but I fancy they were not much edified, for the attempt at argument was rather a lame one: the question debated was, "Is it better for Virginia to cease making appropriations for internal improvements?" Vic Brown and Capt. Simpson took the affirmative and John Johnston and Mr. Overall the negative side of the question. Mr. Simpson's arguments were pretty good, and Johnston made a very witty reply, but I thought both lacked solidity. I enjoyed myself a good deal however in the first part of the evening as Scott and Benton Roy and Mack Wells came around to pay their respects and "Gossip" a little. The juveniles hold their debate this evening but as their "thoughts are very tender" and their "ideas are but just learning to shoot" they do not admit ladies yet.

Cousin Harriet Richardson departed this life yesterday morning at five o'clock and was buried today and cold as it is Father, Uncle Tom and Aunt Betty have gone up there. I feel very sorry for Ginnie. She will feel so very desolate now and Cousin Marcus too: I do not know what they intend doing.

Willie was pleased with the purchase you made for him, indeed I think you have been fortunate in giving general satisfaction in that line. I sent Cousin Sue her

16

books but have not seen her since my return. Do not blame her if she does not answer your letter immediately as it was misplaced when I first arrived and I could not send it to her as soon as I should have done.

How I wish I could have been at the Institute Tuesday evening to enjoy the lecture: you must attend them frequently and write me all about them.

And now dear Irvie, I want to say to you "Remember there is no such word as fail!" I think if you will stick to your business (I am sure you do) you must certainly succeed and then think what a pride we will all feel in your success. I have missed you much since I left and think very often of you in the evening wondering if you miss me or the "saucer" which I used to keep for you. Well I think we will enjoy ourselves when we meet next summer and oh! won't we have fishing parties, horse-back parties and picnics and mountain excursions and "lots of fun". It will not be my fault if we don't.

The little boy *(Evred Buck, a young brother was born Jan. 9, 1860)* is really a bright, intelligent looking infant and may some day take the place that Irvie now does at home. Apropos to that, you scamp! Why did you not deliver up that lock of hair which Ma sent me? I did not hear a word about it until since I returned.

Thank Uncle John for his letter which I have just received and tell him I will respond to it very soon. It was so kind in him to be as punctual as he was. He speaks of Mr. Reeves affliction in it. I am sorry to hear he is compelled to play the invalid. Tender him my sympathies and condolements.

When you see Cousin Clara remember me affectionately to her — and Mrs. Hinman too. Tell the latter how much I regretted not being able to call to see her again before I left. Now Irvie, do try to write us very often and tell us all about your progress, etc.

All unite with me in love to Uncle John, Cousins Mary and Elizabeth and last but certainly not least yourself.

Yours fondly,
Lucie
(Lucy Rebecca Buck, age 18, Irving's sister)

Have not heard from Alvin *(their older brother)* for some time, have you? I send Cousin Mary a little sketch I made this morning just to prove to her that I followed her advice and have not been idle.

Father bids me thank you for the stock cover and says it does not matter about your getting the paper as he purchased such as I am writing on for fourteen cts. cheaper than you can get it in Baltimore. Hurrah for old Front Royal!

Bel Air
Feb. 26, 1860

Dear Irvie:

As Ma is complaining so much today it again falls to my lot to write you this week.

I received a letter by Willie Rust from Cousin Mary and Cousin Elizabeth yesterday saying they were going to Hopkinsville soon. I am sure you will miss them very much. I feel so sorry that they are going away. Mary Miller was married to Rippetoe very secretly this morning. No one knew anything of it and no one was present except Hamp. They were married early and came on down to church and are to return home I think this afternoon. I do not what they intend doing or where they intend going. Poor Mary! I fear, from all I can hear, that he has not espoused <u>her</u> but only her <u>money</u>. She is a nice girl and I should be sorry if her life be not happy.

Cousin Sue *(Sue Buck, of Mountain View)* came over Wednesday evening and stayed until yesterday morning when she and Nellie *(Nellie Buck, Lucy's sister, 16)* and I drove out to Mrs. Simpson's and spend the day, indeed we had quite a dinner party. Miss Jackson, a Miss Williams, Cousin Sue, Nellie, myself, Mack Wells and the three Misses Simpson. Benton *(Roy)* came out in the afternoon but we left soon after his arrival. Capt. Bob *(Capt. Robert Simpson)* made himself very agreeable as <u>he</u> thought but <u>I</u> thought rather the reverse. Charley Buck *(Sue Buck's brother, age 18)* brought horses and we went to Mountain View and stayed all night. I do feel so sorry for poor Cousin Sue and do not know how she manages to be as cheerful as she is. Uncle Newton *(Dr. Newton Buck of Mountain View)* is very low-spirited. Cousin Sue says she sends a box to Cousin Mack by Uncle Marcus Buck and if he does not go on to Philadelphia she wishes you to forward it to him yourself.

Aunt Betty and Uncle Tom *(Ashby of Oakley)* are here and send love to you. Dick (Buck) and Uncle Mack *(Marcus Blakemore Buck of Belmont)* are in the other room but I have not been in to see them yet.

I will not write you any more now as I may write again during the week and besides Uncle Mack can give you all the news.
All send love,
Fondly yours,
Lucie

Bel Air
April 1st, 1860

Dear Irvie,

I guess you think your Bel Air correspondents are very remiss, but certainly not more so than you are. You lazy fellow! Why have you not dropped us a line to let us know how your cold is. I know you are very busy now and after working hard all day do not feel very like writing at night — so upon the whole I suppose we will have to excuse you if you should happen to neglect us.

Uncles Tom and Mack and Cousin Sue Richardson started for Kentucky Thursday. Uncle Mack speaks of going no further than Cincinnati and returning in a week or so but I think he will lodge in Hopkinsville before he comes back. Uncle Tom has business to attend to in the lower part of the state and Cousin Sue will spend her time between her two Uncles Tom and John Richardson. They will be at home in three or four weeks.

I staid three or four days at Rose Hill last week and spent a day with Cousin Sue at Riverside and enjoyed myself considerably. Mr. McEwin's day for preaching. Aunt Letitia *(Jane Letitia Bayly Buck)* and Dick *(her son)* came down this morning *(from Belmont)* and we all went to church together. Ma and grandma were at Zion, but Aunt Letitia came home and dined with us. Poor thing! I feel so sorry for her. She is so much excluded from all society and misses it so much *(living on the mountain)*. She has just received a long and satisfactory letter from Walter *(her son)* of which she is justly proud. Uncle Fayette *(Thomas Fayette Buck of Clover Hill)* frequently hears from Henry *(his son)* and he always writes as if he was well pleased with his situation.

Father was very much pleased with his visit to Baltimore. Oh! I must not forget a commission which I have for you. Father got me a pair of boots from his old shoe maker on the corner (you know him) with the privilege of returning them if they did not suit. They are entirely too large and I wish you to exchange them for a pair the size of the shoe sent and also get me two yards of trimming like the piece sent. I will ask Father where he got it and write you. You can send them up by Mr. Miller, or before if you have a good opportunity.

Perhaps you have heard that Cousin Sue Buck intended uniting with the old school *(hard shell)* Baptist church this month. It is not generally known here and will, I guess create some surprise. There is to be preaching in the Episcopal church tomorrow and Ellen and Carrie Brown and perhaps Col. and Mrs. Jacobs will be confirmed by old Bishop Meade.

Poor Uncle John! *(John Newton Buck, Lucy's father's youngest brother's wife died April 1, 1859.)* I know this is a sad day with him bringing with it so many recollections. I have been intending to write him some time during this week. Thank him for the pretty box he sent me and also the remaining presents.

Aunt Calmes *(Henrietta Chew Buck Calmes, widow of Spencer Calmes [1771-1854] of Kentucky, lived at Bel Air)* is very particular in sending her love and says I must tell you how she wants to see you and what a long time has elapsed since you were here last Christmas.

Well I must close. All unite with me in love.

Hastily and affectionately,

Lucie

Get the shoes with heels. Uncle John has some change to pay for the trimming.

Bel Air, April 1st, 1860

Dear Irving,

As Lucie is writing I thought I would write to you. Little Ma and Grandma went to Zion today. Mr. Simpson spent the day here and is going to stay all night here. Francis Peterson and myself may be will to given to us Easter. The baby is very unwell he has caught cold and Ma has a bad cold so we all have cold. Willie *(William Richardson Buck, age 5)* is as frisky as ever. Nannie *(Annie Neville Buck, sister, age 8)* has got a new song, Lollie Lollie eat my <u>roach</u> ly ly. She brakes out every five minutes and sings it. Alick *(servant)* sprained his back and Father feared that he would be cripple for life. He can work a little now. Harriet *(servant)* has a daughter which is of course is the sweetest, the dearest little thing that ever lived. The baby is tuning his pipes. Ellie is snoring away so happily on the bed.

I must close. Give my love to all. Excuse all mistakes.

Ever yours truly,
Laura V. Buck *(sister to Irving Buck)*

Bel Air Apr. 9, 1860

Dear Irvie:

I know you will be looking for a letter from some of us and as I have not answered your letter received last week, I have concluded to do so this evening, should have done soon yesterday but have neither time nor opportunity. it was a day of confusion and bustle with us. it being our regular meeting day and besides your Cousin Sue was baptised. also Mrs. Vincent. I do not think I ever looked on a sweeter face so calm and placid. it was indeed a lovely sight. many who witnessed it said it was the most impressive scene they ever witnessed. she had taken cold and was sore and stiff in her limbs she could scarcely walk. but after it was over was like a different person. Aunt Gusie was very prudent and insured affection. Uncle N. was gratified but distressed that he could not go with her. said he felt that she had been taken and he left. I have had a quiet day today. Ella and Laura are at Uncle N's. Your Grandma and Aunt Betsy are in town, Orville and Cary have gone to the river fishing. your Father and Lucy took a ride up the grade and I was left with Aunt *(Calmes)* and the little children and have been _____ much nurse as it is holy day. Lucy and your Father have arrived and he has just started to your Uncle Mack's. I received a letter from your Uncle Tom *(Ashby)* today from Lexington, Ky. it was post marked last Tuesday. I do not much think he will go to see Alvin as he is already anxious to get home unless he should be detained by business in which event he may go. it is only sixty or seventy miles. your Uncle Mack returned Friday night but I have heard nothing from his trip. what do you think? John Williams is going to be married. it has only been a few weeks since Lucy received a most disgusting letter from him in which he wanted to die right away. he says he had once hoped to be happy but now he has nothing to live for and is only living because he is obliged but hopes to meet her in Heaven never to be separated. he says he knows he once held a place in her affections but thinks we have prevented her writing to him. but begs her not to grieve for him. I wish you could see the letter. she has answered it cooly but kindly saying her parents never had prevented her from corresponding with anyone and she was sorry if he had misconstrued her feelings for him that was not her fault as she had never been anything than Cousinly. about the times he must have received her answer he sent us tickets to his wedding. we had such a laugh at her and she enjoyed it as much as any of us. she says she was expecting to receive his obituary. I expect Cousin Sam Richardson's estate will make their money out of Patterson as his farm will be sold soon. your Aunt Bettie *(Ashby)*, Cousin Sue and myself expect to go to Winchester soon now if I am well enough. I am and have been quite unwell for some time have something of erysipelas my ankle is much swollen from it and I have a bad cough. your Uncle John wishes to know what kind of shoes Lucy wants. She says she gave you instructions about them. Dick was here today and will be back after awhile. he was talking of joining a fishing party. I heard yesterday that your Cousin Sandy *(William Alexander Buck)* had engaged in business with Geo. B. and Mr. Cattlett and have gone out. I have just written to Alvin have not heard from him for several weeks. I must close. our love to your Uncle John and believe me

Your devoted Mother
E.A. Buck *(Elizabeth Ann Ashby Buck)*

Baltimore, Md.
November 27, 1860

Dear Lucy,

Upon looking over my letters, I find myself two in your debt, but I will write one long one and let that go for both.

Your last letter ended very abruptly, when you were upon a very interesting subject — the intended visit of Miss Maggie, I am at a loss to know if it was mailed before you finished it or if you did it to tease me.

We have had some very cold weather in the last few days, but it has been raining like "blazes" this morning and the weather has moderated greatly. I went to Westminester Church on Sunday and met Mr. and Mrs. Gist and Mrs. Lambdin and went home with them. It is the first time I have seen them for two months. After scolding me, they enquired very particularly after you and regretted that you were not going to return to Baltimore this winter.

There were two or three Palmetto flags hoisted here yesterday and the blue cockades are getting plentiful on our streets. One flag was hoisted on the Liberty Street engine house and there was considerable excitement there last night in consequence of speeches etc.

I suppose that Uncle John is with you by this time — I was very much surprised to hear the death of John Farney.

I have received two or three letters from Alvin. Lately he is getting more punctual than he used to be.

I wrote to Willie Richardson a long letter a few weeks ago but have received no reply. This is the second time that I have written and received no reply — blow him up when you see him.

It will be impossible for me to get up home at Christmas. Not even Miss Maggie's visit (that tempting bait you held out) can get me away. If Miss M. will remain until the 1st of January: I will try very hard to spend a month with you and she may take all the credit of my coming to Front Royal, "great inducement that".

Cousin Elizabeth is living on Eutaw Street, but I do not know what number or I would have gone to see her.

I have not been out to Pikes Peak for a long time but will go out sometime this week.

Have the Warren Rifles received their caps? If they have, I wish they would forward me the money.

Everything is so dull that I have no news.

Love to all — Ever your affectionate brother,
Irving A. Buck

I have postponed that above named long letter until the next time.

1861

My Dear Sister Lou

Lest you again get up steam and come at me for my not talking to you enough, I expect I had better get about replying to your lengthy letter of March 1st which I have perused again, and again, with uncommon interest. Having taken a whiff of the "calumet of peace" you offer me, I find its fumes more fragrant than those of the best "Havannas" of which I should be a good judge, for (to my discredit) many of them have desecrated my lips since they uttered a kind word in your ear. Your grateful messages to Cousin Mollie C and my little ministering spirits, Ret and Millie made them so happy, that I am sorry they were not sent long ago — though this is no fault of yours. They return love enough to break the back of a mule and of course flimsy paper such as this will not bear it. Ret *(Henrietta Major, they were married in 1867 and had 10 children)* says <u>she</u> would be more than delighted to accompany me to Virginia in July, but it seems impossible for her to do it on account of that all pervading malady — "hard times". "Dough" is very scarce in the pockets of your Elder Brother, but if the Lord is willing I'll try to rake enough together about the 15 July to pay my expenses to the "Y" *(Railroad spur in Front Royal)* and I can work my passage from there, across the fields home. Our meeting is still in progress with now and then a convert. Tell Walter, our friend Tom Bryant is a seeker. Oh Lucy! you cannot imagine the interest I take in this young man, and when he could no longer resist the earnest appeals made to him from the pulpit and went forward, I had feelings which had been first stirred up upon seeing Walter take the same step. How I wish our dear Father could be brought under the influence of sermons which seem daily to be thrown away upon this sin hardened and rebellious people.[1] There is a young minister with us from Paducah who preaches the most powerful sermons I ever heard. I am sorry to find from Ma's last that Uncle Tom has gotten into a difficulty with that little puppy Bob Simpson; he has been sadly in need of a good "larruping" ever since I can remember, and the sooner some man condescends to administer it, the better.[2] From your description of Nell she must be a paragon of loveliness, unsurpassed by any one — <u>except</u> the Dolcinea of your Brother Alvin. I have an invitation to a wedding on Wednesday night, but don't think I shall go. Name this to Walter and tell him the parties to it are Mr. McCombs and Miss Julia Glass. Miss G is one of the prettiest girls I ever saw and has wrecked several barks of hope in the hearts of our Boys. Your "<u>Uncle Fred</u>" never went in very heavy with her, and consequently has nothing to lament over. As to my adventures of this kind of affairs, I promise you many hearty laughs when we meet.

Who do you refer to as thinking so highly of Pat *(Irving Buck)* — the Rascal! he keeps perfectly mute upon this subject to me.

Please confer the favor upon me of breaking a broom stick over Walter's skull when next you see him for not writing to me. My thanks to Ma for her letter. Love to each and all. Write soon.

As ever your affectionate Brother
Alvin

Preparation For War
April 18, 1861 - July 21, 1861

Baltimore
April 25, 1861

Dear Father

Your and Lucys letters reached me yesterday evening. I have written home three or four times with in the last week but I doubt about your having received them as all mail communication is cut off between Washington and Alexandria and the branch of the Balt & Ohio RR from the Relay to Washington is in the hands of the government.

I wrote to Dick yesterday at the Ferry, but from your letters I suppose he left a day or two ago. I am very sorry to hear that he was unwilling to go with the rest of the company, but do not believe that it was the want of courage but on account of his health.

It is impossible for me to leave here now, we are doing nothing it is true, but I am so situated that I can not get away. I tended my resignation to Mr. Boyd, night before last, but he would not accept it — he asked me to take a walk with him and during it, I brought up business as the topic, he said that he had a larger force than the business justified, and that although it was against his wishes but that he would be compelled to ship some of them, I then told him that I was of his opinion and made him this proposition, "that I would give up my situation stop my salary and go home, and that if things brightened up that he would let me resume my place" — but he said no that I was very useful to them, and that they wished to keep me, but he is going to discharge <u>two</u> or <u>three</u> that sell <u>four times the amount of goods that I do</u> — he said further (what I consider to be a great compliment) that they <u>never had a young man in their employment</u> that they <u>esteemed</u> more and they would advance me as rapidly as possible. I then asked if they would have employment for me all the summer he said yes, but that I could have a month or six weeks to spend at home this summer. Now don't you think that I had better hold on here?

You all seem to be unnecessarily alarmed about me, if you could peep in and see us all sitting in the counting room, or around the door singing, whittling, and cracking jokes you would not think that we were very badly frightened — its true that the town is full of soldiers, ready to fight till death if the enemy attempts to pop through our city, but I know that things here in Baltimore have been very much exaggerated, as I see by extracts from other papers but we did drive the Massachusetts troops back with nothing but brick-bats throwing stones, as our people were unarmed. If they had have been not one of them would ever have gotten back.

I have been employed for several days in making cartridges. I don't know that I shall ever use them, but like "Toodles" think they are "so handy to have in the house".

Lloyd Logan was in Philadelphia when the Massachusetts troops returned and he pretended that he was a republican so as to hear their account of the fight — you would hurt yourself laughing to hear the old fellow tell it — he says that one fellow said that the boys fifteen years old in Baltimore could whip the devil, he said that if they stooped down to get a rock that the paving stones would meet their hands half way and when they pointed their guns that they would hit them on the head with rocks and knock them down before they could pull trigger. *(On April 19, 1861, the Sixth Massachusetts was on its way to Washington. Southern sympathizers erected barricades in the streets of Baltimore and the troops had to fight their way through. At least nine civilians and four soldiers were killed.)*

I know a young man about my size who lives a few doors above us, who was coming from the Post office at the time the fight occurred, he was unarmed but rushed into the ranks of the enemy and caught one of them by the coat collar, and tore it off, and then took his musket and cartridge box from him, a police officer who saw it stepped up to arrest the young fellow, who told him if he put his hand on him he would run the bayonet through him (the officer) and then shoot the load into him, the officer thought he had better let him alone. The young fellow then brought his spoils out to the store, where they now hang as "trophies". I know a number of instances of young fellows knocking soldiers down with their fists and taking their weapons.

Fifty thousand men could not pass through here to day. A great many families have left the city. Mr. Shipe is ready to leave at moments notice. He wants to take me with him, he will go by private conveyance.

Mrs. Stuart (Aunt Betsy's niece) died on Sunday night. I am not going to enlist in any company but fight on my own, and if I am drafted will go to Va and join the Warren Rifles.

I will follow your advice and keep out of mobs and out of the way of brick bats and C and will not burn any powder unless they attempt to force troops through here, and then I know you would not wish me to stand by and see them go through without having a shot at them.

Say to Ma and the girls that even if I did go home that I would join the Warren Rifles immediately, for I am sure I would not stay at home while all the rest of the young men were fighting for their rights.

Please give the enclosed note to Warren — I may not write again for a week so don't be uneasy.

Send all of your letters via Winchester as I get them two days sooner than the old route. I have just heard that the Port of Baltimore is blockaded.

Love to all — let me hear from you soon

Ever your affectionate son
Irving A Buck

Oak Grove, Kentucky
April 27, 1861

Dear Lucy

I received your letter on yesterday morning just five minutes previous to leaving Town for this place, and will make a hasty reply which must suffice for the present.

Alf Parkins *(Alfred Parkins along with Walter Buck joined Capt. Bowen's Warren County Cavalry Company on June 29, 1861. This became Co. E. 7th Virginia Cavalry)* and I came down for the purpose of getting horses and joining a cavalry company which will leave in a week or less for some scene of action — The community around here will furnish horses and equipments of every sort, and we will be at no expense whatever — cousin Alick and Willie *(Blakemore)* are members and Mack Blakemore *(Marcus N. Blakemore)* will join today — We can't tell yet to what point we will go, but suppose will be ordered to Paducah to unite with a large body there and then move on to attack Cairo, at which place about 6,000 federal troops are collected—or we may be sent to Cin or Washington—If to the latter — I will try to get up to see you all, provided some Yankee don't bag me—

Our company will number about 100 men — Cousin George B and Cous Newt Catlett are very anxious to go, but having families they must stay at home — They have however joined the Home Guard. I am sorry to have to leave H and part with all my friends there — but duty calls — There is a bare possibility that I may yet have to remain on account of not getting a good horse but I am making my arrangements to go—

Will leave for Town this evening to finish preparations — This Country is arming all around and things are gloomy —

Will write again in a day or so — After I am off direct to Hopkinsville as I can get letters better from that point than from any other—

Remember me affectionately to all —

May God protect you all is my prayer —

Truly your affectionate brother,
Alvin

Baltimore
May 13th 1861

Dear Father,

Your note was received on Saturday evening, and I had to read it the second time before I could fully understand it — your views coincide with mine exactly, as I had made up my mind to stay here and let circumstances guide my future movements.

When I wrote to Nellie, I had upon the impulse of the moment concluded to go to Virginia, as I had just heard some very exciting news from Harpers Ferry, but upon reflection, I determined to stay and attend to my business as Mr. Boyd seems anxious that I should remain with them and perhaps I will not be needed at all in Virginia, but if I should be depend upon it I will be at my post as soon as possible.

I do my best to keep my tongue and temper and frequently I say things upon the spur of the moment that I would not upon cool reflection.

I have no idea what our house will do, but think it likely that they will go to Richmond or some other point in Virginia, but where ever it may be I will go with them. I don't know why it is but they seem to place more confidence in me than in any other employee in the house, the book keeper excepted; its done in little things, for instance I have charge of the keys of the store, a thing that no other man in the house ever did, and when they receive goods they always give me the bill to see that they are all right with the instructions not to let any of the other men see them. I only mention these things to show you that its best for me to stay here on a small salary than to make a change, even if I received a little more, in the store I am perfectly respectful to Mr. Boyd, and always obey every order, without stopping to ask why it should be done, but at the Hotel or in our room at night (I am sleeping with him while Mr. P's away) I am perfectly free and easy, and am as "big a man" as he is.

I have reasons to believe that he is going to give me more than he said, first they have discharged clerks, whose salaries amounted to $2500, and secondly I wanted to draw a months salary and instead of saying how much he would give me asked what amount I would want and upon my repeating my first request he said that he would arrange that, but wanted to know how much I needed, at that time.

It made me feel sad when I read Ma's letter stating how you were all economizing. I myself have not bought a rag of clothing yet but shall be obliged to do so, as I am getting shabby, but a dollar never looked so large to me before, and I have not spent a single dollar unnecessarily since my return here.

I owe Lucy and Ma a letter but they will have to take this for an answer as one letter a week is as much as I can afford.

You must not judge any thing by my letters to the girls, as I write just as I feel and my letter partake of the mood I am in, and I often say things I do not think.

I feel the deficiency of my education more every day, but have no chance to improve it now. I would gladly follow your suggestions, but am so frequently interrupted that I could not read to my own satisfaction or benefit. Mr. Shipe has not yet left the city. I see by the Gazette that they have changed the time of the trains upon the Manassas Road.

Mr. Shipe requested to be remembered to you all.

Ever your affectionate son,

Irving A. Buck

June 6, 1861
Front Royal

Dear Dick,

I have been intending to write to you for several days, but you get so many letters from here that I suppose you are posted as to what little is going on in this place.

I have been home nearly a week. I left Baltimore very unexpectedly and will go back one day this week.

I am very anxious to join your company but circumstance I am afraid will prevent it. When I look around and find that all of my young friends are in ranks to fight against the invaders of old Virginia and see that my house is not represented it makes me feel ashamed and when I go back to Baltimore I will try to arrange things so that I can strike a blow for her.

I wrote to you while you were at the Ferry but do not suppose that you received the letter.

Front Royal is very dull, more so than I ever thought it could be, but there are no young men left.

Alvin is still here. I have no idea what he will do.

There are three very nice young ladies at the Hotel. I like them very much.

I expect to get back from Baltimore about the 1st of July and I hope that I may by that time be able to be with you.

Col Bowen is here trying to get up a company, but is progressing very slowly, but as there is a prospect of the Malitia being drafted I think that his ranks will fill up more rapidly.

I was up to your house a day or two ago, all were well. They are very anxious about Walter, but between I and you I do not believe that he is coming back.

I hope that you are having better weather than we have, for it has been trying to rain for two or three days.

I have no news to write, but drop you these few lines to let you see that I have not forgotten you.

Remember me to Benton, Scott, Charlie's B. & R., and all the boys.

Ever your affectionate cousin,
Irving

Taylors Hotel
June 10, 1861

Dear Father

When arriving here we found reports so unfavorable that I concluded not to attempt to carry the horse through.

Mr. Cloud and myself expect to take the cars for the Ferry tomorrow morning and will stage it from there to Frederick.

Everything very dull here — some few soldiers passing. Mr. Shipe will give you the news.

Ever your affectionate son,

Irving

Frederick
June 11, 1861

Dear Father

We arrived here safely about an hour since and will proceed to Baltimore by the 8 o'clock train in the morning and as there is a friend here who speaks of going to Winchester in the morning I will get him to carry this.

We had great difficulty in getting out of the Ferry *(Harpers Ferry)*, had we not met Jim Washington we could not possibly have gotten through.

I suppose that you have heard of the battle near Fortress Monroe — it will be rather a damper to Gen Butler. I saw Smith Turner at the Ferry. We came from there in a stage and expect to be in Baltimore to dinner.

I do not know when I shall be able to write again so don't be uneasy if you do not hear from me as from all I can hear things are more quiet than I expected to find them.

Write by first opportunity.

Love to all,

Ever your affectionate son,

Irving

June 1861
Camp Pickens, Saturday 22nd

Dear Lu

I rec^d your note on yesterday and must acknowledge my delinquency in opening our correspondence, but upon the first evening I was here I sent you all a message by Uncle Mack and the next day one by Capt. S.B. Gardner *(owned farm south of Front Royal)*, so I considered it unnecessary to write until yesterday, and then no one went up whom I knew.

This place suits me to a "T". I am perfectly at home among the Boys and am getting along well in drilling.

Tell Father I send my valise up by the train and would like for him to get the committee to forward me one of Blockley's knapsacks immediately. Have gotten a blanket here. Capt. Simpson is very polite. We are looking to be ordered off daily. Take a prisoner or two every day and some of them are very saucy. Tell Miss Nannie

Taylor I have tried to get the S.C. button for her but have not succeeded. All well. Love to all.

Alvin

Those N.O. Zouaves or "Tigers" Uncle Jon *(John Newton Buck)* spoke of arrived this morning. They are a hard set.

If any letters come from the West please forward immediately.

Camp Pickens
June 24, 1861

Dear Ma

Your note was handed me this morning — I was advised by the officers not to send my valise up, until my knapsack came so I kept it — My box goes up to day—

Please send some sausages if you have enough to spare — We can't tell at what time we may be ordered off — I am ready to go at any moment, for the sooner Washington is taken, the better —

We have gotten tents and are pitching them today — Charley Buck, Dick and I are in the same sleeping squad and will tent together — Troops from the South are continually coming in, and I think affairs in this quarter of the state are approaching a crisis —

Love to all including F̲a̲n̲n̲i̲e̲ ̲S̲t̲u̲a̲r̲t̲ *(Belle Boyd's cousin and Mr. Stewart was proprietor of the hotel in Front Royal)* and the "Taylor Girls" —

Truly your affectionate son
Alvin

Camp Pickens
June 30, 1861

Dear Lu

Received your acceptable note this morning from Billy Richardson *(William Millar Richardson, lived at Rose Hill)*.

It has been raining this morning and camp wears a desolate aspect.

All the troops except those in our Brigade (three Regiments) have left and I suppose we are to lie around here this summer to protect baggage. Our Boys are rearing about it and I really think it hard. When I volunteered it was with the expectation of fighting and not being an army-follower. I was unwell several days last week but am now o.k.

Billy Richardson belongs to our mess.

You can pass the lines on I expect as well as before — Velvet is all right on my pants.

31

We have lots of artillery, and many pieces are mounted around here of large size (32 pounder's). I am without want now except to move on towards Washington.

Love to all

Truly your affectionate Brother
Alvin

Army in Camp near Manassas, Virginia
after Battle of First Manassas
July 21, 1861 - January 25, 1862

Front Royal, Va
July 25th 1861

Dear George *(George Williams)*

Your kind letter was received a week ago and I would have answered sooner, but I know that they write to you from home frequently and keep you posted in what little news we have.

It is needless to tell you how the news of the two victories were received here, tho' at first we got very exaggerated accounts.

I would have been down before this but have been sick, and without a uniform, but I have almost recovered and nearly ready and will certainly be down on Monday if not sooner.

I see by the papers that if persons passing over the road has not a permit that they will have to pay their own fare if it is customary. I wish you would procure one for me, as I am going to fight for Jeff and the Confederacy. I wish them to pay all expenses — please attend to this.

I wish that you could come up for a few days for you would have a good time. All are well. Remember me to Alvin, Benton and all the boys.

Write me by return train

Ever your friend
Irving A. Buck
Can I attend to any thing for you?

Front Royal Warren Co. Va
July 29th 1861

Col. Thomas Jordan[3]
Dear Sir,

The bearer of this my nephew Irving A. Buck Esq. goes to the junction with the view of uniting with the "Warren Rifles" a volunteer company from this county of which his brother Alvin with several relatives are members; but in the past few days has learned there has been a good deal of dissatisfaction upon the part of the company against their commander and very prudently he wishes to defer his connection with them 'till after the disturbance shall have ended. Irving is deservedly one of the most popular young men I ever knew — a universal favorite with all his acquaintances, possessing the happy gift of winning the affections of his seniors as also those of younger years. His moral character is unsurpassed with a most pleasant and cheerful disposition. Having understood you were wanting an additional number of scribes, I would be gratified if you would give him such a situation in that department as may be at your disposal — feeling confident he will render satisfaction in every particular.

Suffer me to congratulate you with others in the command of our army, for the great victory at Stone Bridge upon the 21st inst.

Hoping the "God of battles" will continue to rest with us, I am

Yours very respectfully
Thomas A. Ashby *(Irving's uncle)*

Head Quarters
August 11, 1861

Dear Lucy,

Cousin Willie arrived this morning bringing your and Ma's letters and says that the feed is over at the Depot. We will have them brought over immediately and tend you our thanks.

Our boys were ordered to Fairfax Court House yesterday and not to Leesburg as you suppose.

Say to Alvin that Mosely was taken sick day before yesterday and has gone home on two week's leave. Benton *(Roy)*, George *(Williams)*, and myself have been quite busy in consequence of so many of our clerks being absent.

The Prince Napoleon was here day before yesterday, he looks like a lager beer drinking son of Germany. He is not unlike Sam Thomas — looked quite shabby and dirty and was dressed in a linen coat and straw hat. He and General Beauregard stood and spluttered some kind of jaw smashing French and then rode over the battlefield.

I put my clothes in a carpet bag of Benton's and will send them up this evening.

I think that our Head Quarters is an unhealthy situation. Several persons are sick now and two negro men have died since Alvin left here.

Thank Aunts Betsy *(Elizabeth Almond Ashby)* and Calmes *(Henrietta Chew Buck Calmes)* for the pears and peaches and tell them I will eat and think of them.

When you see Miss Bell again remember me affectionately and piously to her, and ask her why she did not reply to my note (which I never wrote, but you need not tell her that).

I mean to try for a leave to go to Richmond. Every person tells me that I am not a member of any company and do not belong to the army as I have never been mustered in or drilled with the company. I am going to ask Col. Jordan and if I am not, I am going down to F.C. House and join so as to draw my pay, but before I go down, I will come home.

Love to all, ever your affectionate Brother,

Irving

Send me two or three good steel pens.

Head Quarters

1st Corps. Army of the Potomac

Manassa, August 21st, 1861

Dear Lucy:

Benton *(Roy)* and myself have just returned from a walk, we went over to see the Mississippi dress parade and to hear the band all of which was very nice and finely finished by your lengthy and highly interesting letter which was handed me by Alvin a few moments ago (he having taken the first benefit). The contents of your epistle are noted and in truly business like style I will reply to your enquiries in rotation.

As to my health let me assure you that I am eating my rations and am as hearty as a rhinoceros. The day that George *(Williams)* left I believe I was a little unwell, had over eaten myself perhaps you may depend upon it that I will come home if I get sick. We have plenty of time for sleep and recreation, and are not over worked by any means, tho we have more of it to do now than formerly on account of so many of our clerks being absent.

I did not see Bob Roy *(Negro Freeman at Bel Air)* when he was down here, although I heard from him. Was very sorry to hear of the loss of the horses but Father will get paid for them in the first place <u>Lersuer</u> had no right to press it.

In regard to my pants I did upset the ink stand upon them fortunately they were an old pair that I brought along for office use and I think that the map of North America I made on them was rather an improvement, it does not matter any way as we are a very tidy set down here.

I have done nothing in regard to joining a company, everyone tells me that I am not a member and drawing no pay, but I don't care a straw either way.

I am very glad that Dick *(Buck)* got an extension of his leave as I think that he deserves it and hope that he may have a good time.

Receive the thanks of the mess for the coffee, but this morning we succeeded in getting some of the genuine but will keep the rye for a rainy day.

Our mess is composed of ten, three of whom are away and we draw rations for fifteen. We have been living very well since the arrival of the basket, have for breakfast beef hash, broiled ham, toast, coffee, milk and butter when we pay 25 cts. for it — for dinner roast beef, tomatoes, corn, rice, bread and bacon — supper coffee, bread, meat and when Mrs. Hope's *(lived near the mill below Bel Air)* box comes, honey. For dessert we have all manner of jokes and sharp remarks from the smart men that make up the party. Gen. Beauregard's son arrived here yesterday.

Say to Dick that he must stop here when he comes down if he will let me know what day he comes down I'll meet him at the cars.

Benton and myself are going to walk over to the Junction in the morning.

Alvin has given up writing home, and has given that department to me entirely, he is writing now but I do not know to whom, as he has a piece of paper over the name but I think that I could guess, he gets very uneasy about mail time — but as I am generally more successful than he, it makes him jealous, and expects to have the benefit of my letters and let me do the answering which I don't think "pays".

Received a letter from Williams yesterday, he and Roy were both well.

Alvin has written to Grand-Ma, give her my love, say that if I do not mention her name in my letters I think of her none the less.

Have strung my "few lines" to great length and admit rather ashamed of the production, but you, like the Dutchman who was kicked by the donkey, must "consider the source" and after the trouble of writing it must do penance to your brother's sins by reading it — I'll promise you should not have a similar infliction.

Mrs. Proctor has not yet reported but we expect to hear from her tomorrow.

Several of our staff have arrived in the last few days from Gen. Bragg's Army, they left all of our relations well.

Did you receive those pictures I sent? (_____ Essays)

Love to one and all of the family — will send Uncle Tom a paper in a day or two. You had better not let Father or Uncle Mack see this I imagine I can see them lift their hands in horror.

Ever your affectionate Brother,

Pat *(Irving)*

Dear Lu: Deduct 33 pr. cent for lies., Alvin

Do nothing of the kind — its all true. A. does not wish to _____ A. thanks for cravats very nice — says make one of same material like long one—

Aubrey Pearre

Baltimore Aug. 22, 1861

Irving A. Buck Esq.

Your esteemed and much welcomed letter of the 8th is before me, and I can assure you, that, its contents was read with feelings of pleasure and delight. I have often thought of you since you left me, and have wondered if you had endangered yourself upon the battle field, in defence of Southern rights and liberties, or had remained at home as a comfort and solace to your Mother and Sisters.

I see you have selected the former, preparing to die, if necessary, in the cause of liberty, than to live a slave. I sincerely approve of your actions, but, at the same time,

I have to reproach myself on account of my slothfulness. I should be with you in person, as you know I am in heart, to help to gain that liberty, which here after I expect to enjoy. I often ask myself: Am I to remain inactive, and enjoy all the comforts of life, while my Southern Brethren are upon the Field, enduring all kinds of hardships and depriving themselves of all the comforts of life, in order to secure that, in which I am so much interested? Reasoning thus, I am ready to leave all, and share your fate. But when I look around me and see my condition, and with the certain knowledge of bringing the gray hairs of my parents to a sorrowful and untimely grave, what can I do? Nothing! — but silently kneel before the God of nations and ask Him to protect and shield you and strengthen your armies, that you may hurl back your invading foe! and at the same time, ask Him to guide and direct me according to His own pleasure.

But this does not interest you.

McKendree was in Virginia as you mentioned in your letter and would have been most happy to have seen you, but his time was short and not knowing where to find you, he did not obtain his desire.

We are all very well. Johnson has left us and not being successful in getting the appointment in the Customs House, has gone to the country. Wolf is still with us, he having a Maryland trade we thought it best to keep him. Merritt and Billy are still with us. Charley is here and often speaks of you, McKendree saw Bynion, he was quite well. Merritt and Wolf are strong union men. Your uncle Abe is well and was glad to hear from you. He enjoys himself as usual, and rejoices with exceedingly great joy, when we receive any good news from the South. Smith was exceedingly glad to hear from you, and when I related to him the contents of your letter, he exclaimed "poor fellow, how I would like to see him". You may rest assured, Irvy, that you are not forgotten: the hearts of your friends are with you.

Gloom, as a dark pall, seems to hang over our city. The merchants have lost all their energy and seem despondently to enquire, when will all of this end? Our churches are but half filled — our hotels are almost deserted — the armed soldiers around us, frighten the merchants from us and consequently business of all kind is at a stand still. Our citizens feel daily, the iron heel of despotism, placed more firmly upon their necks, and like the Jews, on the banks of the River of Babylon, we mourn. Yea, we weep bitterly when we remember our former sweet days of liberty. If I should come over, could you secure me a good place, among good fellows where I could learn quickly? — write me whenever you can but don't write any thing that is not allowed. Be faithful and true to the cause — it is treason for me to write this letter, but if it be treason "let them make the most of it".

My prayers, Irvy, is offered for you, night and morning, that the strong arm of the Lord may be around you — in battle or out of it — to shield and protect you from all harm. Try to recognize Him in all things, for if the Lord is with you — all the world cannot conquer you. Be faithful to yourself and do not get into bad habits, as most men in camp life will do. If you have any regard for me — don't do it. I have not given any one the directions of sending letters to you. I was afraid your friend would not like to be troubled with many letters. All your friends send their kindest regards. Farewell, May God protect you, and if I should not meet you again upon earth, I hope, when the storm of life is over, to meet you in heaven.

Your affectionate friend,

A. P. *(Aubrey Pierre)*

(Note: He was a Junior Partner in Irving's Company in Baltimore, and later joined Irving in Cleburne's division — See footnote of letter dated November 6, 1862.)

Head Quarters
Fairfax Court House
September 15, 1861

Dear Nellie

Mr. Miller is going up to Front Royal in the morning, and I will reply to your letter, although every thing is in such confusion that I can write with very little satisfaction.

We moved down on Thursday and have not gotten settled, the house that we are now in is the Generals Quarters, and a very nice one but we are going to move the office and our sleeping apartments to one now occupied by Longstreet — and I hope by tomorrow that we will have every thing settled. I have walked through the village several times and seen many pretty ladies, but they all always have half a dozen brass buttoned fellows with them so that I had no chance to "ring in" — its about as hard looking place as Strasburg and I do not think that we have gained much by the move, however I have not yet an opportunity to Judge. I have not yet seen the Miss Richardsons.

Captain Jordan arrived here yesterday evening he said that he saw Father in F.R.

The provisions and clothes came all o.k. I do not know what arrangement to make about sending things backwards and forwards now. I suppose we will have to watch our opportunity.

The boys have all been on picket every since we have been here, but will come off this evening. Charlie Richardson *(of the Warren Rifles, later Co. E. 7th VA. After the war he moved to Nebraska and was elected Sheriff twice in Custer County)* came up yesterday and was here until late last night — he says that Mack is very sick.

I will try to send the basket, and our clothes up by Hamp if I can get them over to the station — in regard to our keeping the boxes sent us, all that we neglected to return were two small paper boxes I left in Manassa and would have sent them up last time but did not have room in the basket.

Our mess has been broken up but we will reorganize it in a day or two — but do not send any thing more unless some one is coming directly here.

You speak of Cousin Sue being in such bad health, and being aware of her condition, — has she the consumption or any thing of that kind?

If Alvin will lend me his cap I will send it up to Lucy. Tell her to cut the pattern and send it back by the first safe opportunity by some one coming directly here, so as to prevent the possibility of its getting lost — she can make it of grey, black, or blue, ask her to cut it a little longer, and the crown smaller, for the more it droops the prettier it looks, and if she can get no other vizor to cut the one off of the grey cap I left — but think that Mr. Blackley would sell enough patent leather for that — two thin pieces put together and bound around the edges like the one on the grey cap is very pretty. I'll pay all expenses, get things right. I am in no hurry she may take her time — I will send her a couple of buttons to put on it — if she will notice there is a little whale bone in the back of the cap sent — to keep it in the right position — the cloth for the "Rifles" uniform makes very pretty caps — had better get Blackley to make the vizor. Lend my cap over to show him how it should be done.

I have not yet decided about my uniform but will let you know in a day or two. Capt. Simpson came to see Col. Jordan about my getting my pay — he and the Col. say that I am entitled to it, and that he had my name on the pay roll, but that some of the company objected on account of my not having been mustered in — it just amounts to this — if I am not entitled to my pay and uniform I am of course not a member — and I am sure I do not care about the pay — as I get $11.50 per month here. Capt. S is very anxious that I should get my company pay which I am very much obliged to him for, but am under the impression that he wants to secure me. I my self do not think that I can claim it — and told the Capt. and Col. both so.

I think that I can get a few days leave after we get settled and will go up home for a day or two.

Our Quarters are about five hundred yards from town and entirely hid by the trees.

11 o'clock P.M. saw some of the Rifles this evening, Will Richardson, Dick and Charlie all well.

Love to all ever your affectionate
Irving

Head Quarters
October 10, 1861

Dear Lucy,

The pants and your letter were not handed me until this morning and I was not aware that you were such a badly treated person by a certain brother, until the receipt thereof. Really, it was not intentional for really I do not know from one opportunity to another who I wrote to last. However, I will not quarrel with you about it.

The cap and uniform came, the former is a perfect beauty, and it is the prettiest that I have ever seen, and I have had numerous offers to "trade". Benton received one from Lynchburg last night, but it is not as pretty as mine, and you may accept my thanks for it. The uniform fit very well and reflects great credit upon Nell and yourself. A. has bought a set of Va. buttons for it. I have engaged a set for my uniform when I have it made. I paid a big price for them, but they are of the finest quality fine gilt. I will try to come up in a week or two to have my uniform cut, and get some bedding as the nights are getting airish.

I have not yet called upon the Miss Richardsons or made the acquaintance of any ladies, although I have had abundant opportunities. I do not know why, but I have not the least desire for ladies' company. One of the Miss Richardsons died a day or two ago. She was not one of those I used to know but a younger sister. Dilce is married. Alvin came very near calling on Miss Ninn the night her sister died, not knowing that she was sick. I met Miss N in the street and if my stock of clean linen and impudence had been larger I would have gone up and introduced myself. I intend to go to see her in a few days.

Moseley has been discharged the service and is now in Lynchburg, we frequently hear from him. He sent us all a gold pen a piece by a member of our mess yesterday. At this time he could not have made me a present more acceptable. He was a great loss to our mess. He says that anytime I will come to Lynchburg he will send me a free ticket, he being in the office of the RR.

I suppose that Charlie Buck gave you a full account of the President and the review. It was a grand sight.

We have a brigade drill nearly every evening, and the Warren Rifles in their new uniforms will compare with any of them and look a great deal better than the majority. The 17th Regiment drills splendidly. We have two or three bands in a short distance of our quarters, and have lots of music among them, the band of the 1st Va. (Richmond) Regiment. I wish you could hear it play "Dixie", "Mocking Bird", "Gay and Happy", and many other beautiful pieces.

I have not heard from "Nannie Dear" (Nannie Taylor), for a long time, although I have sent her several Newspapers.

Charlie reports that Miss Alice Morehead and Mother reached Front Royal Tuesday night from Washington via Fortress Monroe, and Richmond.

The pants sent were the wrong ones, the ones I want are my black cashmere, as they will be too small for me after while. I will send the ones sent, back. You may also send my suspenders, as my pants and vest will not make the "connection" without them, which is rather uncomfortable this weather.

I sent a small package and letter to father directed to Mrs. Jordan. Did he receive and forward them? I also started my carpet bag of clothes.

Alvin gets letters from Ky. frequently and seems to be perfectly contented. I suppose you have seen the notice of the taking of Hopkinsville by the Confederates.

I was over to the 17th this morning, saw Dick, Charlie, Willie Richardson and all the boys. All of them except Scott Roy, and Smith Turner are very unsociable, and Charlie Buck was here for the first time last night.

I am writing this now because I happen to have time, and do not know when I will have an opportunity to send it.

This is a miserable wet drizzly evening, and all the amusement we boys have is to build up a large fire and sit around it and abuse one another.

I will try to get a sketch of our "cottage in the woods" and send you.

I will try to send Father a Baltimore Sun.

The paper I am writing on is some captured from the Yankees, and had printed. We have a plenty of envelopes now, but happened to be out when I last wrote.

Irving

Head Quarters 1st Corps A of P near Centerville
November 2, 1861

Dear Lou

It has been considerably over a week since I have written home, and for me to let my correspondence lag for such a time is unusual, but it has not been my fault for I have had no opportunity. Benton went up last Saturday, but when he left here he had no idea of doing so.

This has been one of the most miserable days I ever knew. I believe that every tent in the 17th Regt. was blown down, but we are very comfortable here, but I do pity the boys in the ranks. I was over to see them day before yesterday. Willie Richardson was quite unwell.

Gov. Letcher has been here for several days. We had a grand review of the Virginia troops, and gave them (each Regt.) a Va. state flag. I had no idea that there were so many Virginians in our Army. I saw Mack Bayly, but did not have an opportunity to speak to him.

Benton returned on Tuesday night, from his account he had a very pleasant trip. Called on "Nannie dear" various times. By the way the next time you write, give her my love. Alvin has a very tender spot under his vest for Clara, and I think that six months more absence from Hopkinsville, the "Major's" *(his future wife's family)* command over him will be lost entirely, and he will quit the military and go to mechanics -ie- will quit "majoring" and go to "tayloring" — however he may find more competition in the latter than the former.

Enclosed I send you the design of the new battle flag. It is an exact copy only the stars are not large enough. It has been adopted, and most of the Regiments have been furnished with them.

I have made up my mind to go to Kentucky when my time expires here. I think that I can make it pay. I will, of course, go by Richmond for the purpose of seeing the capitol.

Alvin has taken a tent with the telegraph operator (a nice fellow and Baltimorean) and between them they have a comfortable bed, and A. says that he would not trade his bunk with the "oldest man in the world". Speaking of this the first good opportunity you have I would like for you to send us both more bed clothing, as we begin to need them. I also want a paper of large tacks. Ask Father to keep an account of these things — we have just been paid off and have lots of money.

It appears that I cannot get time to come home. I have never yet asked for leave but believe that I can get it when ever asked for. I left in my trunk a vest that buttons up high, and is faced with black ribbed silk which is considerable worn, but the vest is good. I wish if you can get anything that you would put a new facing on it. And I have a pair of pants of the same material which if bound at the bottom will do very well for the office. I had thought of giving them away. I have a set of small brass buttons for the vest. I wish these things fixed in case I should come up, for if I do, my stay will be very short.

Monday evening — Was over to the Regiment today. Billy Richardson was better and spoke of going down on picket with the rest of the boys, but I advised him not. Charlie Buck and Charlie Richardson were also in camp on the complaining list.

I received a letter from Cousin Willie Blakemore today. He says that he has wound up his business and speaks of coming to Virginia shortly. Cousin Cad and Clarence have the typhoid fever and Cousin G.W. the chills. Cousin Kate Blakemore was at the Grove and M.H. in Nashville. The letter was dated the 25th of October.

I am very anxious to hear the particulars of the fight at Romney.

Bailey Jacobs[4] is going up this morning — send the bed clothes by him. Nov. 5, 1861.

Irving

Head Quarters 1st Corps A of P

December 6, 1861

Dear Lucy,

Your letter came to hand several days ago, and I would have answered sooner, but Hoblitzell[5] called here the other evening and said that Uncle John expected to be here yesterday or today, but I suppose that he has changed his mind and gone back to Winchester, as he has not yet arrived. I did not see Mr. H. as I was out at the time.

The 17th went on picket this morning and will be gone until Monday. I am glad that they will have such pleasant weather.

It is reported here that Captain Wheatly[6] died a few days ago, is it so?

I got my bed clothes a few days after coming down — and am very comfortable. Alvin has a chimney to his tent and is in no danger of freezing just at present.

There is nothing of interest going on here, and we are leading the same monotonous life.

I suppose you have seen Henry *(Henry Augustus Buck)* and had a full account of his "adventurous and hair brained escapades". I wish he would pay us a visit before he joins the army.

Enclosed I send a letter to Jule *(Julia Catherine Buck, Henry's sister)* which you will send her by the first opportunity. Perhaps you had better get Father to drop it in the office.

None of us expect to get home Christmas, but if we can get the "fodder", we are going to have a little frolic all to ourselves including Richardson, Buck and Co. of the "Bloody 17th". We had a mess of oysters a day or two ago.

The night that Willie Richardson came down we found out that he had brought Scott (Scott Roy) a cold turkey and Dick some sausage. So that night about ten o'clock although it was raining, we went over and made the boys get up and cook us a supper which they did without much grumbling. They came over to sup with us the next night and <u>we</u> did not "say <u>turkey once</u>".

I will send our clothes and the basket up by the first opportunity.

Mack Bayly came over to see us yesterday. He is looking very well and I think that soldiering agrees with him.

Alvin received a letter from Bud Buck a few days ago. He says that Cousin Willie is aid to General Tilgham. I was very much surprised to hear of the death of Cousin Judith. Bud is not in the ranks but on detailed service in the ordnance department.

I believe that our Indian Summer has just set in. How is Charlie Buck?

Ask Father to send my boots down by the first <u>safe</u> opportunity.

I suppose you will spend your Christmas at Clover Hill or will Jule and Em. come to Bel Air?

Hope that Buck the XIII *(Frank "Dixie" Buck, a brother was born Nov. 27, 1861)* is in good health and spirits and doing his share of "squalling". Grandma, I suppose is happy.

Love to all, ever your affectionate Brother,
Irving

Head Quarters Corps A of P
December 12, 1861

Dear Lucie,

I have just received the carpet bag and clothes. They came all o.k. except the catsup froze last night and caused the cork to come out, but did no further harm than to soil the flannel jacket which I will send up and have washed again. I received a letter from you a day or two ago but do not know who brought it.

You need not cut up about the matter for I have a trunk full of clean clothes but it's a little too cold to change so often.

Dave Spengler expects to go up tomorrow and I will try to get him to carry this.

The letter I wrote Jule contained a photograph of old "Beaury" if you have not sent it you may open it.

I wish Father had have come down during the good weather, but we cannot offer him much inducement now as our cook is sick, and we have difficulty in getting our meals cooked.

I suppose Uncle John gave you a full account of everything here — the execution of the "Tigers" etc.

Was over to see the boys this evening. They are all well and Richardson, Buck and Co. are going to commence building W. house tomorrow.

Nothing new.

Love to all, ever your affectionate Brother,
Irving
I received the socks.

Head Quarters Corps A of P
December 21, 1861

Dear Lucie,

Dick is going up this evening and I will drop you a line by him. We managed to have him detailed to bring down our Christmas supply. He will return on Tuesday so that you had better get everything ready.

You have all doubtly heard the European news. Things look brighter now than they have before for a long time.

I have been thinking that it would be a good idea to have two or three shirts made of brown cotton with linen bosoms to wear this winter, as bleach muslin will be scarce hereafter. Ask Ma what she thinks of it.

Alvin received a letter from Cousins Geo. B. and Willie Blakemore last night. All were well.

Tell Jule if she will send old "Beaury's" photograph back that I will get him to write his name under it.

I refer you to Dick for the news.

Love to all. Ever your affectionate Brother,
Irving

Dear Lucy,

Dick and the provisions arrived safely on the 25th. We have a plentiful supply for which we thank you very much and hope you did not deprive yourselves. We have had quite a pleasant time, at least as much so as we could expect.

Many thanks for the cravats, which were very nice.

The boys have nearly finished their house — when done, we are going to give them a <u>storm</u> (i.e.) eat them out.

I send my shoes up to have mended. Ask Father please to have them repaired as soon as possible. My boots have ripped, and I am nearly on the ground. Alvin's also in want of his boots.

I will write more when I have time.

Dick lost my cap coming down. It blew off near Happy Creek Station.

Telegraphic dispatch this morning announces the death of Prince Albert.

I send box etc. up by Geo Hope, who has a sick leave.

I wrote to Ed Buck *(member Co. E, 7th Va. Cavalry)* a day or two ago.

Love to all,

Ever your affectionate Brother,
I. A. B. *(Irving Ashby Buck)*
I find I cannot send the box this time.

Dear Lucy,

Your letter of the 28th was handed to me this evening.

I thought that I had been quite punctual of late, my letters have been very short it is true, but then there was nothing to write, and I am only following your orders for you say "write if its only a line to let us know how you are".

I am glad that you have had such a pleasant time, and wish that I could have been with you to enjoyed it with you. I can give our program in a very few words: we did comparative little writing on the 25th, walked over to the 17th did not have dinner until dark, when the boys came over and helped us to dispose of the good things, and now we are in our usual routine.

I am disposed to think that a certain Mr. Wilson had made a deep impression in a certain quarter, with his "sunny brown eyes", you had better be careful how you make the acquaintance of such persons, from my short acquaintance with Hoblitzell, I was not very favorably impressed, I am maybe, and hope I am mistaken, and do him injustice, but it will be well enough to be careful. I am satisfied that there is some as great rascals in the 1st Maryland Regt. as ever graced a jail — and I know that you all feel a great sympathy for them on account of their being refugees, and away from home, and you must remember also that the greatest scoundrels sometimes make the best impression at first. I know nothing of the young men of whom you write but advise you to be prudent.

If Lincoln, Sewart and Co. could see the bad luck you wish them I am sure they would tremble.

Your bouquet was fresh when it arrived, and Roy has it on his desk now, looking as fresh as though they had just been gathered.

I think you might make me a couple of shirts, and if I like them will have more made.

Do not trouble yourself about making another cap, if I do not get mine I will buy one.

Any one to hear you talk of the "Queen of hearts" ordering up "the deal" etc. would think you a regular graduate of Baden-Baden or the fashionable saloons of Washington City.

The boys will complete their house tomorrow and on New Year's Eve they are to give us a supper. Some of them are over to see us every night — Scott has just left here.

Alvin is not offended with any one, but has a constitutional dislike to writing letters — he is somewhat indisposed this evening, he has been feeding better than usual I suppose, and the change was too great from army rations.

Dec. 31. Alvin has recovered and eating his rations.

The Yankees have backed down and agreed to give up Mason and S.[7] without a doubt — poor degraded wretches!!

Love to all

Ever your affectionate Brother,
Irving A. Buck

Seal and send the letter to Jule when you read it.

---

[1] Alvin Duvall Buck and his first cousin, Walter, were working in Hopkinsville, Ky. His great uncle, John Buck I, Marquis Calmes (IV), Marquis Richardson, Benjamin Coombs and Samuel Price and families all moved to Kentucky in 1802.

There was a "General Christian Awakening" in the United States just before the Civil War. This started in New York City in 1858, spilled out to the various states and over the world. It was known by some historians as the Fourth Awakening in the United States.

"Walter" is William Walter Buck, son of Marcus Blakemore Buck of Front Royal. He lived in a beautiful home, Belmont, on the mountain where the Sky Line Drive now enters Front Royal.

Alvin's father, William Mason Buck, was the grandson of Thomas Buck, one of the founders of Front Royal. W. M. Buck had carried on the tradition of being well respected, a good businessman, prosperous, and a leading citizen of Front Royal. His views were sought by family and friends alike and he was executor of five estates. Yet it took the Civil War, death of a son, business failure and loss of all worldly property to bring him to the point Alvin wished. His decision was described by his daughter, Lucy, who wrote in her diary in 1886 (her father was 77 years of age):

"After dinner, I hurried to change my dress and drive Cousin R. in the buggy over to church. Father told us that in the morning he intended offering for membership in Dr. Water's church and we were so glad to know it. He went forward after the sermon was over and made his application with a quiet self possession in earnest solemnity, wonderful in one so retiring in nature. His reception by the members of the church was impressive and touching. When this was through it was announced that the baptism would take place at 5 o'clock and it was then 4 p.m. So we had to hurry home bringing Cousin Bette Richards with us in the buggy to get her ready to go down to the creek. The rite was to be administered at the pool just northwest of the house bordering the meadow. Father slipped quietly off in his usual way, walked down along the bank of the creek and coming up to Dr. Waters said in a clear tone, "I want the first three stanzas of "Rock of Ages" sung. It was the hymn my son sang with his dying breath when he asked me to meet him in heaven". This request was complied with and then the ordinance administered with the solemnity and simplicity that I've never seen equal. No one could fail to be touched with the beauty of the scene, the clear soft sunset, the calm, quiet prevailing the little assembly, and the central figure, the white-haired patriarchal man in the midst, all combined to make a picture I shall never forget. When the ceremony was over, Father walked back to the house as quietly as he had left it and was sitting in front of a fire in his room and was quietly talking with Mrs. Smith."

At his death in 1895, it was written in the newspaper obituary of William Mason Buck that "he was the last of those great Virginia gentlemen about which we have known."

He closed his memoirs by quoting Patrick Henry who wrote in his last will and testament:

"There is one thing more that I wish I could give them and that is the Christian religion. If they have that, and I had not given one shilling, they would be rich; and if they have not that, and I had given them the whole world, they would be poor."

William Mason Buck then added,

"That wish is the only legacy I have to bestow on my dear children."

Walter's brother, Richard Buck, who was in the "Warren Rifles" trusted Christ as his Savior during an awakening in the Southern Army. Dick was converted in the trenches of Petersburg in 1864.

William W. Bennett in his book, *The Great Revival In The Southern Armies*, wrote that by January 1865 it was estimated 150,000 Confederate soldiers had been converted during the process of war.

2 I am not sure why a conflict existed between Thomas Ashby and Robert Simpson. The former was a Warren County official. Politics probably was the cause and had nothing to do with the fact Capt. Simpson was the school master for the Front Royal Academy and later Captain of the Warren Rifles.

Lucy Buck, Alvin's sister, wrote in her diary on February 12, 1862:

"Saw a stranger riding on horseback along the street — upon his approaching and saluting us several times, I finally recognized Captain Simpson, although his beard has outgrown my recollection. Bowed coolly to him."

Later when General Longstreet visited Lucy's home, Bel Air, in Front Royal on November 1, 1862, the family gave him such glowing reports regarding Captain Simpson that the General replied, "Then 'tis time he was promoted".

Upon hearing of Major Simpson's death at in 1864, Lucy wrote her heart ached for the Simpson family.

[3] Thomas C. Jordan, a West Point graduate became a Brigadier General.

[4] Bailey Jacobs joined the "Warren Blues" which was mustered into service at Front Royal June 17, 1861. He became Captain upon the promotion of Captain Mandly Taylor Wheatly to Major.

[5] Soldier who stayed in Front Royal all winter due to wounds or illness. He became a friend of the Bucks.

[6] Captain Mandly Taylor Wheatly who recruited the "Warren Blues" was later promoted to Major. The "Warren Blues" were part of the 49th Regiment Virginia Infantry. Major Wheatly became sick at Manassas and died at his home in Front Royal on Dec. 1, 1861.

[7] On November 8, 1861, James M. Mason and John S. Slidell were taken from an English ship on the high seas en route to England and France as Commissioners from the Confederate States of America. They were released December 26, 1861. Mason's home in Winchester, Virginia was promptly torn down by the Yankees.

1862

Dear Lucie,

Henry left so hurried and unexpectedly I had only time to toss my clothes in the carpet bag. I intended writing that night but for some reason did not. You and Ma's letters, by Tom Campbell, reached me, I was at the 17th when he arrived. Ma seems to think that I do not write in as good spirits as usual. I do not know why. There is nothing in the world new here, the same routine day after day — and when I pick up my pen it almost mechanically traces the words, "application for 30 days leave on Surgeons certificate" or "Lt — tenders his resignation".

George Williams reached here on Monday, and is now regularly in the harness. He is very efficient. We still retain J. T. Petty *(of the Warren Rifles)* as the Colonel seems loathe to give him up — truly our company has been well represented at these Head Quarters in numbers at least, if not in capacity, but there surely must be some, or details would not be made so frequently on the same company.

I have not been near so busy for the last four days as heretofore, but my business is such that it will keep me always here, and I see the prospects of my furlough fading in the dim distance. The reason of our being more pressed with work than formerly is that we are now granting leaves of absence in extreme cases, and every paper that passes through this office has to be recorded and accounted for. Also all letters received, as if you could see the piles of leaves, resignations, transfers, discharges and applications of various characters that come into the office every day, you would not wonder that we are kept constantly at our desks. This is my department. Alvin has the letters that are written from this office. The General and Special Orders circulars and etc. to record besides a good deal of nice writing for the Col.

Hope, Petty and Williams have the letters, orders and etc. to copy. Roy has the general endorsement and handling of <u>all</u> these papers, which is the most responsible and confining of all — though he and I are essential to one another — as I cannot enter these papers until he has endorsed them. I may add that Geo. Wms. is <u>closely</u> connected with us as we all <u>three</u> sleep together on <u>two</u> cots. But I commenced boasting that I had not been very busy, but the Col. has communicated to me the pleasant intelligence that he wishes me to make another copy of the Battle of Manassas, for the General — which forcibly brings to my mind the old "saw of" not whistling until we get out of the woods, but I console myself with the knowledge that there is but twenty four hours in a day and night (thanks to the Almanac and clock maker) and the law allows a man to sleep six of them.

I saw Henry very little and did not have time for a Kentucky talk, he is a strange mortal and I cannot fathom him. He has not changed a particle by his sojourn at the

Grove. He does not appear to like the West, but from his account it is not the same place it was when I left it.

You all seem to have taken a great fancy to Mr. Wilson. What is the name of the firm with whom he was engaged in Baltimore? It is surprising with what facility the members of that Maryland Regiment procure furloughs in our Corps a man must show that his case is of the most urgent character to get one, even for a few days. I cannot say that I admire Miss Vin Lionberger's taste much, to fancy Mr. H.

I see from advertisements in the papers that Colonel Jordan's pamphlet that Alvin copied for Sir Jas. Ferguson, M.P. at Fairfax C.H. has been published in England, with a nice compliment to the Col.

I sent Nellie a picture of a "Tiger" drawn by our draftsman. It is very accurate.

I think that this spell will put an end to this campaign. How proudly must the Yankees look upon it, to their numerous victories (?) in crushing out the "small rebellion" — another such will about finish them.

I see from the papers that Cameron, the Chief of thieves, has resigned his appointment as Secy. of War, I suppose treasury is empty, and he will seek a place where there is better chances for him to indulge his thieving proclivities. I should like very much to <u>plant</u> him beside his brother, near the famous Henry house.

I do not expect to get home in May, when our company disbands, as I intend to retain my place, but I am going to make some desperate efforts to pay a visit to "<u>Nannie Dear</u>" before that time.

Alvin received a couple of letters from Kentucky a day or two ago. Nothing new in Hopkinsville, all of our relatives were well.

Colonel Jordan went up to Mrs. Weem's this evening to meet Mrs. J. He will return on Tuesday. This is the first time he has been away since he entered the service, and I think that he richly deserves it.

You need not send my shirts back, except the colored one. The next time I have an opportunity, I will send two pairs of Alvin's pants, one to mend and the other to get a pair out of for Willie — as Alvin has discarded them.

Benton is complaining very much.

I have no recollection of leaving a carpet bag at home. There must be some mistake about it, as it certainly is not mine, and I relinquish my claim in her favor — (Cous. Mary)

It is now so dark that I can scarcely see.

Love to all — Ever your affectionate Brother,
Irving A. Buck

Transfer to the Western Army
January 25, 1862

Head Quarters 1st Corps A of P
January 25, 1862

Dear Lucie,

You will please get mine and Alvin's <u>clothes</u> in <u>perfect repair</u>, <u>every stitch</u> that we have both <u>summer</u> and <u>winter</u> — and pack them in my trunk that they will be ready at any moment — so that if needed no delay will be experienced. I cannot now give my reasons for this hasty request but will let you know in a few days. Say nothing about this, but do not <u>delay</u>.

I wrote you a long letter a day or two ago. Nothing new since, except our defeat in Ky. which you have doubtly seen in the papers.

All the 17th boys are well. The sun came out this morning for the first time in nearly two weeks.

Give yourselves no alarm or uneasiness about what I have written — as all will be explained very soon.

Love to all—

Ever your affectionate Brother,
Irving A. Buck

Since writing the foregoing, Col. Jordan has given me permission to reveal the plans. Gen. Beauregard has been ordered to Columbus, Ky. and we are <u>all</u> to accompany him. Benton is going up to F. Royal tomorrow evening and he will give you the particulars.[1]

We will try to spend a day at home before we go, but it is very uncertain.

I will try to exchange my heavy shawl for one finer and lighter — to have a couple of shirts made, as I do not know about our washing.

I will write Father more particularly.

If I should send a shawl home to make shirts, please sew the pockets on the outside thus: *(draws picture)* and trim with some kind of binding.

I send my vest and Alvin's pants to have mended.

Head Quarters 1st Corps A of P
January 25, 1862

Dear Father

As the General has been ordered to Columbus, Ky., the Colonel seems anxious that we should go with them. We have determined to go, but would like to do so with your full consent. My view of the matter is this; we are still members of the 17th Regt, and will be until its time expires (1st May) it is then at our option whether we re-enlist at all or not, we can then enlist for 12 months while here, will be compelled to go in for two — and besides I think that it is only a temporary arrangement and that we will return next summer. This is only my opinion and from nothing that I have heard. If we stay here we will have to go in ranks which would go very hard with us as we are not used to picket duty. Col. Jordan seems to be perfectly satisfied with our services, which he has shown by retaining us, and perhaps it will be of some service in future.

I am sorry that the General is going to leave here, the French soldiers never had more confidence in Napoleon than our men have in him. He is a man and soldier in every sense of the word.

I would be pleased if you would have a conversation with Benton — who will give you all the points.

I shall be very sorry to be so far from you all, but it seems to be the best thing I can do, let me look at it in any point of view.

Will do my best to spend a day with you all before I go, but think it exceedingly doubtful.

The General will start in a few days. Col. Jordan and the clerks will follow soon after.

Benton will give you the particulars.

Hastily and affectionately your son

Irving

Luray, Virginia
February 6, 1862

Dear Irving,

I received yours sometime ago, and owe you an apology for not answering more promptly, as I have no excuse whatever, I have not seen your Father since, but no doubt it will be all right <u>upon sight</u>, I have no idea of our indebtedness to the Howard House, but any amount you say will be all right. I am sorry my pecuniary circumstances will not allow me to carry out my wishes and inclinations, that is, to say to you I charge you <u>nothing</u> but I hope we may all get to Baltimore and I have an opportunity of repaying some of the many kindnesses received at your Father's hands. Please accept my thanks for the Clipper it is the only Baltimore paper I have seen, for six months, I read advertisements and all notwithstanding its duly republican proclivities, I have just learned that <u>Mr. McBoyd</u> had arrived in Manchester via Hancock. I am visiting him today, My wife sends her love to you and often speaks of you and the girls also particularly Miss Thomas, Come up soon. We would be delighted to see you.

Your friend
A. Shipe

I may come to Manassas in a few weeks. How can I find you? Take good care of yourself, and let <u>strict</u> <u>temperance</u> be your Motto. Liquor is the greatest Enemy an army has to contend with, old <u>Abe</u> "aint no where" — Good bye

Spotswood Hotel
Richmond, Feb. 8, 1862

Dear Lucie,

You see that we are still in Richmond — after being delayed at Manassas two days we arrived safely here on Tuesday evening — had I known that the Colonel was going to stay so long, I would have been at home some days more.[2]

We went around to see the ladies immediately after tea and received a hearty welcome and spent a very pleasant evening. They are the same girls as of old and we were perfectly at home.

I think that R is the most disagreeable place I have been in for a long time. I have visited every place of interest and am heartily tired of the place — and have merely lived all day for the hours between 8 and 12 P.M.

Miss Nannie is anxiously expecting a letter from you — they all asked after you all. Mrs. Taylor is complaining of sore throat.

We expect to leave tomorrow morning.

We heard that Alvin and the boys were en route for Lynchburg on Thursday.

You have heard of the capture of Fort Henry — the last news we have received is that Fort Donaldson had been attacked, the result of which we have not heard. I do not suppose however that it will affect us at all.[3]

I have met numbers of my old Baltimore acquaintances — among others, Ellie's Mr. Wilson.[4] I was standing in the office the evening I arrived and noticed a young man whom I had frequently seen on the streets in B., but had never spoken to him. I walked up and remarked that I perceived that he was a Baltimorian. He said yes, I then told him my name and he said his was Wilson and I knew instantly who it was. I have seen him frequently since but had no opportunity to form an opinion. He seems to have no employment here.

Benton and myself have just returned from Mr. T's — we went up to say "good bye".

I will write when I arrive at Columbus *(Kentucky)*.

We heard from the General — he arrived safely at Bowling Green.

Love to all —

Ever yours affectionately
Irving A. Buck

Jackson, Tennessee
Sunday, March 2, 1862

Dear Father,

I intended writing you upon my arrival in Nashville but as Cousin Mack left for Virginia so soon, it made it unnecessary for me to do so in a business point of view, and I thought it best to await the result of The Donelson fight, so as to be able to give correct tidings of our friends who were engaged in it. Cousin Willie and Dick Blakemore escaped and I left the former in Columbia with Cousin Alick. The latter (Cous W) is in Memphis and will be here in a short time to follow the very uncertain fortunes of "Old Beaury" in some capacity or other. It is thought that Mack Newton got safely away from the Fort but no one seems sure of it.

Upon my arrival in Nashville I met Mr. Sears who is a refugee and he advised me to be careful in venturing into Kentucky. At Clarksville I met other friends who persuaded me not to attempt it. Cousin George still remains in H. and intends not be driven from home by the "Vandals".

Genl. A.S. Johnston's army amounted to but little less than a mob upon entering Nashville, and his men seem to have lost confidence in him as a leader.

We have had a pleasant time in this place as far as there are three girls living next door with whom we spend our evenings — The General will put us to work in the morning and we will then be kept regularly at it as there is an immense amount to do in the way of organizing, etc. The Colonel has just had enough writing to amuse Irving and myself for the first week, and the rest of our party have not been able to take a hand yet.

The weather is quite warm and a hard thunder shower visited us this morning. There is more difference between the climate in Virginia and here than I had imagined.

Irving had a dumb chill on yesterday and a high fever last night but is better now. He will be near Doct. Brod. so that in case his attacks shall continue, he will have the very best of medical attendance. Major Snowden (of Genl Polk's staff) who is also here, had a terrific "shaker" yesterday and our whole party may look out for having a siege before becoming acclimated. I think Roy had better have his joints riveted up before they commence on him or he may drop to pieces on the first shake.

I occasionally find an old Hopkinsville acquaintance who has strayed over into Tennessee and joined some Regiment. My friend, Bryant, who was a brother clerk at Blakemore & C's was taken prisoner at Donelson; also Mr. Giles Cobb (Newt Catlett's brother in law) and a son of Cousin Helen Skinner, about 17 years of age.

Irving will write tomorrow. It is growing dark.

Love to each and all.

Truly your affectionate son
Alvin
P.S. George Williams desires to be affectionately remembered to all.

Dear Lucie,

I have been from home over a month and <u>not one line have I</u> received, though I know it is no fault of yours and am certain letters for me at Columbus from which place I wrote two weeks ago.

We like Jackson much better than C. It is situated mid way between Corinth, Mississippi and Columbus.— on the Mobile and Ohio RR — and junction of Mississippi Central — it has some 3,000 inhabitants, four churches, Court House and numerous stores — it is a very pretty place almost every yard is filled with cedars, trained and trimmed to grow in a conical shape.[5]

There are three girls here with whom we are having a gay time, we have had several "big" dances — the youngest is very pretty and resembles Cattie Boone a little. At first I held "four aces" against all the rest — but Ed Skinner came along and knocked me as high as a kite — however it did not hurt me much.

We met Tom Porter before we left Columbus, he was exceedingly kind and insisted on our going out to his house, which invitation Benton accepted, and was much pleased with his visit.

By the way, has Mr. Boyd[6] ever visited Bel Air yet? Ask Father if he sees him to say that Porter and Co. have the money to pay the bill due Boyd Bros. Co. and will do so upon receipt of their note —, if Mr. B has not the note with him, and will enclose me a blank receipt signed, I will fill it up with the original amount and interest — as I do not now know what it is — and collect the money, and tell him perhaps he had better let me get it in a Confederate check as there would be less danger in sending it in that form — at any rate to write and give me information touching this matter.

I see that Alvin has written that I had a chill — I had head ache and fever, which he construed into a chill but give yourselves no uneasiness as he was entirely mistaken.

Hereafter direct your letters to this place as we will establish our Head Quarters tomorrow.

I received a letter from Cousin Willie a day or two ago, he says he will be with us in a few days.

I met old Jno. Seely here a few days ago. I did not make myself known — but he finally found me out.

Love to all —

Ever your affectionate brother
Irving

Bel Air, March 11, 1862

My Dear Boys,

Unless you were here you could not possibly understand the excitement which prevails in town today in anticipation of the advance of the enemy into the valley. You know if a big rock is cast into a mill pond it will make a greater noise and splash than if thrown into the ocean. So it is with villages — excitement such as would scarcely be credited can be raised in a village by circumstances which would be scarcely noticed in a place of any size. I was over this morning and could not help feeling amused, though sad, to see the consternation into which the citizens — the male portion at least were thrown by the order which Snyder received last night to demolish the bridges and hospitals. The gentlemen are much more alarmed than the ladies and are running about the streets like flocks of frightened sheep who've lost their shepherd — some are going to take refuge in flight — among the latter Mr. Haynie. He has been playing such a prominent part in public affairs and has been of so much service to the Southern Confederacy and he is so universally known that it would be dangerous for him to remain here. Verily, "the wicked flee when no man pursueth." The most sensible of the denizens will remain here and stand their ground — among the latter your own family. I suppose there is but little doubt that they — the Yankees will send some of their forging parties in to visit us but they will not station any large force in a place of as little importance. And I don't think they'll injure us much beyond cutting off mail communications and stopping the cars. Only think there has not been a passenger train or mail from below since Saturday last, we can neither send nor receive letters or newspapers until the foe is whipped and driven back, and Oh! What a depravation! But I'll tell you how you must send us letters — put them in two envelopes, direct the inner one to us — the outer to Thomas Almond Esquire Luray — we have a regular mail from that place. Or else you might send them via Culpepper, as we will try to smuggle in a mail from there too. You must write as often as you can. You don't know how anxious we are to know all about you. Only think Alvin has not been heard from since he left the party at Stephenson — and we were so much afraid he had gone on to Hopkinsville and been captured by the enemy — but I will not believe anything else than that you are both together wherever you may be. Letters have been received the last week from George Hope and Williams and from Benton Roy but neither of them spoke particularly of either of you and we could not learn anything about whether Alvin was in Jackson with them or not from them. I do think the boys might speak a little more particularly about each other when they write — 'twould be such a satisfaction to their several friends if they would. Please dear Alvin do not run any risks in trying to get to Hopkinsville — better delay that visit awhile than that the Confederacy should lose the services of one of it's soldiers by your being confined in prison.

Belle Boyd is in town! Nellie and I are on our way to pay Miss Polly Haynie this morning when just as we were crossing the street opposite the hotel she and Alice Stewart rushed out, seized us and went bearing us off prisoners to the parlor, when we made our escape to Miss Polly's room but they pursued us thither and we surrendered at discretion. The terms of the capitulation required being that we should sing "The Bonnie Blue Flag" for them. Miss Belle inquired most expressly after you both, begged us to send you any amount of love and respects or something of that kind, it matters not what. Said she had never met with two brothers to whom she took such a fancy as in your case — wanted your address so that she might know how to direct letters to you both in reply to some which she said you had written her a long time since (which letters of yours, I'm of the impression existed only in the realms of her imagination). I should be very loathe to believe you would have gone so far as to write to her. I do not intend calling on her and hope she will not appropriate to herself my visit of today. Fannie and Mr. Stewart start for the South tomorrow — the one in quest of health, the other of safety, I intend sending this letter by them that they may mail it at some point beyond.

Giles Cook is in the other room talking at a rapid rate to Nellie and Cousin Emma. He has come over to tell us goodbye previous to going into the army — he has joined the Warren Rifles and will in company with Smith Turner, Tom Petty, Johnnie Boone, Charley Buck and Scott Roy start to go across to Culpepper in wagons on Thursday. From this point they will go to rejoin the company wherever they may be stationed — we do not know where the 17th is stationed, though it is believed to be in Gordonsville. I think Scott was over yesterday and again today to tell us goodbye, he is not well enough to be on duty but thinks it best to complete his recovery in camp. He is one of the very best of boys and the more I see, the more I like him.

Tell George Hope that his family are well as usual, so far as I know anything about them. And I believe they are as well as usual at Captain Roy's though Scott said his Ma was sad and lonely — he also said he thought they had abandoned the idea of going to the country this summer to live.

There's nothing new in the way of gossip in Front Royal. I believe — nothing spoken of but war and it would be utterly useless for me to attempt writing to you the rumors we hear relating to that prolific theme. All are well at home with the exception of a few scattering colds in the family. All unite in much love. I must close darling brothers begging that you will write soon and praying God to bless you, keep you and restore you to us very soon.

Yours fondly,
Lucie

It is rumored here that Beauregard died on the seventh instant but I cannot, will not believe it — 'tis surely some sensation report intended to frighten the credulous. If it be true, Heaven help us all! Oh! for a newspaper! Father bids me say in case of any disaster, he wishes you to directly to Port Gibson, Mississippi where you will find relatives and friends.

March 30, 1862

My Dear Brothers,

    The church bells are ringing, but we do not deem it expedient to brave this rain and sleet, even for the purpose of hearing one of Mr. Berry's excellent sermons. Father has just gone through, and as I have finished reading to him, I will devote some of my leisure moments to writing to two dear lazy boys who occupy my thoughts constantly both in my waking and sleeping hours. But indeed you don't deserve a letter from home, for we've written you twice to Columbus and twice or three times to Jackson and not a ghost of a reply to either have we received. Last week when our last mail from Culpepper arrived, _____ letters from you. I vowed not to send you a line till you did write and so great was my disappointment and vexation that I did not dream about either of you that night or the subsequent one, and I believe it's the first time since you left that I missed seeing one or both of you in my dreamland for two consecutive nights. So there now! But now that the mail has stopped and 'tis impossible to receive tidings from you, I've concluded to retract and will avail myself of this opportunity—the last I may have of sending a letter by private hand to be mailed somewhere within our lines. Let me tell you how often we have heard from you since you left us near the first of February. You both wrote us on the route, one from Lynchburg, the other from Richmond. Since then the only letters we've received at all was one from Irvie dated Columbus, February 16—before the fall of Donelson. Only think of that! We have indeed occasionally heard from you indirectly. Mrs. Hope has received two letters from George — Cousin Sue Buck and Miss Annie Simpson, one from Cousin George, and Mrs. Roy and Scott have between them received some four or five letters from Benton, and they were so kind as to give us the benefit of their missives — else we might have fretted ourselves sick with anxious imaginings about you — for we can't even get newspapers and are just as ignorant of the events transpiring around us as if we lived in Ramshatchkon instead of the Valley of Virginia. The last intelligence received from you is through a letter which Mrs. R. received from Benton just Thursday, dated Jackson March 9 in which it is stated you are both well. Irvie having just recovered from the mumps, was so glad to hear it. Did you think of home, Irvie, while you were sick and miss your nurses? I for a long time attributed our failure in receiving letters to the derangement in the mails—but as so many have been received from the West through the same medium, it is not likely that all the letters you might to have written were miscarried. But Ma will scold me if she finds I have commenced writing you a lecture upon your cruel neglect. She won't let me insinuate that you're voluntarily negligent of us, but insists upon it that you <u>have</u> written and that your letters were destroyed in the mail burnt at Gainesville, but you know that's been so long ago, nearly a month. But a truce to upbraidings.

Of a venty "Despots heel" is on our soil now, and I fear it will leave such a "print" as will not be easily effaced from old Warren. The advent of the Yankees took place last Tuesday somewhat on this wise. Father, who had gone to Cousin Marcus Richardson's in the morning, climbed up the Fort Mountain in company with a number of ladies and gentlemen upon hearing of their presence in the vicinity, and saw them winding about the roads looking from that distance like great black serpents; at one time they were so near that he could distinctly hear the Captain give his orders and he was within an ace of meeting them face to face in a narrow defile of the mountain which encounter would probably have proved inconvenient to him just then, for he was mounted on Dick Bayley's charger, a fine horse equipped in military style with "McDonald's Calvary" written on the saddle. They would most probably have taken a fancy to the animal and appropriated it leaving Father to "foot" it home. He seemed a good deal excited when he reached home—he is generally so very tranquil you know. It happened that Nellie was spending several days at Mr. Richard's and when she and Dick made their appearance about dusk that evening, they set up such an ear rendering shout for Jeff Davis as I never before heard and announced to us that they had just had an interview with the Yankees at Riverside, at least <u>Dick</u> had, Nellie would not deign them the light of her countenance. Mr. W. Kendrick's family are boarding with Cousin Bettie R. and Mr. K was home on furlough at the time. He, Nellie, and Dick were just preparing to walk into town—he had preceded them to the river that he might have the boat ready and _____ _____ just putting on her hat when about 50 Feds cantered up and inquired for Mr. R. _____ espied Mr. Kendricks on the way to the river, and in shouting— "There's a Secesh! I know him by his stripes!" dashed after him and soon returned bringing him to the house closely guarded. His wife is extremely delicate and her very existence seems bound up with his. You can imagine her feelings when told her husband, who had left her ten minutes before expecting him to return in a little while—was a prisoner in the hands of our bitterest foes and had returned indeed, but only for a few minutes to bid her farewell and perhaps forever. She went to the Major in command asked for the release of her husband. He replied politely and respectfully but very firmly that when her husband grounded his rebellious arms and became a <u>loyal</u> citizen he would grant her request, but not till then. She said nothing more then, but went to her chamber and they say she is heartbroken. Her little sick boy begs her to bring "Papa" back to him because he "wants to make up with him."

Dick Bayly was very near being taken with the C.S. uniform on—was just in the act of stepping out before them when Cousin Bett and Francis grasped him and soon disrobed him substituting in its stead his citizens garb. The Lieutenant asked Dick why the bridges had been burnt? "To obstruct your progress," he answered.

Well the officer thought we had given ourselves unnecessary trouble as they would immediately rebuild them. He then asked Dick his sentiments. "I'm a true secessionist," was his reply. "Would it take much to make him a Unionist?" He thought it would take a "great deal". "Why are you not in the army?" "I am not subject to the draft." "Perhaps you will join it though at all events?" Dick thought it "highly probable". "Well," said his soldiership, "You'll have a good time getting to your comrades. That's all!" Finding he would not commit himself, they did not trouble him further. They made frequent inquiries about Bowen's Cavalry and were evidently very uneasy lest they should be ambushed — some were in the neighborhood. They called for "spiritual" refreshments and turning to Cousin B. hoped she would like them better upon more intimate acquaintance, said they would probably be neighbors for some time during the erection of the bridges. She did not echo the hope and they touching their caps, decamped going back to Strasburg. They behaved more like white people than should have been expected of men in their line of profession. Their commander said they were a choice company composed entirely of young ministers and pious young men. I presume said hopeful Christians, and purchase the indulgence of swearing from "Fathers" Beecher or Tyng. As they indulged to a degree in that elegant past time. Dick Bayly left for the army two days after that — went to Jim Bowen's cavalry. Poor fellow! He's so careless and thoughtless that I'm afraid he will suffer not a little during his novitiate. Thursday evening last while sitting together chatting with Cousin Mary Pierce, Laura came in to say, "The Yankees are coming!" We rushed to the pavement and truly, there they were, about 50 horsemen riding cautiously and timidly down the road toward town — looking much more like a band of cowardly rogues as they are than a body of victorious warriors. They did manage to raise a canter as they entered town, when they immediately proceeded to Becky Reed's and put her through a system of cross questions. She told them that we were all true and loyal Unionists to a man. It happened that the board of examination for the militia men were sitting that evening, but were warned by Firth and Anderson in time to dispense ere the arrival of the foe, but not before they had heard that such had been the occupation of the people during the day. They rode up to the hotel and one of them (who actually proved to be the renegade son of Virginia — Porte Crayon) inquired for Reverend R. T. Berry— and being satisfied as to his whereabouts they then turned to Dr. Dorsey, Mr. Haney and others seated under the porch and inquired whether or not we were loyal citizens? "We are secession to a unit," was Mr. Haney's reply. They then asked if the draft was successful and added that if our men only knew what they were fighting for they felt assured that it would have been decidedly a failure. They were told that we entertained an idea that led us to believe that we did know what we fought for—whereupon, they touched their caps, wished we might never have a more unfriendly visit and left as quietly with as little demonstration as they had entered. They were in town scarcely fifteen minutes and I'm inclined to believe the exodus was hastened by the information which tis said they obtained from Julia Overall — viz that we had 500 cavalry scattered along the mountains who were acting as scouts and guards and were keeping a strict watch over the affairs of the vicinity. This force of course existed only in her imagination, but it must have had the desired effects for they have not been here since. Don't you think Belle Boyd went on the porch at the hotel and engaged in conversation with them during the little time they were here? She does make herself too conspicuous indeed. I do not know where the Feds are now encamped. Some were on the hill above Mr. Kendrick's house and constructing boats 'tis said—you know Jackson had all the boats on the river as far as Clem's Mill destroyed a short time since and as the river is high, they will have some little difficulty in crossing with the infantry. I believe they have raised their standard on the hill and have things conducted in military style—do not know what they number—some say one thousand but I've no idea there are so many there yet. You should have been standing on the style where we stood this morning and heard the sullen roll of their drums and the distant booming of their guns (we can hear the volley of musketry and the report of cannon very distinctly from up the valley) and I know you would have felt the blood seething through your veins. Had I been told three months ago that we all should have witnessed the triumphant entry of the enemy into our very midst without a sensation of fear, I could not have believed it, but such is the fact. It may have been the affect of excitement which made me daring, but I rather think it was indignation. I used to shudder at the base idea of their coming, but now every feeling of timidity seems to be swallowed up in anger or a sickening longing for revenge such as I never expected to experience. I feel as if all my better feelings were entirely dormant and I'm afraid if this hardening process continue much longer I shall become as heartless as they themselves. To think that we are as slaves to them! That they not only claim our property and persons, but they want to fetter our minds and hearts, our thoughts flow in just such channels as they shall direct, our hearts throb to just such sentiments as they endorse and we are impotent in their hands, depending on their caprice for continuation of life or the enjoyment of the necessities of existence with no chance of redress. Oh! Isn't it hard? And then not dare to tell them what you think of them, to hold in apparently friendly grasp the hand that holds the steel to our breasts, to feed and give comfort to creatures who would burn the roof over your head and not venture to do it reluctantly either! Only imagine we offering refreshments to the man who would gladly in the next battle lay either of you cold in death in the field. I won't do it! They have thus far committed but comparatively few deprivations—'tis not their policy to proceed to violent measures as long as there's a chance of proselying. They had rather lull the people into a fancied security and after winning their confidence the game is easily secured. I believe they are resolved on doing as much mischief as possible and the longer it is deferred the worse it will be when it does come and there is no use trying to keep off the evil by appearing to be willing slaves—it will do no good and they will respect you less for it.

Don't you remember Chenowith—the Methodist minister who once preached here? He it was who conducted the creatures into Winchester and promised to act as guide through Front Royal—said he knew Brother Petty and Brother Trout well—had eaten many a nice meal there and made very large promises as to what he could do for them—. Oh I have not the patience to write about him! You have doubtlessly ere this heard the particulars of the battle at Kernstown near Winchester—but you may not know that though our numbers were forced to retreat it was in fact a victory on our part. Jackson received bogus orders to advance upon Winchester which was represented as having been evacuated. He obeyed, was surrounded on three sides by five times his number, cut his way through them, disabled them so that they could not immediately pursue him and retreated to his former position. 'Tis said the Yankees confessed to the loss of 1400 killed, while we only lost 80 killed and 200 prisoners. Ashby has been fighting for 19 days almost without intermission—has killed 200 and <u>lost two men</u>. He seems to be invincible—there were nine balls sent at one time toward him the other day without effect—he has his horse shot from under him, his hair shaved by the bullets and was not long since invited to dine at the house of an old Tory who had a nest of the Feds concealed at the house ready to pounce on their prey. But he was too smart for them and invited some 20 of his men to accompany him—seeing which unexpectedly addition to the number of guests—the Yankees decamped leaving Ashby to enjoy his repast in peace. When he had finished he offered a reciprocity of hostilities and took the old Tory home with him per force and it is likely his visit will be a prolonged one. You have ere this heard that Cousin Newt Cloud and Tom Buck had emigrated from Missouri and Arkansas and came to join the Army in Virginia. Bowen's Company they've chosen I believe but Cousin Newt is not well enough to join the army yet and Tom has been waiting to pay his old Father a visit. The other day he slipped through the enemy's pickets and going along the mountain reached home. But had only been there a few hours when the Yankees came in one door and he went out the other and running the blockade went to Clover Hill. Cousin Newt is at Cousin Sam Buck's, Henry Buck is home sick and Cousin Mount at Mr. Hall's. So if it be true that the enemy intend crossing to Luray to divide Jackson's forces I am fearful they may capture some or all of them. We received a letter from Uncle John dated New Market the other day in which he spoke of the safe arrival of Alex and Horace there—I confessed 'tis more than I expected of them. I do not know how the change of affairs has affected the servants here—I can detect but little if any change in them. But I believe as a general thing the love of freedom is strong within them that they would risk almost anything to obtain it. I do believe though that they are a little afraid of their "deliverers" You never heard of such cruelties as they've perpetuated in Winchester—they ordered two or three of Mr. E. Bowens servants to do some very hard service in which they demurred whereupon they were shot and bayoneted. They worked them and beat them as no Southern gentlemen would dream of doing, and are afraid to leave them at liberty at night lest they should run away, so they lock them in the jail. Some <u>have</u> escaped and returned to their masters and bring awful accounts of their treatment. I don't believe Bob Roy or Harriet will go with them for Bob is very much afraid of them, but further "desponent sayeth not." They may take the servants, I'm willing to work—wash, iron, scour or ___ shears in the field if need be—but I want them to leave a few farm horses that we may till the land and raise a little bread. There are serious apprehensions entertained by many in regard to this thing—the valley has been drained of its substance for the support of our army, we have no men to cultivate grains—our servants will have left us, our horses taken away and how are we to keep from starvation? This is what Uncle Mack and Uncle Tom and almost everyone says but somehow I and Father are hopeful of better things. Though I cannot tell in what shape to expect relief—I only feel that we are not well enough acquainted with military affairs to judge the plans of our Generals and I think that the abandonment of the valley for a time will ultimately prove to have been the best thing for us though we cannot see it now but above all I believe in a just and merciful God and I do not think He will permit <u>Might</u> long to triumph over <u>Right</u> in this unholy war waged by our enemies; I believe that with His assistance and protection—we will come off conquerors in the conflict and our beautiful Virginia be freed from the power of the oppressor very soon. Or if this be not His will—if it be our lot to suffer longer and more cruel things than we've yet known—then I hope He will give us strength as our day and not give us more than we are able to endure. We certainly have deserved to suffer this much and more for past ingratitude.

Tell George Hope that they're all well as usual at home and that his mother wrote him a few days since at the same time we wrote you—but I doubt if you even got either of them. Have not heard from Captain Roy since Thursday when Cousin Mary Pierce who is staying there came over. She said that Mrs. Roy had been quite unwell for a week with a sore throat but was much cheered by the receipt of a letter from Benton and Scott the same day. The Warren Rifles are at Orange Courthouse in a very comfortable fixed in their new huts there. Scott and Charley Buck have both rejoined the company—the latter has much improved in health. The friends generally are well and always tell me to send love to you both. Uncle T. just left said I must tell you he often and earnestly thinks of you both. Aunt Calmes says the same thing. And now precious brothers, I feel in closing this long letter as if I were taking a long farewell of you both—as if you were just reenacting your last departure from home. Little did I think the last time I watched your forms disappearing in the darkness as you winded your way down the old footpath from the house—little did I think of the changes that would take place within so short a time after our separation. And now I know as little of what may occur the time that must intervene ere we can again hear from much less to see you. We may not have another opportunity of writing until those evil spirits are exorcised from our land—but if it be possible we will endure to let you hear from us sometimes even though we send you only sad tidings. Meanwhile you know not what our anxiety and uneasiness on your account will be. We can only hear from Beauregard through the medium of the Northern papers and of course they will always present the darkest side to our view and we generally have to reverse the news they contain. For instance, if they say Beauregard and his command have been captured, I shall firmly believe he has just given them a tremendous thrashing—so that we may possibly arrive at the truth in that way. Yet this will not be hearing directly from you. We won't know if you are sick or in comfortable quarters or anything about it. Oh it is hard! But there as one consolation that the fact of our not being able to receive tidings from you would not materially influence your comfort and you would be just as well off as if we knew all about you. And our generals can fight their battles just so well and achieve our independence just as well with, as without our knowledge of the march of events. And besides the stoppage of the mail communications may, after all, spare us the hearing of a good deal of bad news (sour grapes).

Think of us often dear brothers, though I [know] you cannot as often as we do of you—think of us, but do not make yourselves uneasy about us for I am persuaded that all will yet be well with us. We have the same Protector that you have and we must all try and cast our care upon One "Who careth for us." I need not say how much love each member of the home circle sends you. They all send messages which I cannot remember now but will leave you to imagine. Give our love to Cousin George and say we hope someday to have the pleasure of welcoming him to Warren again. <u>When we're free!</u> God bless you both and in His mercy restore you to us again—prays your sister.

Lucie

Uncle Tom says if you direct letters to Stanardsville, Green County, c/o Mr. Alfred Almond it is barely possible that we may get them through to some future period. I do wish Alvin that you could see Evred now. He is so saucy and so sweet and says pretty much what he pleases. He knows your ambrotypes and always begs to see them when I open my drawer where I keep them. He calls every young gentleman who comes to the house "Abbie" Mr. Brierwood and Senth both are always "Abbie". Willie makes some sharp speeches too. He tells Grandma that we had all better eat up all of that preserved citron as the Yankees are coming and will get it anyway. For the same reason he wants to wear his best clothes everyday. When he first heard they were coming the other day he commenced crying bitterly saying he wanted to tell himself good-bye "before they came;" he brightened up very much in a little while as if a consoling reflections had preceded his fear and remarked with a high most expression of relief—"well Cora Richards is out of their reach, she's in Culpepper." The thought of the safety of his _____ really seemed to comfort him. That _____ I call disinterested _____ Nellie and Laura have not been to school for several weeks as Mr. Brierwood had _____ not been able to teach. I guess though he'll start again next week and I'll be so lonely again. I continue teaching the boys but fear they do not make such progress as they should. 'Tis so hard for them to fix their minds upon anything like regular study and I don't wonder at it.

I have your letters concealed where I think it will puzzle the Yankees to find them let them search never so diligently _____ contrabands. They won't get your ambrotypes either nor my diary nor the silver spoons nor my jewelry. And if they can find fire arm about the house it won't be because Nellie has not done her best to prevent them.

(She hid her treasures under her hoop-skirt.)

Monday Evening, 5:00, March 31
(1862)

Well Dear Boys, Tis all over! Bel Air has been desecrated by the presence of those emissaries of darkness!

I finished my letter to you yesterday intending to send it off this morning but was disappointed by my opportunity — so I'll open it now and send you an additional account of the proceedings of our compulsory guest. Mr. Richards came up this morning to warn us to take care of our provisions such as potatoes, bacon, lard, corn and poultry and to be on the qui-vive all the time as the wily Feds were not to be trusted with a "coffin seven." He said they had seventy-five at the river yesterday but said they would soon have four or five regiments quartered in Front Royal where they would be a convenient distance from the main army should it need reinforcements. Some ten of the officers staid in his <u>house</u> last night and he does not pretend to know how many were quartered in the kitchen. One of them came in before Cousin Bet's face and asked for "that lady" (meaning old Aunt Charlotte, the cook) and then remarked to Cousin B. that one of her "bands" (contrabands) had promised to bake him some bread and he had promised to reward her services with a whole barrel of flour. He could well afford to do this as they seized all the flour poor Mr. Weston had at the River Station Depot. One of the officers told Mr. Richards yesterday that no private property should be molested and that he would station a guard about the house to prevent any annoyance from "the boys." Nevertheless the next morning he found himself minus potatoes and they had actually taken five of his bee stands. Oh he was so provoked! He called the above mentioned officer to him and told him about the theft as soon as it was discovered — the officer looked very much mystified but we no doubt that he shared in the spoils if he did not participate in the performance. Nellie said if those bees had been anything like true succession bees they'd have stung the Yankees into a sense of propriety. Mr. R. says they brought four Union flags into his hall the first thing, wasn't that mean of them?

Mr. R. left about dinner time, and directly after dinner I was sitting nursing the little babe singing "Maryland" in a very audible tone of voice singing it with the spirit and the understanding — when in a little while they came in and said that three Yankees were here. I went to the window and saw three of them out on the pavement. When Father came out they walked up to him and asked him if he could give them a little dinner. He greeted very coldly and asked if it were possible the officers did not furnish them provisions? "Yes," they said they had rations at the camp but they had been walking around reconnoitering and they were quite hungry. They went down into the dining room and I begged Ma to send Harriet and Bob Roy down to preside at the board — but she would not. One comfort they did not have anything very tempting for their repast. Harriet would not trouble herself to provide very abundantly for them. I was so glad! And don't you think they absolutely thanked Father when they concluded their meal. Mr. Brierwood finding that they were here came over immediately and he and Father plied them well with questions. You know at the late battle near Winchester they refused us permission to bury our dead and Mr. Philip Williams performed the sad duty himself — while he was going over the battlefield collecting the remains of our poor fellows he had an opportunity of observing the number slain on the other side, and reported accordingly. When Father asked the Yankees about it today they remarked that they thought Mr. W. had a great deal of "brass" to speak of it in that way. Father told them that he wanted them to respect the Rose Hill family and mansion and spoke of the amiable qualities of said family. They made many fair promises of forbearance themselves and promised to report to their officers any of their comrades who should transgress. They'll keep their word of course — they always do — they said they were very harmless — would not take anything from quiet citizens except poultry and that "the boys" could not help stealing sometimes. We are going to feast on turkeys for some time to come 'tis the only way to rescue them from their ravenous appetites. Mr. Brierwood talked to them pretty plainly and remarked that he wished our "First Maryland regiment" could meet with their First Maryland regiment in conflict. They said theirs was composed of right "hard chaps". Mr. B. told them that ours differed being composed of gentlemen. Oh! Boys you don't know how degraded I felt at being under the same roof with such creatures and when I saw them sitting on the front porch just where I had so often sat with you both — where we have so often played together — where I have always welcomed you on your return or wept your departure it was as much as I could do to keep back the angry tears. But I was determined not to be overcome by any such weakness, 'twould have gratified them too much could they have known it. The air seemed oppressed by their presence and I could not half breathe till they left and then I was right dizzy from indignation. Would you believe it? I felt no sensation of fear and I have never seen Ma and Grandma calmer. Aunt Betsy was very much frightened — Aunt C. simply wrathful. You would be so much surprised to see how bold we've all grown. I'm as much astonished at it myself tho as you could be. What would you think to see a Yankee paper published at Front Royal? It is not at all unlikely — for they say they intend editing one here. Wouldn't I like to write some articles for them though? The Yankees said that it would be a pity to kill as noble a fellow as Turner Ashby — they only wished he were on the right side and what a gallant fellow he would be! I presume they want to take him prisoner so as to cage him. I've no doubt he would be very profitable to Barnum more so than the "What — was — it?"

Jackson has been largely reinforced and 'tis to be hoped he will deliver us from the hands of our enemies. We have heard heavy cannonading today and hope from the direction whence the sounds proceed that he is driving them back toward Winchester. I have unbounded confidence in this brave commander of ours and cannot help but think he will ere long recover what he has been forced to give up in the Valley.

'Tis, I believe, a mistake about their sending so large a force here from Lincolndom. We heard this evening that Henry Buck is at Cousin Sam's and rather more secure than he would be at home. Father is waiting and I must close with oceans of love from all. The little "Dixie" looks as if he would like to send his big brothers some message but language is inadequate to express all he feels and you must draw upon your imaginations for it. Goodbye dear boys.

Ever your devoted sister,
Lu

I forgot to say that the yankees did not rejoice in the light of our countenance today — did not see the face of a single lady of the family and Nell and I've resolved to be invisible to their sight so long as they remain here.

Oh I just <u>wish</u> I had time to tell you how these yankees have been cutting up here and I reckon Lu and I don't spit fire and wormwood when yankees are named. Oh I hate them and love to hate them as Grandpa use to say. I've seen them four times but they've seen me nary time yet. But I'm so sleepy. How does the mump go Irvie? And Miss Tolliferro Alvin? Good night — write soon to us.

Your ever fond sister,
Nellie

Corinth, Mississippi
May 15, 1862 (arrived June 19, 1862)

Dear Ma,[7]
Yours and Nellies letter received this evening. I have written but it seems without success.

We are all well. Roy (Benton) been promoted is Captain and A.A. Gen.[8]

Cousin Willie, Alick, Frank B, Marcus Newton and Dick Blakemore are here, Dick has similar position to my own.

Feel no uneasiness on our _____ General Jordan will take good care of_____

Lucie's voluminous letter of _____ has also been received —

Hope, Williams, Dick, Alvin and all _____ well

I send this by Flag of Truce with f _____ it may reach you—

Much love to all —

Ever your affectionate son,
Irving

Dick received his mother's letter a few days ago —

Marshall Blakemore is also in the _____ here, though I have seen him but once _____ is _____ hearty and very little change — Billy _____ called to see us he is Captain — Let me hear from you as frequently as possible —
"Irvie"

Bel Air
May 24, 1862

My Precious Brothers,

How can I begin to tell you all that has occurred here in the last 24 hours? My heart is _so_ full, and yet I do not feel as if my cup were full until I can make you participants of our joy. We are in Dixie once more! There is not a Yankee, excepting those under guard (we've a goodly number of _those_) this side of Winchester. We are for the present time _free_ - free to think, speak and act as inclination prompts us, and only those who have been in cruel bondage can know what a blessed privilege this is. This time yesterday morning, we were subject to the greatest petty tyrant in the person of a Yankee Colonel, that I ever saw. He would not so much as let a citizen go out of town or a country man come in, on any occasion though it might be a life and death emergency and we saw nothing but helpless starvation and suffering staring us in the face, because he would not permit any fuel or provisions to be brought into the place and his men were helping to rob us of what little we had there. Oh the hour seemed a dark one! but a glorious dawn was near.

We have known for some time that the Yankees were frightened almost out of their wits because they had seen some of our men in the mountains and fancied that the "Stonewall" was meditating a "fell swoop"! The more alarmed they became the more rigid they grew, until we began to think there must be some grounds for their fears and a "renewal of hope brought us consolation." Although it was whispered among some our "rebels" that several of the Confederate calvary had been scouting in town during the week, still we did not suppose that they were here for any other purpose than to gratify a spirit of bold adventure and to gain information for some remote purpose. And here let me add parenthetically, a word about these same scouts of ours. Walter and Sam Simpson are tyro Ashbys. I wish I dare tell you how wonderfully bold and courageous they've been - all that they've been doing at intimate peril of life - but I must not because, I don't know what Paul Pry of a Yankee this may fall into the hands of and I never would bear the idea of betraying to them any Sesech secrets. Bless the two brave fellows! though I say.*

Yesterday morning Colonel Kenly seemed to be unusually apprehensive, and as we felt assured there was something brewing, Ma and I concluded to run up to Mrs. Hopes and learn if they had received any intelligence of movements on either side. A Yankee, who had happened to be in the meadow below the house saw us go toward town and evidently fancied we were news bearers for the Southern army for he jumped over the fence and stealthily followed us until we went into the house; There we encountered another of the genus of who was anxiously inquiring if he could - "git some 'aigs and buther." His footsteps had scarce grown cold on the threshold ere we heard the sharp report of a rifle and another and another in quick succession and Ma saw the <u>brave</u> Union soldiers scampering about our front meadow in a very undignified manner but we concluded they were in pursuit of some escaped prisoners and expended a vast deal of sympathy upon the supposed unhappy captives. In about two minutes Miss Bettie White rushed in with disheveled locks and almost fainting exclaiming, "Oh my God! the Southern army is coming — they've fired upon and driven in the yankee pickets, and they're fighting on the hill above town. Oh my God! The hills are just 'black' with our calvary! Some water! Quick Julia Ann!" You can guess Ma and I did not tarry to see whether or not she fainted but snatching our up bonnets made for home at "double quick"; for although we knew what a sensationlist Miss B. was still we knew that something extraordinary was transpiring. Upon reaching home we found Nellie, spyglass in hand at the upper window and when she exclaimed, "Oh! they <u>are</u> our <u>dear</u> boys!" I looked in the direction indicated and as long as I live, I never, never shall forget the thrill with which I recognized our "gray coat" rebels, and to refrain from crying from delight was more than we could do. We saw our boys emerge from the woods to the right of the "Manor Grade" above the Court House first. Calvary (and, to our eyes everyone there was Walter) then a few infantry skirmishers. While engaged looking at <u>our</u> men we forgot the enemy until I heard someone exclaim "Look how they scamper!" And truly they did, not even in<u> broken lines</u>, but singly, in couples, in tribes, in quartettes and "ad libitum", armed and unarmed, contrabands and Yankees. Some of them did form into column and make a feint of returning fire, some went up into the Court House and hospital windows and fired away harmlessly at our men, only one shot I believe taking effect killing one of our poor men. But our cavalry (amounting to they afterwards told us to only a General's guard) charged upon them and then commenced a general stampede; the Manassas Races on a small scale. I never did see such "fast" men in my life, it seemed as if each man was endeavoring to gain distinction by putting down and raising up his foot faster than his neighbor; some to save time came out by the carriage house and I don't know whether Aunt L. Blakemore, Nellie or I were most delighted, and you would not blame us for laughing and cheering if you could only know how we have writhed under their insulting taunts about the "Rebel Race from Winchester," the unhappy condition of "degraded old Virginia." I think I was insane for a little while for I don't remember anything more until I found myself on the upper porch waving to our cavalry who had by this time commenced dashing by and Father telling me if I could not restrain my excitement I had better come in where I could not see them. Just then the whole company halted below the house and Walter and an officer rode hurriedly up to the house, the officer to make inquiries as to the route the Yankees took, and Walter to bid us — "Cheer up and be gladdened than we ever were in our lives before," for Jackson and Ewell were coming to whip the yankees from us. You never saw a boy so enthusiastically welcomed in your life, but our interview was interrupted by the boom of the Yankee cannon which opened upon our boys from that little skirt of woods on the right of the road above Rose Hill where it had been planted a week before for the purpose of "shelling the town" when the "rebels" came in. You should have seen Walter coolly riding away regarding the shell and balls as more than he would an April shower. We had one piece of artillery on the hill above the Court House and another nay, I believe two others in the edge of the woods near the road leading to "Mountain View" and these with the two Yankee cannon kept up a continual dialogue. One shell cut a corner of the mill roof off and passing through embedded itself in the railroad embankment without exploding. Another exploded in the barn tearing the weather boarding like brown paper, if it had come on in a straight line to the house it might have played the "wilds." Nellie and I were standing in the porch when one of them passed over the house with a great whiz and cutting off the twigs of the aspen tree went on it's errand of death toward Mr. Hope's mill. One fell in the mill, one on the hill just above their house and one very near Uncle Tom's house. For a time both Rose Hill and Oakley were exposed to a crossfire, but no one was injured fortunately there or in town; it seems almost miraculous that more of the shells did not fall in town for I know the Yankees did not take any particular pains to prevent them having threatened its destruction long since. I cannot tell you how strangely calm I felt all this time and whenever we could slip up out of the basement (where we all took refuge,) we, Nellie and I were with Father on the porch watching the progress of the skirmish and did not realize our danger until it was all over. Grandma, Aunt Lettitia, and Calmes and Aunt B. although alarmed were calmer than you would think for. Ma was not frightened, but the excitement made her nervous; the little ones were some of them very much distressed but I believe Orville and Cary rather enjoyed it. I was more amused at the servants — they were terribly frightened, Bob Roy in particular who was nervous from sickness. and don't you think some of the contrabands in town who have been the most familiar with the Yankees when the firing commenced came right away over here and betook themselves to our kitchen for refuge, glad enough to seek protection at a slave owner's hand. Well, we silenced the battery on the hill and a little skirmish took place in the field immediately by the Rose Hill barn, in those little pines there, and about the old Lehew house. We drove the enemy to the river - across the bridges (which they had completed only the day before) took possession of the bridges and depot. They planted a cannon on "Guard Hill" and poured a brisk fire down on us, but we soon ousted them although they had greatly the advantage of us. You must understand the main body of our army had not yet come into town, that the fight was only between our advanced guard and the enemy - our men almost worn out with forced marches of 6 or 8 days - their men fresh, well fed and equipped, amounting to I don't know what number, for they always kept them marching and countermarching in and out of town purposely to prevent our making any estimate, but I suppose there were several regiments. Do you know, the 1st Maryland regiment C.S. and the first U.S. have ever since the war professed to be very anxious to meet? Well, we had the honor of being the 1st U.S. stationed here and the first C.S. were the foremost in making the charge and I tell you they did meet with a vengeance, our men taking or killing the whole regiment not fifteen escaping, and marching their prisoners into town singing "My Maryland" to them and it was just as much as our officers could do to prevent our men from cutting their throats. Mr. Petty and a number of the older citizens say they never saw such determination in any men's faces in their lives as was expressed by our Marylanders - that they never saw such a desperate charge as they made. I was delighted to think that the Yankee 1st was among the captured, for I tell you they are an awful sett.

The telegram wires along the road were out at eleven o'clock A.M. (how, no one about here knows) so the Yankees below, did not know the state of affairs here and very unsuspectingly sent their two trains of cars (some say three) up here, when Major Wheat of the N.O. battalion, took both of the two trains and pressed them into the service of the C.S. They had been transporting a large amount of supplies to the two depots here and at River Station, and from an unfinished Yankee letter taken at River Station had been intending to throw a large reinforcement over this side of the Shenandoah. We took all their stores to the sum of many hundred thousand dollars - hay, salt (very much needed), sugar, tools, flour, clothing (several boxes of which had never been opened), arms, ammunition, some few horses and a few new saddles, - besides the tents and wagons which they left in their hurried flight. They had pine torches all about the depot here and were just in the act of igniting them when the incendiaries — a contraband and white were discovered and taken I suppose either to be hung or shot. We took all the artillery they had here too, four pieces. When the main body of the army came in we all went over to the street opposite Mr. Petty's and saw them come in. Poor fellows! So dusty and worn they looked, some barefooted, many of them ragged and nearly all ravenous, but far from dispirited, for it was one incessant cheer from one end of the line to the other, whenever the regimental battle flag was borne by we would salute it and it seemed to delight them greatly. They would wave aloft their bread, pickles, meat, pies or whatever edibles they had in their hands and cheer themselves, Jeff Davis, the C.S. and the ladies. One poor little fellow as he passed by turned to us and remarked with a sin-comic expression, "Ah, ladies, I'm too tired to holler now!" You never saw people so happy in your life as were our good citizens, every door was thrown open and inhabitants stood on the sidewalks with water and provisions of every kind refreshing the weary troops as they passed by and every eye gleamed through a mist of grateful tears and every lip seemed wearing a "God Bless You!" It was a scene which must have thrilled the coldest heart and call forth such emotions as are not often felt in a life time. Cousin Mount Cloud rode up while we stood there and he told us that Cousin Horace Buck had a letter from one of you to us and that he knew you were well, but though we have been trying to get that letter all day it has not as yet made its appearance.

We had three of the soldiers to tea, a Mr. Meriweather, Colonel Johnston of the 1st Maryland, and Adjutant Ward of the same. By the way Irvie, the same Frank Ward is the "<u>cousin</u> Frank" you've heard Nannie dear so often refer to; he spoke to them and remarked that though they were really not connected that she had claimed cousinship with him. I'm going to write her a letter for the express purpose of delivering a message which he sent her. Only don't be jealous for 'twas not a particularly tender one. He is farming the Mount Vernon estate - agent, I suppose of the MV Ladies Association - is quite young but one of the most refined polished fellows and very agreeable. He gave me some trophies taken this evening - photographs of Beauregard, McClellan, Burnside and Corcovan; He also had daguerreotypes, one —a lady who's residence is in Baltimore he knows. He declares his intention of giving it to her in person when he gets there and he insists on being there by June 18. Colonel Johnston was also very pleasant. We did not retire till twelve o'clock so delightedly engaged were we in listening to our bands and trying to count the regiments that marched by. This morning I think we had some thirty to breakfast among them some sprinkling of New Orleans Tigers sans the Tonrre uniform. There was among them a distant cousin _____ Ashby, and a Mr. Morton, one of the FirstFamilies of Virginia acting as assistant surgeon. He spent a great part of the morning here while we were repairing his holster and belt and he is not only a throughbred Virginia gentleman but I think a good Christian - very intelligent and converses beautifully. Mr. Hobltgell and his friend Mr. Russell were over early and Captain Gardiner of the New Orleans "Star" battalion. All seemed in the best possible spirits and are confident of success. 'Twas a pleasure to hear them talk. Henry Heater came over to have his strained wrist cared for too.

72

Mack Bayly and Cousin Tom Buck have been with us and give some amusing accounts of individual daring. They had quite a battle at Ninevah and Cedarville and 'tis said the dead Yankees are in heaps along the road - we don't know and never will know how many they've lost for they have carried a great many off. We have lost comparatively few excepting at Bucton where our loss is said to have been heavy owing to the recklessness of our men. Our brave and ever to be lamented Sheets fell there. Next to Ashby and Jackson he was the greatest terror to the Yankees. They called him the "Red Fox" because they said they had had him twelve times in strait from which no one but a fox could have escaped but he <u>did,</u> and at last fell pierced through the heart by a bullet just as he waved his sword above his head giving the word of command. He had received his promotion to a Colonelcy a few days before. I never saw a man so regretted - his death seemed to have dampened the ardor of the whole army. He now lies at Mr. Boone's ready for burial which will take place tomorrow. He ought to have a lofty monument erected to his memory, but whether that be done or not he will ever live in the hearts of those whom he died in defense of. We lost two other gallant Captains in the same regiment. Cousin Tom Buck had a horse shot under him, but so determined was he that the Yankees should not have the benefit of his bridle and saddle, that after the horse rolled thirty feet down an embankment into the creek he waded in under a perfect avalanche of bullets and took them away with him. Sandie Buck had also a horse shot under him and his mother and father were in the depot at the time and witnessed it all. Ship Mitchell took <u>five</u> Yankees prisoners on his <u>own</u> responsibility. They were much armed with two revolvers apiece but yielded like good fellows for all that. Belle Boyd has been here for a week - said when she first came, that she was enroute for Richmond where she was to be married to Dr. Kennedy (one of the medical faculty who had charge of the hospitals here last winter) and settle down. Well, don't you think "they say" when all the firing was going on the other day that she wanted a dispatch carried to our men on the hill, but no one being found to undertake the perilous enterprise, she took it herself and came back with her dress riddled with bullets. I don't know how true this is - only hear the rumor as I've heard it from several sources. I think the story a very probable one.

We heard today that Cousin Sarah Buck, Cousin Ed's mother died last week from cold taken while watching the Yankees pass by; I have no doubt the excitement had a great deal to do with it. Poor thing! She suffered greatly here but I hope and believe she has made a happy exchange. Cousin Ed and Will are up the Valley. There is very heavy cannonading going on up the Valley towards Winchester and I expect Banks has by this time learned of "Stonewall's" approach. I forgot to tell you that the wounded are some of them in town - Cousin E. Richardson had several with her - one had his leg amputated and died soon afterwards. It must have reminded her so forcibly of poor Willie's sufferings; you know he has been paroled and we expect him home very soon now. We feel very anxious about our friends in Johnston's division. I'm afraid as there's so much sickness down there that they'll have some of them to go into hospital and I've such a horror of that. I wonder if any of them remember that this day one year ago they were driven from Alexandria. And by the way yesterday was the anniversary of the ratification of the ordinance of secession. I wonder if the fleeing Yankees thought of <u>that</u>.

I have so intent telling about the exodus of the Union troops that I have not said a word about how we were invested just exactly one short week ago. Ten or fifteen thousand of Shield's division passed through, and as it was raining in torrents they had to encamp here for two days. The first we knew of it all a Yankee officer dashed up one early morning and told Father that he had selected his two meadows below the house for an encampment for General Kimball's brigade remarking at the same time that the General would pitch his tent near the home if he could not get quarters under the roof which, being indisposed, he much preferred doing. Father then concluded as he would have them so near him at any rate that they had better be in the house as a protection; so he told the officer that they could if they chose occupy the West end, which they proceeded to do with all possible alacrity. I never did witness such a scene as was presented after the troops marched in - rails seemed possessed of a strange vitality for they took to themselves wings and flew away. They even went to town and unroofed some of the old sheds there for firewood. I could not help crying when I saw the field of luxuriant wheat all laid open to the incursion of stock particularly when I remembered that this was our sole dependence for bread the next winter. To give General K his dues I will say he made every effort to save the outside enclosures - sent off couriers in every direction with orders that they should not be touched, but you know it is a very difficult matter to induce 4,000 weary, wet and hungry men to sit down and listen to reason without a fire when there is plenty of wood around to give them a cheerful blazing fire. They were a sorry looking sett truly, but some made themselves comparatively comfortable with the tents they pitched and the little plank huts that seemed to spring up everywhere spontaneously. They pitched three tents in the back yard for the orderlies and servants of the General and it afforded us infinite amusement to watch from the windows their housekeeping and culinary arrangements only I was too much vexed with the whole party to enjoy it as I otherwise might have done. Nellie and I had nothing to do with any of them - though the General and his staff took their meals regularly with the family we never went down in the dining room till the second table where we generally encountered one of the attache's of the staff. This same Yankee must have a very exalted idea of our cousin's soldier-boys for we made it a matter of conscientious duty to converse with each other about the "<u>dear</u> brave fellows." And we took too, particular delight in speaking of our "Noble Beauregard" and "Ashby;" and when they had it several times reported that Ashby was prisoner, we agreed with each other at the table that he would certainly die before permitting himself to be captured — and we did not anyway believe any such rumors because they had had Beauregard dead <u>eight times</u>, but he had afterwards revived long enough to hurt the Unionists considerably at Pittsburgh Landing. I never directly opened my lips to one of them excepting an old wolf in sheep's clothing in the person of a chaplain of an Ohio regiment and he told me so many palpable falsehoods that I would not stay to hear him out but deliberately got up and left the room. The General himself administered a handsome rebuke to him at the table one day for his impertinence and afterwards told Father he was the greatest old hypocrite alive and followed him everywhere boring him almost to death. I never have seen more delicate consideration and gentlemanly courtesy in my life than was displayed by the General and his whole staff, while here - they told Father when they left that no efforts on their part should be wanting to reinstate him (he lost some seven hundred dollars by their occupation) but I don't believe one word of that promise as I believe they make it a point to break all they make.

The Yankees don't like this place much - say "it's a mean, bitter Secesh place anyway" I could fill sheets of paper telling you the good things said to them by men, women and children, yes little children scarcely able to talk shake their tiny fists in their face and say "Do dare Yankee!" I'll try to remember something to tell you when you come home. I must not how ever omit giving you an account of a little occurrence that took place a short time since. I think it must grace the annals of war. When we were first invested (infested) one Saturday night. The little baby was sick and Ma had a light in her room. The next morning bright and early three rough old Teutonic Yankees came over and wanted to know why we had been making signals to the rebel cavalry on the mountains, said that they were on guard at the depot and saw a singular light moving about at the window and assuming a variety of significant forms - that the officers had ordered them to fire into all such phenomena and they would have done so if Mr. Turner had not told them we had a large family here and that probably it was a sick light. When Father laughed at the absurdity of the whole affair they became angry and talked so rudely that it frightened us. Father at least succeeded in convincing them of the fallacy of their theory as to the signals and they said, "Well," they "did not care a straw about it anyway just as they got their pay," "but, as they were obliged to obey orders we must either extinguish every light by nine o'clock, have thick curtains at the windows or suffer the consequences." So those minions of "Abraham the Conqueror," not to be a whit behind the great Norman tyrant, instituted a modified system of the curfew. And, Sunday as it was, we had to get to work and put up blinds all the time wishing that "Alvin and Irving could only know to what we are subjected and sympathize in our detestation of our oppressors." Whenever anything extraordinary occurs our thoughts instantly revert to you and "oh, I wish we could tell dear Alvin and Irving!" is echoed by every member of the family.

But I forgot, I intended telling you about one Unionist that I don't cordially despise and the <u>only one</u>. Charlie McGetigen, the corporal of the guard that came over to see about "those lights" he came over soon after they left and apologized for them saying they were intoxicated when they witnessed those pyrotechnic displays. He then went on to speak of the war - said Abe Lincoln was the last Republican that would ever occupy the Presidential chair; that if the abolitionists North and the extremists South had been hung long ago all of this would have been spared the nation — professed a hearty dislike for the abolitionists and showed a scar on his face which he had received in denouncing them at an election riot - . Now I never saw but one Yankee in my life who confessed their abolition proclivities - and I should have believed him no more than the rest only there was something very honest and frank in his manner and face and he spoke so naively - he is quite young, a resident of Philadelphia. Father gave him a tract when he went away and the Corporal said he would bring paper, which he did the next day and continued to do whenever he could. Once, when the Michigan cavalry, the "betes noive" of the army were quartered in the vicinity he offered Father a guard to protect the premises from the thieves which he declared were a disgrace to the army. He came over himself that night and patroled the railroad below the house. When Kimball made his descent upon us — before he had fairly taken possession of "his Quarters" McGetigen came hurriedly up the hill, through the pouring rain — only replying when challenged by the General with a _____ and "I've come on business General" passed quickly on to where we stood grabed. Father's hand, regretted that he was the selected victim to the soldiers and wanted to know if he should not furnish him with a guard. When Father declined, saying the General had appointed one - he respectfully withdrew, he came back after awhile, and seeing Father in a back door tried to come in again but the sentinel refused admission through the gate. He left, and we saw him no more until the army left when as the last troops were leaving the encampment we looked down towards where Father was standing collecting his remnant of rails and there saw the little Corporal shaking hands very heartily with Father; he came on up to the house and seeing Ma on the porch congratulated her on the removal of the army. He received while here an order for marching and left very hastily - never came back again, but Father saw him in town the day that his regiment took its final departure and he told him they had been on picket ever since the day he left first, had but just returned and asked for a pass to come over but Major Tyndale would not grant it because they were momentarily expecting marching orders. I really felt like we had some little protection while he was here for I believe he felt an interest [in] Father's welfare but as he only left the day before our troops came in to deliver us, we could very well spare him and, to tell the truth, I was glad he was not in the skirmish. I really would regret his fall very much. Old Major Tyndale said he took the 28th Pennsylvania away because the Secesh were proselyting them. By the way — if you should see in the Northern papers an account of the "warm union meet- ing" held in Front Royal, [believe] never a word of it. It is all as false as the Unionists themselves. Let me tell you what a Yankee trick this same Tyndale served the "rebel

76

gentleman" here. You must know that Father, when they first came, set his face against asking a pass of the old fellow and staid away from town ten days. At last one morning two couriers and after while a messenger arrived with an invitation for him to meet with other citizens who were that evening to convene at his "headquarters to make some arrangements mutually beneficial to citizens and soldiers" (as if we and they could have anything in common). Well Father went, and the Major then presented a paper for their signature in which they were to bind themselves over to keep the peace, to give no information to the Southern army, and do nothing calculated to bring a collision between the two parties. In return, he would withdraw his pickets - allow the citizens to continue their farming and other occupations and restore to them their former privileges. This was a bitter thing to do, but they concluded as they knew nothing, they could communicate nothing to our army and that they must at last be reduced to a similar necessity by absence of supplies, so they said they would sign it if he would alter the wording - but "not one jot or one tittle should pass till all was fulfilled". And they affixed their name as it stood - Father, Uncle Mack, Jim and Newton, Mr. Berry, Drs. Hough and Dorsey, Messieurs Trout, Green, Richards, Captain Roy and numbers of others. The pickets were <u>not</u> withdrawn and no privileges restored, and the excuse — "military necessity" was in the eyes of the Yankee a sufficient one for the business of the whole proceeding. We have since heard that they've published an account of the affair under the guise of a "warm Union meeting". I truly hope the whole South may prove as strong union as the members of that committee. Tyndale left the very night before our army came in and was superseded by Colonel Kenly who's reign fortunately for us, was of short duration. The Yankees up to that time had been course and rude, but committed comparatively few depredations; but on the day preceding our deliverance went down to Rose Hill, broke in stole the last sack of salt Cousin E had - all her canned fruit, her corn and her bacon. In fact this was a foretaste of what we all would in a little have had to endure. The more I think of what has transpired within the last few days the more marvelous does it seem. The more clearly can I trace the hand of Providence in it all. And never were men worse frightened or more vigilant than the Yankees for a week preceding the advent of the "rebels" — and yet, that our pickets should have been able to come into town a week ago, that Walter should have been for days incog. so near home that he could see his little baby sister playing in the grass before the door. That so large an army could have come right upon them, literally catching some of them "napping" despite all their watchfulness is all more than I can account unless by attributing it to divine interposition in our favor little as we have deserved it. You never in your life saw anyone so completely happy as Walter was the few minutes we saw him that day. I only wish I knew the dear boy was all safe now. Father has not a hand on the place. You know he hired two free boys, Ed and Charlie. Ed went off the day after the Yankees first came in and never returned. Charlie went off a week since, but finding the Yankees supremacy waning came back today. Father told him however that he had deceived him once and he would not place it in his power to do so a second time, so he thought he had best seek a home elsewhere. Rob Roy, poor fellow, is going into a rapid decline — looks dreadfully and cannot speak above a whisper. Uncle Gilbert you know always had conscientious scruples about working - so Father has to depend on hiring chance laborers by the day when he can. I feel so sorry for him -sometimes wish I were a boy myself and had the strength to assist him. Orville and Carey do what they can towards supplying the deficiency but that is very little. Alec and Horace are in our army. The former came over to see his mother when he passed through but the latter went directly on. I can see there is universal disappointment among the servants at the flitting of their Yankee friends. They behaved very well while they were here knowing that they would have things pretty much their own way anyhow, they had even selected residences which they were told would be theirs when their masters were subjugated. Becky Reed honoring Oakley with her preference. But now they see their towering air castles fall smash to atoms and 'tis no wonder they are distressed. I feel very sorry for them, they do not know what to be at. The love of freedom is very strong within them - and I have too much of the same feeling to blame them for that. They are very ignorant don't know how incapable they are of self government, don't know that the very liberty for which they yearn would be the worst thing for them. 'Tis no wonder they should be dazzled by the pleasing future which their pretended friends opened to view, that they would make almost any sacrifice to obtain a position which they fancy they're qualified to occupy and adorn. And yet they can't altogether trust the Yankees. They are afraid to go from the protection of their masters and yet they are anxious to cast off the bonds of servitude. So in this state of doubt and uncertainty they are very unhappy and I feel infinitely more pity than anger toward them. Only I humbly trust the Yankees may never come back here again. If they do they will wrack their disappointed vengeance on us and there's not a servant at home or abroad that I would trust. Oh it would be terrible! You don't know. Don't you think Uncle Fayette's LeRoy led the Yankees to his master's house and was playing spy when our men took him - he thought they were Yankees and told them all he knew of their plans. They have him in Luray now in jail. I don't know what they'll do with him.

(Monday.) I left my letter open thinking I should be able to write you something about the battle of Winchester but 'tis impossible to get anything very definite from there. We only know that Jackson has carried everything before him, cut Banks division to pieces, took more prisoners than were taken at Manassa and would have gotten Banks himself if he had not deserted his staff and fled precipitately toward the Potomac alone. The last we heard, Ashby was in full pursuit declaring he'd take him or kill every horse in the attempt. He has my earnest wishes for success. We've taken some stores at Strasburg, taken Winchester, and Harper's Ferry and have possession of this branch of the B.&O.O. railroad, are rapidly pushing on to Maryland but our men are so completely broken down that I'm afraid they'll have to tarry awhile to recruit and thus afford the enemy time for making formidable opposition. 'Tis said that Shields is returning his steps this way to flank Jackson, but this can scarcely be so unless he has received large reinforcements which is not probable. We had seventeen hundred prisoners here last night but they all marched out to Winchester this morning. Among them was our whilom Provost Colonel Kenly who was wounded; and they do say we have Brockley, Littlefield and Stunkel and Blackwood, a quartet of as deeply dyed traitors as you'd find in Yankeedom, and that's saying a good deal. We have taken some of their "Star spangled banners" too, among them the very one they brought into town so insolently a little while ago.

We cannot arrive at any average estimate of the number killed and wounded in the battle of Winchester. I've no doubt we've lost many brave spirits, but the Yankee division was almost perhaps quite, annihilated. We have some of our men here, who were wounded in the skirmish Friday evening, scattered about town some at Rose Hill, none at Bel Air as it was not so near the scene of action. They have some of the wounded Yankees at Dr. Brown's who received the same kind care that our men there do although they treated the family so badly. They tell me that there are some deceased Yankees in the barn field and one buried down here in the meadow. I don't know how true it is and don't intend to investigate the matter where "ignorance is bliss 'twere folly to be wise." We have a number of broken down sick soldiers in town. Poor fellows! I do feel so sorry for them. Nellie and I are literally on bread and water that we may have the more milk to send them. Many of them can't eat anything else, and 'twould be a shame indeed if one could not make that little sacrifice for those who have done so much for us. I have not drank coffee since the 1st of May because I am opposed to buying anything from the Yankees and when our present supply of sugar is gone we'll have to come to that or go without, so I want it to last as long as possible. When you think we have the ventable "Tigers" among us, they frequently come over to get something to eat and though thus far they have been behaving very well all things considered, yet I'm constantly in dread lest the feline disposition will manifest itself. I must tell you of a prank of theirs. As soon as they arrived here, they found a box of Yankee uniforms at the depot, assuming them as disguises they jumped on the cars which their commander had taken, put off down to one of the stations, Markham, I think - where the news of the skirmish had not reached. Here they strutted about until they attracted the notice of the Yankees who thinking they were some of their own men, came out and accepted the invitation to ride up the road a little ways. They did go, but never went back any more as you may guess.

We have not a great many men in town now, but Taylor's brigade is expected today - will quarter here as a reserve for Jackson. I do hope Shields has not been reinforced. I'm in continual dread lest those hard creatures should get back here again.

Ma was in town this evening and heard there is a rumor of another great victory at Corinth - a very decided one. Oh if it only proves the truth! It would prove a stunning blow to the enemy and a serving cordial to our men. If the Valley is not retaken won't you write us a long account of yourselves and of the battle of which you have been — if not eyewitnesses. You can direct to Richmond care of some of the Rifles, if we hold that place, if not you can direct to Cousin Horace Buck and we will most probably get it some time in the future. Would you believe we have not received more than one letter from Alvin and two from Irving since you left Virginia - the first dated at Columbus 17th of February the other two Jackson March 2. We have heard since then through a letter to Mrs. Roy dated Corinth, March 28 at times we did not even know where Beauregard was, and as the last we heard from you, you were undetermined as to whether you would remain at Headquarters - we did not know even then whether you were with him or not. Since we have heard that Colonel Jordan has been promoted I think perhaps he has been empowered to retain you as clerks. I hope so particularly as Walter told us he had heard from you recently at Corinth. At all events I will direct this to that place in the care of Mr. Roy and if you are not there he'll know where you are and forward. It is too bad that we can't get that letter from Irvie. Cousin Horace Buck and his company passed through so hastily that we could not find out who had it - don't even know where to inquire for it. For the present we must content ourselves with knowing that you were well when last heard from which is a great comfort. I wonder if you've received half of the letters we've written. I rather think not. You don't know how constantly you are in our thoughts dear boys every hour, nay, almost every minute of our waking hours and you haunt our dreams at night. Whenever our prospects look a little brighter and I think "surely we must achieve our independence before another year," the next thought is and then Alvin and Irving will come home and see us and settle down, if not near us, at least where we can hear from them and know where they are. If we do gain our freedom we will be one and all impoverished. We will have to go back to first principles and ply the spinning wheel instead of the piano - wear linsey woolsey instead of silk. I find we can and do dispense with a great many things which a year ago I considered essentials to comfort if not life. And if we have to work for ourselves then we won't have the bother of managing servants and we'll know when our task is well prepared If we make our own goods we won't be quite so particular as to the cut and make of them and we will be spared the worry of following the varying fashions indeed or find a grand chain of compensation running through all the apparently rough, intricate web of our life in the coming "hard times". I do really believe we should all be the happier for being a little more primitive in our mode of living and I for one am willing to make the experiment. If only peace could be restored to our country and our friends returned unscathed morally as well as physically and the wheels of government fairly wound up and set to running smoothly. Oh! It would be _____ wish for.

We have heard they are fighting at Richmond but no nothing of the probably results. I suppose you heard before we did, about the battle of Williamsburg in which our boys were engaged. - heard how poor Willie Richardson had to have his arm amputated from the effects of the wound received there - his left arm - he was taken prisoner and was paroled. Willie Rust and Giles Cook were both slightly wounded and I believe both taken prisoner. Young Painter too. Captain Simpson was wounded on the breast button of his coat. Though if the ball had not glanced it might have gone through his heart. Poor Payton Scroggins was killed. His old mother almost idolized him and is I expect almost frantic at his death.

We saw not long since a paragraph in the paper announcing that such a number of Beauregard's staff as were with him at the battle of Shiloh were uninjured. Among them mentioned was "<u>Captain</u> T. B. Roy of Warren, Virginia" it is time that one of old Warren's son has been promoted to that dignity I am glad and must offer my congratulations. Ma was at Mrs. Roy's yesterday and they showed her where a ball had passed through the parlor window breaking three panes of glass and buried itself in the opposite sill. It seems that Capt. Roy was at the upper window waving to our men when the fight first commenced, and they don't know whether some of the Yankees who were everywhere concealed around his house fired at him or some of our own men accidently shot it. Father, who was on the house while it was going on was mistaken by the "rebels" for a Yankee Vidette and hardly escaped being shot — this we learned sometime afterwards. I send you some of the locust blossoms which the balls cut off here in the yard.

Tell George Hope that they are all well at home. Mr. and Mrs. Moffatt both there and all doing well. Be sure to mention him when you write — they are so anxious to hear from him. Give a great deal of love to Cousin George for us all — tell him I hope his Ma has ere this heard of his where abouts as Cousin Sue Buck wrote her long since. I do feel so sorry for him - he must be more entirely cut off from his home than you all. Remember us all to Benton Roy — tell him that they're all I believe as well as usual at home and that his sister and Walter are there.

I wrote you a letter of eight sheets a short time since giving you the most minute account of everything that has transpired since the Yankees first came in but I've concluded this will be almost as much as you'll care to wade through for some time. All the relations are well and all bare the pressures of the times much more bravely than you would imagine. Uncle Newton is gloomy it is true, but you know that precedes more from his ill health than anything else. Uncle Mack is not hopeful, and at one time it was distressing to be with him but he has changed very much in many respects - is more thoughtful and affectionate than he has ever been before. Grandma too is wonderfully calm - but will cry when they bring the Yankee prisoners in. Ma and Father have both been much depressed and no wonder when anything did look so dark, but I think they're both wonderfully cheered now in view of our recent successes. Aunt Betsy is very excitable, Aunt Calmes perfectly tranquil except when Evred cries. She is perfectly devoted to the little fellow, and he is as saucy as can be to her as well as others. He calls me "Soncie". I've taught him all your names always when asked where you are says - "Abbie and Erbie gone way to ____" knows your picture and I can often stop his crying by merely showing them to him. He is a high spirited little rebel. You would have been amused to have heard him walk about among the Yankees when they were here singing "Way down South in Ditchie". Willie's as sharp as ever — wish I had space to write you some of his and Nannie's ideas on the Yankee question. General Kimball used frequently to caress them when here because he had little ones at home, but he did not succeed in making Unionists of them. "Little Sunbeam" is the pet of the establishment - the brightest, most joyous and the best little fellow ever saw. I know we are apt to make use of these expressions in every case, but they are <u>particularly</u> applicable to him. You don't know how often, when we all would be so gloomy - he could win a smile from us by his cunning pranks when nothing else could. I don't know what we would have done without him sometimes. Nellie helps me abuse the Yankees and laugh at our friends when we talk of subjugation. Sometimes though we get "blue" too and then we go off and shut ourselves up to prevent the infection from spreading until it is all passed away. I wish you could see a parody on "Maryland" which she has written - 'tis ____ she sings herself "Indignant Pulect". Tom Petty takes this to Richmond tomorrow. All send more love than I can express in words so you must imagine how much. Take good care of yourselves and write just as often as you possibly can and we will do the same.

I trust it will not be many more months before we are permitted to meet again - till then goodbye dear brothers, God bless you.

Your loving sister, Lucie

* On June 15, 1862, Lucy wrote, "Mrs. Moffet brought us a paper in which was published a dispatch from Walter to poor Colonel Ashby (killed a few days before) when the former was scouting in the mountains just before Jackson's army came in. It had Walter's full signature on it."

The book "Stonewall in the Valley," by Robert G. Tanner, gives this account which appeared in the New York Herald on June 16, 1862. The report directed to Col. Ashby was captured by the Yankees. It read, "Colonel Ashby — Sir, I have been myself to within sight of the enemy's camp at Front Royal. They have one regiment of Marylanders encamped between Richardson's and old Mr. Garrett's; also, one company of cavalry from Michigan Regiment, and one piece of artillery on the hill between Front Royal and Weston. Very respectfully, Walter Buck, Lieutenant, Co. E."

Accounts of the Battle of Front Royal frequently give Belle Boyd credit for meeting the Southern army and reporting Union strength. It is apparent that Jackson already had this information from Walter Buck. Belle Boyd confirmed that there were no changes in Buck's information.

Head Quarters West Depart.
Tupelo, Mississippi
June 18, 1862

My Dear Sister,

Your letter of the 24th reached me a week ago. I cannot say unexpectedly for I had predicted when I heard "Old Front Royal" had been weeded out that I would get a four story letter from you. Just see what faith will do, particularly when there is a dear sister in the case, like yourself.

Your account of the Yankee escapade was highly satisfactory and amusing. I had been puzzling my brain to think where the battle took place. But now I have it in my mind's eye. Indeed I do not see how the citizens escaped injury. We learned of the fight by telegraph on Monday evening and I will leave you to imagine our delight. Front Royal is now classic ground.[9]

From your letter it has been a long time since you heard from us, nearly three months. Immediately after the battle of Shiloh, I wrote, knowing how uneasy you would all be, and sent it to Richmond by Marcus Newton, who gave it to someone to give to Mrs. Haynie. Since then I have written repeatedly, directing to Luray, Richmond, and in fact everywhere I thought there would be a possibility to run the "blockade", and on the 14th ulto I wrote to you by flag of truce and enclosed the letter in one to Mrs. Heironimus at Winchester. But of course in that I had to be very short and under restraint.

Your letters have, I believe, all reached me. The one of eight pages came to hand about six weeks since and I have had one from Ma and Willie since.

There have been several changes in the office since leaving Jackson. Roy has been promoted, also Geo. Williams, who day before yesterday was appointed Captain and A. Adjt. Gen. to Col. Liddell, Comdy Brigade in Hardee's Corps. I am glad of it, he will make a fine officer and fill his position with credit. He is on duty in his new place, but has not yet left our mess. Dick Blakemore has been clerking here for two months. Burton has gone into the Quarter Master's Department. General Jordan still keeps his original place, will not leave the office. In fact he cannot be spared. He has just returned from Oxford where he has been down with typhoid fever. Is now perfectly recovered and doing well.

Your speaking of Walters riding up to the stile reminds me of a dream I had some time in May, before I heard that he had been selected Lt. I got up one morning, remarked that I had dreamed I was standing at the stile and that Walter dashed up on horseback with an officers shoulder strap on.

I did not write to you by young Marshall from the fact that he was at Head Quarters but a short time. The letter I sent Mrs. Roy was one Benton had left with me to send to Richmond.

Were you not surprised to hear of the evacuation of Corinth?[10] It was a splendidly executed move. We did not lose a man or gun. The Yankees did not know we had left until we blew up the magazines. Gen. Beauregard can retreat as well as fight. It has knocked the Yankees plans all to smash and disconcerted him beyond measure. By the way, what a splendid liar Halleck is. You need never believe anything you see from him.

Roy is in Gen. Hardees staff and the old General is delighted with him. He went to Mobile this morning with Cousin Willie Blakemore who is General Johnston's aid. Marcus Newton was over yesterday. He leaves tomorrow for Selma, Ala. He will soon be commissioned Captain in the Quarter Master's Dept. Cousin Alick is in the same dept. Frank Buck is — one of Gen. Price's body guards. Bud is Captain and Chief of Ordinance of Gen. Clark's staff. Marshall Blakemore was over yesterday. He has changed very little. He is in Gen Van Dorns Army.

I received a letter from 'Nannie Dear' a few days ago. They have left Richmond and gone to Clarksville, Va.

We very seldom hear from the 17th Regt. and up to a week ago were ignorant of the casualties in the battle of Williamsburg. I was sincerely sorry to hear of Willie Richardson's[11] misfortune. Hope he is now at home. I have always felt greater anxiety about him and Dick than all the rest.

I admire your and Nellie's spirit, but you had better be cautious. I fear if the Yanks get into Front Royal again you will all fare badly. Who ever imagined that hostile shells and balls would fly around Bel Air? The rendezvous for juvenile Bucks or that it would be desecrated by a Yankee General establishing his Head Quarters there in, and in my room too. My blood boils when I think of the outrages of the Enemy. The idea of a family, not being able to sit up with a sick child without being accused of signaling to Confederates, by a pack of Dutch drunkards.

"We hear it and heed it with vengeful thrill
And will not forgive or forget"

Alvin (the Count as he calls himself) started to Richmond with dispatches a week ago. He will return about the 1st of July.

This is rather a dull place compared with Corinth. There our pickets were so near that they were continually skirmishing and the report of their guns and bursting of shells would shake the office. One of them, a fastidiously inclined Federal, having ensconced himself in a secure place, sang out to one of our men, "I say you d _ _ _ d conscript, aren't you tired of drinking sassafras tea and singing Dixie yet?" We have a plenty of water here and of excellent quality.

General Beauregard has taken a short leave of absence. He is looking better now than I have seen him for a long time.

I shall write you when ever there is a shadow of chance for the letter to reach you and I know you will do the same. Give yourselves no uneasiness on our account. We have made ladies acquaintances where ever we have gone. I had promises to be taken care of if sick etc. I will still follow the fortunes of "old Beaury".

Dick Blakemore and Geo. Williams send their love. The latter wishes to know if you ever hear from his house. If you get an opportunity, write to his parents. He will be under lasting obligations.

George Hope is well, he sent a letter to Front Royal in care of Sam Thomas in Richmond.

Love to one and all of the family. Trusting we will all soon meet under the roof of the old homestead,

I am ever your affectionate Brother
Irving

You may let Walter read the enclosed letter also. Where is Uncle John?[12]

H Qrs West Department
Tupelo Miss, June 19, 1862
(Received in Front Royal on July 21, 1862)

My Dear Captain, *(Capt. Horace Buck)*[13]

Yours of the 18th May was rec a day or two ago, need I say what pleasure I felt at your prompt reply to my short note by young Marshall?

First allow me to congratulate you upon your promotion and assure you if I had the least penchant for cavorting, old "Doc"[14] would be my Captain and Ashby my Colonel in a very few days. What has become of Bowen since the reorganization? I was not aware that Mr. Marshall[15] had a Co of his own.

Yes indeed, we will take a smile when we next meet. I have not tasted a drop since entering service, but upon such an occasion I will certainly lay aside my rule. And what "yarns" we will tell one another!

We are now in position in which I think the Enemy will not dare to attack us and if he does will get a terrible drubbing.

This climate agrees with us all, and none have been sick of any consequence.

I have left the enclosed letter to Lucie, open for you to read, which you must do without the least hesitation — provided you have the patience to wade through it — and will you be kind enough to send it through by the first "underground train" that starts — perhaps Walter could engineer it.

You must excuse the shortness of this, it is late and I am very tired, but I will write you again in the course of two weeks, but I scarcely know where to direct. I am going to send this in our dispatches to the War Department.

Love to all the boys and tell Cousin Newt that I sent his letter the next day after receiving it, by one of Gen Hindman's staff who was going direct to Little Rock.

Make Will Cloud[16] and Walter write me, a letter from the "Old Dominion" is a treasure out here, I never knew how to appreciate it before.

I insist upon our correspondence being kept up, you must reply at your earliest moment, and will not find me unprompt — direct to this place. Hope we may all be spared through this war to take a drink Bron's.

Ever your affectionate Cousin
Irving A. Buck

Headquarters Department No. 2
Tupelo, Miss., July 19, 1862

My Dear Dick

In the name of heaven and the love you should hear me — write me, this suspense is too horrible. You with the rest of my relatives are engaged in battle after battle, the result of which to you we know not what. I have written you but without effect. Have you forgotten me? Or do you suppose I have no affection at all for you? Now Dick I implore you to write me a detailed account of the casualties. I today received an imperfect newspaper list of the casualties, but a great many are just down as missing whom I suppose have rejoined the company. I was glad that none were killed.

Alvin was in Richmond a month ago, he would have visited you, but he was there on business and did not know what moment he would be ordered back. He heard it reputed that Willie Richardson had died from the effects of his wound, notwithstanding the strong circumstantial evidence, I cannot help believing it to be false. Poor fellow, his affliction was heavy even with the loss of his arm, for him and you. I have felt more solicitude than all the rest of my numerous relatives engaged in this struggle for our homes and liberty, however I am getting too much on the 4 July order to please you.

I suppose you have heard that George Williams has been promoted to Captain and A Adj. Gen to Act. Brigadier Gen Liddle, he is now on sick leave, he will probably resume his duties tomorrow.

Benton Roy has been promoted to Major & Chief of Gen Hardee's staff. If he was only a woman, the General would certainly marry him.

Hope, Alvin and myself are the only clerks left of our Manassa crowd, we do nothing particular but fight flies, fleas and mosquitos, all of which are very numerous and ravenous. The weather here is exceedingly hot and very enervating, though our troops are in fine health.

Cousin Alick and Mack Blakemore are now permanently stationed at Selma, Alabama. Cousin Willie has gone up there on a sick leave. I miss him very much. Gen Johnson's quarters are very near us and I am with him every day. I suppose you are aware that he is Gen J's aid?

Frank Buck and Mack Blakemore are both in Gen Price army and I see them frequently, the latter is much informed in every respect.

Do you ever hear from home or is the "blockade" so effective as to prevent all intercourse?

I shall send this to Richmond by Capt. Jordan, who will find your locality and send it to you.

July 22

Col Brent returned from Richmond yesterday and states that Capt Simpson is a prisoner at Fort Warren.

So Dick please write me immediately and direct Col Brig Gen Thomas Jordan, Chief of Staff, Chattanooga, Tenn.

All the boys are well and send love,
Ever your affectionate cousin,
Irving

Clover Hill, August 12, 1862

My Dear Alvin and Irving,

What work of the "sweet sunny South" is honored by your presence now, I know not, do not even know where to direct a letter, but mean to try and send you this one and trust to chance for your receiving it. We know that Beauregard with a portion of his command was in Richmond during those battles, those awful battles, and 'tis to be assumed that you were with him — indeed we heard through a letter from Newt Petty that he had seen Alvin in Richmond but that was when A. was there with dispatches, we've nothing from either of you since then. I had thought one of you would have written immediately upon your arriving in the "Old Dominion" — but I won't scold, for perhaps you <u>have</u> and the "underground train" failed to make connections and we have not received it. Irvie's letter (so like his own dear self) dated "Tupelo June 18" was received about three weeks since, and I think I need not say how very delightedly it was hailed — the first tidings we had had in such a long time and we had been so uneasy lest the climate should have had a harmful influence on your health, imagining you sick, suffering and perhaps dying, and we ignorant of it and powerless to minister to you. It was all very silly to take trouble on trust as we <u>see</u> it now that we've learned there were no grounds for it.

I have long been wishing to write to you and give you a detailed account of what has transpired since you heard from us last, but the "powers that be" have woefully curtailed and limited our privileges as correspondents — and now I have so much to tell you, that I'm sure I cannot send you an iota of all I want by this post. You will perceive by the above date that I am at dear Clover Hill. Nellie and I coming up on Sunday last to breathe a little the air of freedom and to recruit body and mind both of which have been sadly in need of renovation. There is, comparatively speaking, little difficulty in sending a letter to the lines from here, for there are almost always some of our cavalry here in the "Forks" — just enough you know to keep the Yankees in perpetual fear of a "Stonewall avalanche" from the mountains.

We had the pleasure of seeing them yesterday. Someone came in about nine o'clock and told us that some of our men had galloped down toward Front Royal (about 50 of them we suppose) and in a few hours we heard the ringing of horses hoofs and a great shouting. Looking from the porch we saw from 15 to 20 of the blessed rebels dash across the river this way, and the remainder of the party with some prisoners preceded them up the road toward Luray. By the time our boys had reached the house the Yankees were in sight at the river and although we rushed out to see them they had only time to bid us not fear for them, to say they had taken our Provost, a Colonel and two Captains prisoner and beg us to go into the house as the enemy would presently open fire. A "Minnie" soon came whistling by as we stood in the porch and another, but our boys defiantly laughing at the impotent fury of the pursuers discharged their revolvers and dashed away over the hills. I know the Yankees were delighted to have the boys elude them, glad that the river, which was by the way very shallow, afforded an excuse for not following them, for after riding about the road insanely for a few minutes they turned their horses heads and went back to town. You could not appreciate the affair unless you had been here to witness it. The enemy had a battalion encamped at the lower end of town near the Glasscocks' and no one knows how many they have snugly ensconced in their fortifications at the river; our Cavalry force is variously estimated at from 20 to 50 strong. They entered the town, took the Provost and other officers besides a number of infantry prisoners, but as the latter were not effectively expeditious in their movements they were obliged to leave them and only succeeded in securing those who were on horseback. The Confederates divided their forces and while one portion of them hurried on with the prisoners toward Page — the other remained on the hill here just long enough to attract the attention of the Yankees, inducing them to believe that all the troops were on this side of the river and thus diverted them from their pursuit after the prisoners. Was it not nicely managed? We rather expected the enemy in a large force to make a reconnaissance over here today, but hope their comrades will deter them from strict investigation of the "Forks". The citizens will suffer for this raid I know, though I'm sure they were as much surprised as the Federals at it. Speaking of making of a reconnaissance reminds me that you may perhaps have seen in the Northern papers a glaring account of Geary's grand reconnaissance in the Fort Mountains sometimes since. I think you will agree with me that it was a brilliant affair, when I tell you what I know to be true (a well authenticated fact is a novelty these days) that 20, or less, of our cavalry repulsed 600 of that old wretch's men. The Yankees of course when they scampered and scrambled back down the mountain did not know that they had so small a force opposed to them, did not know that 20 men discharging a half dozen loads apiece in quick succession seemed like a volley from 120 men. Not they, they did not wait to ascertain how many of the Guerrillas those towering rocks concealed but would upon the principle that "Discretion is the better part of valor."

There is one little sentence in Irvie's last letter that always thrills me with pain when I read it. "I was sincerely sorry to hear of Willie Richardson's misfortune and hope is at home". Yes dear Willie he is at home, a home that he will never leave, a home from which the summons to the battle field will never call him. You know of his death — but do you know how well and tenderly he was cared for? He was taken from the hospital at Williamsburg into the house of the episcopal minister there. Mr. Ambler who knew of the family at Rose Hill. There he was well nursed and thought at one time convalescent, but was taken with hectic fever and died the 29th of May. Mr. & Mrs. Ambler both wrote to Cousin Elizabeth most consoling letters in which they spoke of our noble Willie in the highest terms. He told Mr. A. that he had long been thoughtful on the subject of religion and expressed his entire willingness to trust the issue of events to the hands of God — requested that the family worship might be conducted in his room, was frequently heard sobbing during the service and sometimes he was heard in almost inaudible prayer. He was delirious a week before his death and called in the most touching manner on his Ma, his sisters and Cousin Sue Buck. Two ladies — refugees from Alexandria bought him a handsome coffin and his grave was filled with flowers by kind and gentle hands. Mr. A said he never saw anyone make such a favorable impression upon everyone as he did and that he received attention from the citizens who regarded him as a friend. Oh boys! I can now realize in poor Willie's loss how I should feel if one of you were taken — I did not know how dear he was till he was gone. Next to you and Walter and Dick there's no one whom it would be so difficult to give up. He was so noble and true, so gentle and so kind. This poor world cannot afford to lose many such, there would be too few worthy examples left us. Poor Eltie! she and Willie were devoted in life and death did not long divide them. She was sick when the news of his death arrived (which was not till nearly two months after his decease) and they would not tell her of it until she began to grow stronger and as soon as she heard it she said she could not live and really grew worse from that until the 29th of July when she expired with a message of love and farewell on her lips. She bid them all adieu, begged them not to sorrow for her when the exchange she was making was such a blissful one, said she did not it kind in them to wish to detain her here, she had every trust every assurance of a happy hereafter. She told Uncle Tom she had much to tell him but her time and strength were too limited but said, "Oh I love you all, I love you so much." Cousin Sue Buck promised she would never leave her Ma; Cousin Sue took Willie's death grievously — indeed seems more distressed than his own family and has gone into deep mourning for him does not care to conceal the relation which they sustained to each other. Of course Cousin Elizabeth and Sue R. are almost broken hearted and yet they try so hard to be patient and calm. I was at Rose Hill after they heard about Willie and before Eltie's death and when I tried to persuade Cousin Susie to take some refreshment, she said so wearily and hopelessly — "Oh, Lucie why should I eat? Willie's gone and I've nothing to live for." It cut me to the heart. I do not think that either she or her Ma will long survive those who have gone before — they are both sick now, and I believe would welcome the summons to another world with delight. Just think of what a large, happy family they had a few years ago and now what a mere wreck there is left of it. It must be so sad to outlive all that one loves best.

I believe, yes I know Nellie wrote you a letter by one of our paroled prisoners a month ago and directed it to Richmond. Did you get it? She had to write very cautiously and could give you no news beyond that of a domestic nature. I was quite sick when she wrote — and indeed all of us have at times been on the invalid list but I believe we are all well as usual now except Carey and the little baby who are somewhat indisposed. What do you think of my having had a Yankee physician to attend me? It happened in this wise. Colonel Van Buren of the N.Y. 102 Regiment and his clerk and waiter were taken sick at our house and Dr. Bogardus, the surgeon of the regiment attended them. When the Colonel went away he left his two sick men in charge of the doctor who then boarded at our house. He conducted himself in such a gentlemanly manner that Father several times asked me to let him prescribe for me (it was difficult to get our own physician). I at length consented, and have never regretted having done so, since he has put a stop to a troublesome cough and promised to make me a strong and healthy girl if I will follow his directions. He was so kind, was at our house three weeks, attended nearly all the family professionally, gave Father a goodly supply of medicine, such as are not to be had anywhere and would receive no compensation therefor. He was called in to see poor Eltie one midnight when the picquets would not let messengers pass for the other doctors. Went down and ministered to her and continued to go every day and stay there every night, walking to and fro from her, taking out lemons and fresh beef for her, carrying his own medicine and was unremitting in his exertions. When he went away he begged Father to write him and let him know how Eltie was. One of his patients, an <u>honest</u>, polite farmer boy from New York, died at our house poor fellow three weeks ago. By the way, Miss Belle Boyd has been in town for two months, she met with Dr. Bogardus and was dreadfully smitten, actually came over to see him one evening and wrote to him. The favorable impression was not mutual, however, and the young New Yorker left for his regiment with a whole heart. Miss Belle was taken in at least. A sharp Yankee played the part of a paroled Confederate prisoner who was going to our lines and would carry dispatches to our army. She gave him all the information which she possessed and her letters to Jackson. He bowed, bade her good evening remarking that he would see her again, and in a few minutes they returned and arrested her. The next morning she occupied a carriage and was escorted out of town by a large retinue of cavalry where she was carried I have not been able to learn, probably they only took her home, probably sent her beyond their lines as they have been threatening to do. Oh I do wish she would renounce the world and go into a convent!

There has been naturally a good deal of sickness in Front Royal, it could not be otherwise with such a garrison who now occupy the place who do not seem to understand the meaning of cleanliness. Poor Front Royal, 'tis sadly dilapidated and desolated! I do not know of more than three cases in which the sickness has proved fatal. Mr. Jacob Myers and Mrs. Jackson both died last week after a lingering illness, and old Mr. Proctor too died a month from the effects of a fall received months ago. Mrs. Hope and Mrs. Roy have both been very much prostrated in consequence of the perpetual nervous excitement and suspense, but I trust we won't long be thralls now and I think they will both soon regain their ordinary health and spirits with their liberty. We have had a scary time of it since that bright little episode in our experience. I mean the week which elapsed after Jackson's entree. Such orders as have emanated from the Provost office during the last month or two; in the first place if a group of citizens collected at corners or on the sidewalks they were to be fired into and dispersed. Lights shining through windows after tattoo are to be fired into—sickness and death no excuse. Last Friday and Saturday they pressed into service all the contraband "gentmen" who have not "left the country for the country's good" and forced them to throw up breastworks at the river, even taking Uncle Tom's poor old Uncle Lewis. Bob Roy had a fortunate attack of sickness which exempted him. They say they intend next to take the women servants and put them to washing, cooking and sewing for the braves in the "grand National army." This is all inconvenient but endurable, but that order of Pope's is too iniquitous for anything. To think of Virginia gentlemen having set before them the alternative of swearing allegiance to a government against which every principle of humanity, justice and truth _____, to soon sentiments abhorrent to their very souls, or else to be exiled from home and friends and sent forth with helpless women and innocent children to starve. This proclamation is worthy it's source but I trust that Mr. Jefferson Davis may circumvent the old Nero's plans yet.

Were you surprised to hear the Yankees had reoccupied Front Royal? Oh boys never so long as I live shall I forget the awful gloom of that day of their return. Seeing our poor invalids marching out of town unable to protect us, seeing the lurid flame and smoke from the burning depot and commissary stores, and above all the sombre clouded sky and the sullen splash of the cold rain all seemed to make us all feel the more dreary. Father was in town when the Federals came in — we all took refuge in the basement, the little children screaming with terror and clinging to us for protection and Aunt, Ma, Grandma and Aunt B. livid and frozen with horror. They came in like swarms of vultures, every hill seemed alive with them. They planted a cannon on the hill back of the orchard and when they commenced firing the first shell just whistled and shrieked around the corner of the house. I thought for a time it had passed through the passage where I stood. They did not throw many shells but presently they surrounded the whole place and marching by the house encamped in the same meadows where they'd been before. I was very much frightened though I did not "let on" for I expected they would commence punishing the Secesh for aiding and comforting our dear rebels, but they did not do quite that — only took what contributed to the comfort of their encampments. General Kimball again established his quarters at our house remaining until Sunday morning when he and his staff left for the river where they expected an attack from Stonewall. I hope never to see such another day as that Sunday. General K. had told Father that there would probably be an attack on Front Royal. There were batteries on the surrounding hills so that in that case our house would be exposed to a cross fire from our own men. Early Sunday morning the regiments in the front meadow commenced discharging their guns into the hill at those rocks there above the dam. I'm sure there must be quite a lead mine in that embankment for they would fire volley after volley by the battalion, until the windows rattled. The balls whistled around the house biting off the twigs of trees, one struck [the] house about a foot below Ma's front chamber window and one actually going through the officer's quarters. The children were almost frantic with fright begging to be taken away before the cannons were fired and we were so nervous and sick that the slaming of the doors was startling. General K. told Father he could give us an escort if he wished to remove us to a place of quiet and security. There was an attache to the staff — Frank C. (Crippen) of Cincinnati — who had always made great pets of the children and was invaluable to Father in preventing depredations by the men. This boy I first cordially detested, but soon found that he possessed the qualities pertaining to a gentleman in a greater degree than almost any Yankee I ever saw. Father sent us to Uncle Mack's in a wagon — the whole family bag and baggage and "Frank" was unanimously chosen by the children to escort us through. Such a time as we had winding our way through the armies! Frank would ride in advance, clear the road, pulled up stakes and throw down fences that we might go through the fields; when the soldiers were inclined to stare into the wagon he would ride in between us and them and say "I am so sorry but soldiers are very rude." Then when we argued and quarreled about the war (he was the first I ever condescended to argue with) he was so polite and well bred. He told us that they had 180,000 men in pursuit of Jackson and he could not possibly elude them — that they had already surrounded him in Strasburg according to last dispatch in camp, he compassionated him because he was such a "brave man." But for all that I did not believe he would be captured and injured and told him so. Well that week at Uncle Mack's seemed like a dream. We were all so worn with anxiety and excitement that we went to sleep and slept day after day night after night like dumb berated animals only arousing long enough to eat and hear wild horrible rumors which we only disbelieved because we did not wish to credit them. When we came home and heard how annoyed Father had been I more than ever regretted having left. For four days and nights he was on guard on the premises, not daring to go to sleep and not daring to sit down lest he <u>should</u> sleep. Bob Roy was sick and Uncle Gilbert had his wife's baking bread to sell the Yankees, so poor Father had to drive up the cows from the barn field through the rain. After the battle of Port Republic Shields army again passed through and we enjoyed not a little teasing Frank about the whipping which the certainly captured Jackson had administered to the "invincible Shields". He acknowledged the corn and seemed with all so weary and dispirited that we then desisted. This time Colonel Thorborne (commanding brigade — Carroll's brigade, the same that bore the brunt of that battle) had his quarters at our house. He and his staff were all so called Virginians — traitors as we told them. I tell you it hurt me to see such recreant men at our board, but it could not be helped and ere comforted ourselves with quarreling with and singing Southern songs for them. With one or two exceptions they behaved pretty well. Irvie, you remember Hattie Gillespie? Well don't you think her father and brother have joined the Federal army and the whole family came through with Shield's army. Hattie and her sister came over to our house to call on Colonel Thorborne but we did not make our appearance and she did not inquire for us. One of the clerks told us that she and one of the young officers boarding were carrying on a flirtation but he thought she would be disappointed in her conquest as Captain L. had already a young wife in Wheeling. I believe Dr. G (Gillespie) expects to settle in Wheeling. We were sincerely glad when these were gone and hope they'd be the last, but just as Father had harvested his wheat Banks command came through in route to Serryville. This time we had Colonel Schlandecker commanding brigade. So you see Irvie dear, your room has not been desecrated once, not twice, but four times — why the venitable — Banks, Shields and Cooper themselves have been at home. The two latter I saw but the former I did not trouble myself to go to the window to look at. I can't bear him! Don't you think they took the wheat Father had gone to the expense of harvesting to feed their horses! And he does not expect to thresh the remainder. You ought to see how, they've mired the yard and destroyed the fields. Father, poor Cousin E. Richardson and Mr. Richards have probably suffered more than anyone in the country yet you don't know with what a patient fortitude Father endures these things and while the last four months have whitened his hair and bowed his form, he is still calm and tries to infuse his patience into our spirits — poor Father. Ma and Grandma too bear it wonderfully and neither of them are adverse to speaking their mind in season to any of the heretics. By the way you would not believe how the Yankees of one division detest those of different commands — they sometimes say they hate each other more than they do the rebels. Boys I'm afraid it was not kind in me to write such a catalogue of grievances, but you know it is not always near so bad, and we do manage to have more amusement than you'd think for and those pleasures we do have are so much more keenly appreciated than they used to be. We have boarding with us now a Dr. Marshall of Delaware who seems to be a gentleman. He is very kind, and having been a great traveler is quite an entertaining man. He stands on guard at home while Father goes to town — on Sunday last we were enabled to go to church for the first time since May.

Mrs. Hampson Miller and Miss Spengler have just come to spend a day with us and I must stop.

Thursday. I must tell you dear boys that we heard from town yesterday and learned that in consequence of the raid on Monday that they arrested Mr. Jacobs, Mr. Stinson, Captain Roy, Mr. Petty, Mr. Buchen, Uncle Mack and some others. I know not who and are to hold them as hostages for the officers captured. They have released the citizens on parole on after signing an obligation of some kind, however. Father was not taken, so you see we have a good deal to be thankful for. The Yankees say our men had the audacity of His Satanic Majesty himself when <u>twenty-five</u> men were dashing to a garrisoned town, take 30 prisoners and escape the same way they came. They could not bring many of their captives away as they were mostly infantry. Walter was not I think one of the party, but he is not inactive wherever he may be. He has been doing good service and I wish I could tell you some of his exploits. One of his latest was to take three prisoners one night by himself and came into the house where he was staying at two o'clock a.m. with four or five revolvers, five naked sabers and his prisoners — he was almost exhausted poor fellow. The Yankees go out constantly and bring in their paroles signed by Walter. Some were genuine and some of course of their own counterfeiting. I am so proud of the gallant boy — he is as well known as most of our superior officers and it does me so much good to hear them talk about him. He was near Ashby our own brave Ashby when he fell and has as a relic a fragment of wood stained with his blood. Ashby was certainly accidently shot by one of our own men. You may probably know more about our boys in the 17th than we do. We have heard that none of our immediate friends suffered in the late battles before Richmond. Charley R. had been wounded at Fair Oaks but is reported well. Marcus Richardson and Mr. Wells were both wounded at Port Republic and though disabled for service for a long time to come are yet hobbling about. Our friends have been so fortunate I believe the relations generally are as well as usual. Uncle Newton has been much annoyed and yet is not nearly so much disturbed by it as you would imagine. He has just heard from all his children — Cousin Kate at Port Gibson, Mississippi and Cousin May in Ohio are all well. Through a letter from Dr. Kirkbride we learned that Cousin Mack was doing very well and quite contented and Dr. K. says he means to take every care of him come what will — is not that kind? We have had a letter from Aunt Cattie who writes that they've suffered comparatively little in that section. Poor Eliza Columbia is dead. Cousin Bettie Richards was at our house on Sunday said her Ma and all were well and said we must send her love to Dick B. when we write.

When you write to Cousin George say to him Miss Mary Simpson has received a letter from his sister Martha in which she speaks of having received a letter from him. The family all well and Cousin Lucy in Rockeport on a visit. That's all I've been able to learn from the letter. I have written to his Ma as you requested and tried to make her feel easy respecting him.

George Hope need not feel uneasy about his mother for she is only nervous and not really much sick. I suppose Cousin George and "Captain Roy" are neither of them with you now— you must miss them. Dear Beauregard the report of his misfortune shed a gloom over us all, but we hear that he is about resuming his command and trust all is well with him. I wonder why you were sent to Richmond with dispatches Alvin? We feel so anxious to know about it.

I'm afraid you're anathematizing me for imposing such a "tall" letter on you but you don't know what a pleasure it is to write you once more. I'll promise to be a more lenient correspondent when the war is over, meantime indulge my weakness and read it in installments if it please you. They laugh so much for worrying you with my documents.

We are very hopeful notwithstanding oppression and hope to be a free people ere the coming frosts have withered the woods. Are we too sanguine? You will, I hope, write whenever you can. I think you will; we will certainly do the same. If you should fail to hear from us for a long time you will not be uneasy for you cannot appreciate the difficulties of sending letters to our lines. I hope this state of things may not last long and pray that God may ere long restore my darling brothers to us unscathed mentally or physically. All send much love.

Ever your loving sister,
Lucie

(This was at the end of the previous letter by Lucy dated August 12, 1862. The rest of this letter is missing.)

October 21, 1862

Dear Boys,

This precious bit of gossip was penned two months ago and dispatched by young Frankhouser to our lines — instead of delivering it to Dick Buck to mail he brought it back here the other day, so, as you say the last six months are a blank to you, I will send it yet to assist in filling up that blank. Surely I have got two of the best rebels for brothers to be found in the Southern Confederacy and you may thank those two long letters, received last Saturday night, for it. Alvin's dated October 12, was the first we have had from him since early last Spring — it was a long nice letter dear Alvin and we all thank you just as much as if it were not your duty to have written it long ago, and Ma is going to answer it before very long. Yours Irvie to me was equally acceptable. I'm so glad you are so well off and trust we may all weather the gales of the coming Winter in spite of the war. Alvin's idea of economy may very readily be adopted by this "shin plaster" generation. I wonder if silver currency is so scarce everywhere as here! I like your proposition with regard to Miss Nannie's visit very much Irvie. I suppose as she has been acting the kind sister to you so long you are going to bring her here to act in the same capacity for me. Very good, you have <u>my</u> free will and consent to that arrangement — <u>hers</u>. I presume, is not wanting. As to the estimations in which you are held by your superior officers, we feel perfectly satisfied having too often heard through others of how your services were appreciated.

Bel Air-22nd, 1862
(August)

Dear Brothers,

It is such a beautiful evening and I have no work at present. I am going to scribble a little. Ma, and myself have just gotten home from a very pleasant visit to River Side. I do wish you could come home, we have so many things to tell you which will be forgotten by the time you come home. It seems like a dream to be rid of the abominable Yankees. We are not afraid to talk and tell about the war now though we could sauce the officers whenever the different armies were here, as we seldom <u>condescended</u> to speak a word to the privates. There was <u>ONE</u> truthful and gentlemanly Yankee in all those vast armies that were here, and that was Frank Crippen and the only one I would like to see, I wish he could be slightly wounded and taken prisoner so we could show him some kindness and laugh at him. Suppose you have heard of the death of Cousin Eltie. There's a soldier talking to Ma has put me out and I forgot what I was going to say. Annie has gone and spilt the ink all over Grandma's steps and Father who has the toothache has been giving me a rowing up about wasting ink these times. I used to be so proud to tell the Yankees that I had two brothers in the armies. please write to me sometimes I like to have a letter to myself if I can. It is the first letter I have written for nearly a year as I never take a pen in my hand for months together. You ought to see Evred he can say anything he pleases and Aunt is a perfect slave to him. And makes her ride him on her back up and down the stairs and when he cries and Father goes to whip him she runs as feeble as she is carries him about until he is quiet. Lt. O'Farrell came in and had to go and see about supper and now there is no lines and it nearly time to go to bed. I would copy this but I have _____ to do attending to the children and more particularly tonight as the girls are away. So goodbye from your sleepy sister,

Laura
The Yankees are at little Paris and persons are expecting them here.

Bel Air, September 30, 1862

My own dear brothers,

July, August, and now September has passed without bringing a letter from you. How little I thought when reading Irvie's letter of the 18th June that it would be such a weary time before we should welcome another from the same dear source. I keep that letter conveniently near me in my drawer and to it I often go for consolation when I begin to despair of receiving any more now. You don't know how jealous I have been of Mrs. Hope to think she has had <u>four</u> letters from George in the last fortnight and we not one from you in the last three months. It was right provoking to see them all gloating over his letters and I could only vent my vexation in quarreling with you and the postmasters. But I am sure the fault is more theirs than yours. We have written you frequently. Ma sent you a letter last week.

Through George H. we learned of your safe arrival in Charleston and from all he said I judge you are not very well pleased with the place. We were very very sorry that your pleasant little coterie of relations has been dispersed and that you should have to go so far among entire strangers. I think though after you make acquaintances there you will find it very pleasant. I hope so at least. Only you must be very careful not to contact any fevers or diseases that may be prevalent there now.

I had a letter the other day from Nannie Taylor, the first since the Yankee occupation here. She has returned to Richmond and spoke of a letter she had just gotten from Irvie alas "Pat" merely mentioning that you were well and that you had written requesting her to let us know how and where you were. She also said that Belle Boyd was being lionized there now having been sent there with the exchanged prisoners. I hope she will be so well pleased as to wish to remain always.

Ma wrote you how unexpected was the arrival of Cousin Marcus Newton about 10 days ago. We were so sorry you had not known he was coming that you might have written by him, but I believe his visit was rather a surprise to himself as his determination was very sudden. He expects to leave the day after tomorrow for Bragg's command — wherever it may be, but he says he contemplates his return now with much less pleasure since hearing of your removal. Indeed he seems to regret your change as much as we do. We have seen a good deal of him since he came and I think he has improved more than anyone I've seen from the army — improved in every respect. Perhaps I think so all the more because he is so expressly like you dear Alvin, indeed I can sometimes almost imagine it <u>was</u> you instead of Cousin Mack, so entirely has he your very expression and gesture — his very smile makes me sad it so resembles your own. Nellie and I spent a couple of days very pleasantly at River Side last week and our pleasure being enhanced by a visit from Dick Bayly at the same time. He is altogether the most thorough going soldier and what is better the best of boys. His furlough expires tomorrow when he will rejoin his regiment in Winchester. We have but just returned from a most delightful little excursion. On Sunday evening last Nellie and Scott Roy and Cousin Mack and myself "pressed" some horses in the neighborhood and rode up to Clover Hill. Scott immediately returned but we remained overnight and yesterday had a long ride following the Shenandoah where it is turned from its course by a spur of the Fort Mts. We discovered a little fairy island in the river and Cousin M. and I ventured to, and explored it — 'twas a charming little nook overshadowed by great sycamores and elms and embowered in almost an impenetrable maze of smaller groves; then the views of the combined efforts of the grand wild old mountains and the blue, placid river were enough to craze an artist. As I was <u>not</u> one I fortunately retained complete possession of my faculties and descended with a very good grace to the enjoyment of the substantials of life in the dinner which Aunt Lizzie had smoking on the board for us on our return. We started home just before sunset yesterday evening but as we rode very slowly we did not reach our destination till long after moonlight and starlight were abroad. We so often wish for you both to share our enjoyment with us. Never mind, General Lee says we will have peace in 90 days and I am a devout believer in General Lee both as a prophet and a warrior, and if he prophecy aright now I trust our next Christmas festivities will be gladdened by two whose presence would contribute more than anything in the world to our happiness. We have cheering news from the west now — General Bragg seems to be bent upon giving the enemy — "a little more of the grape." Beauregard I believe competent to take care of Charleston. Price will keep them "agitated" in Missouri and now if we could only sweep away every vest of them from Virginia soil all indeed would indeed seem well. As it is there is some movement in the army of the Potomac not exactly satisfactory to those who like us can't comprehend it.

Mr. Proctor, you know, died during the summer and Mrs. Proctor is going to Charleston to live with her son — she leaves in about a fortnight and in the meantime we are endeavoring to make you up some linen to send by her — and some little necessities which I'm sure you'll need. I don't know how in the world you manage on so small a salary to clothe and board yourself — wish my ability to do for you were equal to my inclination.

Dick Buck has been engaged in recruiting conscripts for a month past, but has been but little at home in the meantime. Poor boy! Never had I thought to see our merry, careless Dick transformed into such a sad, careworn man. I don't know what is the matter with him, when he first came home he was more his old cheerful self than I've seen him since the war, but it only lasted a few days and now he is oh so gloomy. He <u>may</u> have heard something when he was at Mr. Sampson Bayly's that disconcerted him — he <u>may</u> think Walter has been taking advantage of his absence, these things <u>may</u> trouble him to a certain degree, but I'm satisfied there is a better cause for it. He seems very much grieved at the changes in the place and speaks as if he had nothing but desolation and ruin to look forward to all the days of his life. Poor Dick! I wish I could see through it all and if possible do something for him. He has been in Fauquier for two weeks and we are expecting him home every day, after which he will report himself at Richmond and then rejoin his regiment. Charlie Richardson thinks his arm will recover far enough to permit him to re-enter the service before very long. Charlie Buck too is at home now and very cheerful. His foot was amputated but it is thought with an artificial foot he may be able to walk as well as ever. Giles Cook is at home wounded slightly in the head. Uncle Tom was appointed by the county an agent to purchase salt from the salt works and started two weeks since on his mission, is expected home every day and Mrs. Tensia Tyler will probably return with him. Many of the refugees are returning to their homes now glad to be back once again. Mrs. Stewart and Fannie came home a few weeks since.

Did you hear that poor Mr. Charles H. Green died of apoplexy last week? He was quite well one evening, ate a hearty supper and was the next morning a corpse. Poor fellow! I'm afraid he was not prepared for the solemn change.

Laid my pen down to go see Scott who had come in — came to make a call about ten o'clock this morning and left at three P.M. He has been at home sometimes being unable to march upon a very lame foot; is just as full of fun as can be and I've laughed more today than for a long time before — wish I had some of the "consequences" that we've written today to send you. They are very amusing. He too goes back to his regiment tomorrow. They are holding "quarterly meeting" here now and are having something of a revival among the soldiers. I hope they may do them some good poor souls, for they suffer so much here that it would seem very hard for them not to have a better world in prospect. I never before appreciated the trials of a soldier's life, but during the last three weeks thousands of disabled and wounded have passed through town, nearly all of them poorly clad and the most of them weak, sick and almost starved. It was pitiable to see how eagerly they begged for a little bread and milk — always offering to pay for what they got when they had the money, though of course no one feels like taking anything from one so worn and battered in our country's service. Nellie dressed the wounds of a poor Alabamian who stopped at River Side, the wound was a dreadful one through the cheek and ear, and it made me deadly sick to stand by and hold the basin for her, but you would have been surprised to see how skillfully she performed the task and how gently too. She is a great girl, that Nell. You must not fancy we are suffering for food, it is true that this constant demand for provisions has reduced us to a very frugal style of living, but we shall have bread enough for the winter — we can do very well without meat while we have milk and butter. We are peculiarly fortunate in this respect for we have <u>cows</u> and many have <u>none</u>. Thus far we have had vegetables and have done very well. I regret though to think that when you all come home we will have so little with which to spread the board of welcome, but I hope the warmth and sincerity of that welcome will in some degree atone for other deficiencies.

We have arrived at the dignity of a mail once more, a semi-weekly mail, and as I intend sending this out by it I must close before it leaves town. All friends well and cheerful. Mrs. Hope has been complaining a good deal but is I think better now. Aunt Calmes says I must not forget to send you her love, and all the rest of the family unite most heartily in love to you both. May God bless you both dear brothers. Yours ever affectionately,

Lucie

Just now for a few lines to my dear boys tis so seldom we can write. I do not like to let any blank paper go. Do write and let us hear from you personally. We have heard through Geo. Hope but it is not like getting a letter from _you_. He writes much about himself — why is it he is so favored? He has been to the springs with General Jordan and speaks of rooming with Beauregard's nephew. Let us know all about yourselves how you manage to get along with such small pay. I cannot understand why the General has not done better by you. I should think you were entitled to more than eleven dollars per month. We feel uneasy about your getting the yellow fever. This is the season for it. I am so sorry you have separated from the boys, and more so that you do not like your present situation but you may like it better after awhile. Little Willie Hall died last week with diptheria. We are not fearing that we are to have the yankees again — our army is now in Winchester and 'tis thought they will go to Gordonsville if so we are certain to have them. The cause of our falling back the defficently in getting forage and provisions all of this country has been drained and if they get here I fear we shall not ever have bread and meat and if we have nothing for our cows to eat, cannot have milk and butter — but we must trust to Providence. He has left us here to live and I hope will not forsake us now — we have had a long drought — wish it would rain — Grandma is at Uncle Tom's — God bless you my dear boys asks their fond mother.

E.A.B. _(Elizabeth Ashby Buck)_

Bel Air, October 1862

My Dear Alvin,
    Your letter of the 13th reached me in just a week which is the first and only one we've had from you since you left Virginia. the one you wrote the week before never came to hand. Lucy received one from Irvie at the same time. I should have answered yours by the first mail but Lucy had written to you both in August and sent it to Dick to forward but he never got it and a few days ago it landed here so we concluded if it's contents were old it might be uninteresting to you so we sent that with a few additional lines. we try to write to you once a week for you must know we are only indulged in having a mail twice a week now and are even thankful that we can send and receive letters at all. Old Major Lewis keeps the mail in Mr. Weaver's store — do not know what sort of an officer he will make as he has just commenced. we received last night Beauregard's dispatch of the skirmish at Charleston and thought while reading it that perhaps you or dear Irving might have copied it — hope you may always be able to drive them back. we now hope to not to have the yankees here at least for awhile they are sending a good many sick here. I believe mostly Longstreet's men and tis said we are to have a large number — they took the academy yesterday. John Lovell had just cleaned and fixed it up nicely and had a good school it is almost a pity to turn him out. I am afraid the sick cannot have such things as they need here

as there is no provision made for them and the citizens have distributed til they have scarcely anything left for themselves and yet they cannot see our soldiers suffer without trying to relieve them. our sympathies are constantly excited by the sight of suffering in almost every form. Mary Pierce has just come in to spend the day and says Mrs. Roy received a short letter from Benton yesterday the first she has had for some time — he says she has not heard a word from home since April, he must be very anxious, he says but little about the Perryville affair. we cannot get the truth about it. indeed it seems almost impossible to get the truth about anything even our own army as near as it is to us. Walter came up with the girls from Colonel Larue's. the first we have seen of him since last spring though he spent most of the summer on the Mountain he says he never was as happy in his life as he has been the last eighteen months. Henry is at home, sick but is getting better. he is not fond of the service. Mrs. Sue Donald was here this morning she asked after you and spoke of the visit we paid her, and was very pressing for me to repeat. she says the yankees caught a cat and some kittens at Lena _____ Mason's boxed them up and sent them North and they proved to belong to Rob Steele. The "Rangers" are stationed near Colonel Larue's. the girls had a nice visit there and but for the death of poor Cousin John G. *(John Gill Buck)* would have enjoyed themselves more. we heard last week of the death of poor Mack Buck, he died in August, was buried in Laurel Hill to be removed. we did not learn any of the particulars. you speak of Marcus N. having some fine qualities. I think he is a noble fellow and you haven't a better friend in the world than he it made us quite proud to hear him speak of you and Irvie. I am sorry he cannot be with you. Lucy is suffering dreadfully with neuralgia, indeed she is never well. the baby has been quite sick for a month. Evred is the worst child above ground. I have to whip him like a colt and then have to nearly drown him. the other day Billy Rusk came here and he wanted to know what in the h'll was riding around the hill for. the ink is so bad I can hardly make a mark. would you or Irvie wear fine yarn socks? If so we will try and knit some we cannot get the cotton. give much love to dear Irvie. I will try to write to him soon. hope you may both keep well. Mary P. sends her love to you both and says make haste and get done fighting and come home. all unite in much love. may God be with you and keep you, prays your fond mother.

E.A.B. *(Elizabeth Ashby Buck)*

Mrs. Hope is better and has been on a visit to her brother for a week. Mrs. Andrew Almond has many acquaintances in Charleston and says she will give you letters to some nice young ladies there.

My Dear Boys,

Irving's letter of October 1 came to hand on Tuesday — the first we have had for a long while. Alvin's, I suppose, was sent through Staunton and is ____ ____ at Strasburg waiting for someone to go for it. for we must know we only get a mail from there when someone gets on a horse and goes up for it. the last we had John Lovell sent <u>Johnny Anderson</u> for. Mr. Jones is not <u>the</u> man for the place. he has been frightened so ever since the yankees came that he seems to be afraid to do anything and makes no effort to get the mails. all we get is <u>twice</u> a week on horses. you speak of not knowing what is doing here since the occupation of the yankees. had you gotten all the letters we have written you would have known almost everything we were particular to write everything we could knowing how it would interest you. what we have encountered since we saw you I can never tell you but should we be permitted to meet again can tell you a great deal I cannot write. but with all were more fortunate than we might have been. whenever the army was here in force we had headquarters here for the officers and they were a great protection to us. some <u>few</u> of them were I believe <u>gentlemen</u> but they were scarce. we had two surgeons who stayed with us for weeks and I really formed a strong attachment for them. one of them, Dr. Bogardus of the 116th. N.Y. was a young man. he attended all nearly all the family while here and was as kind as he could be and gave us a quantity of medicine. he was sent for in the night to see poor Eltie Richardson when they could get no other physician and although he had never seen one of the family he went and nursed her as tenderly as a brother could have done and when he left us he seemed <u>disappointed</u>. Evred was devoted to him as soon as he would hear his step on the pavement and would run and get in his arms and lay down on his bed and go to sleep. the other was Dr. Marshall of the 3rd Delaware one of the most social pleasant men I ever met. he was taken prisoner while he was here and I was really displeased but he soon got released. you perhaps saw an account of a dash our men made in town while they were here. I wish I could give you a full account. one night the doctor remarked that he had had a dream that had made a great impression on him. he dreamed that he was taken prisoner by four of our men that he was unarmed and expostulated with them about their taking him. it seemed to disturb him so that I said, "Doctor you ought to wear your green sash and that would protect you." the next morning he started over to town as usual to see his patients. about 11:00 we heard the cry "the Confederates are in town." we ran out and saw the yankees running to the river at full speed and the children saw two of our men dash down to Billy Bowling's and engage a number of the blue jackets. they had an encampment just a few yards from there. another party of four took the pickets just above your Uncle Tom's dashed into the Baptist Church where their Cavalry were picketed took them then dashed down to Captain Jacob's store where the Provost Marshall's office was took the guard, the Provost and a Captain then followed Dr.

Marshall over to the hotel, took him (he had a bottle of vinegar in his hand for me on his way over to dinner) then went up to the hospital and released Amos Groves and Newt Dorset and rushed out of town with thirty horses and about as many men. two of them came down by Perry Crisers to Mrs. Jones tollgate took all the pickets there but one and him they shot and he died in about a week. in a few minutes the yankee cavalry from the river as well as town were in hot pursuit yelling like Indians. the artillery was placed on the hill above Cousin E. Richardson's ready to shell town. our men dashed up the Luray Road and when they got to the bridge and a part of them with the prisoners kept up the road, the balance of four or five crossed the river at Clover Hill rode up to the barn and made a demonstration the Yankees thought they were all there and fired across the river but took care not to cross. the girls had gone up the day before and saw it all. our men consisted of 25 men led by Lieutenant Baylor. their horses were so broken down they let most of the men go, but kept the officers and horses. the doctor got off near Colonel Tripletes and came home to supper. it was one of the boldest raids of the war. the yankees were very much alarmed and incensed and would have shelled the town but for Colonel Reddon who was supposed to favor the people. the other officers were so angry with him about it they had him arrested. the next week the whole party moved off and that was the last we heard of them except for a few cavalry who came down from Winchester twice. Lucy wrote a full account of it. I would so like to hear what has become of Dr. Marshall he had applied twice for a discharge or furlough and said he was going home the last of September if he had to be court-martialled he almost shed tears when he left. Bell Boyd was arrested while she was here and sent to Winchester escorted by 50 Cavalry from there she was sent to Washington and confined in the old capitol for some weeks she was then released and the last I heard of her she was in Richmond boarding with General Joe Johnson she took a desperate fancy to Dr. Bogardus and said she had found he was her cousin she used to come over here to see him. I teased him well about his <u>cousin</u>. she spoke in the most extravagant terms of you both. she is as one of the officers said here at the table a great rascal or crazy. she did the people here an injury. she was as well known by the yankees almost as Beauregard. one little yankee was brought here sick and died on the red lounge in the other house. another one was very ill but got well. your Father sometimes did not go to town for three weeks. kept him all the time watching to keep them from stealing everything. we had to keep our cows in the yard for two or three months. the shrubbery is all broken down and the grass trampled in til the yard hardly looks like the same.

We had the parlour filled with barrels of shelled corn and covered over with books and as many as 30 of them slept in there and did not know it. after the battle here when the Yankees came in after Jackson the eye could reach in no direction that it did not rest on 1000s of them. the house, yard and fields were full of them and they were discharging their guns by 1000s.

One ball struck the house just under my window and another went into the other house where the officers were and the whole family except your father had to leave home and go up to your Uncle Mack's for a week and your father had even to drive up the cows in the rain. they went into the kitchen and stole the wood we had to get supper and while Mahalar went for more wood they stole the dough out of the tray but they never searched the house and never gave us imprudence but once when one of them went in the garden to dig potatoes and I went after him he abused me dreadfully and quite an amusing scene took place. I do not think I ever was as mad in my life. your Uncle Tom so far from being arrested seemed to be a favorite with all, made many personal friends and always told them his opinion of things. your Aunt Bettie made over $100 in gold and silver besides notes and a great many presents such as pickles, canned fruit, spirit, sugar, coffee, candles and a great many other things. one of the officers gave Allie a nice silver watch, an elegant hat and left a splendid sword there worth $60 to $70. we have since heard he was dead. when Jackson's men came in they captured two trunks of jewelry, watches, chains, deguerotype cases. they gave your Aunt Betty some of them and when your Uncle Tom went to Richmond he sold them for $150. she is flush of money. she sells a great deal to the soldiers at good prices such as milk, butter and as your Uncle Tom sent to Washington by one of them the wife of an officer and bought a box of goods such as calicos, handkerchiefs, dye stuffs he and Gen. Deever (the officer who was so kind) had the box brought on the cars <u>free</u> directed to him he got the goods at the old prices and gave each of us a calico dress and some other things. they seem to prosper in every thing and is very kind to us. at the time our men made that dash into town nearly all the citizens were arrested and he was in a squad of them and they never troubled him but were at all times respectful. so they were to your father. we used to laugh and say he froze them by his manner. they broke into Weaver's store repeatedly and stole a great deal from elegant silk dresses at $1.50 per yard. they stole and sold for $5.00 a pattern but no one seemed to pity him for he is extorting in every way he can and had he sold his goods at reasonable prices he would not have had so many of them to steal he bought some goods from the sutlers but they stole most of them. at one time their trains were hauling stores from Winchester to Culpepper by here and a party of our men pitched into them near Tom McKay's and captured them. they were so mad they arrested Tom McKay and Ben Hicks and old Mr. Bartlett and they knew nothing more about it than you did. they have confined in Washington ever since til a few days ago they came home and gave terrible accounts of their treatment. they have injured Mr. Petty very much seems to have gone at spite against him. they went to Mr. Marshall, searched his house, broke open their drawers, stole their handkerchiefs, stockings, collars and even their money and their clothes that were in wash. you never have seen a place so desolate as Rose Hill. and to crown all last Thursday evening their servants house in the yard took fire and burned down. and was near taking the smokehouse and house. I took two buckets and started down and Nellie after me. by the time we got there it was generally known in town and they had taken nearly everything out of the house. the family were much more composed than I expected. your grandma and Lucy soon followed me but we could do little else but be with the family. when the _____ _____ battle took place here a Louisianian was wounded near there. he was taken to the house and had his leg taken off and has been there ever since. he was an Irishman and was the most grateful creature you ever saw. he had gotten so that he could walk everywhere on his crutches and they clothed and fed him like he had been one of their family and he was very useful to them but he seemed to feel that he was an encumbrance to them and after he found there was a prospect of the yankees getting back here he was afraid to stay said they might take him prisoner and put him in some place that he would freeze to death so finding an opportunity to go home he left there a few days ago. they miss him very much. his name was Howe. they had another taken there at the same time who had his leg amputated but he died the next morning. they are now entirely alone except for your cousin Sue who will always make it her home. she has only been at her father's twice for a few hours. she is looking badly black is not becoming to her. Charlie Buck is walking about but cannot use his foot. he takes great interest in the farm, trying to help his father. Charlie Richardson has gotten well and talks of joining the army again soon. he will I expect go to the cavalry service. Dick Buck has gotten back from his trip to Salem and Richmond and expected to start out again today. he says he never received but one letter from Irvie and could not answer it he was a good deal disturbed that you should feel hurt with him he does not know where he will join his company not till he gets orders. W.M. Cloud and Edwin went to their company on Friday. Walter, Henry and the other boys are with their company it was somewhere between Winchester and Berryville the other day. your Uncle John has been assistant quartermaster all the time he is now I expect in Gordonsville getting clothing for his family of some _____ thousands. Lucy, Nellie and Cousin Bet went to Colonel Larues on Friday in a wagon that was going to Charlestown for salt. your aunt Catty said she had some fruit and yarn, etc. for the children and as Cousin Bet has some things Aunt Elisa left her there will return in a wagon and bring them. the girls have been so confined I was glad for them to have a visit I expect they will be gone about a week. Colonel Larue lost a number of his servants but they were all captured and he sold them. Uncle N., Jake and Stewart, your Uncle Tom's Thornton and Uncle Mack's Mose all went. nearly everybody in the neighborhood lost some but us. many of them have been taken. if old Abe's proclamation is carried out I suppose the balance will leave the first year whether they want to or not. since writing the above, we have heard the sad news Cousin John Gill's *(Buck)* death he died at Colonel Larues on Sunday night. he went down to the camps to see his boys on Monday before and went there in the evening complaining. they thought he had quinsy until Sunday evening when they found it was diptheria. W. Cloud has just come from the burying and said it is the most distressed family he ever saw. Sam did not get there till he was dead. I feel uneasy about the girls they write me that Henry is complaining — I wrote to you by Mr. _____ and sent you some clothes which I hope you will get before this reaches you. some soldiers were riding in a handcar on Thursday and just as they got to the cattle stop at our mill, the car turned over killing one and hurting another so he died the next morning. Grandma and the children send much love to you. so do write while you can we cannot tell when we may have the Yankees. General Toinble has been at Mrs. Cloud's for three weeks. he is wounded his wife is Mr. Presmon's aunt. they left yesterday. may God protect my boys, asks their mother.

E.A.B. *(Elizabeth Ashby Buck)*

Head Quarters
Department of South Carolina and Georgia[17]
Charleston, S.C. October 30th 1862
(Arrived November 27, 1862[18] *)*

Just a few lines, Lucie dear, in reply to your letter. I have a violent aversion to seeing an envelope start homeward without having some of my "fist" in it.

It was a good idea of yours sending that old letter — it contained a great deal of news and I am gradually becoming acquainted with all that has transpired around home during those long, dreary months of silence. To give you an idea of how our friends in the 17th keep us informed I'll say that your letter gave us the first particulars of the death of Willie Richardson — we heard that he was wounded and afterwards that he had died — both of which were vague rumors and I had hoped that he was still alive until a month ago when I heard from home and even now cannot realize it, and always associate him with my contemplated visit home. In my dreams I constantly live over some of our past times together but these sweet illusions are soon dispelled and I awake to mourn the sad reality, oh that I could change it for the dream. It is not right that we should question the actions of Providence, but it indeed seems hard that he should be taken, when there are so few like him — such thoughts and reflections make me sad and to think of him is truly "a painful pleasure", but I try to reconcile myself, by my knowledge that he has only exchanged this for a better life, and blame myself for selfishness in wishing it otherwise and trust that if it should be the will of God, that I too, should be called from this world as suddenly, that I may be as well prepared for the change.

Do you not think that Alvin has improved wonderfully as a correspondent? He has written letter for letter with myself, so you see it is never too late to mend.

Was very glad to hear of your safe return from Clarke, had begun to entertain serious apprehensions that the Yankees would again have possession of my "Rebel" sisters.

I am proud to hear of Walter's exploits. Uncle Mack has two "Bowld sodger boys" of whom he may well be proud. Walter has become considerable of a hero. I agree with Alvin, who says he "never heard of a Buck, whose "gourd" (head) was worth $10,000 — I would sell out for half price".[19]

We are no better pleased with Charleston than at first and wish would be ordered elsewhere or anywhere else, I have an idea of trying a hither to infallible method of accomplishing this desirable end: vis. to make some lady acquaintance — to show that I am correct I'll give you a short chapter of my experience: 1st at <u>Columbus</u> after being cooped up weather bound to the house for days, we at length "rung in" with a "feminine" when the next day down came a telegram ordering us to Jackson, this was not so bad as she was on the shady side of 35 and a damaged article in point of beauty — At <u>Jackson</u> we met certain Vics and Mollies, after wavering some hours between the two I finally attached myself to the former, and was getting along "hugely" when <u>Alvin arrived from Nashville,</u> I introduced him as my "brother", I do not know whether the word "brother" produced an unfavorable impression in my behalf (I tried to think so afterwards) or what, but my suit was on the wane from that moment, notwithstanding the various hints thrown out about certain engagements in Kentucky, but am under the impression that Alvin (the ungrateful scamp) whispered into her willing ear, something like a blow in the dark, I could not return, however I held on with tenacity worthy of better success, until I accidently heard that the old man said to Vic "if all of the young men were like that one — meaning A. she ought to make all the acquaintances she could." Now what produced this favorable impression with the watchful "parent" I am not prepared to say, but think A must have had foresight enough to pay his bill (her father was the hotel keeper), or perhaps presented him with sundry "Havanas" — be this as it may I saw that I would have to "carry my pigs to another market" and with this praise worthy conclusion became desperately enamored with Mollie but it was no go, the cold shoulder was soon apparent. I had been too assiduous in my attentions to her sister and found it was a waste of time and <u>affection</u> in that quarter for me and was considerably <u>non-plussed</u> and in doubt how to proceed to get out without giving the boys a good joke on me — but determined to follow Hoyles instructions in whist "When you are in doubt play a trump" and in hearing of the rest of the party, gave Mollie to understand that she must not place any serious construction on my conduct towards her and hinted at a prior engagement etc. for which piece of gratuitous impudence I was assured I need not be uneasy on that score, and boxed until blind, but afterwards got a <u>kiss</u> to make friends (I forgot to mention that before introducing A to Vic, I recommended to him a cousin of hers there at the time, who was as ugly as the devil ("old nick" I mean) but my representation was a Venus for beauty, and Croesus for riches, in reality — her finances were in a state generally compared to the condition of a church mouse or a fowl owned by Mr. Job. After this we quit the hotel and went to private boarding with a very nice lady — a "pensioner" who had that invariable piece of boarding house furniture a "brick topped" (red headed) daughter but one of the best girls I ever saw and had no designs on any one, for on the contrary she "blew our trumpets" so strong in the ear of a Miss Alice H that after sundry hints about getting acquainted with Miss H which the memory of my last love (?) was too fresh to permit me to agree too readily — the said Alice, finally one day made it convenient for us to catch her at our house while "visiting her friend Susie" and "had no idea it was so late", etc. notwithstanding we had seen her leave the day before a few moments before we arrived — our landlady having afterwards acknowledged she had given us out, in her excuses for a cold dinner. This time we of course got a "knock down" to Miss A. Here I had the inside track on Alvin (who had meanwhile been cut out with Vic) — much to my satisfaction — by a Mississippi Captain and poor "Court" *(Alvin)* here learned that his <u>goatee</u> and <u>caterwauling</u> were unavailing against <u>brass</u> <u>buttons</u> and <u>gold</u> <u>lace</u>, the lady having discovered that I bore a strong likeness to a "dear friend", cousin or something of the kind, and I for said likeness was rewarded with a bouquet which for dimensions reminded me forcibly of one of those round flower beds Ma used to have in the garden. She left with a promise from me that I would call soon. I went — into the largest brick house in town and the finest parlor I have ever set my foot in anywhere — up went our cards and down came the ladies — Miss Alice radiant in a nicely fitting brown silk and diamonds enough to set up Tiffany on a small scale. I also learned that their father was a thriving merchant, doing a heavy business in the "rag trade" — was a <u>consumptive</u> with his life heavily insured, and noted for never paying a debt (the latter part I did not get from them). Upon the strength of all this I became desperately smitten, spouted Shakespeare and Byron, and positively denied any acquaintance with V and Mollie, declaring it was all a mistake and was not me but Alvin (A. not being present or my hide would certainly have paid for this fib, but I bound Burton, who accompanied me over, to secrecy and felt tolerably secure, and was reckless as to consequences). I flattered myself that I was producing great impression on the fortress, and would reduce it when called upon to surrender and was actually planning how I would complete the back of the house, which was in an unfinished condition, I brought up other guns to bear for a final attack, when unfortunately the conversation took a religious turn, here I did not know my ground, not being <u>au</u> <u>fait</u> in the doctrines of the various denominations, from her conversation I supposed she was an Episcopalian — she was a Methodist, and knowing the antipathy that generally exists between the two — I proceeded to make some facetious remarks about Methodist ministers, their chicken eating proclivities, etc. I found to my horror that I had nearly annihilated myself in her estimation — where upon my bow and exit followed after some stammered exclamations about my family being of the Methodist denomination (the Lord forgive the fib). That night visions of brick houses, pianos, diamonds etc. floated through my head in glorious confusion which at length settled down into a dream of entering the parlor and approaching the sofa upon which sat the adorable Alice, when lo! she was suddenly transformed into an immense rooster, with a white cravat on and Methodist hymn book under its wing and which proceeded very unceremoniously to throw me out of the window, I lit among the poultry and — awoke and found myself on the floor, old Buck asserts that I rolled out, but I have an idea that his fist assisted — as I had a bruise on my shoulder that very much resembles his knuckles. Tried to reinstate myself by accompanying Miss Alice to church next night and by my devotion and patience, during the infliction of a sermon, strongly tincture with <u>sulphur</u> and calculated to scare a person into heaven and when I arose from prayer with my eyes filled with tears (caused by her letting a large hymn book fall on the place where old Buck struck me the night before) I so far succeeded that I entertained strong hopes of getting the house the next visit, or at least a diamond ring — when alas! for human expectations when coupled with military affairs, an order arrived for us to "repair to Corinth without delay," we left that afternoon, after a <u>heart</u> <u>rending</u> scene from old Buck and Vick, which I witnessed through the shutters — I soon healed my "wounded heart" in the bright eyes of a pretty brunette — here was but one obstacle that was insurmountable, being in the shape of a big husband, who was likely to outlive a rich bachelor uncle and not liable to conscription on account of some exemption, which I tried in vain to convince him was done away with by the new law, and became quite eloquent, painted in glowing colors the advantage and glory of volunteering to being conscripted as he <u>most</u> <u>certainly</u> would be, and even went so far as to suggest a very "nice company whose duties were light and would just suit him", but no, he knew better, "they could not conscript him" — and the matter ended by our retreat from Corinth — whilst at Saltillo, we introduced ourselves to a couple of girls and the next day were ordered to "trot". My next blast was at Chattanooga with Miss Nannie V. a very pretty girl with a very large mouth, but which was filled with beautiful teeth — she told me she was 16 years of age, I do not think she was older, had gotten well enough acquainted to admire her hair (which was really very pretty) and while so doing would twist around my finger, and while standing in the night air, advising her to wear hoops, (something the East Tenn. girls never do) I caught a cold that like to have finished me — from which I had not recovered when ordered here — this was the "last feather" and gave me a big disgust, and shall foreswear the "softer sex" until I meet a pretty something I have not yet seen here — from the foregoing you will suppose those I have met were very "soft" about the head. But <u>sub rosa</u> this must never reach Richmond — there thanks for your kind consent to certain arrangements and there may be more truth in it than you suppose.

Have been trying to get you some music but there is nothing new — there is a piece published in Augusta, heard it sung by the "Queen Sisters" will try to get it for you it is called the "Volunteer or Weep Not Dearest" the words are not very good, being too much repetition in it — but the air is pretty.

Received a letter from Williams yesterday, he and Roy were both well.

Alvin has written to Grand-Ma, give her my love and say that if I do not mention her name in my letters I think of her none the less.

Have strung my "few lines" to great length and am rather ashamed of the production, but you, like the Dutchman who was kicked by the donkey, must "consider the source" and after the trouble of writing it you must do penance to your brothers' sins by reading it. I'll promise you shall not have a similar infliction.

Mrs. Procter has not yet reported — but we expect to hear from her tomorrow.

Several of our staff have arrived in the last few days from Gen Bragg's Army, they left all of our relatives well.

Did you receive those pictures I sent? (Pope's Essays).

Love to one and all of the family — will send Uncle Tom a paper in a day or two — You had better not let Father or Uncle Mack see this, I imagine I can see them lift their hands in horror.

Ever your affectionate Brother,
Pat *(I.A. Buck)*

Dear Lu:
Deduct 33 per cent for lies.
Alvin
Do nothing of the kind — its all true, A does not wish to open it.

Head Quarters
Department of South Carolina and Georgia
Charleston, South Carolina
November 6, 1862

Dear Ma

Your letter to Alvin reached us yesterday and I intended replying last night, but was more engaged than usual, my regular work kept me busy until after 10 o'clock.

Mr. Bowman "reported" yesterday and Hope and myself went out to see Mrs. Procter in the afternoon — we spent the evening and had a very pleasant time — she is staying at her son Caleb's house — it was very kind of her to trouble herself with such large packages.

The shirts do fit admirably — please accept our thanks for them — but Ma you should not have sent the money, we really did not need it and it was painful for us to think that perhaps, you had deprived yourself and the children for us —, we are now well supplied with clothing. A and myself are going to buy a suit of blue army cloth, jacket, pant and vest, from the Quarter Master's office, which will cost us $25.00 — at any other place they would charge at least $100.00.

We have broken up our mess and gone to boarding, it is cheaper and more pleasant — at my house there is three young ladies one of who has discovered that I am very much like a Cousin of hers, so I suppose I'll not remain much longer in Charleston (see Lucie's letter).

I received a letter from Dick Blakemore and Benton Roy a few days ago, both were well. Benton was bragging that Gen. Hardee was unwell and he was having some rest and was luxuriating in marble, rosewood and spring mattresses at Knoxville. I have no doubt but that he appreciates them to their fullest extent after his Kentucky experience. I also received a letter from Pearre[20], he was applying for a clerk ship in this office, but all the places were filled — which I was very sorry for, as I am exceedingly anxious to have him with us.

Evred *(Evred Buck, born January 9, 1860, a brother)* is a very precarious young man, he had commenced swearing so early that perhaps he will become disgusted (as I did) and quit before he is a man.

Thank Mrs. Almond for her kind offer, when I want a wife I am going to Georgia for her, they are the prettiest, kindest people I have met south, both times I went through, at every depot there were crowds of ladies with every thing nice for the soldiers and were untiring in their attention to the sick — the girls are fine, and healthy looking and have small feet and not round shouldered, the latter is a characteristic of southern ladies, at least as far as my observation goes — I know the reason of it though and will tell you when I come home.

Am sorry that Uncle John *(Falstaff)* was . . . *(The last of this letter was lost)*

Bel Air, Tuesday, November 18, 1862

My Dear Irving,

Your letter to me came by the last regular mail we received. it reached us just as we were in the greatest excitement and alarm expecting hourly an attack here and which if it had been made it would have involved us in the greatest danger. I never saw your father so alarmed and excited in my life — no wonder then that we should not have been calm, but Lucy wrote to you at the time and also the next week both of which I hope you received. our mails are again cut off ere at least disarranged — the enemy being in the direction of the Culpepper courthouse prevents our getting it regularly in that way but there is no reason why we should not get them by Strasburg if they will only take the trouble to send there so I hope you both will continue to write and we may get them sometimes at least as long as we hold the Valley and if you should not get letters you may know it is not our fault as we will write by every opportunity.

We hear so many rumors about our army that it is impossible to get any truth — two weeks ago we expected to be in the hands of the enemy — now many think they will not be here at all others think they will. I do not think they can possibly

111

stay here in force, they have nothing to subsist on and they will be afraid to come in small numbers but they may make occasional dashes and destroy the little we have left which they can do in a little time this I fear at the very best and it will be as much as the citizens can do to live through the Winter without much suffering everything is so high and scarce the soldiers have consumed nearly everything and our army have taken all of the provisions that could be spared so as to leave none here as inducement for the enemy — Last week Early's division were here and tore up the Rail Road and destroyed every little bridge I thought it very unnecessary to destroy the "_____" for should they determine to build the other part of the road it will be a small job for them to repair that — It did make me feel sad when I thought of the labor and money that road had cost and the many dear ones that had passed over it some never to return and others I had hoped soon to see but it is gone and <u>our walk</u> to town is <u>ruined</u>. the yankees can not now get subsistence for themselves or their horses without hauling it and if they try that they will have a <u>good</u> time this <u>Winter</u>. they brought in a yankee prisoner yesterday who said they were 200,000 strong below the ridge. I do not believe that but there is no doubt about their being in large force are trying to get to Richmond. tis said McClellan was asked if they would get to Richmond this Winter. he said, "No." they then asked Burnside, he said "Yes." they then told McClellan they had no more use for him. Henry Buck expected to join his company yesterday but it rained and he did not go — they are still in Clarke or Jefferson. I heard they had quite a skirmish near Rippon the other day in which the "Rangers" figured tis said, the seventh and one or two regiments of infantry kept off I'm afraid to say how many thousands, killed seventy and wounded several hundred and took a number of prisoners. I do not know how true it may be. Walter <u>is happy</u> — Dick made a narrow escape the other day — he has been as you know getting "conscripts" — he and Lieutenant Zimmerman were in Middleburg the yankees dashed in and they ran to a house, rushed in and tis said Dick ran in a room where some young ladies were preparing for bed and ran under <u>their bed</u>. Zimmerman went to another room and did likewise — they were not detected but a young man in the same house was caught. Dick could not get home and so had to join his regiment. I expect it goes right hard with him after being out so long especially as his clothes are all at home. Charlie Richardson goes back tomorrow. Colonel Corse has promised him some position he does not know what. poor boy I am afraid he is gone. he, Joe Miller and Baily Jacobs tis said were spending all last week at Joe's his wife was from home Baily Jacobs has nearly lost the use of himself from rheumatism. walks with great difficulty and looks dreadfully. Charlie Buck's foot is nearly well but he cannot use it he walks on two crutches it looks strange to see him but it is no uncommon sight now. Charlie is quite fat and well and is head man at home bids fair to make a manager. Newton Petty and Johnny Boon are at home. they have gotten a transfer and are going to join the cavalry Captain O'Ferrall but I do not suppose they will add a great deal to the <u>credit</u> of any company so far as bravery is concerned. Tom Petty has been in that company for some time and is said to be a good soldier — Mary Pierce and the girls spent several days at Mr. Richards' last week and had a nice time Mack and Sam Buck and a number their officers were there. General Jackson has had his headquarters about Jessee McKays for some time and it has given the young men a chance to visit a little. Sam is a nice fellow, has just been promoted to First Lieutenant by his officer tis said to be a very honorable promotion. your father has just been in and told us Kate Long was dead we heard she was not expected to live with typhoid fever poor young girl! in the bloom of youth. Turner Ashby and a number of others are dead. Nellie had a letter yesterday from Dick Blakemore from Knoxville, he says he had not heard from you though he had written. Lucy had one from Benton last week they had just found that communication was open here. your Uncle John says that Mr. Pearre told him that John Smith had thrown himself away. that his association was principally with the Union men and federals. we had hoped Mr. Pearre would have been to see us before this but I suppose as the army is near Winchester he cannot well come. your Uncle John says his aim seems to be to find you and we hope yet to see him. your Uncle Tom said when he was in Richmond that Nannie Taylor was in black we have since heard that it was for a brother who was in the Northern army and died in a hospital in Baltimore. they had disowned him but I suppose that since his death their natural feelings for him have revived. tis said his course nearly killed his mother. your Uncle Tom did not see her or Clara—from her letter to Lucy I fear their circumstances could not be good as they have trouble in some way. she is a sweet affectionate girl and I love her much. I think the reason your Uncle Tom fared so well with the Yankees was his being a mason a great many of them were — I wish you and A. were in a situation to join the fraternity but I know it is too expensive for your means now. Give much love to my dear Alvin and tell him I answered his letter as soon as I received — his to his Father then came with mine. your Grandma often says you and he have forgotten her that never write or even send her a message. Aunt Betsy is quite sick — she and Aunt send much love to you both I am writing in her room — Lucy is a great sufferer with neuralgia, her health is not good—she is never well — all would send love if they knew I was writing — Good night—may God bless both and keep you I ask in his name.

Your mother,
E.A.B. *(Elizabeth Ashby Buck)*

Say to George H. *[Hope]* all are as well as usual at home. Old Unle Ben has not been expected to live for some time he has almost entirely lost his mind. The Rose Hill family and all friends in usual health.

The following is written on "captured" stationery with an American Flag stating:

"Our flag, (that used to be) the constitution and the union
Much Chunk Rangers, Captain L.F. Chapman Company E, 28th Regiment P.V.

Colonel Tynsdale alias Nero

State of Suspense
Month of Dec. 3rd day, 1862

Dear Irvie,

If the mails be true to their trust you will ere this have received a letter which I wrote you on your birthday, but that six page letter of the 30th of October deserved a special reply. You would have laughed could you have seen me when Father handed me the pacquet. A <u>double</u> letter directed in <u>Alvin</u> <u>handwritten</u> was <u>such</u> a novelty, and my face flushed, my eyes grew dim with tears and my hand trembled so that I could scarce open it. And then when it <u>was</u> opened and <u>two</u> letters instead of <u>one</u> and such a delightfully long one too as yours was fell out it was too nice. We had not heard from you for three weeks until just the night before when we got one from Alvin to Ma and getting such a batch of letters all at once threw us into a perfect flutter of delight. I hardly knew whether to cry or laugh when I read yours — twas so characteristic of the dear writer and I could just imagine how you looked when penning it with your head bent over the paper and that saucy smile hovering around the corners of your mouth. Why don't you write in that way always? Don't you know you two are the most interesting subjects you could enlarge upon in your correspondence? We had rather you would tell us of yourselves than to give us any amount of war news which the newspapers themselves would furnish us. You know we would never weary of reading your letters even were they twice as long as some I write <u>you</u>. Alvin <u>has</u> improved wonderfully as correspondent and you don't know how fond we are of his letters. Grandma hoards hers up as a very treasure and keeps it in her Sanctum Sanctorum where she can occasionally have a p___ of it all to herself. Dear Alvin, we were so pleased at his writing so seriously — though we <u>knew</u> he was often more thoughtful than he appeared; yet tis a pleasure for him to express himself thus. I think there are few persons who understand my brother, but those who <u>do</u>, appreciate and love him so warmly. It does me as much good to meet with some of his friends to hear their expressions of enthusiastic regard for him — such persons for instance are Cousin Mack, J.T. Petty, Scott Roy, <u>Captain Peyton</u>, etc. etc. My poor Irvie, what sad experience has been yours. Little did I imagine what my merry hearted brother had been undergoing since he left us — little imagine what damage his heart has suffered since then. Why I don't often know how, after such a lavish expenditure of affection you can have any left to bless your home friends with. To think how often I have boasted that you were above such weakness, that you were invulnerable to all the artillery of the mischief-making little god; so little was I prepared to judge of human nature in general and Irvie-nature in particular. I don't know whether your experience was ____ a comedy or tragedy with regard to Miss Alice — and there is some inconsistency in your course of proceedings that I can't exactly reconcile. You would induce me to believe that you are earnest in the consummation of certain arrangements with a Richmond friend — nay would actually leave me to think that said arrangements had been brought to a successful issue, at the same time you give quite a graphic description of your Herculean labors in the efforts to vanquish a certain Tennessean Amazon, and even go so far as to make your plans for the future remodeling of her establishment. You certainly could not have seriously entertained the idea of discarding either of the ladies after matters on both sides had progressed so far, and yet to settle the affair in any other way you could not that I can see which <u>did</u> you intend to favor with your final preference Alice or Nannie? By the way, how your imagination had developed and improved since your residence in the South and West. That description of your dream about the clerical rooster was mostly of Baron Munchausen himself — however it has afforded us a subject for ceaseless merriment and there is just enough of the truth in your narrative to elicit my sisterly sympathies in your behalf. But you might have known that I always told you there was no place on earth like Virginia, no girls like Virginia girls, no boys like Virginia boys (except Maryland boys) and consequently no "affairs de colur" like those contracted and carried on in Virginia. Had you been "true to the auld line" and confined your operations to the vicinity of Richmond how much you might have been spared! Has Alvin consoled himself of the loss of his Vic (Tim) in the bright eyes of some daughter of the Palmetto state, or is Kentucky still in the ascendancy? I begin to think, from his evident anxiety to get back to Hopkinsville that he is going to astonish us all by becoming a very model unmitigated constancy. I, myself, am sadly in need of advice — I have been so accustomed to depend on the judgement of others that I could never choose so much as a ribbon for myself, and now when matters of greater moment present themselves for consideration, I am such a slave to the pernicious habit of dependency that I can't for the life of me make a definite decision. The matter 'tis between Maryland and Eastern Virginia — Captain L. and Dr. M. I do not believe though Maryland could carry the day but for my pride of State and my wish to appear consistent in my assertions of her superiority to every other state in every respect. But, I'm writing you so much nonsense just because I have nothing else with which to fill my sheet. I have written you so recently. Captain L. decidedly in ascendancy no mistake Uncle Tom *(Tom Ashby, City Official of Front Royal, lived at Oakley)* is in Richmond again, it's too bad old Governor Letcher to make positive promises to let us have our supply of salt and then to disappoint us — it keeps Uncle Tom continually on the <u>wing</u> to attend to it, and him with all his exertions I'm afraid they will not agree to let us have our portion of the seven and one half pounds per head, till February when the Yankees will have invested the place and prevented the reception of any kind of supplies. I can't understand why it is that when Warren *(County)* has suffered so much from both armies, when she has been so true to our cause has done all she could to aid and abet it, that she should be one of the last to receive favors at the hands of Government. I have been staying with Aunt Bettie during Uncle Tom's absence and have enjoyed my visit very much. Nellie is with us tonight and Aunt Letitia Blakemore, and if you want to imagine my surroundings while penning this, just, in imagination, step into Aunt Bettie's south chamber *(Oakley)*. It is night, a fire burning on the hearth the crackling of which, with Nellie's breathing is the only audible sound for the household has retired. I am seated very unceremoniously on the floor before the fire and enveloped in my wrapper with candle in chair near me and my portfolio on my knee scribbling now a few lines and now falling out into a long reverie from which the crackling of the fire invariably arouses me. Nellie is in the arms of Morpheous long since and I wish you could see how sweetly she is sleeping. No one to look at her face as it lies there on the pillow shaded by her long dark curls would imagine it belonged to a maiden of eighteen, but rather fancy it that of a petted child wearied of play who has sunk to sleep dreaming of the sports of the day. May it never wear a look of deeper care! Dick has again returned from Salem but was unsuccessful in getting his horse. I think however he must have been successful in some of his essays to judge from his bright expressions and great cheerfulness. He was to have met us here tonight and I don't know how to account for his non-appearance except on the score of the rumored proximity of the enemy, he may have been afraid to come to town. Cousin Newt Cloud came in very unexpectedly last night on business, his regiment was then near Berryville. He looked well but is very homesick and anxious to hear from home. He said all were well in the regiment except Walter who was slightly indisposed. This morning our cavalry left town and the enemy were said to be quite near but this was an exaggeration. Mack Erwin came in about twelve o'clock and said he was on his way to Clover Hill where he wants to take refuge from the Yankees — reported a skirmish near Berryville yesterday in the cause of which the Confederate force being small had to retire whereupon the place was occupied by their troops. He is both very deaf and nearly blind and therefore unfit for service. Dick Bayly *(Co. E., 7th Va. Cavalry)* came in this evening and gave us further particulars. Said the Yankees advanced with quite a force of cavalry, artillery and infantry while we had but parts of four companies which were in such a position as to be exposed to their raking fire of shell and grape which however did no mischief excepting to wound one or two of our men. Our men being overwhelmed by superior numbers retired a short distance in "good order". Poor Alfred McKay was badly injured by his horse stumbling and rolling on him in the charge, but tis thought not to be serious. Our army has formerly evacuated Winchester and the enemy are taking quiet possession of it. I suppose for the purpose of building the B and O.O.R.R. Our brigade is at Strasburg and there Dick will rejoin them. We are awaiting our fate with disparaging calmness and every day

116

after today still expect a ____ of the Yankee cavalry unless Burnside may have use for his troops in this section and cause a withdrawal of them — tis our only hope.

I send this out tomorrow by Dr. Turner who is going to seek Smith who is sick in the hospital somewhere within our lines. It is impossible for me to say whether or not one shall have any more mails — you can but write and try to get the letters through. After you <u>know</u> all communications to have ceased — direct your letters to Captain Buck who may be able to smuggle them in. Captain Simpson has been promoted to the Lieutenant Colonelcy of the 17th. Wesley Lehew is Captain of Company B and Smith Turner First Lieutenant. Dick *(Buck)* Second and the Junior Second lies between Scott Roy and J.T. Petty. Charlie Richardson, Johnny Boone, and John Johnston have joined *(Horace)* Buck's Company *(Co. E., 7th Va. Cavalry)*. None of them I fear very great acquisitions to it. Charly Buck[21] remains at home — sends his love to you both and says he will write soon. All are well as usual at Rose Hill. I believe I never told you that Colonel (now General Corse) stayed all night there when Longstreet passed through and told them all about his being wounded while riding Fan (Willie's horse) in battle and how the same ball that struck him killed a poor fellow. Both master and horse fell in the same cause and both nobly. The family were so much pleased at the way in which you and A. mentioned dear Willie in your letters. All well at Belle Monte except Jacquie who has the jaundice. I did not tell you poor little Charlie Boone died last week of diptheria — the family are much distressed. The family are all well and send love. Aunt Bettie *(Elizabeth Almond Ashby)* and Letitia *(Letitia A. Buck Blakemore)* send their love and the latter hopes you will not omit to mention her boys[22] when you write. Mrs. Hope is quite unwell, but I do not think is more so than she has been heretofore. The rest of the family there are well. I need not tell you how much disappointed we are ____ ____ ____ come home Christmas but we look for a "brighter day coming" and until that day, darling brothers we must wait.

Thank Alvin in all our names and say to him Ma intends replying to his letter very soon if she has an opportunity — has not been at home this week — or would probably have done so before. We are glad you have your clothes and keep the ____ till you do ____. Good night. God bless my brothers till we meet again.
Lovingly Your sister,
Lucie

December 4, 1862

I sat up till twelve o'clock last night writing to you Irvie dear, but this morning before breakfast Cary came in bringing me your letter of the 24th which came in last night's mail. Although Ma has written Alvin a letter to send with mine making quite a package, yet I must enclose an "addenda" in acknowledgment of your four. I received also a nice long letter from "Nannie Dear" in which she spoke of receiving a letter from her "brother" Irvie and promised me to be a good sister to "Pat", when we shall be again allowed the privilege of holding communication with him, and give him all the information she can. So if your bulletins shall increase in frequency hereafter — have the grace to ascribe your good fortune to the right source. I sometimes since met with an acquaintance of her — Dr. Clarkson in South Carolina and he told me that a friend of his from Charleston was very much enamored of _my_ friend and _would_ address her if he had not _already_ done so. In my next letter to Nannie I dropped some hint of what I had heard and I suppose it is no breach of confidence or good faith to give you her reply only you must promise it shall go no further — "I was quite startled at seeing — ___'s name in your letter, could not imagine how you had heard from him. He is a most charming acquaintance and one of my best _friends_, but is _in love_ with a young lady here — _not_ your friend Nannie. Don't suppose he ever thought of such a thing." She _is_ a dear girl, and no mistake. I'm glad you're forming acquaintances in Charleston — that make your sojourn much more pleasant — do not trust your own strength of resistance too much though in warding off the attacks of Cupid, for you know it has proved insufficient of you. I will, when I see Willie Buck again, prosecute my inquiries about your North Carolinian friend and hope the mystery may yet be satisfactorily solved. I was very much surprised of your account of George Williams visit to your friend Randall's. I believe I will give up the plan of forming an opinion of the disposition and character of my acquaintances. I find I'm such a bungler at it. Now for instance, I would as soon have thought of old Diogenes himself having an affair ____ as Cousin George. I'm glad though to learn he is not above the weakness common to us poor mortals — it is such a comfort to have "companions" in misery (she is just getting uneasy and a little "jealous"). I wrote you on your birthday and remarked to Ma at the time — "perhaps dear Irvie is thinking of us now as it is his birthday." But I did not know you were writing to me even then. I don't think there are many minutes in any day when you could think of us that there would not be a perfect communion of our spirits — a perfect in interchange of heart thoughts.

Irvie dear, I don't know how you could have heard that Captain Simpson thought we were displeased with him. I give him credit for too much delicacy to suppose _he_ mentioned it to you — if he _did_ did he tell you that we had ever refused to speak to him? Because we have not, though I heard he said we had. It is true that we _did_ hesitate before doing so, and that the greeting was anything else than _cordial_, but, to the best of my recollection I never have declined bowing to him when I've met him. Once when I had not seen him for a long time, and his beard had grown beyond my recollection, he spoke to me on the street and I did not immediately recognize him, but when I did I returned his bow. Aside from his private character, he has sustained such a reputation as a _brave soldier_, that, had he been much else worthy of notice, I could not refuse to acknowledge his claims to my recognition as _such_. Yet under existing circumstances, I could not feel like receiving him upon terms of intimacy and friendship. Since your explanation with regards to his order to have Alvin bayoneted, I'm glad I know he was only slandered, but until he can explain his very rude conduct with regard to Uncle Tom, my next to father, I do not think a nearer intercourse would be productive of much pleasure to either of us. So far as, I, myself am concerned, Captain S has acted the part of a gentleman only, and if anything else more wanted to bind us more firmly to him, that want would be fully met in his kind attention to those brothers, dearer to us than anything on earth. But while Allie and Uncle Tom are resting under imputations such as Captain S cast upon them, I don't think he can expect us to regard him as a true friend. I would not injure him for the world, rejoice in his success, and, were it in my power would enhance it — more. I cannot say — unless it be that I hope he may allow his many good qualities influence his future in such a manner as to lead us to forget what has occurred.

Aunt Bettie says you must, if possible, eat your Christmas dinner with her — says she will give you a fat turkey — sends ever so much love. Aunt Letitia says she looks as anxiously for your letters as if they were from her own boys as she always expects to hear from them through you. We are having such a cozy time of it here today — it is lovely weather without bright as a May morning and we, Aunt L and B, Nellie and myself are sitting in Aunt B's nice comfortable sitting room with warm fire and plenty of nice apples for the eating. We have been discussing the merits of our thousand and one friends and relatives and of course you two came in for a share of the entertainment. Didn't your left ear burn? I do wish you could step in upon us now, I should like for you to see Nellie and myself in our new calico dresses which we cut and made ourself. They do fit beautifully and with our white cambric ruffles complete a _____ ensemble (with regards to costume) that, as a Confederate girl, I should not be ashamed to appear before Mr. Davis himself with. Well I must releave you now. Ever your own sister,
Lucie

(Later) Have just received a letter dated November 5 from you to Ma suppose it came in last night's mail. Dick Bayly just brought from home. Your report to Father I have heard nothing of — they may have it at home though. Nellie has been down the street and met Willie Buck there. She asked him to describe your friend whom he met at the store. Says he was of medium size, dark eyes and haired and with eye lashes as long as his finger. Does not remember his name.

We hear cannonading in the direction of Strasburg — guess they are having an artillery dual in which there is seldom anyone "hurt". Dick Bayly says Dick Buck went to Strasburg last night to see Walter. Only think, they've not met for sixteen months before. We've been expecting Uncle John this week but are afraid now that he won't be down as the army is retiring. No news from the Yankees today — hope they will be "non est" for some days longer.
Yours perserveringly,
Lu

[1] General Beauregard fell into controversies with Jefferson Davis and Judah Benjamin, then Secretary of War of the Confederacy after First Manassas. On January 26, 1862, he was ordered to Kentucky under Gen. Albert Sidney Johnston.

[2] After five days at home, Irving, Alvin, George Williams, Benton Roy and George Hope headed west.

[3] On September 13, 1861, Maj. Gen. Leonidas Polk, C.S.A., seized Columbus, Kentucky. Brig. Gen. U.S. Grant counter attacked by taking Paducah, Kentucky.

Early in February, Commodore Foote, U.S.A. and Brigadier General Grant moved up the Tennessee River and after a naval bombardment, Fort Henry fell on February 6, 1862. Its garrison moved to Fort Donelson on the Cumberland River.

On February 14, 1862, Fort Donelson's guns drove off the Federal gunboats, but the fort fell after four days of siege on the sixteenth to General Grant.

The whole line across Kentucky gave way after the fall of the forts on the Tennessee and Cumberland rivers. Bowling Green, Kentucky, fell February 14-15, 1862. Gen. Albert Sidney Johnston retreated to Murfreesboro, Tennessee; Nashville was occupied by the Union troops.

Columbus, Kentucky, described as the "Gibraltar of the West," was evacuated by Beauregard's forces on March 2, 1862.

[4] Mr. Wilson had been a patient in Front Royal and often visited Bel Air.

[5] Following the Confederate reverses in Kentucky and Tennessee, Gen. Albert Sidney Johnston moved from Murphreesboro, Tennessee to Corinth, Mississippi.

Maj. Gen. Henry W. Halleck, U.S.A. was named commander in the west. Grant was ordered south on the Tennessee River. Brigadier General Buell's forces in Nashville were ordered to join Grant at Pittsburg Landing in Tennessee.

General Johnston, C.S.A. elected to strike Grant at Pittsburg Landing before the reinforcements arrived from Nashville. The Confederates left Corinth April 3, 1862. Rain delayed the march but on April 6, 1862, at Shiloh, the Union army was completely surprised. Gen. Albert Sidney Johnston's forces attacked the Federals on Sunday morning and scored a victory but the Federals received reinforcements from Buell and on the seventh of April held the field. General Johnston was killed on the sixth and General Beauregard assumed command and retreated after the seventh to Corinth.

U.S.A. . . . Grant had 42,682 men and reinforced with 20,000 of Buell's men from Nashville; Killed . . . 1,754; Wounded . . . 8,408; Missing . . . 2,885.

C.S.A. . . . Johnston had 40,335 men; Killed . . . 1,723; Wounded . . . 8,012; Missing . . . 958.

[6] Mr. Boyd, Irving's employer in Baltimore visited Bel Air February 12, 1862. (See *Sad Earth, Sweet Heaven*)

[7] This letter was torn and difficult to decipher, so consequently is incomplete in content.

[8] AAG to General Hardee

[9] Irving was speaking of Stonewall Jackson's victories in the Valley of Virginia and especially Front Royal on May 23, 1862.

[10] Confederate General Beauregard took command of the Western army after Gen. Albert Sidney Johnston was killed at Shiloh. Beauregard pulled out of Corinth, Mississippi, May 29 and 30, 1862, and headed toward Tupelo, Mississippi, in the face of Union General Halleck's 100,000 troops. Halleck started for Corinth April 29, 1862.

[11] William Millar Richardson was wounded in the Battle of Williamsburg, Virginia, May 6, 1862, and died May 29, 1862, at the age of twenty-one.

Sue Buck, daughter of Dr. I. N. Buck, (Uncle Newton) of Mountain View, was the fiance of Willie Richardson. She moved from her home to Rose Hill and lived with Willie's sisters and widowed mother. To his memory she remained faithful throughout her life. She became sick every May 29th.

[12] John Newton Buck was in Co. E, 7th Va. Cavalry along with six other members of his family.

[13] Horace Buck was named Captain Co. E, 7th Va. Cavalry when the Company was reorganized May, 1862.

[14] Horace Buck was a doctor.

[15] Thomas Marshall raised a Cavalry Company in Fredrick Co. and was assigned to Ashby's command. He rose to the rank of Colonel and was killed November 12, 1864 near Cedar Creek. He is buried in Winchester, Va. beside the Ashby brothers.

There was a Thomas Marshall, son of Robert Morris Marshall of "Happy Creek" near Front Royal. He was killed at Brandywine Station. He rose to a Lieutenant.

[16] Cousin and cavalryman who recovered Walter's body when the latter was killed at Upperville on June 21, 1863.

[17] Beauregard, due to illness, turned over his command to General Bragg in Tupelo, Mississippi, June 20, 1862. Beauregard then went to Mobile to rest. In September he was in charge of the South Carolina - Georgia area.

[18] Lucy wrote in her diary, November 27, 1862, "Father handed me a pacquet today which upon unsealing proved to be a letter — 6 pages of foolscap from dear Irvie, giving me an amusing account of his moving experience since he left us. I never was more amused in my life and could scarcely read it for laughing. Bless his dear heart."

[19] Walter Buck, a brave scout and member of Co E, 7th Va Cavalry had a price on his head. Walter Buck had scouted the Yankee forces (incognito) in Front Royal for Colonel Ashby and General Jackson days before the Confederate Army attacked on May 23, 1862. His report to Colonel Ashby read:

> "Colonel Ashby — Sir, I have been myself to within sight of the enemy's camp at Front Royal. They have one regiment of Marylanders encamped between Richardson's and old Mr. Garrett's; also, one company of Cavalry

from Michigan Regiment, and one piece of artillery on hill between Front
Royal and Weston.

Very respectfully, Walter Buck, Lieutenant, Co. E."

This message was published in northern papers. The Federals had discovered it and several of Jackson papers in a burned rail car after Jackson's retreat south, up the Valley.

Therefore, Jackson was fully aware of the strength of his enemies in Front Royal from Walter Buck's report and before Belle Boyd sent her message.

[20] Aubrey Pearre, a young Marylander, was a junior partner in Irving's company in Baltimore (Note letter August 22, 1861). He joined Semple's Alabama battery and was assigned, with Irving's help, a clerk in Cleburne's office (see letter dated February 8, 1863).

Later he became ordinance officer in Liddell's brigade.

After the battle of Franklin he was named field ordinance officer of the army.

[21] Charles Newton Buck of the Warren Rifles was accidentally wounded in the foot in April of 1862. He was captured in Front Royal on February 20, 1864 and not exchanged until after the war.

[22] Marcus N. Blakemore and Richard M. Blakemore.

1863
Tullahoma, Tennessee

Head Quarters
Cleburne's Division
Tullahoma
January 13, 1863 (arrived Jan. 26, 1863)

My Dear Sister,

Your letters of the 25th of December and 1st of January reached me today, and although I wrote to Ma a few days ago, will reply at once.

I gave you an account of my Christmas and the battle. Since our arrival here we have been comparatively comfortable, but very busy. The last month appears like a dream — though some of the scenes are very vivid. The more I look back upon the battle and think of the showers of death passed through, the more I wonder at my escape, and feel my inability to return my gratitude and thanks to a kind Providence for thus bringing me through unhurt and attribute it in part to the prayers that I know are daily sent up in my behalf at home.[1]

Alvin returned to Charleston a week ago — and suppose he has written you before this. Disliked parting with him very much. Almost wish myself back as clerk with him. I have obtained the object for which I was working — a commission — and would willingly relinquish it, as soon as I establish my competency to fill the position, could I get any other place that would support me until the close of the war. Since accepting my present place, have experienced a sense of depression of spirits before almost unknown to me. This will wear off I think. Have a great deal to attend to — a Major General is entitled to two Adjutants — a Major and Captain. We have not the Major, consequently all of the work falls upon me. Gen. Cleburne and staff are a very pleasant set of gentlemen and allow me to write things my own way.[2]

Took a ride this afternoon with Cousin Willie to see Cousin Robert — he wished to be remembered to you all. Cousin Geo. B. left here a week ago for Staunton. He said if possible he would go to Front Royal. Hope he may be able to do so.

Geo. Williams is at War Trace about 18 miles from here. Benton is here, but I seldom see him — each of us are too busy to visit the other.

About the time you were writing me the New Years letter — I was up by a camp fire writing orders and expecting an attack from the enemy. Wish that I had time to give a detailed account of the fight, but like many other things will have to reserve it until after the War.

Enclosed is the promised photograph. Am sorry it is not a better likeness. Everyone says it does not flatter and my vanity whispers the same thing.

I have shamefully neglected my correspondents lately. Just to think I have not written to "Nannie Dear" for six weeks, but intend to do better when I get some little leisure.

Would like to have Alick *(servant at Bel Air)* very much. Need a servant and find it very hard to procure one.

Can form no idea as to what will be our next move. The feeling against General Bragg is very strong, with both officers and men since the late retreat, and I join with them in wishing that Gen. Beauregard may be sent to supersede him. I esteem Gen. Bragg as a brave and gallant soldier, but no strategist. As a subordinate he will do very well, but cannot be trusted alone, the past six months have fully demonstrated this. Should he be removed, I hope he may be placed in some place where he may retrieve his lost glory. Public opinion is against him. My feelings towards him is that of pity — believing him to be patriot — working to the best of his ability.

Enclosed are some more photographs. It would be a good idea for you to paste them in your album.

Love to one and all. Direct your letters to Tullahoma, Tenn. for the present, as we do not anticipate a move from here soon.

Ever your affectionate Brother,
"Irvie"

The loss of our Division alone, in the late fight, was more than that of our whole Army at the first battle of Manassas. Here I am at the end of my paper. You have no idea how much I dislike to finish and sign my name to a letter home. It is like breaking off a pleasant conversation, or taking a long leave, as every letter I send or get may be the last — on account of the mail communications. If ever I get home again, it will have to be a mighty power to move me from there.

Head Quarters Dept. of S.C., Ga. & Florida
Charleston, S.C.
Thursday, Jan. 15, 1863
(arrived Front Royal Jan. 26, 1863)

My Dear Lu:

Upon my arrival, on Sunday last, from Winchester, Tenn., I found your nice letter of the 19th ult. It is with pleasure that I always anticipate the epistolary remembrance of my birthday. There is one day in every year when I can feel an assurance that I occupy a distinguished place in the minds of those at home, and that some one is penning fond words to the wanderer — for what else am I? Roaming around for six long years it is but natural that some of the finer sensibilities of my nature should have been blunted, but not one living emotion of my too impetuous or impulsive heart, for the dear ones of the old homestead, has been lost, and if, as you complain, you have not been honored personally with a letter, it has been unintentional upon my part. Indeed I do not now know to whom my last was written, so little difference did I think it made to <u>whom</u> it was directed if you were all equally interested in the contents. Now to make atonement for past delinquencies you shall have the longest communication ever made above my signature, and if it abounds too much with the pronoun "I", attribute it to the fact that this is a very dry climate for news and small talk, and nothing more worthy in the way of a subject can be found than myself.

As Irving was successful in obtaining an appointment in Gen. Bragg's Army it was thought I might possibly secure a position by visiting in that quarter. So, with a handsome letter of recommendation from Gen'ls. Beauregard and Jordan, a furlough was granted me for two weeks, for the purpose of visiting "Army of Tenn." and the morning of the 21st December found me en route for Tenn. Arriving at Murfreesboro, and going out to Roy's camp, he informed me that every vacancy had been filled, but that he had worked faithfully, and the first position offering would be reserved for me if possible. I then went over to Williams' Camp and found Cous. Willie nearby. Spending two days with them, I returned to M., having been assured by Generals Hardee and Liddell that their influence could be relied upon to aid in my advancement. They are both officers of high standing and will be of value to me. Irving came on a day or two afterwards and reported for duty in time to serve in the great battle of the 31st Dec., which, he avows, cured him of any love he ever entertained for fighting, and it was certainly the most terrific scene of slaughter and bloodshed I ever saw or imagined. Irving's *(Cleburne's)* Division was on our left and from that point the Enemy was driven with most prodigious loss, the ground being filled with Yankee corpses. Gen'l Cleburne, his commander, fought as usual, like a lion. Not having a horse I was unable to gratify my desire to go on the field as a Volunteer Aide, so that, with two young men from Gen'l. Bragg's office, I set off on foot to join a Regiment near the center of our lines, but upon getting within 3/4 of a mile of the field we were advised that to reach it we would have to pass several hundred yards through an awful artillery fire. This was rather <u>tight</u>, if true, but we pushed on and upon walking to the summit of a little knoll in rear or our lines, the truth of the assertion was no longer to be doubted. The Enemy had a battery (said to consist of 20 guns) which ploughed lanes through our front, while the tremendous masses of infantry around it poured deadly showers of minnie (sic) balls through our ranks and the air was filled with whirring, hissing shells, which exploding high in the blue vault above, scattered death-dealing fragments over and in the rear. We now halted and agreed, as the chances were about ten to one against our getting to the front amid such a storm of lead and iron, to remain on the hill and witness the tide of battle. Our boys charged repeatedly to capture the annoying guns in the battery just spoken of, but were each time forced back in confusion — and night came on with no definite result to the conflict at this point.

Getting the range of our little party the Enemy dropped his shells around with such accuracy as to compel a change of position to a more secure point where the artillerists could not have so distinct a view.

From all other parts of the field the Yankees were driven back and the next day commenced retiring, having lost, according to their own newspapers, 30,000 men — it will certainly be found that their casualties exceed 15,000. I saw 5,000 prisoners and the whole number will amount to 7,000. Besides, our Cavalry gained their rear and captured 3,000 mules and burned 600 wagons. We also took 31 pieces of artillery and several thousand small arms. Our loss was 9,000, in killed, wounded and missing. Gen'l. Breckenridge attacked them a day or so afterwards with his division, and was repulsed with heavy loss. As the Enemy commenced reinforcing largely, and his own men were worn out, Gen'l. Bragg fell back, some days afterwards, to Winchester, some 50 miles distant, but has again moved forward to within 30 miles of M *(Murfreesboro)*. I marched 33 out of the 50 miles from W *(Winchester)* to M through mud and rain, leaving M in the morning at 5 min. past 12 and making 13 miles, long before daybreak.

Cousin George B. and Newt C., were at M with us, having been forced from K'y. My kind remembrances to him. Cousin Robt. Newton was there but I didn't see him.

Have just received a note from Irving, ordering some uniforms for his brother officers. He writes in good spirits but says his work is very heavy and keeps him close. No one will ever find fault with him on the score of his wanting industry, for a beaver is an indolent animal in comparison with Pat *(Irving)*. By the way, you have made a mistake as to my <u>sobriquet</u> — it is "Court", not "Count" for I have none of the requisites for the latter character and the former you will doubtless recognize as peculiarly appropriate, in view of your elder brother. Pat is frequently addressed as "Little Court", to distinguish him from the "Old Court". Even Roy and Williams, when in the office, did not escape from the application of a good-humored nickname for each.

Poor Roy, the cares and incident to his station have given a thoughtful, taciturn tinge to his once buoyant disposition and it requires an hour's effort in the way of hard talking to bring him up to his old standard of cheerfulness. Williams is still the sensible, rollicking, good-tempered fellow of yore, who would "let all the world wag as it would". To complete a trio of my best friends, Cous. Willie is unchanged, and it would take a long war to roughen him any, and in point of generosity, were I to ask him for a couple of his fingers, he would at least consider the request before refusing.

Well, Lu, I am, as you say, nearly a quarter century old, but do you mark any changes in my character within the past seven years? I am sure if a person's own feelings were a test of age, not over fifteen would be awarded me, and should I run out the allotted period of three score and ten, the succeeding generation will likely to denominate me the "Old Boy".

Nelly shall be remembered when the next letter is mailed for home. Her claims to a special missive have been overlooked, like yours, in the supposition that all would consider themselves stockholders in anything from Pat or myself. One of Laura's earnest, saucy, off-hand squibs affords me exquisite amusement. She will yet make a good correspondent and, by the way, it is nearly time Cary and Orville were figuring with the pen.

I will send you my photograph but will wait a short time before having it taken, as I know you would prefer seeing it with b<u>ars</u> upon the uniform, and it may not be long before I may be entitled to them.

Saturday 17th. News reached here last night that the Yankees were advancing in two columns in North Carolina, headed by Brute Butler — the latter is very doubt-ful.

Now, having complied with my promise to give you a long letter, and hoping the "Yanks" have not yet reached you, I must ask you to give my love to all and believe me

Your affectionate brother

Alvin

Head Quarters Cleburne's Division
Tullahoma January 28, 1863

My Dear Nellie,

Yours of the 7th has just been received, in the midst of my sassafras tea and molasses and mixing the flattery contained in it, with that savory mess, has put me in such a Christian humor, that I'll reply while the spell is on me. Ma's letter of the 16th was received two days ago — the reason of which was, it was directed to Tullahoma and yours to Shelbyville — was just on the point of replying to it, but will give yours the precedence — as I am sure she will not care to whom the letter is directed, so she hears from her "bad boy".

Was very sorry to hear of the visits of the Yankees, it was transient to be sure, but then they will of course repeat it, and mayhaps will capture some of our interesting correspondence. So my poor old shot-pouch has at last gone to satiate their thirst for taking war-like (?) equipment from defenseless citizens and will not be surprised to see a paragraph in the N.Y. Herald announcing the capture of an immense amount of secreted munitions. Grand-Ma, was recompensed for the scare they gave her, for taking the old gun out of the boys reach, — I frequently catch myself smiling, when I remember the many lectures she used to give Alvin and myself on this subject. <u>Now</u> I object to the report of fire arms and the smell of gun-powder as much as she does, having had enough to last me the rest of my life.

This is the <u>fourth</u> letter I have written home in <u>three</u> weeks — so there can be no complaint on the score of punctuality. My photograph I enclosed several weeks ago.

Was surprised and pained to hear of the death of Frank Buck and can scarcely credit it. I saw him at Tupelo, about the 20th of July. I will write to Gen'l. Price immediately to know the circumstances — he was in Gen'l. P's escort and had been strongly recommended as 1st Lt and Adjt of one of the Regiments.

Hear frequently from Alvin, and have written him on an average of once in three days since he left.

Do you ever hear anything of Ella Price, of Winchester? If so, tell me something of her — my reason for it is, that one of Gen'l. C's aids, Lt. Jetton, met her in Staunton last winter and became desperately enamored of her and finding out that I used to know her, makes it his constant theme to me. I promised to make these inquiries — if you get an opportunity give her <u>my</u> love for him — and if she is as pretty a young lady as she used to be girl, you may drop the latter part of it, and give it to her on my own responsibility.

Our staff consists of the following gentlemen — Major C. Benham, Chf of Staff, from California — Captain <u>Irving A. Buck</u>, A. Adj Gen. Va — Lts. I.R. Jetton and Lt. I.R. McClellan Tenn. and Lts. S.P. Hanley and L.W. Mangum, Ark, Aides de Camp — Major J.K. Dixon (wounded) Miss., and Capt. B.F. Phillips Tenn., Inspr General — Major T.R. Hotchkiss (wounded) Chf of Artillery — Lieut Chas Hill (Clara Taylor's cousin) Md Chf of Ordinance — Major A.L. Landis, Qr Mr and Major Issac Scherck Chf of Subsistence.

Cousin Willie Blakemore has been quite unwell for several days — but nothing serious.

Williams is still at Wartrace — he telegraphed me on Saturday that there was some dozen girls from Shelbyville at his quarter having a frolic and that I must come up, accordingly up I went on the next train, but when I arrived found them just embarking for S — was introduced, <u>wrote</u> <u>myself</u> a pass, jumped on the cars and went with them — spent a very pleasant evening and returned at daylight the next morning "without prejudice to the good order of military discipline".

The weather is very cold and disagreeable, so much so that I am perfectly contented to stay quietly in the house — the snow is thick on the ground, but what do we care so long as we keep such roaring fires as we do.

Yes, it has been nearly a year since we last saw each other, will it be another before we meet? You say you wish to know if we are "changed" — personally very little, my heart not a bit, otherwise if there is none for the better I trust there is none for the worse — and when we <u>do</u> meet I think you will find that I let "care dance with the devil" as much as formerly — for you know I am a firm believer in "letting the wide world wag as it will for I'll be gay and happy still" etc. — as for Alvin he will be a boy at 80 years of age — and just as fond of mauling me into submission as now.

General Joseph E. Johnston arrived here yesterday, we all hail his appearance with pleasure and we think perhaps there will be some change for the better.

Have just returned from a visit to Cousin Willie, whom I found much better — he desired to be remembered to you all, and spoke of writing to Father. I see Cousin

Robt N. occasionally, he always enquires after you all and sends some affectionate message.

Truly Front Royal must have degenerated generally and the Hotel[3] in particular — compare it now to the balmy days of Blakemore, Smith, and even Fishback! but enough, this subject is apt to call up gloomy reflections.

Now for the first time since the war began I have some hopes of peace — everything seems to have a tendency that way — when it does come to pass, I shall return home and devote one week to talk to you all in.

Have not heard from Mack or Dick Blakemore[4] for a long time. Dick is, I believe, at Columbia, with Major Severson.

Roy and Williams are both well.

Love to all at Bel Air, Bel Mont, Oakley, Rose Hill, Mountain View, and Clover Hill. Write frequently. I wrote last to Father.

Ever your affectionate Brother

Irving

Head Quarters Cleburne's Division
Tullahoma Feb. 8, 1863

My Dear Lucie,

Yours of the 24th and 27th have been in my possession for several days, and contrary to my usual rule, were not answered immediately, but have been so employed that I could not write with any satisfaction to myself, still less to you, but today is Sunday and it seems that some of our Brigade Commanders are Christians, as they have not crowded me with work, so I'll see what can be done in the way of a reply.

You speak of my letter having been written in a sad tone — at the time it was done — the day after the battle — the circumstances were well calculated to depress, but now think I have regained my usual flow of spirits — but never expect to experience such hard campaigning again, as I am informed it was the roughest the Division was ever subjected to.

The juvenile host of Bel Air seems to be imbued with the military spirit — I sincerely trust the corn-cob missiles will never be replaced by the musket, though as "Capt Carey's"[5] Battalion is all rank and no file, have no doubt but that he could obtain any number of recruits and would soon rise to a Brigadiers commission.

On the 1st of Jany, by reference to my diary, I find that I got up at daylight and in company with Gen'l. C rode along our lines, which the enemy shelled at intervals. That night I started out to find one of our officers and for several hours rode over portions of the battlefield, thickly covered with the unburied dead, occasionally I would come upon some party who had found and were interring a comrade, by moonlight (the brightness of which formed an agreeable contrast with the stormy scenes just closed). Those beautiful lines on the death of Sir John Moore came forcibly to my memory, but I was far from being in a mood to appreciate poetry or the scene and my time was employed in spurring and encouraging my horse, which would start and shy as he came upon a corpse in some obscure spot. I was alone and confess that these things unsettled my nerves and called up some gloomy reflections, after an unsuccessful search, returned to camp and then went over to see Cousin Willie and drink a cup of coffee, as my appetite was not in the least impaired.

Feby. 9. Had just gotten this far in my letter when I was ordered to Wartrace on business. When I arrived found it would be necessary for me to go to Shelbyville, "pressed" Williams into service, we arrived a little after dark and immediately called on some ladies, had a very pleasant time and returned this morning in time for work.

Mr. Pearre arrived here several days ago, he was from Charleston, where he had been in search of me, he has not changed the least and is so much like Willie Richardson, that if possible, it makes me fonder of him than ever, he will remain with me for the present. He is quick, intelligent and energetic, and hope he may obtain some place commensurate with his merits. *(See footnote in letter dated Nov. 6, 1862.)*

You asked about Gen'l. Cleburne, this question has been partially answered by a slip cut from a paper, which I enclosed last week. He is very quiet, has little to say, and any one to see and not know him would take him much sooner for a private than a Major Gen'l. He very justly bears the reputation for being one of the best fighters and bravest men in the army, has been shot three times, in the body, mouth and foot. As an instance of his daring: The day after the battle he went out in front of our pickets and in easy range of the Yankee sharpshooters, to pick up some guns — whilst we were there they commenced firing, he seemed to be perfectly cool — although the bullets were flying within a few inches of us, and did not leave until he secured the gun — as for myself I felt very uncomfortable but as a matter of course, did not leave until he did — I thought of this exploit as I did of the goat that attempted to knock the locomotive off the track, "I admired his spunk but had a very poor opinion of his judgement". Gen'l. C is one of the few men who have risen from a private to his present position by merit. The company of which he was Captain has turned out two Majors and one brigadier general — Gen'l. C, Gen'l. Hindman and Brig. Gen'l. L. E. Polk. If we should ever get within range of a photographing establishment, will get the picture of himself and staff.

I was interrupted here, to go on a review given by Gen'l. Hardee, to some ladies from Huntsville — after riding around with Gen'l. C, was introduced to them, very much pleased but am sorry to say, they leave in the morning.

You speak of my photograph having a care worn expression, it was taken under very unfavorable circumstances — just as I was starting from C. I ran into a gallery and had it taken without looking to see if it was good, I was tired, vexed and wore a very unbecoming coat, besides you must remember that I am a year older than when you last saw me, that year has been spent bending for hours each day over papers, and then you know I am getting "old, prim and particular". When I get on my new grey Confederate coat with the lace on the sleeve and three little bars on the collar, my big boots and sabre I fancy that I look quite Napoleonic (Alvin would suggest Lewis McDaniel on "big muster day" but as the Court is absent, I am spared any such malicious and mortifying allusions).

Have received two letters from "Nannie Dear" lately, which I answered promptly — she will do to lie to —

Truly Alvin has improved wonderfully as a correspondent, when he wrote the 5 sheets of fools cap the spirit must have moved him greatly.

No, I have not contracted the habit of smoking, chewing, swearing (accomplishment) or drinking, indeed I am less inclined to these vices now than at any period of my life. However I do not boast for I am far from being a saint.

Have had several sobriquets added to my original one of "Pat" — for instance, "The younger Buck" and "Little Buck" (Gen'l. Jordan) "Towser" (Alvin, on account of my canine properties) "The Young Court" (A being the "old Court" I am naturally the young one) and now it is the "little Captain" —

All relatives and friends well — Love to all. Say to Grand Ma, that she must not be distressed at the sight of my likeness, for the original will return to worry her for many long years, after the war is over. What has become of Cattie Boon[6]? (that was)
Ever your affectionate Brother
Irving

Head Quarters Cleburne's Division
Tullahoma, Tenn.

My Dear Nellie,
The Major General _____ (as I say in official letters) has just ____ wishes me to copy his official report of the Battle of Murfreesboro, so if your letter of the 18th just received is to be answered, it must be done at once, and ____ mine that you will have to put up with ____ than usual.

I am the envy of all of my _____ as their families are all within the enemy lines and they seldom receive letters and never such a ____.

Have a clerk by the name of Bailey, Charlie Bailey, from Arkansas is about my age and shaped very much like old Sam Spengler, has no more respect for a Captain and AAG than he has for a private and no more respect for a Major General than a Captain. As he swears as long and loud when he is sitting beside General C. as when we are alone. And he is not at all niggardly with his profanity before either. But with all he is one of the merriest best hearted fellows in the service and the life of our Headquarters. When I opened your letter tonight he commenced swearing because he could not hear from his sister Mollie Bailey, all family names you see. You will readily perceive that I am not the most "unlucky" fellow in the world, notwithstanding Fathers early prediction, relative to certain "Murals".

You need not distress yourself about _____ a for I _____ you delightful, much coffee and plenty of sugar all the time and first rate __ have a <u>French</u> cook from <u>Germany</u>, who in _____ of $40 per month prepares the daily food _____ rations for the staff of the Division __ staff. The General says we live so d——d _____ he will not eat with us, but messes with our doctor, Dr. Johnson, from Kentucky, formerly a member _____ Senate — he is a curiosity in his way _____ and one _____ old gentleman and always near us in the battle to take care of us in case we should _____. If I ever get <u>back</u> I'll have thousands of incidents to relate that it is impossible to confer. My diary is very unsatisfactory, merely giving the main incidents of the day and does not go into the minutia.

Alvin writes but seldom. I supposed that he has been prompt about writing to you. Cousin Geo. B. has arrived and is writing in the Engineers office. He had a letter from Cousin Clara a day or two ago — all relatives were well in H. *(Hopkinsville, KY)*.

It has been raining incessantly for two weeks.

Yesterday evening Gen. C. came into the office and tried to back his staff by proposing to go out to a cascade three miles distant two of us, Lt. Crittender and I responded and told him "we would see him out". Accordingly we started — it was raining as it only knows how in Tennessee — when we arrived at the falls to tease us he proposed we should all take a shower bath. So into it we went and had a delightful bath — I imagine I can see Grandma shaking her head and saying how "imprudent" but _____ of overcoats and a very suspicious looking _____ we rapidly created _____ and then the best of it was I could not get my boots on and had to ride 3 miles barefooted. The General was not off as he had to _____ put his socks in his _____ without socks. The cascade is very much like the one we used to visit on the Mountain. It falls some 60-70 feet. When the weather is _____ ride every afternoon. I have a splendid horse "Beauregard." He cost me $250 — saddle Gen. Hardee told me yesterday he was the best he had seen in the Army.

While reading letters from home I lose myself to the world and while smiling over some passage in the letter am frequently recalled to myself by having a dispatch thrusted under my eyes or by some son of Erin's asking if "here is where you keep the Adj. Generals" — no doubt expecting to see the said AAG in the shape of a wild beast chained to a post, fed in raw beef and guarded by a pitchfork as the Adjutant has a good deal of disapproving of applications to do, he is of course not a great favorite with the troops.

Lt. Jetton says he will avail himself of your offer and _____ a dispatch to his charmer.

It is very gratifying to me to learn I have gained the appreciation of my friends and relatives and no one appreciates it more particularly of the Rose Hill family for none of my relatives have a greater love or respect.

_____ is very efficient and I am in hopes he _____ self into a _____ when I got this far was interrupted _____ but I will not complain as it _____ mention of your brother it says, ___ "I found _____ officers of my staff very efficient in this battle their posts all the time and discharged their duties with courage promptness and in not often equalled." After which he enumerates _____ which I figure I have written so much _____ I am quite ashamed of it and begin to _____ egotistical, but I know of nothing else _____ you as much ___ received a letter from Alvin this evening he said he had just written you.

Cousin Geo. B. and Cousin Willie rode out to the cascade this evening.

I dined out today at our commissary's, had a magnificent dinner, after soup, meat and desert, we topped off on <u>real</u> coffee — ala St. Nicholas.

Met three young ladies during our ride, intend to call on them in a day or two.

Enclosed is a letter from Jetton to Miss Ella Price, try to forward it to her and get a reply.

Cousin Rob N. *(Newton)* is stationed within a few hundred yards of our H.Q.s.

Geo. Williams was down on yesterday — he wishes to be remembered.

Love to all

Ever your affectionate brother,

Pat

Do you ever see the Southern Illustrated?

Head Quarters Cleburne's Division
Tullahoma, February 19, 1863

My Dear Lucie,

It has scarcely been a week since I wrote you, but will reply to yours of the 8th (I suppose as it was not dated) received on Monday, for which Father will accept my thanks. I would be sorry indeed for him to tax his eye sight in writing me, as much as one of his letters would be prized.

Received letters from Alvin and Hope of the 14th. Both were well, but hourly expecting an attack upon the city. I still adhere to my first opinion and do not believe they will ever attempt it.

It seems that I always anticipate your questions. In one of my last letters was a list of our staff, as to the duties on the field, there is nothing regular, but all act as aids, etc. to carry messages from Gen'l. C. to the Brigade Commanders in directing moves and rallying troops. The adjutant should always be with the General to issue orders, write letters etc. and is frequently up at night engaged on these duties when all the rest are asleep. In Quarters the aids do nothing but ride with the General. The Adjutant issues the orders, disposes of papers, approves or disapproves them, writes letters, makes out returns, signs requisitions etc. in all of which he is guided by the orders from superior Head Quarters. The Inspector General, as the name indicates, is a sort of overseer of the Army. He sees that orders are executed, discipline kept up, camps are kept clean etc. Ordinance officers are charged with arming and supplying the troops with ammunition both on and off the field. The Chief of Artillery has all of the artillery under his command although the batteries direct the firing and moves them from one position to another. The engineer makes reconnaissance and draws maps of the country, lays our fortifications. The duties of the Quarter Master and commissary are too well known to need any account from me.

In my statement in my last letter I said that General Cleburne's old company had turned out three Generals — it should have been <u>five</u> Generals, Tappare and McRae in addition to the other three I mentioned. Gen'l. C. has promised me a picture of himself and staff.

Cousin Willie Blakemore is not a volunteer but a regularly commissioned aid and a gallant fellow in the bargain. I am one of the <u>few</u> who know and appreciate his many good qualities. When we are together, it is the only time I forget the war. We talk of the relatives and laugh over our old times at Oak Grove, until we imagine we are living there over. He wishes to be remembered affectionately to all of his relatives and those at Bel Air in particular. He never fails to inquire after the families at Rose Hill, Clover Hill, Mountain View, Oakley, and Bel Mont. Geo. Helms is 1st Liet. of Engineers and a number one officer. G. Hardee thinks very highly of him and has recommended him for a Captainery. He is quite sick at present.

In event of another battle I will telegraph "Nannie Dear" *(In Richmond)* the result to myself and she will immediately write you. I have made this arrangement by which you will get tidings of me some days sooner than by any other means. I am keeping Mr. Pearre with me, so that in case of an accident he will take care of me. On the eve of an engagement he will receive full instructions in the premises. I can depend upon him.

You say you have something to tell me of great importance when I return home — is this intended to excite my curiosity or used as an incentive to bring me home? If the former let me assure you I have not a particle of it, if the latter, I need no other inducement than I already have. Now if this question is of such monument you had better communicate it by letter as the day for my return is far distant.

Lately you have referred in a very mysterious manner to a certain Capt. L. in Gen'l. Longstreet's Staff and to your preference to Maryland, allow me to say that you are wasting your ammunition on me, as I am wholly in the dark as to your insinuations. Who is Capt. L. and what has he to do with Maryland? The only Capt. L. I know from Baltimore was leader of the "Plugs" and was anything else but "Sans Freur Et Sans". Upon <u>reflection</u> I <u>believe</u> his name was Latrobe(?).[7]

Cousin Geo. B. is expected here every day, has taken a clerkship in the Engineer office.

What has become of Cousin Sue? I have made several attempts to write her, but always break down. To tell the truth my pride has some little to do with it. She very unceremoniously broke off a correspondence with me while in Baltimore, and ever since I have imagined (perhaps it was only imagination) she has manifested a decided coolness towards me. I have carefully scrutinized my conduct to see if I could discover anything to have caused this between such friends, but have been unsuccessful so far. You know I have always been one of her warmest admirers. I admit that this gives me no little trouble, more now than it used to as every relative I lose draws the remainder near to me. My love to her when you next see her, also the rest of the Mountain View family.

Have you ever heard of the death of Cousin Thomas M. Buck? It is reported and generally believed here among the relatives that he was killed in a encounter with the Yankees. Have had no confirmation of this and hope may not be so. It is also reported that Marsh Blakemore has been paralyzed.

Does Rode Jackson ever visit Front Royal now? I never saw her but once — but do you know that one sight had about the same effect upon me as a shell would if it exploded in my vest?

Do not know where Mack and Dick are but think they are in the vicinity of Columbia.

Send me the words to "Trancodillo".

Love to everybody, never forgetting the Rose Hill family.

Ever your affectionate Brother,
Irving

Head Quarters Cleburne's Division
Tullahoma
March 11, 1863

Dear Lucie,

Yours of the 27th February, reached me some three or four days ago, but the "spirit" did not move me to reply, and at such times it is a task for me to write, besides I have not time to compose my thoughts sufficiently — Your letter, if possible, was more welcome than usual, as some apprehensions were entent   that old Major Lewis' blow up with mail carrier might result in no more letters for me, but hope they have come to an amicable adjustment.

As our Corps has not been ordered to Vicksburg and I trust it never will, our summer in Mississippi is sufficient for me, besides before another month will pass we will have as much as we can attend to here as I believe a fight is inevitable within that time, and much sooner if the weather and roads will admit of the transportation of artillery — it is reported and believed that old "Rosey" has been reinforced by Siegel and 20,000 men, I do not fear their numbers, but believe we will whip them at any odds, but with due deference to our present Commander, would rather see some one else at the head of our men, a Beauregard or Lee, would be equal to 5,000 men.

What do you mean by saying that Gen'l. Cleburne's H Qrs is the "Mecca" of Bell Boyd's pilgrimage? Are you jesting or is she really travelling in this direction? Was rather surprised at your requesting me not to cultivate her society, of course I will be glad to see any one from Virginia particularly a lady (?) acquaintance, but seriously speaking, as you would say, I do not think she will come and if she does, her stay will not be long in this God forsaken country, as we are all entirely too slow to suit her notions.[8]

I spoke just now of this being a God forsaken country, if any place ever deserved this appellation, this certainly does, it is second only to Tupelo — we have ridden five miles in every direction and have never yet seen a comfortable house, all small single room cabins.

Received a letter from Alvin, of the sixth — it was principally on business, and gave no news.

Benton *(Roy)* had a letter from Scott *(Roy)*, from Petersburg, so it seems they have gotten the old 17th out of reach of home at last — I wish they would send us Longstreet, to help whip out old "Rosey" — was Newt Petty captured by the Yankees? How is Smith Turner Captain?[9] Where is Wesley Lehew?[10]

Saw Cousin Robb N. and Willie this evening, both wished to be remembered, the former said he had seen Dr. Catlett who was just from Hopkinsville, he contradicted the report of Cousin Tom Buck's death, and says he is in St. Louis, Sam went home and was captured, he is now in Camp Chase — Mrs. Pendleton came through with him, to see her husband who is Quarter Master of Forrest's Brigade.

Who is Gen'l. Jones[11] and where is he from? Never heard of him until within the last two months.

Roy is very well, he keeps very close to his quarters and I never see him unless I go up there.

Remember me to all relatives, and love to all at home—
Ever your affectionate Brother,
Pat

Head Quarters Cleburne's Division
Tullahoma
March 21, 1863
(arrived Front Royal, Va. April 1, 1863)

My Dear Father,

Yours of the 10th has just been received and read, It's needless for me to express my gratification, which is only marred by the thought that you have taxed your

136

eyesight in so doing— I have an hour before dark which I will devote to an answer.

It affords me much pleasure to hear you all have formed such a favorable opinion of Mr. Pearre, every one who knows him thinks the same, and he is not over rated by any means. He is acting as Ordinance Sergeant of the Division and the ordinance officer to day remarked, in reference to him, that the more inter course he had with him the better he like him — and would do all in his power to have him promoted. Have strong hopes for him, as officers of this department (ordinance) have to stand a rigid examination and few can stand it, but am sure he will, as soon as he gains a little more of the practical parts of the service — which for his present position will afford him a fine field. Will send Laura his photograph as soon as he can get where one can be taken.

You were correct in your supposition that I only spoke disparagingly of Capt. L to provoke Lucie — never heard of him before, and it seems I <u>accidentally</u> guessed his name, and the "Plug Ugly" story was the coinage of my prolific brain.

All our young relatives are well and I can assure you that your feelings towards them are heartily reciprocated, they all ways speak of you affectionately and with reverence which convinces me they are sincere in the expression of these feelings of which I am so proud to hear.

You say you feel that you have nearly "acted out lifes drama" upon this subject I cannot bear for my thoughts to dwell. My earnest prayer is that you may live to a peaceful old age to see myself with the rest of your children arrive at the positions your fondest desire could hope for, although I should be well contented to be such a man as my father. I can say for myself that the desire to afford you pleasure has been at the bottom of all my ambitions and aspirations. You cannot conceive my happiness to hear you express "that hope which alone can give peace and safety" and more so because of the knowledge that your life has been such as to give just grounds for these hopes. When your letter was handed me this afternoon, one of our staff remarked that he "wished he had a good father like Buck", he then stated that he had not had a pleasant word with his for five years, and during the whole of his life could not remember of his having done him a kind action. I stated that on the contrary, I could not remember an unjust or unkind word or action from mine during the whole course of my life. To know that I had contributed to make your life happy and pleasant is the greatest reward I ask for any exertion on my part.

Frequently in my letters to Lu and Nell I say things which I do not desire to be taken in earnest, and generally make them so extravagant or ridiculous that you may know how much truth to attach to them — although my letters may be light and perhaps foolish yet I have my hours of serious reflection when the business of the day is over and all hushed in sleep — a soldiers life is one well calculated to call up such reflection — and a man who is liable to go into a deadly conflict any hour, must be thoughtless indeed, not to give some attention to the after existence.

This war has had its good, as well as its bad effects, and if it should stop now, individually, I would not regret the past, it has done much to develop to me the world and mankind, I have made many pleasant acquaintances, and in some instances true friends and but for the separation from the loved ones at home would be perfectly satisfied.

Do not think an action can long be delayed here — have no doubts as to our ability to whip the enemy — in case of an accident to myself Mr. Pearre will have full instructions as to the condition of my affairs — for your information as to my pecuniary situation I'll, state, that equipping myself to make an appearance suitable to my rank and position was quite expensive, and I am in debt about $700.00 — to off set this, I have due me about $500 pay, having never drawn a cent since my promotion, and a good horse worth $300 — so I have enough to put me square with the world. I shall draw my pay at the end of the month and pay up about $400.

So far I have been unable to procure for Alvin, a position commensurate with his merits —, but I will do every thing to accomplish it.

Much love to all relatives and friends —
Ever your affectionate son,
Irving

Head Quarters Cleburne's Division
Tullahoma
March 22, 1863
(arrived in Front Royal, Va. April 1, 1863 with letter to Irving's father)

Dear Lu,

Another day has been carried through — with all the hardships of dining out on turkey, fish, eggs etc. For start not when I tell you I had two invitations to eat Sunday dinners today, the one from Cousin Robt. W's mess was accepted, with the above result.

Do not flatter yourself that you excited my curiosity by that "something" you had to communicate, it was only casually mentioned, and I should never have thought of it again had not your letter have recalled it. It appears that your "woman's weakness" was excited by the "Laura" and the flag. Would you not like to know who "Laura" is? Well she lived in Shelbyville. This night one year ago I attended church in Jackson with Miss Alice. Your hints as to the probability of Flora's conquests fall harmless. Aim your gun in another direction. Throw your shells at Jackson, or "onward to Richmond". *(Nannie Taylor)*

Acknowledge yourself out generaled for once Miss Lucie, you who have been so mysterious about a Capt. L., Balt., etc. I resorted to strategy (learned from soldiering), was fortunate enough to hit his name by a chance shot, vilified him aroused your ire, provoked a retort in which the said Lucie acknowledges his name. There now don't you feel cheap? A very little like a cent pie — and further more she appeals to me "upon my word" as to the truth of my assertion — well for your peace of mind and to prevent my obtaining a reputation similar to the one enjoyed by John Teely, let me state that the "Plug Ugly" story was a fabrication made for a specific purpose, which succeeded admirably. There now I have confessed my sin and hope it is forgiven.

So Dod has made up his mind to commit matrimony. His "Cara sposa" does not exactly agree with the Vicar of Wakefield, when he says "Man wants but little here below" however she is a woman, I suppose, and this will make the difference. I disagree with Goldsmith in the continuation of the verse, i.e., "Man wants that little long" for when I went to school I did want that little (Mary) Long.

We had a splendid review of the entire corps on Thursday, and are to have another tomorrow. Wish you were here to witness it.

Saw a letter from Dick Blakemore to Cousin Willie a few days ago, he was well and at Columbia with Major Servenson. His brother Mack was in the same boat, the upsetting of which drowned Mr. Pendleton — and made a very narrow escape. He did not state the locality of Mack, but I inferred from his letter that they were near together. Will write to Dick in a day and will scold him well for neglecting his Mother as he has.

Geo. Williams was down to see me a few days since.

All friends and relatives well. Much love to all.

Ever your affectionate Brother,

Irving

You were right in not mentioning to Emma the reported death of her Uncle Tom, as it has since been contradicted.

Head Quarters Cleburne's Division
Tullahoma
April 11, 1863

Dear Lu,

Your voluminous letter of the 31st and first reached me this morning. From the length of time which had elapsed since the reception of the last one, had begun to fear that the Yankees had again gotten south of the river. I am in such good spirits that my body is not large enough to contain it all and will try to make you as happy as myself.

Gen'l. C returned from Shelbyville nearly a week ago, in a most heavenly mood, which still continues, a Corps review was ordered for yesterday, accordingly, day before yesterday Gen'l. C sent me to S — after a load of ladies — (the best looking officer is of course always selected for such duty). I called upon several and brought them down yesterday morning, gave them a fine review, horse race and tournament — and a good dinner — in the evening I returned with them —. It is useless for you to ask how I escaped, I was utterly demolished, but am unable to discern whether it is Maggie W. or Maggie C. but as the latter gave me my supper, am disposed to decide in her favor — but was not very successful, as she informed me that I was the most impudent young man she had ever seen. However, to make up for all of this, I received a pressing invitation to call to see her whenever I visited Shelbyville. She sang the "Gypsy Countess" for me, the first time I have heard it since leaving home — she lisped out "My Own Gypsy Maid" just like Nellie: So you need not wonder at my overflow of spirits, besides we keep a good table, and have comfortable quarters and really I am getting so fat and "demoralized" that I contemplate running for alderman, or playing Falstaff (a character for which I am peculiarly fitted to impersonate) after the war.

Was not aware, until I received your letter, that Jones' Brigade, was in the vicinity of Front Royal, hope they may hold their ground and thus allow us communication with home all the summer. My love to Captain Horace *(Buck)*.

The notice of Gen'l. Hardee's marriage was incorrect, indeed I believe he is waiting to see if some kind fairy or spirit will not metamorphose Roy into a beautiful young lady (like the cat in the fable) in order that she may marry him.

I like Gen'l. Hardee — next to Gen'l. Beauregard, he has been always kind to me, so much so, that I think Roy must have been at work for me. I wish to deserve and sustain a good reputation so that when Alvin tries for a position my cause will have a beneficial influence in the matter.

My love to Walter, and say to him that he may look out at our next meeting. I shall put myself in a vigorous course of training to thresh the whole "kit" — except cousin Horace.

Enclosed is Pearre's photograph, for Laura, at her request he had it taken in uniform. He is studying for a Lieutenancy in the Ordinance Department, have no doubt as to his ultimate success, and ability to fill the position, when obtained.

Is Uncle John a bona fide Quarter Master or only acting? He deserves a Majority — at least.

Have one very pleasant lady acquaintance here, the wife of a Mississippi Captain — she says if any of us get sick or wounded, and will come to Jackson, that she will board us until she supplies us with a wife — that is a great temptation to play "old soldier", and she is a particular friend of one of my aides, she told him, that she had said to her husband, that if he got "knocked on the head" that I would be his successor, but he is a confounded Quarter Master — and does not have to expose himself in battle, so he rather holds <u>aces</u> on me. I am such a fool that I become smitten with every pretty woman I meet married or single, wish I were a <u>Mormon</u> so as to <u>marry</u> them <u>all</u>. Am glad to see you have such confidence in my protection from Providence, Camp is very impervious to morals and religion — do not wish to be irreverent, but will give you an illustration of this., Lt. Crittenden, our signal officer, is the only church member our staff can boast of, and he frequently lectures us; a short time ago he concluded a long harangue whether it was more impressive than usual, or at any rate — it set me thinking, and after retrospecting my past life, concluded I would reform, and commence at once by a prayer, accordingly I adjusted myself comfortably in the bed, and from force of habit commenced "Head Quarters Cleburne's Division, Hardee's Corps," when this far I recollected myself and it made me so mad that I commenced grumbling, when Pearre wished to know the cause, when informed he told the rest of the staff and it is now a standing joke on me.

The enclosed fragment of letter is from Williams, Gen'l. Liddell "blockaded" Shelbyville, whereupon he got off this, which you will readily recognize as a parody on Hood's beautiful, "Bridge of Sighs" — Williams desires to be kindly remembered.

Will reply to Cousin Sue's letter in a few days. Love to all,
Ever your affectionate Brother,
Pat *(I. A. Buck)*

Head Quarters Cleburne's Div.
Hardee's Corps.
Army of Tennessee
Tullahoma, Tennessee
April 21, 1863

My Dear Father,

I scarcely know how to reply to your note, I dislike to see the building go into stranger's hands, but of the necessities of the case you can best judge, if it could be rented, would much prefer it, I have no definite plans for after the war, the end seems so far off that I do not trouble myself about it, besides the chances are that I may never get through it, it is, I think, it becomes natural for a soldier to look no further ahead than 24 hours. Have had several propositions to enter into business when we shall have peace, but have no idea that it will ever be in Front Royal, must go some where, where a living can be accumulated more rapidly having lost so much of my life already, so do not let my future have any weight in the premises. My point will be New Orleans, Memphis or Arkansas. I feel myself incompetent to give advice, and am satisfied that whatever you do, it will be best.

Would not be surprised if we had an engagement any day.

Cousin George B begs to be remembered and has promised to write you.

I saw a paragraph in the paper some time ago, stating that the Capon[12] property had been burned by the Federals, but as you did not refer to it suppose it was false.

Love to all,
Ever your affectionate Son,
Irving

Wartrace, Tennessee

Head Quarters Cleburne's Division
Wartrace, Tennessee
April 26, 1863

My Dear Lucie,

You will observe that we have "changed our base" since my letter to Ma of the 21st inst. — we left Tullahoma three days ago and are now sixteen miles nearer Murfreesboro, the change is delightful, we are in the midst of field, forests and rivers, all of which we enjoy to their full extent, The General, our Surgeon and myself are in a very comfortable house immediately in the turn, the remainder of the staff are coupled in the woods about 1/4 of a mile. Williams is about three miles off, at "Bell Buckle". Since my arrival here, in addition to my other duties have been acting as Provost Marshal, Passport and Transportation agent, but am happy to say that the above named functionary has finally been appointed and I relieved.

We are now only seven miles from Shelbyville, have moonlight night, and I can ride to see "My Maggie" at pleasure — have not done so yet, on account of the unsettled condition of my office — but will not be slow in improving my facilities.

The night before we left, our house caught fire and notwithstanding all our efforts was entirely consumed, we succeeded in saving every thing.

Came up in the cars with Miss Battle. She and her sister have been engaged in smuggling goods from Nashville, her sister attempted to pass on a <u>forged</u> permit, and was detected, she had letter which implicated <u>both</u>, the one with the pass <u>was</u> <u>sent</u> <u>to</u> <u>Camp</u> <u>Chase</u>, and this one through the lines with written instructions not to return on pain of being treated as a spy, she certainly is the "spunkiest" female I have ever met, says she is going to try it again, and will wear a pair of <u>boots</u> out for me. She is only waiting until the battle is over, as she wishes to take care of the wounded, I have had some very tempting promises, in event of being promoted or shot, so you see there are even inducements to get wounded.[13]

Cousin Willie had a letter from Cousin Kate, dated 17th inst — all were as usual.

Have had no letter this week fear it is a bad sign, but hope and pray that the soil of Warren is still free from the "blue legs".

Saw Major Roy today, he is well, and getting as fat as a seal.

The temperature is delightful, we have a stream near us which is filled with fish, can catch enough in an hour to last for several meals — every thing is so beautiful, that I feel an elasticity and buoyancy of spirits in a greater degree than I ever before experienced, fear I am too light hearted, and that some misfortune will befall me, to remind me of realities.

"Nannie" has dropped me entirely as a correspondent. Will not ask you to write as I know you will embrace every opportunity, for the present I'll continue as usual.

Love to one and all,

Ever your affectionate Brother,

Pat *(I. A. Buck)*

Head Quarters Cleburne's Div.
Wartrace, Tennessee
May 7, 1863

My Dear Nellie,

Ma's letter of the 24 reached me this afternoon, which makes two from home since I have written, as Lucie's of the 20th was received about a week ago, and upon reflection I believed one from you of the 11th arrived the day I wrote to Lucie last, will try to answer them all at once—

For the last two days we have had the most awful, rainy, damp, disagreeable weather imaginable, such only as Tennessee can afford, all this too just after the departure of half dozen young ladies from the neighborhood, with whom your beautiful brother had a merry time but I am not in despair at their departure it is only temporary and they will return in a short time, mean while bouquets remind us that we are not forgotten.

Our Cause seems to brighten every where, the victory of Forrest in Georgia, was a brilliant affair, and will make him a Major General, at least it should do so, will send you a paper containing an account of it. Lee has again administered a threshing to them near Fredericksburg, the glory of which is dimmed by the accident to the noble Jackson, the Christian warrior, for whom a sympathy is felt by every heart in the Confederacy. It will be our turn next, and I feel every confidence that we have the ability to meet the foe, and will have him back, I hope, to the Ohio. His subjugation polity has "played out" and they are impelled by fear that if they let the war, and excitement consequent hereto cease, that the inhabitants of the north will have time for reflection and turn upon them — hence they seek to do us all the harm they can in a small way, destroying and desolating wherever they go.

Say to Lucie that I thought we were at quits about Capt. Latrobe, but she continues to stir the subject, which she perhaps had better, for her own peace of mind, leave alone, as assertion <u>might</u> be proven to have been correct — and as to her correspondence with a "certain member of Longstreet's Staff" to which she refers so mysterious, I feel no interests in the matter at all, she had better "sail on another tack" to speak nautically.

Was at Shelbyville last week although it involved a ride back home of eight miles at 12 o'clock at night, I was compensated by the expression of sundry, dark eyes!

Am distressed to hear of Grand Ma's bad health, trust it is not permanent.

Had a letter from Alvin, a few days ago, written in a very happy style, he seems to become inspired sometimes, and at such periods I get the benefit of it.

Williams, Blakemore and Roy are all well,

Love to all,

Ever your affectionate Brother,

Irvie

Bel Air

Tuesday, May 12, 1863

Your letter dear Irvie of the 21st came to hand a week ago - it was on the way several days longer than it should have been - but we only get the mail when someone goes to Rileysville for it or as someone happens to be passing it is not surprising. Lucie has just returned from your Uncle Toms and says the mail is in but no letters for so I will not wait but write while I have a chance to send. I do not know what has interrupted the mail arrangements but it was supposed the expected conflict at Fredricksburg had something to do with it and as that is over now I hope they will be resumed. Lucy, Nellie and Emma spent last night and today with your Aunt Bettie Lucy has just returned the others stayed. your Aunt Letitia Buck spent the day with us yesterday it was quite a treat it is so seldom she comes down except to church and she is so affectionate. we have not been there for nearly a year we have no way of going anywhere except to walk and indeed are afraid to go out of sight of home not knowing when the yankees might come — and it is amusing to see the amount of hiding that is done when it is assumed they are coming. a ladies weight is generally increased to about double - they went Jessee McKays last week and took off quite a small girl belonging to Cousin E. Richardson. they have treated the people on that side of the river dreadfully and will do us no better should they come here - so far fortune has favored us. they have been at the river frequently and twice come on the side but did not get to town. we are however all the time in dread. the river has been high nearly all the time it will be fordable in a day or so and then we will begin to look out again. it is terrible to be kept in such suspense. we are anxious to hear from Tullahoma though you may not be there now as it is the impression here that you have work to do there soon if it has not already been done. we are always glad to hear of your being cheerful and enjoying yourself you are now at the time of life for such things in a little while cares and anxieties to which all are more or less liable will come but I trust alas Irvie in the midst of your pleasures and enjoyments you will remember that "This is not our rest" — that "beyond this veil of tears there is a life above." you are exposed to many dangers seen and unseen and the warning applies with peculiar force to the soldier. "be ye also ready for in such an hour as ye think not the son of man cometh" but you are in the hands of <u>one</u> who's able to do all things for and to his care and protection. I try to commit you - I know He doeth all things well and we should strive to be reconciled to all his dealings with us. there is nothing like mirth or merriment here and were you to drop down here now you would feel like you were in a strange place. I do not think it possible for you to imagine the many changes that have taken place and I am certain but for your friends you would not be compelled to stay a week in the place on any account. indeed I do not feel satisfied to spend the few years that may be left me here. I would like to be "down south in Dixie" sure enough and not be left on the borders but never expect it as your Father as much a fixture here as the mountains provided he is able to keep the old place which we often think doubtful. I dreamed two nights since that <u>Major Roy</u> had been sick and came home and I asked him if he was not struck with the changes around. the wave of fortune seems to be with him as from all accounts he is a great favorite and stands high wherever he is known — poor Alvin, we are so grieved to know he is so dissatisfied — it is natural he should be separated from you and all who started out with all promoted but him - no doubt his pride is wounded but I know he has been faithful to his duties and hope he will yet get his reward - Lucy spent several days at Rose Hill last week all were more cheerful than she expected. I fear Sue will not be able to continue teaching do not think it will agree with her — Nellie spent last week delightfully at Clover Hill - Mr. Jackson has gone up to see about poor Willie he is in the enemy lines and we cannot hear from him but have an idea he is living - six of company E had their horses killed and seven wounded. Sandy Buck's, Mount Cloud, Willie Buck's, Charlie Richardson's and Sammy Simpson's among the number. Walter is detached for special duty and is scouting all the time. Mrs. Ed Moss is not expected to live. your Grandma is better and Aunt Betsey has been at Rose Hill for nearly 4 weeks she has been sick. the yankees took some of Colonel Jacob's horses. he went up to Winchester with Mr. Beecher and got three in the place of his and says he never was better treated in his life. it generally supposed he took the oath but he says he did not some say he took bacon and sold them — he must have done something to get off so well. it is hard to know who to trust these times. I was at Mrs. Roy's yesterday. she was looking a little blue but soon got to laughing. your Grand Ma and Aunt join in love to you and all relatives and friends. may God be with you and bless you asks your fond

Mother
E.A.B. *(Elizabeth Ashby Buck)*

Home
May 12, 1863

My Dearest of Brothers, *(Alvin)*
    'Tis not your fault I'm sure that we have had no direct tidings from you since the reception of your welcome dispatch to Father immediately after the grand recon-

naissance, in the Charleston harbor. The mail agents and not our correspondence are anathematized for all our disappointments in that line. Tonight I heard there will be a mail sent out early in the morning and, with the agreeable auxillaries of a thunder shower, an oppressively warm atmosphere, fatigue and a slight headache, I seize the opportunity of sending you a report of the proceedings at Fort Bel Air. It will be not very voluminous one running somewhat on this wise, Since last communication from this place nothing of importance has occurred - all quiet along the lines. There has been some slight skirmishes in the garden through operations there have been very seriously impeded by the continuation of bad weather since the opening of the spring campaign. Major General Father has, however succeeded, in planting a very strong advance guard of peas that are beginning to make quite a show. Then there are divisions of potatoes, beans, beets, onions, parsnips, carrots, tomatoes and so forth but waiting the action of sunshine and showers to spring forth to the rescue from want. I regret to say that our most valued assistant in the cause - the corn regiment is not yet in the field owing to the unfavorable season, however, preparations are being pushed forward and I hope soon to make a favorable report to you of these forces. The troops generally are in good health - Grandma's cold is much better. Ma suffers greatly from vertigo or something very like it but she too is better tonight. Father had intended sending you a communication when we wrote you but has gone to bed with a headache - one of his neuralgia attacks - will be well in the morning. Nellie and I obtained yesterday a furlough to accompany Emma Cloud to Oakley where I remained till after tea this evening. They will stay there overnight - I returned home for the express purpose of writing you tonight - credit me with so much thoughtfulness. I never saw the country looking so beautiful as it does now despite the ravages of war - very few of the fields around town are being cultivated - none at all indeed and the whole earth seems one mass of rich emerald carpeting. This week we're having our first spring weather and today I could almost fancy I heard the leaf buds unfurling and the grass rustled as it grew. I reveled in the warmth and glow - cold weather seems to congeal one's faculties, spirits, energies all seem frozen fast to by a spell - 'tis no wonder that the influence which breaks the spell should be gladly hailed by us all. Only think it is just a year since Shield's army occupied town, since Kimball's brigade encamped on us - it seems a long time and yet a very short one too.

You have received 'ere this full particulars of the second battle of the Rappahannock - although the enemy has been completely repulsed with heavy loss on every side the victory is not so decisive a one as we were at first led to believe - however we are not at all disposed to deprecate our success or be unmindful of the gratitude due our Heavenly Father for having once more crowned our efforts with success. Sometimes I fear it is presumptuous in us to feel such entire such, implicit confidence in fallible morals as we do in General Lee. The idea of his ever entertaining a defeat - is never dreamed of in our philosophy. Heaven bless him! We've heard of no casualties among our friends engaged in the fight and indeed I doubt if Pickett's division took any part in the affair although some of Longstreet's division at one time bore the brunt of the battle. Scott and Giles have not been heard from for ten days owing to the non-arrival of the mails - at last advises they were doing well and being ministered to by kind friends. Of Willie Jackson we can hear nothing more, though it is generally believed he is dead. He is in the Yankee lines which accounts for his friends having no intelligence of him, his father and Miss Sallie Kendricks started last week to see him in case he should be still alive.

Spent several days at Rose Hill last week — it was the anniversary of Willie's receiving the fatal wound and although I knew they remembered and in their secret hearts observed the anniversary still each one tried to make the other cheerful by appearing so herself. Cousin Sue Buck appeared more natural than I've seen her since poor Willie's death. Is it not good of her to confine herself as she does teaching the children with no other reward in view save the pleasure which rises from the consciousness of having done a kind deed - a very considerable compensation I grant yet these are the fewest who would not need a greater incentive to the trying task. Laura, Bell, Nannie Buck, Bob and Jim are her scholars, she teaches in a little cabin in the grove at Rose Hill and only keeps school from 8 till 12 a.m. She would make a most excellent teacher did her health equal her qualifications in other respects. I still try to instruct Orville and Cary but find it impossible to do by them as I could wish. Did Ma tell you that Willie and Nannie were attending Sunday School? They're delighted — are members of my little class and I feel much interested in teaching them. Willie poor fellow is very succeptible and his tender feelings are all the time making a martyr of him. I could but be amused a few mornings since, at the breakfast table I sat opposite to him and I noticed how he kept stealing shy glances at my face and laughing and blushing. Presently he dropped his head and with crimson cheeks faltered out, "Sister Lucie, you don't know how much you look like my sweetheart!" Poor child!

We have had but one letter from Irvie for several weeks. This last one was written in great haste and apparently under the influence of great excitement. He seems perfectly engrossed with the gay society in which he mingles - charmed with its pleasures. I can't tell you how much it saddens me to read his letter for I felt how soon he might be hurried from the festive hall to the field of death and ____ _____ a preparation were the scenes in which acted for meeting the grim monster. Not that I would abate one iota of his enjoyment. Heaven only knows how far I would go to promote his happiness or yours but I would not have your happiness here render your forgetful of the importance of laying up for ourselves "treasures where moth and rust does not corrupt nor thieves break in and steal." But it does not become such a delinquent as myself to pluck "motes" from my brothers eye where mine are so full of "beams."

We have been wondering that you had not thought of forwarding letters to Kentucky through Irvie's instrumentality. He frequently speaks in his letters of having heard from Hopkinsville and I've no doubt could smuggle your dispatches and probably obtain for you replies. Does the plan appear feasible?

Alvin, dear brother, you know not how large a share you have of my thoughts and earnest prayers. We have been observing with unalloyed satisfaction your career during the last eighteen months. Working so faithfully, discharging your duties so conscientiously to your country and to your _____ in rank — that you have done this without reward is all the more to your credit and in no sympathy for your unrequited labors we think of you oftener, love you better and honor you more than we would did you rank ever so high. The world may not applaud and admire as much but all whose opinion should be of most value in your eyes appreciate and approve your efforts. I can well understand how lonely, how isolated you must feel in the absence of those who have been your congenial companions ever since you entered the service. Can well understand how hard it seems to you that <u>others</u> who enlisted after you did who have not been a whit more prompt in the performance of their duties - not a bit more deserving than you, should be promoted while <u>you</u> are still confined to the old treadmill routine. It <u>is</u> hard, but don't be discouraged.

"Still aching, still pursuing learn to labor and to wait" a little while longer and I'm persuaded it will yet be all right. Only think how much worse it might be — think if you were immersed in those horrid swamps, exposed to every variety of hardship and trial and see if you have not some cause to be thankful for even your position. I do wish you would write us more unreservedly enter more into minutia, for do you know we've no idea how or where you are living, whether you're boarding or form one of a mess, tell us what friends you have, give us some idea as to the state of your wardrobe and finances,. Your salary must be very insufficient for your needs. I'm afraid, and I don't know how you get along without some inconvenience - you don't know how many misgivings we've had on this subject. It seems that the Yankees are _____ of trying another visit to Charleston Harbor - 'tis thought doubtful whether they'll make another attempt this summer - wish you and our "little Sampson" could be appointed another field of action in the meantime. Then there might be a chance of your elevation or at least 'twould withdraw you from the Southern Seaboard during the hot, sickly season. We feel anxious about you all the time — feel as if we wanted to be doing something to aid you, but if this cannot be we can at least send you our earnest assurances of approval and affection. Cannot you write us a little more frequently just to say those assurances have not been entirely useless?

The Yankees in Winchester do not seem inclined to bestow even a passing notice on us - oh if they will only remain away long enough to permit us to plant some corn for next year. Father has a field on the mountain above Mr. Fox's which he is planting so if they do come here often they won't find it so convenient to burn the enclosure from around it or destroy the corn.

Nellie spent last week at Clover Hill where she met Mollie Buck also on a visit there of several days - says Mollie is very lively, just as full of fun and frolic as ever, that she made particular inquiries concerning you and remarked that you and she used to be great cronies.

There! it has struck eleven o'clock. I shall be stupid as an owl tomorrow - so good night. All unite in messages of love. I forgot to tell you that a day or two since Ma's sunning yours and Irvie's clothes and your pet "beaver" -Willie walked to the window, took up the hat and brushed it tenderly with hand while the tears rolled up in his eyes - he did it so quietly not knowing that he was observed by any of us. I never saw a child so perfectly devoted to another as he is to you. God Bless you dearest Alvin,

Devotedly Your sister
Lucie

Head Quarters Cleburne's Division
Wartrace, Tennessee
May 19, 1863

My Dear Lu,

Yours of the third inst was received day before yesterday, having been fifteen days en route — but none the worse for that, as it was a letter such as only you can write, I always feel better after reading a letter from home, it has a soothing effect, and all of my sins rise up in my memory and are magnified to an extent greater than they really are, am sorry to say however that it wears off, and the same offences are committed until the reception of another letter.

We are still at Wartrace, and I trust will be for some time, it is a delightful place, and as it is supposed old "Rosy" has sent a portion of his force to Mississippi, it is likely we will remain several weeks yet.

The same day you wrote me I was up at the Camp of the staff, after dinner and was wishing you all could have a peep at us, the weather was delightful and the various members were sitting and lying on the ground smoking and "spinning yarns," Whistler was a violin in the middle of the circle, and every few moments the woods would echo with the merry, ringing laughter, to judge from the happy faces, no one would have supposed that care ever entered their thoughts.

We in common with the whole Confederacy mourn the loss of our noble Jackson, to you of the Valley, his loss will be particularly distressing.

Dick Blakemore called and staid all night with me last week, is very well and looking rough and hearty — was on his way to Morresville, Ala. where Major Serverson was stationed, but think he will soon return to Columbia — he sent many kind messages, all of which I have forgotten.

My lady friends were here again yesterday evening and promised to call and take breakfast with me, but for some reason disappointed me, overslept themselves and even left by the cars I suppose, all this after getting me out of bed an hour before my time. Gen'l. Hardee's daughters arrived yesterday, they will be a great acquisition to our circle — have not called to pay my respects but will do so tomorrow — our staff procured a band and serenaded them last night.

Have not heard from Alvin for several weeks, his silence is unaccountable.

The news from Mississippi is not so cheering, but some think that it will yet turn out to our benefit — the papers report the death of Gen'l. Tilghman, Cousin William T was his aid when he was captured at Fort Henry — wonder where Cousin Kate went while they were fighting at Raymond. The lady I wrote you, who made me such kind offers in case I was wounded, while at Tullahoma, is a resident of Raymond, and don't you think I was so stupid that I did not think of Cousin Kate living there until she left, have been mad with myself ever since.

My wardrobe is in very good condition, have more clothes than I am allowed to carry by orders — and our larder is very well supplied, have beef, mutton, fish (sometimes), eggs, coffee, tea occasionally, butter, rolls and strawberries.

I am well with the exception of a very fashionable disease known as "Army itch" — how it differs from the "seven year" I do not know, but thank goodness it is considered no disgrace, it is contagious, and does not arise from the same causes as the old fashioned "Scotch fiddles". I have a new hide on me every week, as it takes just that time for me to scratch the old one off. I am sure it is equally as annoying as the aforesaid "seven year". How this confession would be received as "refined and polite society" I do not know, but with us is a common topic — and condolence.

Saw Cousin Geo. and Willie this afternoon, both well.

Much love to all

Ever your affectionate Brother,
Pat *(I. A. Buck)*

Home, May 20, 1863

Dearest Irvie,

Julie and Henry Buck, who have been spending the day with us are gone and I have stolen off up here in my room to have a quiet little chat with you before it grows too dark for me to see. Yours of the 25th received last Friday and that of the 7th which should have been forthcoming long since only made its appearance today. I proceed to answer both.

Well last Saturday morning our pleasant dreams were all put to flight by the rude announcement that the Yankees were in town. 'Twas the advance guard of cavalry—some one to two hundred in number and these were succeeded a few hours afterward by as many infantry — a small portion of their command with their artillery they were obliged to leave on the other side of the river. They came over to search the house before breakfast and we were very much surprised. Nellie, Emma and I while sitting at the window reading and waiting for the bell to see our room invaded by two of the torments who had come to look for Southern soldiers. Their search was a mere form though as they contented themselves with opening the doors of the rooms and glancing through them with but one or two exceptions where they looked under the beds. There was a large box of house linen in the upper passage which they conjectured <u>must</u> contain some tabooed articles — having satisfied themselves on this point they made their adieux and departed. They certainly behaved very well considering who they were. 'Twas an officer who conducted the search his only assistant being a fresh faced Yankee youth whose duty, apparently, consisted in keeping strict watch over the faces of the family trying to detect something of the treason in eyes, nose or lips which the tongue dared not utter, every time my warmly lips would twitch out place I had but to look up and find his eyes fixed rebukingly upon them. However they did not make any offensive remarks to any of us so far from it they made no friend by paying a fitting tribute to the memory of our noble Jackson. There was one exception, this was a traitor Virginian whose natural language seemed a species of Yankee billingsgate — he with many oaths made his threats of vengeance on Mr. Hope's family declaring he would burn the house to the ground but for the sick woman there (Mrs. Hope). 'Tis said they were provoked to this by the unbriddled license of Miss B. White's "warmly member". Mr. Moffatt staid at home the night before they came in and made his escape by the narrowest chance. His horse would have fallen sure victim to their rapacity had not Alex incited to action by the promise of a bribe from Mrs. M., mounted it and run the blockade successfully. They stole Mr. Hough's horse—the only one he had and took one or two others from different persons — old ones and indifferent they were. They remained in the square in town all the time, being afraid to venture beyond the protection of the houses. Their barracks were Father's store and the old commissary building next to it. Don't you think they took the drawers from the store to feed their horses from, and then burnt them. Wasn't it mean? —however we are very willing to let them off with the various injuries inflicted there so long as they did not destroy our fencing, crops, and carry off the cattle and horses. They brought their rations with them and when they applied to the citizens for anything they offered compensation for it. With exception of the squad here early in the morning there were not as far as I know, a single Yankee on the premises during their stay here. The cavalry — always the most mischievous — left town immediately after breakfast and proceeded over the mountain. The infantry remained behind in fear and trembling, expecting every moment, as did we all, that they would be attacked by some of our cavalry who had been lurking in the neighborhood a few days before. But they were not and remained with us from early Saturday morning to late Sunday afternoon all unmolested. Their exodus was made so suddenly before the return of the cavalry that we at once concluded they heard that their scouts were captured by a body of Confederates over the mountain. They <u>had received</u> information to this effect as the signal proved — but 'twas a mistake. It seems that on Thursday a body of our men to the number of fifty went down to Charlestown and succeeded in surprising and capturing some sixty Yankees in garrison there. The Yankees in Winchester learning of the exploit determined to punish the daring offenders and sent this detachment through Front Royal to intercept and capture them. They surprised our men in a most disadvantageous position near Piedmont and succeeded in retaking the prisoners and capturing four of our men — Poor Charley Richardson among them — but lost one of their captains and how many privates we do not know. Henry Buck who was in the melee says he saw Lt. Carter shoot two in a breath himself — he also says that all the arms taken with the prisoners to the amount of several hundred carbines, revolvers and rifles we succeeded in carrying safely away with us. Only think how much "ado about nothing" when they had to send a detachment of several hundred men with wagons and artillery just to take four men and to retake some of their own pitiful soldiers. Would you believe it? They only arrested four men in town and released one of them. First Mr. Miller (J.W.) was not quite so fortunate for sick as he was they hauled him off in an ambulance. 'Tis a great wonder the slaves did not go with them — there were but three or four who ventured at all and they were noted — one for his indolence, another very old, etc. I do not think they will occupy Front Royal again very soon or if they do we shall not feel the same dread of them that we have heretofore. Their infantry here was a part of the First Virginia (_____) regiment and their cavalry the notorious "Jessie Scouts". The officer who was here on Saturday morning was dressed in full Confederate uniform and so were some of his men even to their gray military overcoats. You should have seen little Frank's indignant rejection from any attempts of familiarity on their part. 'Twas amusing to see, and justified their declaration that "rebellion" was instilled into the Southern children from their cradles. This selfsame Frank is a bright little rebel and to hear him cheer for "Jeff Davy" you would not suppose our President had a more enthusiastic admirer in the Confederacy than he. Then to hear him sing "Dixie" and "The Bonnie Blue Flag" and to see him go through with the sabre exercise which he has learned from the boys — you would not believe a gentleman of his inches could accomplish so much.

I must not neglect to tell you how Walter a week since in company with three others went to within a short distance of Winchester and captured nine horses, two wagons and several prisoners — he has a perfect mania for horses and is never satisfied unless he is purchasing or capturing them. I only hope he may not be led into danger by this penchant of his. Poor Willie Jackson is certainly dead. Mr. Jackson returned yesterday from his search for him. He was completely perforated by the ball and only lived 36 hours after he received the wound. It is a great comfort for his friends to know he was kindly cared for and everything done for him that possibly could be. Poor fellow! They said he was so brave in action and so patient in his suffering —was perfectly conscious at the time of his death but whether _____ aware of his danger I do not know. Mr. Moore — our former editor — died yesterday evening. He had been sick a long time and death 'tis thought was a happy release to him. His wife and little boy will return to her Father's now.

Oh Irvie, what a loss have we met with in the death of our brave Jackson. The whole Confederacy loved and revered him and he won admiration and respect from his bitterest enemies, but I do not think any people have cause to venerate and cherish his memory as we Valley Virginians. He was identified with us so peculiarly, his field in action was here to a certain extent, we looked up to him, trusted and loved him as a superior being, and now that he's gone from us we feel utterly forlorn. Sometimes I can scarce realize that he in his pride and glory has passed away and everything going on so like nothing had happened — apparently so but I'm afraid that 'twill be a long, long time before we'll ever get anyone to take his place with any and render the service that he did. It seems almost hard that he who had toiled and suffered so unremittingly in his country's cause should not live to witness the glorious fruition of his labor. But 'tis selfish of us to wish him back to the trials and troubles which we know were his here when we've every reason to believe his exchange is such a happy one. If there was not some good in our bereavement God would not have permitted it, and that we have no longer our leader to look to we may turn our eyes to the Source whence that leader himself derived his power and from which we may have been blindedly _____ relying upon the instrument instead of the arm that wielded it.

Lt. Kearney is in Luray — he leaves for Charleston next-week and we sent by him a small package to Alvin. It was reported here the other day that Beauregard with a portion of his command had arrived in Richmond and we would not have been surprised at any moment to see Alvin walk in — we were almost wild with excitement, but there wasn't a word of truth in the rumor anymore than in one we had a few days previous to the effect that Rozencranz had been badly defeated in Tennessee. It's cruel to promulgate such false stories and yet these are those who seem to take delight in nothing else so much as circulating them.

We had a pleasant day with Julie and Henry — something like the sociable old time reunions. The former sent many affectionate messages to you and bids me say how very, very often she thinks of that pleasant winter when you first became well acquainted with each other — of our poor Willie and the sleigh rides and merry evenings at Bel Air and Rose Hill. I tried to induce her to say as much herself in a note to you as she is your debtor in the epistalary line, but she said the "spirit did not move" her. However, if she spends next week with me as she promises, perhaps I may coax her into it. Speaking of renewing correspondence reminds me of "Nannie"— what can have come over her I wonder to cause such a sudden cessation of intercourse with us both. I cannot think she has so soon grown forgetful of us —

perhaps she is sick — perhaps in trouble — at any rate I do wish she would let me hear from her once again and resolve my doubts on the subject 'tis so painful to be in suspense thus. Should you hear from her before I inform you of my having had tidings do not fail to mention it to me. There's a good boy. I think a certain soldier brother of mine is in much more danger of being subjected by a pair of "brown eyes" than subdued by the Yankees. I'm so glad you are enjoying yourself so much and have an opportunity of mingling in ladies society.

You are right to seek such society Irvie — there's nothing more improving than intercourse in a pleasant social way with the refined and cultivated of our sex. This I've often told you. But my brother there is only one thing I fear in it — that you will come so perfectly absorbed in the pursuit of pleasure, as to lose sight of— not your duties to your commanders — but of higher and more important things. Do not let the gaieties and fascinations by which you are surrounded unfit you for appearing on the battlefield at any moment prepared to meet cooly face to face your enemy man — prepared — as far as in you lies, to obey the summons to the presence of your Maker. "Be ye also ready, for in such an hour as ye think not the Son of man cometh." That's all.

My dear Irvie, I _too_ thought we were at "quits" with regard to the "Chevalier" — but tis _you_ who stir the subject now. I never once mentioned him in that letter to which you refer, in at least am not aware of having done so. And as to my ascertation that I corresponded with one of General Longstreet's _staff_ —' tis altogether a mistake. I said one of his _corps_. A wide difference you perceive between the two, one which I do not see how you ever managed to reconcile. Now Irvie, _had_ it been _I_ who made that blunder instead of _you_, Nellie would have pronounced it very natural — as it is I don't know what to think about it unless to conclude that you've been _dreaming_ about the Captain. Never mind we'll have all this over when we meet next summer — till then a truce — I'm already beginning to count the months till the probable end of the summer campaign when you know what you have particularly promised us — hope you'll keep your vow rather better than some others you've made.

Grandma is so much better that she speaks of going to Uncle Tom's tomorrow. Ma and little Nannie went to River Side this morning will probably be absent several days — she left her love for you though. Only think 'twill soon have been a year since the battle of Front Royal — the 23rd of this month. Poor Jackson.

All — Nellie, Grandma, Laura and the children, Aunt and Father unite in love to you. Good night dear Irvie — may God keep you in safety.

Yours fondly,
Lucie

Head Quarters
Department of South Carolina, Georgia & Florida
Charleston, South Carolina
May 22, 1863

Dear Girls,

You both have heavy claims upon my pen, and being at a loss to decide who is best entitled to a letter, I've struck upon the idea of squaring off with both at once — not that a letter of mine is equal to two, or even one of yours.

Lu fired the last shot, and made some inquiries touching the state of my wardrobe — condition of finances etc. Having been rather careful with my apparel there is enough on hand to serve me for a long campaign — this is a fortunate thing for one holding the grade of High-Private (a most honorable rank, but not calculated to afford a man facilities for growing purse-proud). Congress has passed a Bill allowing men on detached service 3 $ per day. Of this we spend unavoidably 60 to 65$ per month for boarding — with two meals a day, one at 9 A.M., the other at 3 P.M. — room rent consumes $3.50 and washing 5$.

We, (I and four others), board at a restaurant kept by a free darkey. The hotels charge one hundred and fifty dollars a month, or eight dollars a day for a less period than one week. We tried messing at one time, but it came near starving, and breaking us besides.

I am truly glad to hear that edibles have a fair prospect of being plentiful with you all, for it has been impossible for me to repress forebodings that there might be actual want of food in the Valley during the summer. May the Lord enable our men to keep the rascally Yankees from ever crossing the Shenandoah again.

Fears are entertained as to the safety of Vicksburg. Gen'l. Johnston may succeed in holding it and the whole State of Mississippi, but it will require a vast expenditure of strategy and blood. Oh that old "Stonewall" Jackson's mantle might fall upon some one of our leaders! — Beauregard, Lee and Johnston are left to us — three sagacious Spartans, who compose a trio unrivalled for carrying on military movements on a grand scale; but who could take thirty thousand men, march as far, appear in so many unexpected places, fight as often, and be uniformly victorious as old Jack. Poor old fellow! We believe he is now in good quarters, and that all truly good soldiers will join him after a while.

Pat's division has moved up to Wartrace, some twenty miles nearer to Murfreesboro, and he seems to be playing the gallant in fine style with the Tennessee maidens. Cousin George B., favored me with a long letter a day or so ago — writes in very spicy figures, but seems lonely since Irving and Cous Willie left him behind — he being still at Tullahoma. Cous Alick has joined Morgan's cavalry and is now on a raid into Kentucky. Wouldn't your eldest brother like to take a scamper in that quarter and include Hopkinsville in the round? Don't you commend my steadfast devotion to objects in that locality? Two years ago this day closed my career in Ky.

and at this very hour of the day I was employed far more agreeably than in wielding a pen in an Adj't Gen'ls office, and certainly had a more pleasant vis a vis than this hard looking scamp (Goolsby) sitting near. Oh dear! but for an india-rubber temperament what would have become of the "Old Court" long ere this? Poor Latham, who has little of this faculty of adapting himself to circumstances, suffers intensely from home sickness — most lamentably bewails his hard lot, and heaps insurrections upon all Puritans, and those in Ky particularly. We are Damon and Pythias, minus a tyrant to test our friendship. I have two other confre´res — Hincks and Tontant (pronounced Tooton) — a couple of young creoles — the latter a nephew of the General.

A brace of rather pretty girls appeared in a window just opposite a few days ago. Upon instituting some inquiries Latham arrived at the fact that they were returned refugees, who would remain permanently. His information was correct, and when they bring their chairs out upon the balcony to enjoy the evening breeze, the rascal hurries off and gets the General's spy glass, creeps behind the window shades and admires them tremendously.

You have no idea of the gratification and pride Irving and I feel in witnessing the fortitude with which those who are so dear to us, bear the privations incumbent to this wicked war, and it is painful to know we are powerless to avert them. Pecuniary resources fail at such a time to furnish many of the comforts of life, and wealth, so magically potent in time of peace, is now frequently a foe second only to the Yankees, for it often proves a magnet to attract attention to its possession, and the more a man has, the greater the disposition seems to be to offer indignity and insult to his family on the part of our Northern "brethren". It is a rough joke to congratulate one's self upon the meagerness of his possessions, and the above is rather dry philosophy but none the less true for all that. Poor Willie's silent but eloquent tribute to my memory, elicited by the vacant "beaver" is more highly appreciated than the dear little fellow would believe, and if I smiled upon hearing of it, 'twas because the scene came up very vividly to my mind's eye and made his roguish face peculiarly interesting. Carey is my debtor for a voluminous dispatch bearing date some two weeks ago. Laura and Orville are losing all their reputation as correspondents.

On Wednesday night three vessels ran in, and last night another. It is now nearly late enough for the booming of the Yankee guns to announce that one is trying it tonight. They make it a point to blaze away though seldom doing any damage. One vessel, 'tis true, they succeeded in capturing some weeks ago — the first in a long time.

Oh, the weather is so desperately hot! It is wonderful that persons living in such a climate have energy enough to talk politics. The ladies are fluttering around in Swiss muslins lawn, organdies & c, in spite of the Blockade prices. A good pair of men's shoes now cost from 34 to 40 dollars — boots from 55 to 70. When the times arrives for the Israelites to return to Jerusalem, the census of Charleston will undergo a large and most beneficial reduction. They now hold supreme power in all our cities, relieving the unsuspecting soldiers of their loose change, and taking scrupulous care to keep out of the way of the conscripting officers. They can easily pay over a thousand or fifteen hundred dollars for a substitute, and do so unhesitatingly when the enrolling officer insists very urgently upon having their names upon the muster rolls.

Well, I'm very sleepy, and the probability is that you will be also before following me through this torturous letter.

Love to every one.
Truly your affectionate Brother
Alvin

Wartrace, Tennessee
June 12, 1863

My Dear Lucie,

Your letter of the 20th of May reached me several days ago and Ma's of the 31st this evening, I will reply to both at once.

General and myself have just returned from Shelbyville where we went yesterday evening, had a very pleasant time. "Maggie's" brown eyes looked prettier than ever, and my reception was such that it will tempt me to repeat the visit before many days, but I am afraid I shall become very much "demoralized" and unfit for service.

I received a letter this evening from Cousin Kate Blakemore dated the sixth — she writes very affectionately, and I am going to answer her letter at once — she states that she has written to our family several times but receives no reply. The lady who brought me the letter was Mrs. Shearer who kindly promised to nurse me at Tullahoma if I should get shot — she has returned to the _____, is well acquainted with Cousin Kate, says when the enemy passed through Raymond Cousin Kate refused to allow them to search house unless they produced a written order from the Provost Marshall to be executed by a commissioned officer — and when they found she was so determined they declined to search — and when our men were there she cooked and drew water for them for several hours.

This day a year ago I received letters from you announcing Jackson's Victory at Front Royal.

I received a letter from Nannie about a month ago, but have not yet replied to it ("brown eyes") — she wrote rather sadly.

Tell Aunt Letitia (*Letitia A. Buck Blakemore*) that Marcus Newton[14] (*Blakemore*) is Captain and Commissary of Woodward's Regiment — heard from him today, was well. Mr. Pearre is still here, working with the energy of a locomotive, he is without doubt one of the most reliable and interminable young men I have ever known — he has been recommended by the Division Ordinance officer for the position of

Lieutenant and Ordinance officer of Gen'l. Liddell's Brigade, with very good prospect of success.

Since writing the above I went out to Gen'l. Hardee's to see the ladies, while there Cousin Willie came over with a band and we had a grand serenade. Johnson's Brigade has been taken from our Division, so that I rarely see Cousin Willie now, he wished to be remembered, and was delighted to hear from Cousin Robb Marisen.

Cousin Newt Catlett has returned from Kentucky — and brought a letter from Rett to Alvin — over which I have no doubt, the said "Court" went "nigh" into fits. Received a letter from him today.

I am suffering with the tooth ache, the first I ever had, but am only waiting the return of our Surgeon, when I will most certainly sacrifice the offending "grinder".

I sat down with the intention of writing a long letter but find myself at the end of my rope now.

We moved out to the front last week, and were within four miles of Murfreesboro — our advance had light skirmishing with the enemy — and gave them a terrible scare — they beat their drums and kept up a great racket.

Love to all—
Ever your affectionate Brother
Pat *(I. A. Buck)*

Bel Air, June 19, 1863

My Dear Irvie,

'Tis no easy task midst all this turmoil and excitement to settle down to letter-writing, yet if your weekly letter is not begun now there is no guessing when it will be finished or reach you. I wrote Alvin a week since, just for the letter which Ma sent him, giving an account of the "servile exodus" from Bel Air, she will write him again this week and I am doing the same for you, as I believe my name is on the "Debit" side of your account. General A. P. Hill's Corps[15] is passing through town now, and the welkins rings with cheers from the troops, while as one band at the lower end of the street ceases playing "Dixie" the strains of "Bonnie Blue Flag" are taken up by the one just entering town, until we have an unbroken swell of soul-stirring music. Now it is "The Lone Rock By The Sea", so plaintive and soft, so sweet and so frought with memories of a happier past, that tears well in my eyes while listening to it. Ah me! Well, after all, one could not well appreciate the Confederate cheers and this Confederate music unless they have been listening so long as we have, to the tramp of hostile footsteps!

Really, Irving, there is so much to tell you that I do not know where to begin. Oh! for a private telegraph-wire!

You have doubtless, in times past, marveled at the mystical story of the labors of Hercules. Well, I can tell you that, in a miniature way, we have reviled him in these exploits. The basement and servant's rooms which we had to thoroughly clean were pretty fair samples of those "Angean Stables", with this difference, the old demigod had but to clean the stables once, while our task of <u>keeping</u> the subterranean apartments in order seems interminable. We do not have to coax <u>Cerberus</u> up from Tartarus but we have subjugated a most refractory <u>cooking-stove</u>. We captured none of Diomedes cattle but have civilized some of the most savage cows and words fail to tell how often the settlement — headed Lernaea hydra has been slain in the many-crested difficulties that have been encountered and overcome by us all. To speak in plain terms we have had a tough time of it and can say with profound gratitude, "I am glad it has been no worse." Still I have not regretted the last fortnights experience since it has taught me more practical useful lessons than would, otherwise have been learned in years. At first I presided over the culinary department. Nellie the dairy, and Laura the nursery while Ma and Grandma assisted in each of these branches of the family work. You should have seen how we labored. At night our feet pained so we could not rest, and in the morning our hands so blistered and stiff we could scarcely handle a broom, but this trouble is in a degree a thing of the past, for we have a perfect giantess in the kitchen now who does the drudgery, so we are having a much easier time of it and this important personage is Miss Nancy Parnell by name. Our hands and feet are growing harder so hurt us much less now, when we work. You should partake of some of my priceless biscuits and sip my ambrosial soup. Indeed I am growing vain of my attainments in the culinary art, and the enconuens of my family almost induce me to believe that I have achieved some wonders. Our friends have been kinder than I can tell, and I sometimes think that if no other good comes of these misfortunes we will have the satisfaction of knowing that they have been the means of proving the number and quality of our good friends. Reverses do not always play so kindly a part for us, do they? Aunt Lizzie *(Elizabeth Peake Buck of Clover Hill)* was here Sunday while we were getting supper in the kitchen, and next morning here came little mulatto "Lucy" as a small assistant to remain just as long as we want her, and many a step she saves us. Aunt Letitia Buck *(Jane Letitia Buck of Belmont)*, Aunt Bettie Ashby *(of Oakley)*, Cousin Elizabeth Richardson *(Elizabeth Millar Richardson, of Rose Hill)*, Mrs. Hope and Mrs. Roy *(Benton's and Scott's mother)* we can never forget for their many evidences of kindly thought, and there are dozens of others I could mention who have interested themselves in our welfare in an entirely unexpected manner. After all, there is something rather attractive and independent in this sort of living, our work when done, is just as we wished it to be performed and if any failure occurs we know just where to lay the blame. Once or twice when worn out and sick, I have felt despondent and asked myself — "Is this after all my portion in life? This vexation, toil and weariness; is this my mission, my only one here?" But the thought was unworthy and I hastened to put it from me by recalling how often I had lamented my comparative usefulness and longing for something to call forth the superfluous energy I felt latent within me, and now that this wish was granted to rebel because the work was not exactly in accordance with my taste! So far we have accomplished a great deal and all without physical injury from exposure and over-exertion — so Oh! but how that shout from the passing troops thrilled my very soul and seemed rending the skies! The excitement is too painful enough to make one almost fanatic. So you see writing is almost impossible. We had expected Longstreet's Corps here and were in ecstatics of the prospect of meeting our Regiment, and the afternoon before their expected arrival had arranged a small tub full of flowers to shower with them with a fragrant welcome, but lo! and behold! Bright and early the next morning our hopes were rudely dispelled by the appearance of a courier who had come to inquire his way to a point lower down the river where he had been ordered to intercept General Longstreet with a dispatch from General Ewell. Then we knew that the Corps had passed on by the lower route, and a bitter disappointment it was! However, if "Pickett's Division" did not come to us, the Washington Artillery in the same Corps did, and were the recipients of our floral greeting. We have since learned that Corse's Brigade[16] made a two days-march in this direction, but was then ordered to return to Hanover Station as guards. 'Tis an inglorious and rather mortifying duty for the glorious old 17th Regiment *(with the Warren Rifles)* and the dear boys are wrathful enough, over it, but they may follow the main army in the rear, and may pass through here yet in route to Pennsylvania, so we'll see them, after all. At any rate, wherever they are located, they are doing their duty mindfully, I know, near enough for us to hear from them, and, comparatively safe, so we think we can afford to let them repose for awhile upon the laurels they've already, so nobly won. And, by the way, Capt. Latrobe has been promoted to the Majority. But you would rather I would write of something more nearly concerning myself. Ma wrote you fully as to events up to last Sunday evening, so I'll take up the record from that time onward, and just give you some extracts from my diary. You will have learned from the papers all that I could tell you of the bombardment and fall of the fort at Winchester *(to Ewell's Corp)*. We at first, thought and hoped that in the engagement "Murdering Milroy" *(Maj. General R. H. Milroy, U.S.A.)* and his marauders were captured, but every man of them, but with true Yankee subtlety he made his escape, with 2500 of his cavalry. The whole attack was conducted with so much General Jackson's quiet dexterity and clarity, that the Yankees must image that leader still with us in spirit. Milroy knew nothing of the movement upon Winchester till the Saturday of the opening attack. Even when informed by his scouts of the proximity of the large troop or rebel cavalry he treated the report with scorn, _____ that is was "only some of Jenkins' guerillas whom he would, soon have in custody." There was not, a venture to say, then a greater surprise sprung during this war than was experienced by the hoary sinner when he discovered that he was surrounded by and powerless in the hands of the "contemptible rebels" as he always dubbed our troops. His escape was almost, a miracle and could only have been effected by the bold measures he adopted, cutting through our lines where they were weakest. But never mind Milroy! The arm of justice is long enough to reach you yet, I trust if not in Washington, then in Philadelphia for there is where our army is aiming to penetrate, if we may believe the report of those who profess to know the purposes of our leaders.

Ma, doubtless wrote you that Mount Cloud and Charlie Richardson were on the track of our fugitive bondmen and bondwomen and should they be captured would reclaim and restore them. Well, last Monday night we were all sitting in the back-door awaiting Father's return from town with the news, and when he arrived there were other footsteps with his, and directly, Charlie R. entered the front door having left Bunker Hill this morning, called in Winchester recovered Father's boy — Horace *(servant)* — and had him lodged in jail in town. It seems that the latter, with Alec *(servant)*, waited on some of the Yankee officers and were captured with them. He says the last he saw of Alec was when he had been ordered to charge through our lines with his officer, that he dashed ahead and thinks he must have been killed or captured as there seemed little chance of his escape. The other colored people had taken the alarm Friday morning, obtained a pass from Milroy and fled in government wagons to Martinsburg in route for Alexandria. So it is doubtful if we ever hear from them again, till old Belle Haven shall be in our possession once more which, it is thought may be at no distant day. As to Alec's death, I am sceptical, he is so sharp and active that I think he would escape a Mini-Ball with the same dexterity that he used to elude detection in his now well-known villainies. Father and Charlie went right over to the jail and released Horace, who seemed mortified and repentant. We said nothing to him excepting to ask the most natural questions and he went to his work the next morning with as much interest as though he had never left. He said he would never have seceded save for the fear of being sold, and he tells the children how foolish this was of him to run away and how he hopes the rest of his family will be reclaimed etc. Father told him, the night he came home that if he would be willing to remain and behave himself, he would promise never to part with him. The proposal was readily acceded to and I suppose will for the present, remain here, though many of friends think it scarcely advisable to have him so near the border. I scarcely know what to think of him. He seems to feel no resentment towards us, is respectful and seems to realize that we were right in bringing him back home, but there is a restlessness and moodiness entirely foreign to his natural manner, though this may be the result of loneliness and mortification, and I believe, now if he leaves again, it will be because of missing his old society and associations than anything else. Old Uncle Gilbert *(servant)* seemed so delighted to see him. I had felt sorry for the old man and you may know the effect which the departure of the others had upon him, well I'll tell you he entirely took to work for the want of amusement there is very little farming to be done this season and by employing white labor occasionally we can get off pretty well with the outside work.

But I must tell you of Charlie R's *(Richardson)* trip to Winchester. He cap-

161

tured one prisoner, a beautiful horse, some clothing and brought me some Yankee stationery by way of spoils. He met there, among the prisoners, the Captain who had taken <u>him</u> prisoner a short time since. The officer accosted him with — "Well Richardson, you hold me in the same situation in which I had <u>you</u> awhile ago." "Yes," replied Charlie, "and I am delighted to meet you." Another Yankee approached and asked Charlie — "How do you like your new General?" "<u>What general</u> are you inquiring about?" "Why, General Starvation," answered the facetious Yankee. "Oh!" replied Charlie, "he has not yet taken command and the stores which Stonewall Jackson drew from Commissary Banks have not yet been consumed."

There were numbers contrabands *(escaped slaves)* killed in this engagement and about 100 captured. Among these were some from this neighborhood. One of Cousin Ellen Richardson's little maids, Captain Roy's man, old Mr. Spengler's woman, and others. By-the-way our poor old neighbor, Mr. Spengler died here two days ago, truly an object of pity. For a long while he had been dependant upon his old servants for support, without another friend in the world excepting his old wife who he had never been kind to, no one will ever know what he suffered from neglect and disease, and poor old man lived, apparently, little hope for a better life in the future.

Last Wednesday was a fatiguing time with us. Nancy was at the mill washing our clothes so Grandma and I, with Ma's assistance, cooked all the dinner for the family and workmen. Will give you a leaf from my diary that you may have some idea of our routine of duties upon such occasion.

"June 17 – Nellie's foot was so painful last night and this morning that I relieved her of her dairy-maid duties, while the others cleaned house and got breakfast. Was at my post early, and yet there were already applicants eager for milk. While filling the canteens a courier rode up, and inquiring for Father, informed him that he had dispatches from General Ewell for General Longstreet who was supposed now, to be at Beny's Ferry. And asking for directions for reaching that point as soon as possible so as to intercept him there. This announcement disappointed me greatly for I knew if this were the situation it would be useless to expect to see the dear old 17th Regiment now. After we had finished up breakfast there were 7 or 8 more applicants for milk, so dinner was necessarily delayed while we served these soldiers. Then they begged for music and Nellie and I played the piano till time to gather the peas for dinner. Just as they were leaving Charlie R. came in bringing the stationery which he had gotten from the Yankees and I was glad to get it, as tis a prize, now. All the morning since dawn, Longstreet's artillery and ordnance trains have been passing. About nine o'clock the Washington Artillery from New Orleans appeared, and from that time forth there was one unbroken stream of soldiers at the doors, dusty broken-down poor fellows, begging for bread and milk or water, everything that could be thought of in the way of refreshments. Our buckets of water sent down to the road from which children supplied the thirsty, and those that came to the house we supplied with everything edible we could spare, even to a portion of the dinner cooking on the stove. It was so pleasant to hear their grateful "thank yous" — and "you are very kind," or, "I'm so much obliged to you," while their faces would brighten and their steps grow quick and light as they walked away. So constant was the excitement and so warm the day and so wearisome our labors that when dinner was ready we could not eat a morsel of it. I was in the kitchen during the meal attending to matters there when two soldiers called at the door to ask for a luncheon. Without thinking, I invited them into the kitchen, gave them seats and hurried into the dining-room to ascertain if there was any chance of getting them food there. While placing this on the <u>kitchen</u> <u>table</u>, I for the first time noticed them closely and was impressed with, their quiet, gentlemanly deportment and appearance. When Ma came in, she learned that they were members of the Washington Artillery from N.O. The spokesman was a delicate-featured, slender and graceful young fellow who conversed fluently. He remarked that his cousin, Miss Herbert had married a Dr. Horace Buck of Mississippi. We remembered then, that <u>our</u> Dr. Horace Buck had married a Miss Herbert some years ago and this was the young man's name. He spoke of a young brother who had died from the affects of his wounds in Warrington a year ago — the same boy of whom we had heard Mrs. Moffatt speak. He had been tenderly nursed by the lady of the house where he had been carried, and when he realized that he was dying said to his benefactors and said — "You have done for me all that my Mother could have done except one thing. You have not <u>kissed</u> me. Will you do that now?" She pressed her lips to his forehead, and he sat back on his pillow contentedly as a little child and whispered "I am ready now," and soon passed away. It was a pathetic ending, of his brave young life. Upon taking his departure young Herbert very cordially invited us to visit him should we ever go south. I was busily engaged upon a batch of bread this evening, kneading the dough vigorously, when Nellie came bounding in saying — "Lucie, a Mr. McCauley *(R. L. McCauley, 4th Alabama)* is here, and he's asking for you." It was a great surprise, for we had well nigh forgotten the little Alabamian who called upon us last Fall when Longstreet passed through. After his inquiring again for me I sent him an invitation to come and see for himself, why I could not make my appearance. Into the kitchen he came, laughing mortally at my excuse, but sat by me while I made out my loaves, asking questions concerning the compound and chatting upon many subjects till the dough was ready for baking, we fixed the oven, lifted the lid and drew out the fire very much as he might have helped unfurl a parasol or don an overshoe two years ago. This done we sent him to the parlor freshened up our toilettes and rejoined him in a few minutes. Found there with Father two very attractive looking soldiers who were introduced as Messrs. Baker[17], brothers and also, member of the Washington Artillery from N.O. Also acquaintances of Cousin Cornelia Black's. They proved fine young men, well-bred, intelligent, and very pleasant, evidently seen a good deal of gay life. The elder sang well and we had quite a concert, followed by a general discussion of music, poetry and fiction. That Mr.

<u>Baker</u> should be conversant with all the standard publications of this class was not surprising, but it was somewhat unexpected to hear Mr. M. *(McCauley)* speak as equally well-informed in regard to them. When the latter learned that Irvie was in constant communication with Huntsville, his place of residence, he seemed delighted and begged that he would send an invitation to him to visit his family there. Avering that his friends would be glad of the opportunity for extending the rights of hospitality to a member of Father's family, when they had learned of our kindness to himself.

By five o'clock the soldiers had all left and we addressed ourselves to getting supper and feeding the poultry <u>and children</u> and putting away the milk, and now I am so sleepy and tired, with scarcely energy to drag myself to bed. I think I can safely say that I've not sat down five minutes today with the exception with an hour or two stint in the parlor with our guest." This ends the extract from my diary.

There was a Major Kirkland at Rose Hill last week. He inquired if a family of "Buck's" living in this vicinity, and being answered in the affirmative, said he was well acquainted with one, Captain Buck on General Cleburne's staff. He was conceded to be the best officer on that staff. Do you know anything of this officer, — brother mine? There was also, another gentleman here with Uncle John, the other day, a Captain Armstrong from Baltimore, he heard us talking about you and wanted to know if you were not the "little Buck" who lived opposite him in Baltimore. Uncle John said you knew him there.

Jimmy Blakemore came in, very unexpectedly recently to see us. I had entertained the idea that his body and intellect had outgrown his heart, that he was a perfect specimen oracular young American, for so he had appeared when I last had seen him three years ago, but he seems to have greatly improved, and was really quite affectionate. He is courier for General Anderson in A.P. Hill's Corps, and as ruddy and robust a young rebel as one would wish to see. His figure reminds me a good deal of Cousin George Williams. He only remained with us a few hours, as his Division was passing immediately through but promised to return later if he could. I am sorry to learn there are treacherous souls in Winchester who are trying to make future friends of the Yankees there, the prisoners. Our soldiers complained bitterly of the partiality shown them, thought this sort of thing is only found among the parvenus, of whom there are a number. You remember Miss Catherine Hooper, don't you? She is now "Mrs. Stewart" and whilom mistress of Dr. Funsteinsfine old residence. They are Tories, and while the Yankees occupied Winchester her house was kind of half way stationed for spies and similar cattle. Uncle Mack and Charlie Buck stopped at their place to feed their horses a short while ago, and they say no Duchess ever assumed more lofty airs than she did, upon the occasion, ordering her children around to the "Nursery"— (her father had <u>two rooms</u> in his house, I believe) and complaining that she had not been able to have her "lawn" properly mown etc. You will note now, that those who are most prosperous now, North or South,

Yankee or Confederate are invariably of the inferior class those who do not scruple to compromise their honor to gain coveted wealth. These social and political agitations remind one of a whirlpool in which sustained things are lost sight while chaff and straws always swim to the surface.

Our mails are so irregular now that we can not expect to receive our usual quota of letters, nor can you. There is _____.

(same letter continued later)

Wednesday, June 24, 1863

My Darling Irving,

It is all over, and I resume my letter, interrupted days ago, to write such things that will cause you to abhor the sight of it. Oh Irving! Irving! To think that never, so long as we live, shall we see our noble Walter again![18] That a little lock of hair and some flowers from off his bier are all that remains to us of the white still form over which such bitter tears were shed in our old parlor yesterday. It is hard to sit down calmly and write collectively the particulars of this tragedy, and yet, we can think and talk of nothing but our lost one and have been spending the morning trying to recall every incident, every word and every act of the dear boy during his last visit to us.

The battle of Upperville, of which you will see accounts in the papers, was fought Sunday between a large force of the enemies cavalry and infantry, opposed to a small number of Virginia Cavalry. Before the engagement was launched the Colonel had dear Walter detailed for duty in the quartermaster's department, thinking thus to detain him from active participation in the coming battle, for he knew how fearless and daring he was, and feared to trust him to exposure of such a conflict as he was aware, was impending. But he quickly discharged these appointed duties and took his place foremost in the charge. This was not incumbent upon him for his company was not in the engagement but his gallant spirit could not brook inglorious idleness while others were fighting for the cause he loved so well. His comrades say that, as he rode into the fray he seemed in exuberant spirits, was mounted upon a favorite horse and frequently directed their attention to her fleetness and beauty. The struggle was a terrible one, the slaughter sickening. About four o'clock P.M. our forces seemed wavering, the enemy gaining. Dear Walter seeing this called to them — "Boys, don't let them drive us off. Come, let's charge them back!" They rushed impetuously forward and just as they reached a gentleman's yard (Mr. Thompson) *[Mr. Thomas]* a ball pierced the back of his neck, the horse which wounded at the same time, gave a few bounds and the rider reeled and fell to the ground. Then our men fell back and left the place in possession of the enemy. Some young ladies of the house saw the poor boy fall and heard him exclaim — "I'm a dead man!" They rushed out and begged that they might be permitted to retain and bury the body. This, the Yankees refused to allow and they took his arms, rifled his pockets of everything they contained, money, trinkets and paper, and even took from his finger a little ring which I had seen him wear till it seemed almost a part of him. They then stripped the very boots and socks from his feet. After robbing him of everything that could be removed, they rolled him in a blanket about him and dug, not a grave but a shallow trench and covered him over. Cousin Will Cloud and several others of his company as soon as they knew of his death, resolved to upon recovering the dead boy's remains, and the knowledge of this happening came to them when his horse appeared in camp with his overcoat on the saddle and they knew he must have fallen in the charge. As soon as the Yankees abandoned the battle-ground, (which was done as soon as it was discovered that we were being reinforced) these comrades returned to the place making inquiries and seeking the grave. When they reached Mr. Thompson's *[Thomas]* house the inmates told them that there had been a brave young Lieutenant killed in their yard, and pointed out the place where had laid him, and when they uncovered the body they recognized him. This was Monday evening. The news of the battle reached us vaguely early Monday morning. Monday at noon Father returned from town looking pale and distressed bringing the report of Walter's having fallen. At first we would not believe it at first because he had been so often delivered from imminent peril that we learned to think of him as we had done of Ashby and Jackson, that he bore a charmed life. But the wounded from the battle continued coming in, confirming the sad news, till disbelief was impossible. Oh! Irving such a shock it was! We were stunned by the suddenness of it, and then to know that his body was in possession of such brutal men, imagining that he might have died in lingering torture at their hands and his dear body hauled upon the heaps of the unholy slaying. Father directly, upon hearing the tale in an authentic dispatched a note to Uncle Mack *(Walter's Father at Belmont)* stating that Walter was badly hurt and he had better come down prepared to be absent from home for a day or two. He and Jacquie *(Jacqueline M. Buck, aged 15)* came about three o'clock, heard the truth as far as we had learned it, sent Jacquie to break the news to Aunt Letitia and started for Upperville. Ma and Nellie went immediately up to Bellmont to remain with Aunt L. in Uncle Mack's absence. All that evening we were in painful suspense, hearing conflicting reports, not knowing what to believe. Late in the evening came letters from Cousin Horace Buck and Newt Cloud confirming our worst fears. We spent a sad, wakeful night and early next morning Uncle Mack returned with the news that the remains had been recovered and would be brought here in half an hour. I can't tell you what thankfulness mingled with my sorrow when I found we would be permitted to pay the last orders to one so dear and so deserving of every respect that could be shown him. Uncle Mack went home to consult Aunt Letitia about what arrangements to make for the funeral, and very soon Nellie and Jacquie returned and later Ma. They said Aunt L. could not bear to look upon her murdered boy. The news of all this had reached town almost as soon as we had heard it and the house was soon thronged, ladies bringing baskets and wreaths and flowers and every face sad and tearful. It was so heartbreaking to see him brought to us slowly in the little covered wagon *("great black wagon" in her diary)* instead of having him dash up to the door boldly and fearlessly upon his beautiful horse as always before, looking so graceful and manly. It was the first time he had ever entered the house without words of cheerful greeting and smiles and caresses for us. And how often had we watched for his coming as for a ray of sunshine, while now his inanimate presence casts such a shadow over us. He was born here, loved this next to his own home while he lived, and t'was fitting that he should rest here in the interval before being consigned to his last eternal rest. Aunt L. wished it so, and we all esteemed it a sacred privilege to have him with us and perform the last, sad duties for him. I shall never forget how he looked when they called me in to see him. They had placed him on the lounge under the Southern window and surrounded him with flowers, and as the breeze rustled their leaves I could almost imagine the dead breathing. Such a calm, peaceful white face as it was there among the lilies and jasmines! The blonde hair was brushed back from the broad smooth brow, the eyelids lightly covered as in natural slumber. About the mouth an expression of firm resolve, merging into a pleasant smile. There was nothing deathlike about him, either in color or expression, and all that looked upon that face said it was the most natural and serenely beautiful they had ever seen. There was a slight contusion on the upper part of the nose, a cut on the side of the head, neither noticeable, and whether produced by falling from his horse on the stones or by the stroke of the saber, will never be known. I never so fully realized before the beauty of Bryant's lines — "Approach thy grave as one who wraps

the drapery of his couch about him

And lies down to pleasant dreams" — as with looking upon that form lying there with folded arms, the attitude one of such calm, majestic repose it, at first inspired a feeling of awe, afterwards I could only look upon what remained of our darling cousin, and think how all unconsciousness of our grief then, when, had he been living he would have been the first to offer comfort and sympathy in any of our sorrows. It was so hard to give him up, tender and true brother as he had ever been. It seemed that any of those who were with him could have been better spared. But it was a consolation to reflect that he had died nobly at his post of duty, as became the true soldier, to know that he had given honor to his name while living, and no blemish upon his fair reputation now, that could cause pain in remembering his past career. But, to have him whom we so admired and loved snatched from us when he had become so essential to our happiness, was such a trial as we shall never again endure unless we are called to yield you or Alvin a sacrifice to our country's cause. Truly, Irving you don't realize what Walter has been to us, these past three years. Just at the time when we most needed brotherly love and sympathy you and Alvin were called away from us, he stepped into the place as no one else could have done, entering into our lives and sympathizing naturally and fully in our troubles. It was true, that he had so often told me — "Lucie I believe I have more the heart of a woman than that of a man." Anyway, there were, with all his admirers, very few who really knew and appreciated his fine nature fully. Those who <u>did</u> understand how such a sensitive, refined soul as his could suffer in contact with the world at large. He had dreamed so many beautiful dreams of life as he would love to have it, had lived so constantly in the realm of imagination that mere existence in this harsh world could not yield him satisfaction, so, perhaps it was Divine Wisdom that removed him when he was taken. At the beginning of this war he and Willie Richardson were equally impressed with the belief that neither of them would live to see its conclusion. And Walter's conviction grew in force after Willie's death. I thought so much of it yesterday, of the intimacy between them and their brief separation by death. We thought so much about you and Alvin too, each of you has lost the kindest truest friend a man ever had. And when Ma bent over to kiss him, for the last time, she said "He was dear to me next to my own sons." Our Father sobbed like a child. I never knew such universal regret as was manifested by the whole community and his passing away has cast a gloom over all the neighborhood. The mountain people to a man, were devoted to him as ever were clansmen to a futile chief and would have followed him anywhere. Yesterday I saw one of them, an old, grayheaded man standing under a tree in the yard, weeping as if his very heart would break. Very few could attend the funeral because of the lack of horses. Uncle Mack came down about eleven o'clock bringing the little children and Jacquie with him. Mr. Berry read the 90th Psalm, offered up a prayer, a hymn was sung and then we looked our last on the dear face, and then they took him away. What a different departure from any he had ever made before, when he had been want to turn, upon reaching the gate and wave his hand or blow us a merry kiss from his fingers. Only Uncle Mack, Father, Jacquie, Mr. Smedley, Nellie, Cousin Sue Buck, Cousin Sue Richardson and Bell went from here to Water Lick. But the Clover Hill family and others joined them there. Could he have expressed his wish concerning this thing, I believe he would have asked for just these friends to attend him at the last. Nellie had more of his confidence than any other human -being, more even than Willie and is deeply grieved. And what a blow this will be to Dick, they were so devoted, and Aunt Letitia is almost heartbroken, but Ma says she tries to bear up with true Christian fortitude. Uncle Mack is calmer than we expected, though he feels nonetheless for this suppression of his grief and has not fully realized the full meaning of his bereavement as he will do, later on. Poor little Jacquie worshiped his brother Walter and seemed so lost and out of heart with everything.

Though we mourn this our great loss we "do not sorrow as though without hope," for we have every assurance that he is resting free from all his trials and labors. [See letter dated April 8, 1861 regarding Walter's conversion.] There are among his friends those who remember such satisfactory conversations with him, in which he expressed his trust in God and his readiness, with this faith to meet Death with all its terrors. He told Cousin Bettie R. last fall that, if he could not place, with confidence, all in God's hands, he thought he could little trust his own powers to meet the fate which daily menaced him. To Cousin Sue Buck who a short time ago spoke with him upon the subject, he said — "Cousin, I have felt, within the last few weeks, that I should not live very long and am trying to order my life in such a manner that I may be ready to obey the summons when it comes." And even without these evidences, how could we believe that so bright a spirit as his could ever be quenched in utter darkness. Without this faith his loss to us would be almost unbearable. But now, we feel that he is not "lost" but simply "Gone before us."

Irving, would this source of comfort be ours now, if we're forced to give you up forever? Could you say, at any moment, "I am equally ready for life or death?" It would be an assurance that we should prize beyond anything you could give us. It is not believed that poor Walter lived many minutes after he was shot, but I would give anything in the world to have been with him at that time to have learned his last thoughts and to have heard him say what his countenance expressed so plainly — "All is well."

Cousin Will Cloud and Henry Kline came up as escort to the hearse and from the former we had the particulars which I have here given you. Cousin Ed Buck was here, also yesterday. It would have seemed fitting that dying as Walter did on the battlefield Walter should have been buried with military honors, but I do not know that this would have been his wish. He always said — "Put me away as quietly as possible" and never desired display in any way.

I have written you so very minutely because I judge you by myself in thinking you wish to know everything concerning one so dear to us all. We were just closing a long letter to Alvin when the first tidings reached us Monday and we were unable to give him any details, so you perhaps had best forward this letter to him as it will give him a fuller account than we shall be able to furnish him soon. This has been written under considerable difficulty as I've interrupted, I think fifty times since commencing.

We've had no letters for nearly two weeks, the mails are so irregular. Do write us very often. Every link broken from the chain that binds us closer in affection with those that remain, and we shall feel more anxious than ever, about you now. General Cleburne has the reputation of being such a daring officer, I'm afraid he will be as reckless of his staff as he is about his own safety. Be brave, but not rash. Above all, do not allow excitement or pleasure to make you forget that this life is only a preparation for that which is to follow.

Alvin and Walter are associated so closely together in our minds, and in some respects resemble each other so much in character, that we cannot help feeling more than usually anxious about the former, as long as this sickly season of the South continues. Dear brother, I do want to see you more than I can tell and it is hard to be so long separated from you with so little prospect of seeing you again. There is

Scott too, who always reminds me of Walter and he was very sad the last time he was at home. This cruel war! I sometimes wonder what we really had to trouble us before it developed —. We are all well but very, very sad. All unite in love to you and in begging you to take care of yourself.

May God bless and protect my brother —

Ever the prayer of your dearest sister,

Lucie

Later — the mail has just brought your favor of the 12th thanks for the autograph. I must let this postscript be my reply, as this letter is already unreasonably long. I'm sad to know you are suffering from an ailment which generally afflicts me every week and this neuralgia is not confined to my temples, by any means. My face is now swollen from tooth-ache of some days duration. I want to tell you that I have just received from "Dear Nannie" such

(the rest of this letter is missing)

Bel Air

Monday, July 27, 1863

My own dear Irvie,

Your letter to me of the 7th reached us on Thursday having been over two weeks on the way. I suppose it must have laid over at Luray. it was the first we had had from you for more than a month and knowing your usual punctuality were at a loss to account for your silence, especially as Mrs. Roy had received several from Benton. we had heard that someone had seen in the papers that General Cleburne was dead and we could not help feeling some uneasiness although I searched the papers diligently and could see nothing of it. am glad to find it untrue. we had seen but little of the skirmishing out there as our papers are so irregular. we do not get one fourth that we're due. Front Royal has become a place of importance it would seem in military affairs. since I last wrote you only a few days ago nearly all of our army has again passed through. it commenced on Tuesday morning the 17th regiment being in advance it would have saddened you to have seen how it had been reduced. it did not stop in town but went right out by Dr. Dorsey's and engaged the enemy near Happy Creek station where they were trying to get through by Manassas' Gap to intercept the passage of our army through Chester's Gap. they skirmished all day and succeeded in driving them back through the Gap. we had three men wounded they lost a number killed and wounded — in the meanwhile our army was passing as rapidly as possible. on Thursday evening there seemed to be every prospect of a considerable battle the enemy were said to be in force and we knew our men would certainly contest their coming. we were sitting on the house late in the evening watching our men who had covered the fields around Johnston's Lake. we could distinctly see the men, horses and artillery. the musketry had been incessant all the evening. suddenly we saw an immense column of white smoke arise accompanied by a flash. the boys exclaimed theres the cannon. I tell you there was old scampering off the house but we soon all returned accompanied by two of General Wright's staff who were anxious to see. we watched it til nearly night. after we went to bed, Johnston's division under Ewell passed here and camped in our field but in the morning all had gone up the Luray road and so nothing of the army could be seen but a few cavalry. soon after firing commenced again just out by Dr. Turner's and this side. our men were seen riding in various directions and in a little while we were again startled by the booming of cannon on the hill above Aunt Letitia's old house. all the time the guns were going pretty briskly. we went down into the basement but did not stay long as we were too curious to see what was going on. it did not last long as it was only intended by our men to detain them til the army was out of the way. as soon as they accomplished this our men left and the yankees came dashing in to find our men. we could see them galloping in all directions and firing as our men would ride ahead of them. but it all amounted to nothing as they only took two of our men and we took three of theirs. they went to Rose Hill and took the only two old horses Cousin E. had and all of her bacon but four pieces and were very insulting. they have ruined nearly everyone in their track. took all of Dr. Dorsey's horses but the old black mare. killed every hog, sheep, turkey, geese, chicken and duck, all of their preserves and pickles and did not leave them an ounce of meat even for dinner. destroyed their garden and took his nieces nightclothes, put them on and walked about the house. Mrs. D. asked what they wanted with the clothes. they "said" to tear up for towels. they cursed her to every thing they could think of. they went to the poor man's near there who had two children, broke up every piece of furniture, ripped open their beds, tore up all their clothing and left nothing but their house and so they did as far down as we can hear of. they fought all around Johnson Lakes - George Armstead's and Dr. Dorsey's. we lost on Thursday about two or three hundred. the yankee officers own to two hundred in killed but 'tis said they lost about five hundred. the ground now is covered with horses lags and many yet not buried. they did not remain long in town and did not disturb anyone. went to Mr. Cook's and saw Giles at the table but did not molest him though he told them he was a soldier. only two were in our yard and they came for water. 'tis said if our army had been one day later in crossing they would have come in here in full force and played the wiles. they expected to capture our wagon trains and pontoons but they missed it. we have a good many wounded in town - the hotel is full but most of them are slight and they are all cheerful and say they never saw such a place for kindness. the people do all they can but haven't in their power to do much. for it is all the time one army or the other and in truth we've found a great difference in our men since going into Pennsylvania. the first night they came here they broke open our dairy, took out every drop of milk, cream, butter and even the crocks cream jar and cream jug and that after we fed them as long as we could find anything to give. we were very much provoked at first but often seeing their sufferings I could not blame them. many of them had been for days with nothing to eat strange to say they said they did not find provisions as plentiful in Pennsylvania as expected and that was one reason we did not stay there longer but you would be amused to hear the boys tell how the women were scared and how they brought out all their nice things and begged for them not to burn their barns. they said they had nothing to do but to call for a matchbox and they could get anything they wanted. we had many of our army acquaintances to call among them, Mr. Herbert and his friend. I believe Lucy wrote you about him. Mr. McCaulley of Huntsville was wounded and left at Gettysburg but the best of it we had our dear old chief General Lee. he with his staff called and staid about half an hour. the family were charmed with him. he drew Lucy up by his side like she had been his daughter and _____ the girls and had them to play for him. he is a specimen of a real gentleman as well as patriot and we do feel proud of him and I think justly. I trust he may be spared to see the end of this struggle and reap the reward of his labors. I do not think it will be many days before we will have another big battle over the ridge somewhere. I forgot to tell you that on Tuesday Scott Roy mistook a squad of yankees for our men and did not find it out til he was a prisoner - but they did not keep him long as he made his escape on Wednesday night bringing a yankee horse with him. he says the major and the captain were very kind to him and gave him the best they had to eat. he told them he was going to get away and that when they came to town they must call on his Fathers and get their dinners. your uncle Mack and _____ witnessed all of the fight on Tuesday. Dick called and took leave of us. Newt Cloud called to see us the other day - he saw poor John Johnson after he was shot says he never saw anyone suffer as he did — he took Charlie Henry out of the road after he was wounded. he lived two days. he saw Tom Buck two days after he was shot - says he was very cheerful but his wound was such the doctors say nine cases out of ten they will not recover. we have not heard from him since. Sandy was slightly wounded also Henry Heater, Rush Lacy was not killed but is very sick. Little Carrie Buck is married to Major Hill on General Holmes staff. Estie Buck is very low. your Uncle Mack has gotten Walter's horse. I do not expect ever to hear from our servants. 'tis said all the contraband in Greencastle were recaptured by the _____. your father has sent to Colonel Larue for a woman and we expect her this evening unless the yankees prevent it. we may look for them in any and all times now as there is nothing to prevent it but I do not think they will be here much. hope they will have something else to do O I am so tired of this war which separates us from our loved ones. Jimmy Blakemore called to see us the other day. Will Cloud has acted very bravely on several occasions lately. Cousin Bet calls her baby Walter Buck. Cattie Samuels has a <u>daughter</u>. I wish you could see our Frank. he is so good I do not know what we should do if he was not. he is talking so sweetly and calls all of our names and brother Abby and brother Irby. Evred too is much better since the darkees left. remember us to Mr. Pearre - when the yankees came in his likeness is one of the first things secured. Bailey Jacobs was wounded at Gettysburg and was brought to Winchester and died in a few days. the skirmish here is considered a very considerable affair. 'tis said when Meade heard of our safe arrival over the mountain he was nearly crazy. he was sure of taking Ewell. had a letter from Alvin a few days ago - wish we could hear from Charleston. we have had rumors it had fallen — but don't believe - 'tis now thought the great battle will be in Mississippi - write as often as you can and may you be kept from all danger and you have a speedy and safe return home — prays your Mother,

EAB *(Elizabeth Ashby Buck)*

P.S. Love from all to you and affectionate remembrances to our friends and relatives who may be near you — all friends in usual health. the girls saw Mrs. Roy at church on Sunday quite an event for her. Estie it is thought cannot live till morning. Horace has been complaining for two weeks - your letter of the 3rd just at hand. Mrs. R. had one from Benton on the 16th.

Tyner's Station, Tennessee

Head Quarters
Cleburne's Division
Tyner's Station
August 8, 1863

My Dear Lu,

Ma's letter of the 27th July reached me three days ago, relieving me very much as I was apprehensive that Front Royal was reoccupied and our correspondence for a while cut off, I had delayed writing from day to day, in hopes that I would receive one so as to reply.

I had noticed in the papers an account of the engagement of Wright's Brigade with the Enemy at Manassas Gap, but had no idea that it was Chester's instead and so near home, the position near Johnson Lakes is to the best of my recollection a very favorable one for a fight, and the gullies could well be used as rifle pits — To you all from the house top, it must have been intensely exciting. Front Royal will have been quite a prominent place, after the war. However I believe the whole country from Richmond to the Potomac is one immense battle field — General Lee made a fortunate escape. We have sometimes indulged the hope that we would be sent to assist him. How I wish Hills Corps would be assigned to the Valley.

Was in Chattanooga day before yesterday and took dinner with Cousin G.W.B. He made enquiry after you all — he had not heard from Hopkinsville for a long while — he is very uneasy about Cousin Alick who was with Morgan in his Indiana and Ohio raid and from whom he has not heard for six weeks, he fears he has been killed or captured, I think the latter is very probable. *(Alex Blakemore was captured and imprisoned at Camp Chase.)*

Received a letter from Benton a few days ago, he is not at all pleased with Mississippi, and gave a gloomy account of every thing. Gen'l. Hardee was in command of the entire Army, in absence of Gen'l. Johnston, who was in Mobile. Scotts'[19] usual good fortune seems to attend him. I believe this is the second time he has escaped from the Yankees.

Am truly sorry to hear of Bailey Jacob's[20] death — he had some noble traits and he was his worst enemy. Was he still Captain or had he been promoted?

It was reported, about the time of the Liberty Gap fight, that General Cleburne was killed, the Yankees are determined if they cannot kill him in reality they will in imagination, on paper, but he is alive and will worry them yet before he "gives up". His men are very fond and proud of him, and call him "old Pat, old Dad" etc.

Was very much surprised to hear of Corrie Buck's marriage — she was a little girl when I last met her, but a very sweet one, and I have no doubt will make a good wife.

Did you hear anything from Ella Price while the route was open to Winchester?

174

Tell me all you know of her, as Lt. Jetton is getting very importunate on this subject — and talks strongly about accompanying me home next winter. He seems very much attached to her, despite two or three other sweethearts of his, scattered over various portions of Tennessee. You need not tell Miss Ellen this, should you chance to meet her, as it is a soldiers prerogative.

In a recent letter to Alvin, which he enclosed to me, you speak of building certain "Chateaux" "to be occupied after the war" while for me, I am consigned to the cold walls of "bachelors' hall" on the ground that I "always seemed such a boy that to appreciate the idea of matrimony with me seems absurd" — this letter was not addressed to me it is true, but I cannot forebear to put my "shovel" in and protest against being so summarily disposed of. You have not seen me for a long time, and do not know what a big ugly fellow I am, or how industriously I am cultivating my beard, and may surprise you yet by beating Alvin in the matrimonial race, at least some of my friends predict it for me — but to tell the truth I love every pretty girl too much to tie to any <u>one</u> now if they would let me have three or four (as they will after war) I might try it — But as it is I dream of Bachelors' halls, with Laura at the head of the domestic arrangements. Have always marked her out for the old maid of the family for two reasons — first, her industrious and housekeeping qualifications — and two because if she had a sweetheart and was engaged to him, I believe she would whip him before the marriage could be consumated unless, it was a very short engagement.

Gen'l. Hill has a pleasant staff, his Adjutant General, Lt. Col. Anderson, says he ate dinner at Bel Air, as the army retreated from Maryland last fall. His other Adjutant — Major Cross was raised near White Post.

One of my old school mates, Tom Bartlett, is in the Ordinance Department at Chattanooga.

In a fit of remorse, occasioned by your letter, I wrote "Nannie" a long letter a day or two ago — but for a few insurmountable obstacles, I would give her a chance to call you "sister" very quick — this may as well be "<u>sub rosa</u>".

Have heard nothing from Alvin for over a week, will write and enclose him Ma's letter. One of my clerks is in Charleston, and will be back tomorrow or day after when I will hear by him.

Tyner is an awful dull place, no ladies at all. I amuse myself by reading, writing, riding.

Much love to all —

Hoping you may remain clear of the Yankees — and that our correspondence may be uninterrupted.

I am every your affectionate Brother
Irvie

And where her brothers were. She told him about you and then he said he was an old school mate of yours though he supposed she did not remember him. She replied that he really had the advantage of her and then he gave his name - "Thomas Pratt!" Wot ye ought of the man? He is in Anderson's division - Ewell's Corps. Mack Richardson (the youngest) is at home on parole - surrendered with the Army at Vickburg - have not seen him yet but hear that he gives a sickening account of their trials during the terrible siege - professes to relish mule meat very much. He says Marsh Blakemore was also in the surrender but he did not see him and did not know what became of him after he was made prisoner.

Alvin, you just ought to see Evred and Frank go in the creek and bathe - we put them in the race these warm evenings and they swim, splash, and paddle to their hearts content crying bitterly when taken out. Often when it is sultry and feverish — Frank takes me by the hand and leading toward the little gate looks coaxingly up into my face and says "Wash - wattie". Evred came running up to the porch the other evening where Mr. Berry and all of us were seated exclaiming gleefully - "Oh Mr. Burry. You just might see me swim" and then went on to give a description of the modus operandi to Mr. Berry's infinite amusement.

The 24th - Was interrupted the other evening by the Misses Marshall coming in to spend the evening and not having had an opportunity either of finishing my letter or sending it out I've just kept it in reserve. There's a mail in but it brings us nothing from you. Oh! <u>What</u> can be the cause of such long silence? Do you know the 25th of the next month is my birthday that I shall be free, white and 21! Now Alvin, I want you like a dear good brother so you are to celebrate my arrival at majority by sitting down and writing me a good long letter - remember such and epoch occurs but once in a lifetime and I never forget to observe <u>all</u> your birthdays - HEIGH HO! almost a spinster! I can scarce believe it — not that I don't <u>feel</u> old enough, but then the years of my life are so entirely barren of any fruit - I have been gleaning so little of the harvest for the "mental bread of life" that it seems almost incredible that 21 years have been trifled away. Isn't it a humiliating thought for me that should I cease to exist today there is not one who could say - "My life was the brighter for hers!" But a truce to moralizing.

Did you observe our national "fast day"? We did - in the <u>letter</u>. I mean, am afraid the spirit was somewhat wanting to make it perfect. Mr. Berry preached and I could not help but think of you and Irvie as I sat there in the old church and wonder whether you were mindful of the day and were even then celebrating so -- we were _____ your thoughts of us. 'Tis not very probable that you <u>did</u>, as I believe such customs are not generally adhered to by the military in general.

T'was too bad your disappointment with regards the position on Stuart's staff. Never mind, I hope by some means you may be able to get a position in our army of the Potomac - the glorious army of Lee that <u>never has been</u> whipped. OH! I do so want you and Irvie to be in that noble army. I would rather were I a soldier, a Virginian, be a private there than a private's Captain in any other army the sun ever shown on. Still you don't forget the old trite copyplate "act well your part" whatever it may be on the stage of life. "<u>There</u> all the honor lies." You've one proud memory connected with this war should you never occupy any other situation than your present one - You were in the first grand act of the tragedy - the Battle of Manassas - there of your own free will and choice. Ah, me! I fear you may have ample time for promotion and risk enough yet before this horrid war is over for peace seems to have been so afrightened as to be shy of returning to us again and when it does come twill not restore to us our loved and lost those who've died to win it. I often think how sad will be the in coming of the few friends that will remain to us after the war, how different their return from what we're so often pictured it, when we thought of welcoming with you and Irvie and two other brothers, Richard and Walter. Dear Walter, he will not have to witness the mournful changes, will not grieve for the grasp.

Harrison's Landing, Tennessee

Enclosed is several autograph letters, to add to the others I have sent

Head Quarters, Cleburne's Division
Harrison's Landing
Augt 29th, 1863

My Dear Lucie,

The first mail we have had for ten days reached us today, while in the middle of our soup and molasses, bringing your welcomed letter of the 9th, I wrote Ma a hasty note several days ago giving a statement of our move from Graysville to this point, at the time it was written a battle was considered as imminent — it had not transpired, although the enemy is still in our front and shells our position every day or two — but so far have succeeded in killing only one man, a sharp shooter attached to these head quarters, he was shot through the brain several days ago, but strange to say survived until a few hours ago. Gen'l. Cleburne was watching the firing of one of their batteries yesterday, when they threw a shell which fell about three feet in front of him, but fortunately did not explode. I was not with him at the time as I was in bed with a high fever and head ache. Am afraid his intrepidity will cause his death yet. A battle may be fought any day. I think they will certainly attempt to cross the Tennessee, and if so we will just as certainly pitch into them. I do not care how soon we get at it so it is a general affair — do not mind it half as much as I do this petty fighting.

Your description of the Sabbath on which you were writing recalled to mind vividly some I have passed at Bel Air, I sometimes wonder if you have such Sundays now as we used to, the sun always seemed to shine bright at that time than any other (and the fish to bite better) sotto voce.

We are almost out of the world here, we get the paper occasionally, and learn just enough to wish to hear more. I have not made a single female acquaintance, not wishing to have the pleasant memories of Chattanooga, so I am tuned with new acquaintances. We were exceedingly kindly treated in C — and the wife of a man who has been ordered from home by the Confederate Authorities, on account of his union proclivities _____ was foremost in extending to us hospitalities — and has offered to attend me in case of a wound.

It seems singular to hear you speak of the capture of a robber chief in the Fork. Poor Walter and I used to picture in our imaginations during our moonlight strolls from Mr. Halls to Front Royal, that the caves on the river were the rendezvous of bandits and speculate what we would do as weary travellers in case of an attack, we little thought that in a few short years the idea would be more than probable — and that robbers would really be _____ in the Fork. Front Royal has become classic why may not the "Fork" be the scene of some of same story! the "Forty thieves" for instance. (I am sure there is fifty in it), suppose that Dick Lovelace or Otho Ridgeway, to be the wood chopper Alibabi — and discover the secret cave and the "open sesami" why not? there is all the material even down to the honest (?) cobbler (Capp) — Tell Laura she will have to commence a second series of *The Arabian Nights.*

The country above this and just across the river is infested with just such bands as you describe, only worse, they are made up of deserters from both Armies and Navy and rob indiscriminately, they are called "bush whackers" and when caught are shown no mercy but hanged to the first limb.

Where is Mrs. Morehead? When you write to Alice remember me with kindness — what has become of Fannie Maddux? Tell Alice if she is in Salem to give her my love.

Oh I must tell you I have the nicest little Tennessee sweet heart you ever saw, she lives in Chattanooga, is almost sixteen years old, is not very pretty, but so sweet and so lady like in her manners Gen'l. Cleburne says she is the image of myself, of course if this is so she is not beautiful and it would seem very poor taste in me, but I cannot see the likeness and it is all right, her name is Ida — pretty isn't it — she will be just the right age for me when I have made my fortune after the war is over. I felt some apprehension on her account after the shelling in Chattanooga, and as my friend Lieut. Hanly would say, I "jerked her a few lines" asking her how she came out of the "grand ball so unexpectedly opened in Chattanooga by Mons Rosencrantz" and received the gratifying intelligence that body and bones were all safe.

Am happy to hear of the recovering of Esten Buck — was afraid his case was all a desperate one. How I would like to spend one quiet day at Clover Hill, with Uncle Fayette and family.

You speak of a new "help" who or what is it? Hope it may be something to relieve you of some of the drudgery of the housework. While it is gratifying to know that you can meet such exigencies it is at the same time anything but pleasant for me to reflect that it is necessary for you all to submit to it.

General Cleburne is sitting in the opposite side of the table under a tent fly answering a letter written in a very delicate hand I strongly suspect that Mars is yielding a little to Venus. I often think of all my relatives, one by one and amuse myself at, or admire some peculiar trait of _ and I long for the time when I shall see them all. Such reflections invariably lead to sad thoughts as the various _____ are connected with some pleasant event passed in what some persons who participated ere no more — primarily among these is the memorable sleigh ride we had to Mrs. Hall's that beautiful moonlight night. You remember Willie Richardson and I, Nellie and yourself went up in the sleigh and met Cous Will, Clara and Walter — and as we returned, the songs we sang; four lighter hearts did beat than ours that night — we returned to Rose Hill and remained until next day — two of us out of that four have already fallen in this war.

What became of Tom Buck who was wounded at *(Fairfield, PA.)* ?

Enclosed I send my notification of appointment. It was made out through a clerical error for "SA Buck". I have a corrected copy in which my name is written in full, and the date of appointment goes back to the 13th of December, the date of the Generals, — I wish you to keep this for me.

Love to one, and all relatives.

Ever your affectionate Brother

"Irvie"

Was a little unwell, a couple of days ago, but have entirely recovered. Mr. Pearre wishes to be remembered.

Bel Air _____

September 13, 1863

My dear Irvie,

I have been thinking so much about you in the last two weeks and have heard nothing from you so long I have concluded to write to you today to send out by the first mail. the papers all seem to coincide in their belief that a great battle <u>is</u> to <u>be</u> fought near you if it has not already taken place and it is but natural that we should feel anxious about you. though we know you are as safe now as you have ever been. you have the same kind protection who has hitherto watched over you and has kept you safe through <u>dangers</u> seen and unseen and I trust will continue to shield you and while His protecting care is over you there is <u>no</u> <u>thing</u> can harm and to him I try to commit your keeping and feel that I am so ungrateful for the many blessings I have enjoyed that I fear many of them may be taken from me. we wait most anxiously from day to day for news from Charleston and Chattanooga and each day brings disappointment we do not average more than one mail a week and when they come bring papers from one to two weeks old. our last letter from Alvin was the second of July. we received three papers from him last week of the 24th-29th. I expect in the great excitement there he has but little opportunity for writing. we greatly fear for Charleston. have every confidence that our loved and brave General will do all that man can do to save the city - should it fall I do not know where they will go — to some place of importance and danger. I feel of sured. our army here gives us comparatively little concern. skirmishes occur almost daily and some prisoners are constantly taken. several squads from below taken by White and Moseby have passed through here. Mount has been on detailed service and was with them when they were taken. he was here this week and is more fleshly than I have ever seen him. his regiment is about Culpepper Courthouse. it is rumored that General Jones has resigned General Lomax takes his place. Henry Buck is at home — has been in company T(?) since the first ____ fight. he has I suppose done as little in this war as any man in it. your Uncle John says he is the only one of the name he is ashamed of.

Little Walker had been very ill and your Uncle John has been down to see him he only staid two days as the yankees were all around there. he returned on Wednesday - has been up at your Uncle Mack's since day before yesterday — he left Walker better. he is looking as well as I ever saw him. he does not live quite as high as he did at the Howard and it agrees with him. your Uncle Larue and Aunt Cattie have been very ill but have recovered. Julia Buck is there. Mack Irwin is more desperately in love than you ever saw one. he goes down about once a week to see her and seems the chance of being taken by the yankees — poor fellow he is in dreadful health. I came upstairs this morning and had a few moments of quiet and wrote the above — since then your Uncle John, Dick, Lucy and Nellie who have been up at the mountain for several days came in then down went the pen and we fixed for church — when we got on the pavement we met your Father and Uncle Tom just from town who said Mr. Berry did not preach and as it was quarterly meeting knew there would be a crowd at the Methodist church so concluded to stay home and enjoy their company. then followed a general confusion - the boys with the addition of Russell and Bob Buck so you may know what chance there has been for writing. your Father and Uncle John have gone over with your Uncle Tom. the boys have gone to play - Dick I found upstairs in the little room so I have followed them up and am now sitting by the window while the girls are showing Dick their little mementos and treasures. Dick has been home nearly two weeks and will be here a week longer. he is engaged in the _pleasant_ duty of getting absentees from the company of whom there are a few. he sends many kind remembrances to you and wishes much to see you. he is looking very well talks a great deal of poor Walter and reminds me so much of him. it is really touching to see the feeling manifested for him by the community especially the poor - dear boy, may he rest in peace. Charlie Richardson just was up here. you know he hurt his hand very badly — still has no use of it. Fielding Calmes of Clarke and Mack Richardson have raised a company here — Fielding is Captain, Mack First Lt. Little Mack is with them. they have detailed for this county. Alice Parkins jumped on a horse a few weeks ago and in folly attempted to ride under a shed — it was too low and she was pressed between it and her saddle and mashed her dreadfully. it is said that it was only three to five inches between her saddle and the shed so you may imagine how she was bruised and crushed. her spine was dreadfully broken. I heard that the doctor said if she kept perfectly quiet she _might_ be propped up in bed in three _months_. poor girl she is I suppose, a cripple for life. Cousin Bett had a letter from Mack Bayly last week saying Sam Buck had joined the Presbyterian Church. I knew that he had professed a hope but was surprised at his joining that church. have not heard the particulars yet. Sandy has recovered and is in Richmond awaiting his furlough having been exchanged. Tom is still in Gettysburg - Josey Grantham is in and saw him and says he was very cheerful and anxious to be in the army. the ball has not been extracted yet and he suffers a great deal — but we now hope he will recover though at first it was not then thought possible. Mary Ann Lionberger was married a few weeks ago to Willie Harris who is some years younger. he is a son of William A. Harris, former member of Congress. they were married in the morning and he started in an hour or so for the army. Fanny Buracre is to be married to her cousin young Wheat. she went to Maryland this spring and bought all of her wedding finery and had all of her trunks stolen. Alice 'tis said is to marry Pitman Carter, a son of the Mrs. W.A. Carter near New Town. Flora is said also to be much admired — their father has made an unexpected fortune since the war — has or expects to buy 3 elegant farms. the whole of Page County 'tis said is engaged in speculation. Mr. Borst 'tis said has made over a hundred thousand dollars. Susie Tyler is on a visit at Dr. Turner's. Charlie Leach Miss Tensias beau is a prisoner in Fort Delaware. Nellie received a letter from Henry Heate the other day but since saw him at our Uncle Macks — he has been wounded. Lucy received a long letter from Nannie Taylor the other day. she is in Campbell country visiting a friend. she said she received a short letter from you just before leaving Richmond. the first she had had for months so short she did not know whether to answer it or not. I fear she feels your neglect. she still expresses the greatest anxiety to visit Front Royal says her mother and Clara were much pleased in Danville. she is a nice affectionate girl. Lucie says she has a good scold for you. the sick and wounded have been taken from town except one at Mr. Overall's and one at your Uncle Tom's a Mr. Buchanan a member of the seventeenth. he is from Alex. Miss Mary Simpson has opened a select school in town. twelve scholars, Elisa Hope and Ginnie Jackson are among them — both are thinking too much of other things to learn much. Lucy had two large teeth drawn the other day and I hope now she will suffer less with neuralgia, though has several others that ought to be out — hard work agrees with her. she has fattened and I think is in better health. I have been so fortunate in getting one of the best girls she is Lucy the sister of your Uncle Macks William. he sold her to Mr. Green and Laura now owns her. she reminds me so much Eliza Ann — but is more active. I fear I cannot keep her long and Laura wants her now and will go to housekeeping as soon as she can get a house. I shall regret giving her up so much that it is the misfortune of not owning them. I dream so much of ours, but if I had Eliza Ann and the money for the others they might go and welcome. I have such a miserable pen and ink I can hardly form a letter — but hope you may be able to read. I wish you could only join the group I have named. when will it ever be that we shall have our loved ones with us again? where is Mr. Pearre and have you heard from Sandy? all join in much love to you. we are still waiting anxiously to hear from you. may God bless my dear boy asks his mother,

E.A.B. *(Elizabeth Ashby Buck)*

Dear Alvin,

Ma's writing you, but as she has not time to elaborate much she's going to give you the general sober news and I'll do the gossiping.

You don't know how refreshing it is to hear from you once more through Mr. Bowman as it has been about three months since we had any tidings from you. Glorious old Sumpter! Unyielding to the last and three times three for our noble Beauregard! How his name trembles on our lips mingled with blessings and prayers. May he cull such laurels from those sea islands as will completely overshadow the hard learned ones of Manassas memory. We've written and rewritten you all without eliciting one word of reply until last Saturday when the mail came in again minus a letter. I told Nellie I would certainly do something desperate if such a course of proceedings continued. But we know you are well, have not been thrown into the ranks by the new order relative to clerks etc. etc. and that you're a terrible nice fellow after all. It's all such good news. Irvie too is getting lazy - nearly four weeks now and no letter. Don't you feel sorry for us?

"All's quiet on the Shennandoah" - not a Yankee has shown his face in our midst since they "caught a Tartar" here in Chester's Gap — at least none save prisoners. It's almost too monotonous. Dick is at home and has been here alone for a fortnight conscripting. I rather think his recruiting has been carried on more successfully in Salem than here - at least 'tis very certain he values the little black-eyed conscript from Salem more than all the mountaineers together. You would be sure to think he and Sue Bayley were "one anither's ain" could you see them together. She has been here a week now and will probably remain some time. Has improved very much since you saw her - we expected her down on Thursday after Dick leaves. Poor fellow! How we shall miss him when he's gone! So free and affectionate such a noble boy as he is and all the dear boy we've got to love in Virginia now - Walter and Richard together.

You heard that Sandie Buck was wounded at Gettysburg and left in the enemy's hands? Well he has recovered been paroled and is now at home. He called here with Charlie Richardson last week looks quite well and gave some interesting particulars of his visit "___ Robin Hood's barn" as the "Northern Tory" is described. While in confinement on Davis' Island he met with Mrs. Wheat by formally Miss Ella Bowen of this place and she told him she wished she dared say all she wished - but told him her sympathy was all for us and that she only wanted to be down South now. Sam Buck has joined the Presbyterian church. I'm so glad. Mrs. Kiger, who is in the neighborhood, had a letter a short time since from Cousin Thomas Blakemore in which he speaks of Angie Smith having been married on the 20th of August to a Mr. Lincoln of Plattsburg, MO. Poor Angie! To think of her having to go through life burdened with such an infamous name. I pity her sincerely. Yesterday I called at

Mrs. Robert Turner's to see Ginnie Davidson and Mrs. Baker (Lou Davidson). The little Baker was of course introduced — a sober, sensible juvenile of six months blue-eyed and full faced looking grave as with the responsibility he has assumed in having put upon him such a name as "Jacob Christian" - yes "Jacob Christian Baker" - was ever such an unChristian name heard of? And is it any wonder that that baby should be grave? The mama is looking more interesting than ever and is apparently a quite sensible mother making no fuss over the child but not by any means indifferent. While upon the subjects of your old "flames" did you ever suspect what a warm admirer you have in one of the fair damsels of this place - even Miss Ann Eliza Scroggins? I had often been puzzled to know why she was so very obsequious to me as I have never tried to render myself particularly agreeable and while drawing some flattering inferences from the fact out came the secret - "How more you are like your brother <u>Alvin</u>?" And now it matters not where I meet her, if she can manage to edge in a question crosswise 'tis invariably — "When did you hear from your brother Alvin? Where was he? - how is he? You look so much like him." She almost had a "duckfit" over Evred the other day when Ma had him in town with her because he was the "image of his brother Alvin!" We all laugh about this mania of hers but 'tis wrong I'm afraid, the poor girl she has few enough to show her any favors so 'tis not strange that she should hold in grateful ___ one who was kind and polite as she says you were always to her while in the store here. "Cast thy bread upon the waters," "Send forth the word it shall not return unto you void."

I've written so much nonsense and now I'm too sleepy to follow it up by something better — the letters are all dancing "perpetual motion at a great ___ before my eyes." Oh! I forgot to tell you that Orville was going to school to Cousin Sue Buck and is very much pleased. I think he will learn very quickly now at least hope he will.

I wish we had something nice to send you by Mr. Bowman but until you all lick the blockade at Charleston I'm afraid we will not be able to find material for doing work for you again shortly. We send you our best love, our wishes — a package of each and prayers that you may be blessed and protected now and ever.
Yours fondly,
Lucie

Bel Air, Monday, October 19, 1863
My Dear Child, *(Alvin)*

It appears almost useless for us to write as it seems our letters never reach their destination. still I can not find us making the effort to finding <u>some</u> may by chance get through. it has been now nearly five months since we had a letter from you and none from Irvie since the eighth of August. you cannot imagine our uneasiness on his account particularly since the battle we had all taken up the notion that he had fallen - we saw in the paper that General Cleburne was wounded and know that Irvie must have been in great danger — and we have been in the most painful suspense til a few days ago Miss Mary Simpson received a letter from George Williams saying he was safe but that a ball had passed through his cap. oh what cause of thankfulness that he was spared. we tried to realize the worst and I believe did as near as could be. and O what a void it seemed to make in our feelings one that could not be filled. he is a dear boy and I pray God if it is his will he may be spared to us. it is so strange that we cannot receive our letters. Mrs. Roy gets hers regularly and others too. I sometimes think that someone must have a hand in preventing it — but Mrs. Hope cannot hear from George. I suppose Mr. Bowman has gotten out ere this and our letters by him reached you. we have had no yankees yet. they occasionally make a dash into Winchester but only remain a few hours. Imbodans command passed here last week and we heard yesterday that they were in Charlestown fighting. we had a fight at Brandy Station last Sunday in which poor Tom Marshall was killed and Tom and Newt Petty were slightly wounded. Tom left a wife and a very interesting little boy. they are at his father's. his remains were brought home. they staid in town all night and had another coffin made and redressed him in his wedding suit. your Uncle Tom saw him and says he looked perfectly natural poor fellow. he only lived three hours. we had a fight at the same place some weeks ago in which Chew's Battery lost a gun and Willie Buck was taken but was released upon the _____ in that he was only one of the boys and he has been in the yankee lines at Culpepper Courthouse ever since til last week. we drove them from there and a negro informed on Willie and they took him. we do not know where he is. Tom Buck has gotten home and is well. his is a most remarkable recovery as no one thought he could live. I wish we could see him. I know he had his own fun while a prisoner. Robert and Smith Turner are both at home. Smith has come for clothing for the company. they are now at Petersburg and expect to remain there some time. they went to Tennessee and were in the Zolicoffer fight. Mr. Davidson has lost one of his daughters (Cornelia). she was seventeen years old. Mrs. Baker (Lou) and her little boy have been at Mrs. T.'s for some time. the yankees broke them up — he is chaplain. Old Mrs. Lahew died this week and I suppose the Boones will be a little higher than ever as I expect they will get some money. though I do not know how she left things. we had a freshet two weeks ago and it took our dam entirely off. it is particularly unfortunate at this time as Lewis Smith has a machine for our crushing sugar cane there and it has stopped it for the time. he has made some mighty fine molasses. we have not made ours yet — will do so as soon as the dam is finished — it would have been done on Saturday but for its raining. there will be a great deal of molasses made in this neighborhood — and it will be a great thing for the people. your Father cut his foot very badly three weeks ago and has not been able to get about much since he rode to town today for the first time it being court. Lucy went up to Cousin Sam Buck's on Saturday with Emma. I wish you could witness some of the girls working

185

operations. I think they will be quite adept after awhile. I forget to tell you that Angie Smith is married to a Mr. Lincoln, a cousin of old Abe's 'tis thought she has done well she says though a cousin of his <u>he is all right</u>. she was married twentieth of August — since writing the above Imboden's men have returned and encamped on the other side of the river. they went to Charlestown — drove the Yankees out and took 432 prisoners. they remained in town several hours but the yankees reinforced and they had to retreat with their prisoners. two Baltimorians staid here last night. they came out last Monday - do continue to write and maybe we may get them sometime and when you do mention George hope his mother seems hurt when we get a letter and you say nothing about him. all join in much love to you. we fear for Charleston but hope for the best. may Heavens blessing rest on you and may you be kept in safety and the time not be far distant when we shall meet again prays your fond mother.

E.A.B. *(Elizabeth Ashby Buck)*

Should this reach you and you to be able to communicate with dear Irvie tell him how anxious we are about him and that we have had no letter from him since 8th of August — but have written to him constantly and fear he has not gotten them.

October 23, 1863

Dear Alvin,

We have written you so often apparently to no purpose — that there's but little encouragement to try again but I will as Smith Turner goes to Petersburg tomorrow and will mail it for me there. We think perhaps the obstruction of our mail communications lies somewhere between here and Richmond so that we can get a letter posted at some other point nearer the latter place there may be some chance of your receiving it. There must be a great deal of repetition in our letters as we do not know which of them you will receive and sometimes for fear you may not hear what we wish you to repeat some portions of the former letters. Ma wrote you two or three days since by mail and it has been but a short time previous to that that I sent you one. When do you suppose we had letters from you? <u>Four months</u> since - and nearly three since we had any from Irvie. Mr. Bowman told us you had written so when we didn't receive your letter instead of quarreling you for a negligent fellow we abuse the whole race of mail contractors. We have even gone so far as to accuse some unknown enemy of intercepting our letters — it seems so strange that everyone but ourselves should receive favors by mail. We were so uneasy about Irvie after the battle of Chickamauga, but we have since learned how narrowly he escaped with a bullet through his cap. I tell you, Alvin, much as I desire to see your persevering efforts rewarded, much as I'd like to see you occupy the position your merits entitle you to — still I hardly know whether I would willingly have you exchange your present situation of comparative security for one of so much danger. That fortnight of miserable suspense after the battle has sickened me of glory. Ma told you how Father had been for several weeks confined to the house and grounds by a wound received on the foot from an ax with which he was endeavoring to cut up a rebellious log. That so nearly well now though and he walked to church on Sunday last.

A freshet which we had some weeks carried off the old dam leaving not a vestige of it. The bed of the creek was so completely changed by this removal that you would have scarcely recognized it for the same little Happy Creek of other days. However that too has been reconstructed and will have been completed in a day or two. The old mill has been converted into a molasses factory under the management of Mr. Lewis Smith (ahem!) and everything in the place seems quite a busy aspect whenever they're smashing and boiling down there. We have had some cornstalk syrup made which was quite nice and our little crop of sorghum will be worked up next week. Persons in the neighborhood are giving a great deal of attention to this branch of domestic manufacturing and generally the subject you hear broached when a couple of farmers or housewives meet is "How about your sorghum molasses?". We expect to subsist principally upon that this winter and if you come to see us we can give you a variety of molasses cakes and molasses candies, molasses sauces and even molasses pies! Will it be an inducement? I wish something would as Mr. Macauley says — "turn up" to afford us of an opportunity of seeing you before the Spring Campaigns open. Some persons seem to be of opinion that we will <u>have</u> no Spring Campaigns, that the American Eagle will droop his wings and retire to some obscure Northern _____ to in sullen anger over his defeated plans of subjugation long before that time. I'm afraid though that story is "over _____" to be true. But in sober earnest <u>don't</u> you think our Confederacy seems to be entering upon the Fall and Winter Campaigns with rather brighter prospects than heretofore? If Bragg can but (with General Longstreets's assistance) succeed in giving Rosecrans another blow with a rod of correction - I believe the tide would be turned completely in our favor and we might then begin to talk about "When this cruel War is over." We await in fear and trembling of the fate of Charleston, Vicksburg and Port Hudson have taught us to distrust the impregnability of our defenses anywhere. General Beauregard will do all in the power of mortal man I believe and we hope on while we fear. And even if she should fall — her defenders have already vindicated their prowess and skills in so many successfully repulsed attacks that 'twill detract nothing from their fame and add but little to the conquest of the enemy. We shall lose another seaport but 'twill enable us to concentrate our armies in the interior where defeat of the enemy will be almost inevitable. In Virginia we're quietly awaiting the issue of the shifting phases of affairs on the Rappahannock and trusting so implicitly in the success as to give ourselves little uneasiness save as to the lists of "Wounded and Slain".

Poor Lt. Thomas Marshall was killed in an engagement at Brandy Station almost two weeks since. Poor fellow! He was brought home, but they would not have him opened at Happy Creek although he was said to be looking very natural. His wife and little child were there at the time - had been staying there for some time but I suppose will return to her friend's in Woodstock as soon as possible. Old Mrs. Lehew died last week too. Poor old lady, her breath was scarcely out of her body ere her sister Mrs. Boone was up and demanding her _____ book of Mrs. Evalyne Jones in whose hands it had been placed by the deceased. Mrs. B has done herself but little credit in the affair and the whole town is ____ in it's censure of her unfeeling conduct. 'Tis not known, I believe, where there was any Will left, but 'tis generally supposed she desired the property to go to her stepchildren. I hope they'll get it for they're clever, deserving young men from all accounts — especially Wesley.

I just returned yesterday evening from several days visit to Emma at Cousin Sam Buck's and left Cousin Jim and Sandy Buck there when I came away. I wish you could see Cousin T and hear his account of his sojourn in Yankeedom. You know he was supposed to be mortally wounded at Gettysburg, but his animal spirits as much I believe as his strong constitution triumphed. He was in the hospital not expected to live in Fairfield near G., was from there sent to Balt. and Fort McHenry, thence from Fortress Monroe to Richmond and arrived at about nine o'clock one night last week. Cousin Lucy was upstairs when he arrived and hearing a voice below inquired if there was news from Tom and where he was. "Tom's here, Miss Lucy!" was the expected reply, and he said she just "pitched" downstairs and into his arms. He looks better - handsomer than I ever saw him yet is suffering very much still with the wound from which the bullet has not yet been extracted. Notwithstanding all this he could keep you in convulsions of laughter for a week straight ahead with his dry antidotes and descriptions of his imprisonment. Was very well and sometimes very kindly treated by both Succession sympathizers and "Union blues". He is one of the most genial, warmhearted fellows and I do admire him so much. Sandy is almost entirely recovered and is a very gentlemanly nice little fellow as straight and trim as a young pine and brave as Julius Caesar. Indeed, Alvin, we have some very brave young relatives. There's Charlie Richardson for instance, a reckless dissipated young fellow and yet as brave, generous and kindhearted a boy as ever lived. Uncle Fayette says he thinks he deserves the title of the "Hero on horseback" as rightly as Lamar Fontaine that of the "Hero on Crutches." He has not the use of either of his arms at all and his neck is almost useless to him yet in the army he will be and was very near being shot the other day at Warrington — the bullet entering and lodging in his saddle. Oh! if Henry Buck had only some of his daring! Mack Irwin went to Clarke a week ago to see Jule was there when Imboden had the skirmish at Charlestown — was in the melee and very near being struck by a shell and when our forces retired he came out with them. You would laugh to hear how he foiled the Yankees and frightened them out of stealing his horse with stories of the proximity of Gilmore and his "scouts".

The Warren Rifles were said to be at _____ Station near Suffolk. Smith Turner, who is in town, goes on to rejoin his regiment wherever it is, tomorrow and we are all busy making up dispatches to send by him. I've just finished a letter about as long as this and have another to write. Ma is writing to Irvie too. Nellie, lazy thing! won't take any of the family correspondence upon herself because, as she ____, "Alvin and Irving can't care much to receive her letters since they don't value them enough to answer them."

All friends at Clover Hill, Rose Hill, Bellemonte, Riverside, Mountain View and Oakley are well. I will not entreat you to write believing that you do so at any rate but let me suggest that you forward your next letter under cover to Clara Taylor at Danville, Virginia and request her to send it to us. I do not know her exact address but her mother is matron of the new hospital there and I think she would get it if you would direct *[it]* to her mother's care. Others of the boys have been sending letters through in that way and I don't see why you need not succeed as well as they. All the family well and unite with me in thousands of "good remembrances". God bless you dear boy.

Fondly,
Lucie

Bel Air, Sunday, November 8, 1863

Dear Alvin,

Nellie has written and has given you the little news — still I do not like for George to go without saying something to you as it seems a private conveyance is the only way of getting letters through. I am so glad George got home that his mother could see him for I fear it will be the last time, her health is so bad — but he has had but little satisfaction on account of the miserable yankees. they were here a day or two before he came and again yesterday. we never know when we are safe — and for this reason I cannot insist on you or Irvie coming home now — when you do come I want you to enjoy your society and have you to enjoy yourself. they took Mack Bayly yesterday and John Boone. Mack had only gotten home the night before. they also got our mail which I regret as it may have contained something for us. I think if you would write and direct it to us — and then enclose it in another envelope and direct to Miss Kate Graves with a note requesting her to forward we might get it — tis the only way letters reach here. she lives near Gordonsville. we have made you two merino shirts —thought they would save you washing and be warmer than white. they are not as nice as we could have wished were made in a great hurry. we send you four collars and two pairs of socks. the latter is a present from Cousin E. Richardson and were poor Willie's. they send their love with the request that you will wear them. it is a compliment as not many could have gotten them. I wish we could send you a pair of shoes or boots and a nice pair of pants but we did expect

George to stay long enough to have any made and it is almost impossible to get any kind of goods here. Lucy made you a cap that the materials were so indifferent she has declined sending it. I have a few plugs of tobacco which I wish to send — but am sorry you will use it — let me beg you to be moderate in its use — it is so high now and I am convinced it is injurious to you — George tells us you are looking thin. he was very kind in coming up to see us and let us hear from you though he had not seen you for some time.

Sue Bayly sends her love to you. she is an odd mixture but is a better girl than the world would give her credit for. when you write let us know when you heard from Ky. all join in much love to you. George can tell you much we can not write. I think he has improved. we are anxious for the fate of Charleston but trust to God and Beauregard. I must stop. may you ever be kept by an all wise and good God and may we soon meet again prays your

Mother E.A.B. *(Elizabeth Ashby Buck)*

---

[1] Bragg, who had retreated from Perryville, Kentucky, was at Murfreesboro, Tennessee along Stone River near Nashville. On January 2, 1863, Bragg struck the Union army and was successful in driving them back and winning a victory, but the next day he withdrew to Tullahoma, Tennessee.

U.S.A.		C.S.A.	
Effectives	41,400	Effectives	34,732
Killed	1,667	Killed	1,294
Wounded	7,543	Wounded	7,945
Missing	3,686	Missing	2,500

[2] Lucy R. Buck wrote in her diary, "Father came from the office bringing a paper and two letters — one from Nannie Taylor to me — one from Irvie to Nellie. I was almost beside myself with joy at their arrival particularly when upon reading Irvie's we learned that he had been promoted to the rank of Captain and AAG of General Cleburne's staff in Hardee's corps." (Appointed December 13, 1862.)

[3] Lucy Buck wrote that Front Royal "is quite lively now . . ." Mr. Stewart, who has succeeded Mr. Fishback at the hotel, has the reputation of keeping a very good house and already has a number of boarders from the cities, among whom are some five or six young ladies — "wild as antelopes".

[4] Richard M. Blakemore, Adjutant Morton's Battalion Artillery, Forrest's Cavalry.

[5] Robert Carey Buck, younger brother, age 12.

[6] Cattie Boone married Lt. Green B. Samuels Feb. 19, 1862. They were divorced after the war.

[7] Lucy R. Buck wrote in her diary "So father did write him about Capt. Latrobe really. Its right funny." Captain Latrobe who was on Longstreet's staff stopped at Lucy's home, Bel Air, at least twice with his general.

[8] Belle Boyd, age 19 was a famous Confederate spy. She visited her uncle's hotel (Stewart Hotel) in Front Royal after being exiled from her home in Martinsburg. There she had shot and killed in self defense a Federal soldier. Lucy Buck and others in Front Royal questioned her character and behavior, because she was often seen "on the arm of a Yankee soldier".

[9] Smith Spangler Turner was a V.M.I cadet from Warren County but left with his professor, Stonewall Jackson. He became Jackson's drill officer, was wounded and twice breveted on the field of battle for gallantry. When Lee surrendered Major Turner escaped through the lines and headed for General Johnston's army in Carolina. The train he was travelling blew up and he was seriously injured but recovered. He practiced law in Front Royal, served as delegate to the Virginia assembly and was a U.S. Congressman for two terms.

[10] Captain Francis Wesley Lehew succeeded Major Robert Simpson as commander of the "Warren Rifles" in November of 1862.

[11] General W. E. Jones was Commander of Ashby's Brigade.

[12] Capon Springs Hotel in Hampshire County, West Virginia, was owned by William Mason Buck, Irving's Father, John Buck, Irving's uncle and J.R. Ricards. It boasted a dining room capacity of 900 and 500 room accommodations.

It was not burned by the Federals, but the cutlery and silver was removed before the invaders arrived. Later some of the linens were sold.

Part of the building burned in 1864.

[13] Office Special Commissioner, Camp Chase, Columbus, Ohio, April 23, 1863

Maj. L.C. Turner, Judge Advocate:

As to Miss Fannie Battle, aged nineteen years, of Davidson County, Tenn., arrested on the 7th day of April, A.D. 1863, by order of Colonel Truesdail, chief of police at Nashville, and brought to Camp Chase on the 15th day of April, 1863, charged with being a spy, with smuggling goods and with getting a forged pass, I have the honor to report that the prisoner denies the allegation of having been a spy but admits that she is a rebel and she had a forged pass. She further denies that she was smuggling goods at the time she was arrested. There can be no doubt from the manner of the prisoner in replying to inquiries that she has been engaged in smuggling. The prisoner is affable and attractive and well qualified by manners and mind to be influential for evil to the loyal cause. She is a daughter of the rebel General Battle. I recommend that she is to be exchanged and sent beyond our lines as soon as it may be convenient to our Government.

Respectfully,

Saml. Galloway, Special Commissioner

Office Special Commissioner, Camp Chase, Columbus, Ohio, April 23, 1863

Maj. L.C. Turner, Judge Advocate:

As to Miss Harriet Booker, aged twenty-four years, of Davidson County, Tenn., arrested on the 7th day of April, A.D. 1863, by order of Colonel Truesdail, chief of police at Nashville, and brought to Camp Chase on the 15th day of April, 1863, charged with being a rebel, a spy, with forging a pass and altering the same and with smuggling goods through the lines and conveying letters and information to the enemy, I have the honor to report that the prisoner denies the charge of smuggling, of being a spy or conveying letters to the enemy, but admits herself to be a rebel and to have altered a forged pass, knowing the same to have been forged for the purpose of being fraudulently used. The prisoner is less intelligent that Miss Battle and more ingenuous.

She has been obviously under the control of Miss Battle. There can be no doubt as to her active and cordial cooperation in the acts of Miss Battle. If she could be removed from the influence of [that] designing woman she would be harmless. I recommend that she be exchanged and sent beyond our lines, and if convenient and practicable that she be separated from the companionship of Miss Battle.

Respectfully,

Saml. Galloway, Special Commissioner

O.R. II, 5, 514-515

Executive Office, Tullahoma, Tenn., May 4, 1863

Hon. James A. Seddon:

Sir: I send you herewith a note which I have just received from Col. Joel A. Battle upon the subject of the arrest and imprisonment at Camp Chase of his daughter Miss Fannie Battle and Miss Booker. They are refined and very excellent young ladies belonging to the best families in the county, and were arrested alone upon the ground of their strong and openly avowed sympathies with the Confederate cause. Miss Battle has had two brothers killed in battle and her father dangerously wounded at the head of his regiment (the Twentieth Tennessee) at the battle of Shiloh. General Bragg tells me that he can do nothing here in the premises and advises me to address you upon the subject. I trust that the peculiar character of this case will be held to justify the most speedy and decided action. If these ladies are not liberated is it not legitimate to retaliate by placing in close confinement a number of Federal officers?

Very respectfully,

Isham G. Harris

[First indorsement.]

Mr. S.

Answer Governor Harris and inform him of what I have done.

J.A. Seddon, Secretary

[Second indorsement.]

May 11, 1863

Mr. Ould:

Another shameful outrage of the enemy in spite of their promise to cease such arrests. Do all you can to procure the release of these ladies.

J.A. Seddon, Secretary

[Third indorsement.]

Office Exchange of Prisoners, Richmond, May 19, 1863

Respectfully returned to Hon. James A. Seddon, Secretary of War.

Miss Battle and Miss Booker were delivered at City Point, Va., May 13, 1863, via flag-of-truce boat.

RO. Ould, Agent of Exchange

[Inclosure.]

Winchester, Tenn., May 4, 1863

Hon. I. G. Harris.

Dear Sir: A rumor reached me some days since that one of my daughters, Fannie, has been arrested by the Federal authorities and would probably be sent to a Northern prison. Yesterday I learned for the first time that the report was certainly true and that she was confined closely at Camp Chase in a room adjoining a hospital. Another young lady, Miss Harriet Booker, a daughter of one of our friends in my neighborhood, was arrested at the same time and is confined with my daughter. I have no personal acquaintance with either General Johnston or General Bragg and I would take it as a very great kindness in you if you will see them and know if anything can be done by which my daughter and Miss Booker can be exchanged or the Federals induced to give them up. I am not advised as to whether we have any ladies prisoners in the South, but if their newspaper accounts are true there are some in our lines who ought to be if they persist in their policy of incarcerating our women and burning our houses. A copy of the Nashville Union now before me of a late date gives an account of the cordial reception of Federal prisoners by the ladies of Shelbyville. For a less offense my daughter is to be closely confined in a loathsome Northern prison. Will you do me the favor of attending to the fore-going request at your earliest convenience and write me at this place?

Respectfully, your friend,

Joel A. Battle

O.R. II, 5, 943-944

[14] Marcus Newton Blakemore lived in Van Buren, Arkansas after the war.

[15] Ewell's II Corps had entered Front Royal June 12 and headed for Gettysburg. The Warren Blues of the 49th Virginia Infantry entered Front Royal on June 12 and were not allowed to break rank. Captain Bailey Jacobs marched by his father's door on Chester Street without stopping.

[16] The Warren Rifles was Company B of the Seventeenth Virginia Infantry Regiment of Corse's Brigade, Pickett's Division.

Corse's brigade left Gordonsville, on July 8, 1863 and began its march to and down the Valley to join the rest of Lee's army. The march took them via Madison's Courthouse and on the tenth of July they began the ascent of the Blue Ridge. The brigade left Luray on the eleventh and bivouacked on the night of July 11, 1863, at McCoy's Ford above Front Royal. Many of Lucy's friends in the Warren Rifles were permitted to visit home, but by the thirteenth the brigade was at Middletown. The march ended at Winchester where the particulars of the Battle of Gettysburg were learned. The brigade remained in Winchester until July 20 when they moved south toward Front Royal. On July 21 the brigade became engaged in the defense of Manassas Gap where it fought gallantly and helped to push back the Federal regulars.

[17] After the war, Major Page Baker was owner and editor of the New Orleans Times Democrat. Carey (Dr. Robert Carey Buck) visited him after the war and Major Baker was visiting Carey in Virginia when he was stricken with the illness that caused his death.

[18] Lt. Walter Buck was in Company E., Seventh Virginia Cavalry Regiment, of the renowned Laurel Brigade, Colonel Ashby's old command. C. T. O'Ferrall was with him when he was killed. O'Ferrall became governor of Virginia and wrote a book *Forty Years of Active Service* in which he wrote, "On the march Lt. Walter Buck, of the Seventh Regiment, who had been delegated to gather forage for his regiment, joined and rode with me . . . as we rode along chatting, we both expressed a desire to see home folks, but we concluded there was no chance unless we could get a wounded furlough, and we both expressed a willingness to receive a little wound so that we could see our loved ones. . .he wanted his in the leg so his arm would be free to embrace the girls who would greet him. I decided to take mine in the arm, so that I would have my legs to get away on, in the event it became necessary in the Union country in which my home was located. All the time we could hear firing in front . . . neither of us ever dreamed what terrible fortune to both was just ahead.

"When we made the charge he was by my side in the front of the squadron. He was a tall, handsome young fellow, near my age; he was well-mounted, and was a typical Southern cavalry-man; he had been trained by Ashby the first year of the war, and had won his lieutenant's spurs by his chivalry and daring.

"I do not remember seeing him at the stone fence, but he was there, as attested by his dead body. I was told he saw me fall and started to me, when he was struck by a ball and instantly killed. So, as I have said, we both received wounds . . .'furlough wounds'; his wound furloughed him forever, mine for months; and almost eternally. His body was recovered and buried at home in Warren County, and on no mound should grass grow greener or roses bloom sweeter than upon his grave. He added a leaf to the laurel wreath of the Bucks, whose members of the Confederate army were many, everyone of whom was entitled to a medal of honor. It was most truly a family of fighters."

[19] Scott Roy was a member of the Warren Rifles, Company B. Seventeenth Virginia Infantry Regiment. He was captured during the action at Chester's Gap and escaped on July 22. This account of Scott's escape is described in *History of the Seventeenth Virginia Infantry, C.S.A.* by George Wise. He writes, "On the night of the 30th, Lieut. Scott Roy, Company B, of this Regiment, whose escape from the enemy has been referred to, returned to the Regiment, greatly to the surprise of all, as he was generally supposed to be dragging out the weary term of a prisoner in some of the Northern strongholds. When the squadron in charge of the prisoners, captured at Manassas, halted the night of the 22nd to rest and sleep, the fearlessly brave Lieut. Roy, undaunted as usual by surrounding circumstances, promptly laid his plans to circumvent the kind intentions of those having him in custody, watched his opportunity, and, after they had fallen asleep, he rolled himself out of the circle of slumbering guards, made choice of the finest horse in the group, and rode off without molestation, enriched by the possession of a valuable steed and a full cavalry outfit, a result which amply repaid him for the inconvenience endured in obtaining them.

Lieut. Scott Roy, who had been captured while scouting within the Federal lines, returned to camp on the 15th, having for the third time outwitted his captors. It appears, that after he was captured, some Federal officer recognized him as one who had escaped once or twice before, and to make themselves doubly sure of retaining him this time, they placed him, with his comrade, (one of Company B) in an upper room of Fort Norfolk, and deputed a heavy guard to take care of him. Roy had advised the Federals to watch him closely, as he intended to leave them, if possible. So, after remaining several nights in the Fort, he and his companion cut through the roof of the building, and sliding down the lightning-rod, passed the sentinel's beat in the darkness, and finding a canoe near the Fort, on the river, quickly availed of it and paddled up the Nansemond to a convenient landing, whence they came into camp.

[20] Bailey Shumate Jacobs, aged 28, was Captain of the Warren Blues, Company D. 49th Virginia Infantry, and was mortally wounded July 3 attacking Culps Hill at Gettysburg. His father had followed the army north and brought his wounded son as far as Winchester before he died. His mother had been summoned from Front Royal and arrived in time to witness his death.

Bel Air is located on an elevation less than a quarter of a mile east of Front Royal, Virginia. The two-story structure was built in 1795. Fifty yards in front and to the right side of the house at the base of a sloping grassy hill runs Happy Creek. The Hope family lived on the west bank of this creek and nearby was the mill. The front of the house faces southward toward the town and beyond it the beautiful panorama of the Blue Ridge Mountains. Lucy gave the best description of this view in the winter of 1861.

> *"The evening was lovely and I turned to look on the landscape spread before. In the fore-ground the smooth, lawn-like meadows and the little Happy Creek like a silver thread me-andering through them. Then the quiet village with the crimson sunset on its windows, and its bright wreaths of curling smoke, and beyond the undulating hill—and in the distance like a fitting frame to this sweet picture stretched the blue mountains all with a cloudless heaven overhead, painted with the sunset pencils . . ."*

William Mason Buck (1809 - 1895) was a merchant and leading citizen in Front Royal. His great grandfather was one of the first settlers in that part of the valley. Mr. Buck and his wife, Elizabeth Ann Ashby (1820 - 1904), had thirteen children. His mother-in-law, Rebecca Richardson Buck Ashby (1792 - 1878), also lived at Bel Air.

Aunt Calmes' (Henrietta Chew Buck Calmes, 1770 - 1872) was William Mason Buck's great aunt, the widow of Spencer Calmes (1771 - 1854). She formerly lived in Kentucky, but lived at Bel Air after her husband's death. She came for a visit and remained until her death.

Mr. Buck lived to the year 1895 and it has been written in a Front Royal paper that William Mason Buck was "the last of that generation of old Virginia gentlemen, of whom we have read."

The children at Bel Air were:

> Alvin Duval Buck, 1838 - 1922
> Irving Ashby Buck, 1840 - 1912
> Lucy Rebecca Buck, 1842 - 1918
> Ellen Catherine Buck "Nellie," 1844 - 1902
> Laura Virginia Buck, 1847 - 1921
> Orville Mauzey Buck, 1849 - 1877
> Dr. Robert Carey Buck, 1851 - 1916
> Annie Neville Buck, 1853 - 1907
> William Richardson Buck "Willie," 1856-1947
> Thomas Evred Buck, 1860 - 1911
> Frank Latrobe Buck "Dixie," 1961 - 1909 (*He was named for a cousin, Frank Buck, killed in battle and H.B. Latrobe of Longstreet's staff and a favorite at Bel Air.*)

Two other children died in infancy. Cora Blakemore Buck and Marcus Newton Buck.

Uncle John (John Newton Buck) was a widower and youngest brother of William Mason Buck. His wife, Amelia Ann Buck (Millie), died April, 1859 leaving one child, Walker, who was raised by Aunt Cattie Larue. After the death of his wife, Uncle John made his home at Bel Air.

There were approximately twelve slaves at Bel Air. Mahala was the cook. Horace, Alex and John Henry were her sons; Liza Ann, Allfair and Mary were her daughters. Mahala was the housemaid. Dummy or Dumb Mary was the nurse who was deaf and dumb. She responded to the vibrations from a knock on the floor by a cane kept for that purpose. Allfair was a Negro baby and Rob Roy a free Negro. Gilbert, a freeman, lived near the mill. "Uncle Ben" and "Aunt Betty" were servants who lived in a cabin near the mill on Happy Creek. After the slaves deserted the family, Mr. Buck hired a white girl to help with the family chores. She was described as being a "gawky, strong, sturdy and willing to learn, country girl."

Mr. Buck had three brothers, one uncle and many other kinsmen living in Front Royal. The population, including slaves, was approximately 500 inhabitants.

William Mason Buck (1809 - 1895)
Alvin, Irving & Lucy's father
Lived at "Bel Air"

Elizabeth Ann Ashby Buck (1820 - 1904)
Alvin, Irving & Lucy's mother
Lived at "Bel Air"

Alvin Duval Buck (1838 - 1922)
Oldest brother of Irving & Lucy Buck
Served on General Beauregard's Staff

Irving Ashby Buck (1840 - 1912)
Captain, General Cleburne's A.A.G.
Wounded at Jonesboro, Georgia

Irving Ashby Buck
(picture made c 1867)

Irving Ashby Buck

Irving Ashby Buck

Irving Ashby Buck

(l to r:) Lucy Rebecca Buck (1842 - 1918)
Ellen Catherine "Nellie" Buck (1844 - 1902)
Sisters of Irving and Alvin

Laura Virginia Buck (1847 - 1927)
Younger sister of Lucy, Irving and Alvin Buck

Rebecca Richardson Buck Ashby "Grandma" (1792 - 1878)
Married William Richardson Ashby (1789 - 1843)
She lived at "Bel Air" with her daughter.
She was the ninth child of Capt. Thomas Buck.

"Oakley"

OAKLEY, just west of Front Royal, was the home of Uncle Tom (Thomas Ashby) and his wife, Aunt Betty (Elizabeth Almond). Uncle Tom was a brother of William Mason Buck's wife. Their children were:

Allie, (Thomas Almond Ashby) 1848 - 1916
William Richardson Ashby, Aug. 8, 1864 - 1942

ROSE HILL, just north of town on the highway leading to Winchester, was the Richardson home. Mr. William Richardson died of typhoid fever in 1859. His widow, Cousin Elizabeth (Elizabeth Millar Richardson) lived there with her son and three daughters.

> Sammie died in 1860, age 10.
> Willie, (William Millar Richardson) died of wounds May 29, 1862.
> Eltie died July 29, 1862
> Belle
> Susan
> Mary died in 1849
> Ann Rebecca died in 1855

Sue Buck, of Mountain View, was the fiancee of Willie, and after he was killed she moved into their home. She never married and became sick every May 29th.

RIVERSIDE is located two miles north of Front Royal at the junction of the North and South Forks of the Shenandoah River. The locality is called Riverton. The home was owned by Maj. James Russell Richards (1806 - 1895). His wife was Cousin Bett (Elizabeth M. Blakemore Bayly Richards, 1825 - 1891). Their children were:

> Russell, (James Russell, Jr.) 1854 - 1914
> Annie, 1857 - 1925
> Henry, 1860 - 1914
> Walter, 1863 - 1904
> Thomas, 1869 - 1941

Richard B. Bayly (1844 - 1921) and Marcus (Mack) Bayly (1842 - 1886) were sons of Cousin Bett by a former marriage. Cousin Bett's brother, Thomas F. Blakemore (1822 - 1896), lived in Philadelphia. Her brothers Marcus N. Blakemore and Richard M. Blakemore (1843 - 1924), were in the C.S.A. Army. Their mother was Letitia A. Buck Blakemore who also lived at Riverside (1803 - 1885).

Major James Russell Richards (1806 - 1895)
Lived at "Riverside"

Elizabeth Mauzy Blakemore Bayly Richards (1825 - 1891)
She was called "Cousin Bett" and lived at "Riverside"

Letitia Amelia Buck Blakemore (1803 - 1885)
Youngest child of Capt. Thomas Buck
Married John Mauzy Blakemore
Lived at "Riverside" with her daughter Cousin Bett

(left) Richard Mauzy Blakemore (1843 - 1924)
(right) Marcus Newton Blakemore (1835 - ?)
Youngest sons of Letitia Amelia Buck Blakemore
Both first joined Kentucky Cavalry Units, then joined General Forrest

Thomas Fayette Blakemore (1822 - 1896)
Oldest son of Letitia Amelia Buck Blakemore and John Mauzy Blakemore
He lived in Philadelphia during the War.

Susan Payne Bayly Blakemore (1827 - 1913)
Wife of Thomas Fayette Blakemore

BELMONT, three miles to the south of Front Royal on the slopes of the Blue Ridge mountains, was located near the beginning of the present Skyline Drive. It was surrounded by one of the largest vineyards east of the Mississippi River. Uncle Mack (Marcus Blakemore Buck, 1816 - 1881) was another brother of William Mason Buck. His wife, Aunt Letitia, was Jane Letitia Bayly. Their children were:

> Walter, (William Walter Buck) 1842 - 1863
> Dick, (Richard Bayly Buck) 1844 - 1888
> Jacquie, (Jacqueline M. Buck) 1848 - 1907
> Gussie, (Catharine Augusta Buck) 1852 - 1877
> Elliot, (Elliot Mauzey Buck) 1855 - ?
> Mary, (Mary Richardson Buck) 1857 - ?
> Eltie, (Elton C. Buck) 1860 - ?
> William, (William Walter Buck) 1865 - 1933

Jane Letitia Bayly Buck, "Aunt Letitia" (1820 - 1898)
She lived at "Belmont"

Lt. William Walter Buck (1842 - 1863)
Co. E. 7th Virginia Cavalry
Eldest son of Marcus & Aunt Letitia Buck of "Belmont"
Killed June 21, 1863 near Upperville, Virginia

Lt. Richard Bayly Buck (1844 - 1888)
Co. B, 17th Virginia Infantry
Wounded at Dinwiddle Court House March 31, 1865
Second son of Marcus B. Buck and Jane Letitia Bayly of "Belmont"

Distillery at "Belmont"

CLOVER HILL (burned 1891) was located six miles southwest of Front Royal on the west bank of the South Fork of the Shenandoah River. It was the home of Uncle Fayette (Thomas Fayette Buck, 1803 - 1874) and his wife Aunt Lizzie (Elizabeth Peake, 1814 - 1864). He was a brother of William Mason Buck of Bel Air. Their children were:

        Henry, (Henry Augustus Buck) 1842 - 1888
        Julia, (Julia Catherine Buck) 1843 - 1909
        Neville, (Linton Neville Buck) 1847 - 1912
        Esten, (George Esten Buck) 1849 - 1913
        Carroll, (John Carroll Buck) 1851 - 1918
        Fettie, (Thomas Fayette Buck) 1853 - 1875
        Lily, (Lily Elizabeth Buck) 1855 - 1920

Thomas Fayette Buck (1803 - 1874)
"Uncle Fayette" lived at "Clover Hill"
Brother of William Mason Buck
Owned Elizabeth furnace named for his wife

Elizabeth Lane Peake Buck "Aunt Lizzie" (1814 - 1864)
She lived at "Clover Hill"

Julia C. Buck (1843 - 1909)
Daughter of "Aunt Lizzie" and Thomas Fayette Buck of "Clover Hill"
Married Marcus Blakemore Irwin in 1866

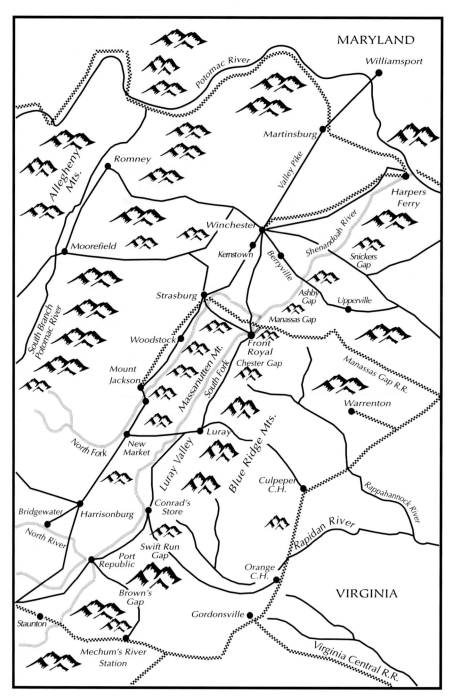

Shenandoah Valley and Environs

Miss Lou M. Furlow
Daughter of James W. Furlow
She nursed Capt. I. A. Buck when he convalesced in Americus, Georgia.
She married Kincheen A. McKinnie on July 5, 1871.

1864
Georgia Campaign

Head Quarters
Tunnel Hill, Georgia
January 3, 1864

My Dear Sister, *(Lucy)*

Your letter of the 24th November, reached me a week ago, but in winding up and disposing of business of last year I have been so busy[1] that I could not write with satisfaction, but everything is so quiet and still this morning, so much like the Sabbath mornings in Front Royal that I will at least make the attempt to write you a long letter. I write now about once every ten days and the last two or three have been sent in care of Miss Graves, I see so frequent account in the papers of mails captured by raiding parties of the Yankee's especially about Luray, that I am almost afraid to write. I feel certain that someone at home will write me today, now would not it be nice, if we could only know what one was writing the other so that we could answer each others questions? I find myself smiling at the childishness of such a supposition, and have no doubt but that you will do the same.

We had a very <u>sober</u>, quiet Christmas, on Christmas eve I dined with some friends, after which we adjourned to the Masonic Hall where some dozen girls were assembled and attempted a dance but we broke up at a very early hour. The next day I dined with another friend, he had invited some five or six of the Ringgold girls and as many more from the rural districts to have a dance. I was sailing around in this somewhat motley crew, I was halted by a gentleman who wished to know if I had a partner for the first dance, upon a negative he proposed to introduce me to "one of his country lassies" I assented. And suddenly found myself confronting a female, whose age I am sure no one could guess within 75 years of, with a tooth brush stuck in her mouth and unmistakable signs of snuff on her face, "Captain Buck Miss " I made a spasmodic motion with my hand and threw my right foot out behind and asked if she was engaged; "Yes but didn't expect the man will come back, <u>Youams</u> in the army tell such stories <u>weams</u> can't believe you, but I'll dance with you any how". The music struck up, Miss _____ friend did not return (and indeed as much as I wished it, I could not blame him) and we took our positions; heaven's knows I felt the degradation, and my fingers unconsciously grasped my coat collar with the idea of turning it down and hiding my bars, I looked around the room and saw stars by the dozen, this reassured me and I even felt at ease and with a faculty I possess found myself conforming to the manners of my company; The next time I was fortunate enough to obtain a more interesting partner and enjoyed myself no little, we broke up about 12 o'clock. The rest of the week popped off quietly and we have now fallen quickly back into our old habits. We have three ladies here from Nashville, who are refined and quite accomplished, they sing and play sweetly on the guitar, so we are not quite cut off from all civilization.

Yes Lucie dear we are getting to be men over women fast, twenty three years old; only think I have already read one third of my book of life through — unprofitable I am afraid. In the retrospect of fifteen years, covers a mingled feeling of pain and pleasure, but I can say that I can trace the causes of pain all to myself. You have no idea how much I felt humiliated when I read your letter, in which you asked me in regard to my past life, and whether the twenty third leaf would at the end of a year present any fairer record than those preceding. I trust it may, am painfully sensible that my past life has not been such as it should have been, and at the beginning of the year I made several grand resolutions which will be rigidly adhered to.

I received a nice long letter from Alvin a day or two ago, containing much good advice and scolding me for some of my tricks, he really made me feel quite mean with all his lightness. I believe him to be a true Christian.

George Williams was up during the Christmas, I do not think he likes his new situation as well as he did his old one. General Johnston[2] is in command now, and has brought his staff with him which will probably make some change with George, and I expect he will go with General Hardee. I saw Roy since ten days ago, he was very well, and had just received a letter from you. General Hardee will go to Alabama for the purpose of marrying, in a few days, and will I suppose, carry him along. General Cleburne is to wait upon him.

The only present I received this Christmas was a pair of yarn gloves, from a young lady in Georgia, and I have been so ungrateful and ungallant that I have not yet acknowledged the receipt of them, but will do so today.

We are having the first really cold weather this winter, but we are well housed and defy Jack Frost, as long as we are inactive.

Has anything been heard of Mack Bayly since his capture?

I saw one of Morgan's Captains who escaped with him from prison and asked after Cousin Sandy, one of them knew him but could give me no information in regard to him as the officers were confined at Columbus and the enlisted men at Johnston's Island. Morgan's escape was a desperate and laborious undertaking and may with less energy than himself would have been deterred from it by the magnitude of the difficulties.

Love to every one.

Ever your affectionate Brother,
Irving

Bloomfield, January 3, 1864
(Berryville, Clark County, VA)

My darling brother, *(Alvin)*

I knew not whether to laugh or cry when your nice long letter was handed me, so I did a little of <u>both</u>, such a treat I don't have every day and coming so <u>unexpectedly</u> made is doubly welcome.

You will perhaps be surprised when you see by the heading of this, that I am spending two months with Aunt Cattie. Jacque, Orville and I started from home today three weeks ago and they were weather bound and only left us on Thursday last taking Laura home she having been here <u>seven weeks</u>. (An <u>age</u> for her to be away from Frank). They had been here so long with me that I was dreading when they should leave me, and the night before they left we were all sitting around the fire thinking of the "morrow", Jim from Uncle Mack's came in and brought me your letter together with one "from home"; <u>you</u> know what it is, do you not? Well I can't begin to tell you <u>how</u> I felt. The children had left me and I did not know how I should miss them. I was sitting this morning reading aloud to Uncle Larue and Aunt Cattie when the door opened and a young Confederate who is wounded and staying with Josie Grantham came in. I left him to entertain them whilst I stole off here to the dining room to write to you though fear what little I can say will not interest you. Have had a <u>quiet</u> time since the children left excepting on New Year I was invited to a dinner party at Mr. Shady Moore's, went and had a pleasant day. I wondered whilst enjoying the turkey, vegetables, plum cake, mince pies, potato puddings, peaches, float and wine where my dear brothers and Dick were eating theirs. The people down here don't know anything about war times, 'tis true the Yankee soldiers and ours have camped on them burnt some fencing and stole some horses, but (other than a few who have lost their friends in battle) they are just as gay and are <u>living</u> just as well as they always did. dinner parties are not infrequent and there is a great deal of visiting done through the neighborhood. At Christmas Aunt Cattie gave us all as much egg nog, cakes, apples and cider as we wanted. Jacque and Orville enjoyed it hugely and were on their "high horses" all day. Cousin William and 'Nelie are <u>quietly happy</u> you never saw two persons more devoted and make as little <u>fuss</u> about it. I have become quite attached to both of them. think Cousin William has done so well. They have been for a week at her mother's and I shall look for them back now every day. Walter is a stout little fellow, and though he is a great pet and much indulged has a fine disposition and one of the most generous, affectionate children I ever saw. I do believe that Uncle Larue loves him better than he does his own sons. Cousin James is living up the valley being afraid to remain here on account of the proximity of the Yankees. He has the rheumatism so bad as to compel him to quit the army, and 'tis said that he and Miss Katie Grantham are to be married but I cannot vouch for the truth of it. The Yankees frequently send a scouting party to Berryville, but there has only been <u>one</u> here since I came down. We met eight drunken ones on our way down on their way back to Charlestown and excepting a few saucy inquiries they did not molest us at all. Your sermons (as you term them) I hope may not be in vain. for I need such sadly and after the perusal of one of your letters I make many promises of amendment in my future course of life, but human nature is too strong. I try to pray to Our Heavenly Father to teach me so to live that when I die I shall not fear death and it's strings. that my wicked heart be changed and I may love Him above all things earthly, but my very prayers seem a mockery, and sometimes fear to repeat them.

Dear Walter's death has taught me to think upon these things as I never did before. I often wish I was prepared to die and be with him in Heaven. oh! you do not know how everything here on earth seems changed to me since he has been taken from it. Often when I am laughing and jesting, my thoughts turn to the new made grave at Waterlick, and I remember that he is no longer one of us. I feel that it is wrong for me to grieve thus for him when I hope he is so much happier than if he were here, but I miss him so much. Dear Aunt Letitia, her's has been the sore trial. May we not hope, my dear Alvin that it be the means of drawing her and Uncle Mack to the mercy seat. She is so sad and I think changed from what she used to be. Dick's visit home last fall was a pleasant one to us. He is always so cheerful and buoyant, and excepting in years and height is the same boy he always was. Sue Bayly left us two months ago and left behind her two warm friends and defenders more than she had when she came to us. (I mean Lu and I) Some of the relations I think did not understand her buoyancy of spirit and thought her both thoughtless and frivolous but beneath the surface there is a depth of feeling that few dream of her possessing.

(January 17) Not having had an opportunity home by which to send this have neglected finishing this till now. We look for someone to bring Dummy home from Clover Hill this evening and for fear I may not have it finished in time to send have concluded to close up now. Uncle Larue and Cousin 'Nilie received letters last night from Cousin James and Miss Kate Grantham who were married at her brother's residence Albemarle County it was very unexpected both to his and her family as they were not appraised of their arrangements previously. I received from home by a blockade runner a package of nine letters from Irvie and one from Ma saying she had six of yours which she would send me by Dummy. The first tears I shed since the children left me, were over those letters. Irvie wrote so seriously and Ma was telling me how hard they had to work during the holidays having to do all the work excepting the cooking and milking. even to bring wood and water. They are so uneasy about Lu who is very low spirited and sad. I feel as if I ought to be home helping them but this is impossible. Uncle L and Aunt C are so kind to me, and often beg me to let them adopt me. Do write me again a long letter like the last. You write me just as I like to be written to and oftener than anyone else. Aunt C and Uncle L desire to be remembered to you. I suppose they have written you from home, of the Yankees having paid them another visit. Gregg's Division from Warrenton. Hope you will come home sometime in February and spending your furlough and now I must close. With much love I am ever your devoted sister, Nellie

Bloomfield, January 21, 1864
(Berryville, Clark County, VA)

My Darling Brother, *(Irving)*

I shall never again quarrel with you for not writing to me after the budget of letters received from home, in which there were four from you to me dated September, October, November, December. You have been so long from home but have become weaned from it in a measure and therefore cannot appreciate getting <u>nine</u> letters from home at one time (being more cut off <u>here</u> than you are in <u>Tennessee</u>) from communicating with them at home. I have been with Aunt Cattie since the 14th of December and expect to remain till the 15th of February. I am perfectly <u>at home</u> here. Aunt Cattie and Uncle Larue treat me more as a daughter than niece. since both been so complaining I have done most of the housekeeping and even to sitting behind the coffee pot, and doing the honors of the table. Cousin William and, 'Nelie are here too and the most quietly <u>happy</u> couple you ever saw. She is a fine woman and suits him exactly. I suppose they have written you from home of Laura's return home from here having stayed away from Frank <u>seven whole weeks</u>. Estie walked in unexpectedly bringing home Dummy who went up with Laura, and another package of letters from home (12 in number) a <u>rare</u> one from Sue Bayly, Lu, Ma, Laura, you Alvin and Jule and others. I laughed and cried alternately so perfectly delighted was I. Estie speaks of returning tomorrow and having them all to answer have commenced with yours.

You speak so calmly of wounded, dead and dying on the battlefield I cannot get accustomed to hearing of it and have you become accustomed to those things? Lucie's pride must have been sorely hurt at your rather <u>slight</u> mention of her Major. I don't think you had a fair chance of judging since you were not introduced to him, besides it was not his <u>personal</u> <u>appearance</u> we admired so much as his gentlemanly deportment and finely cultivated mind. He is certainly one of the most intelligent refined gentleman I have seen during the war — ("Johnnie" <u>always</u> excepted), by the by, have heard from him too. He has been <u>honorably</u> promoted (for gallantry and brave conduct) Lieutenant of the Navy and is now in <u>Europe</u>. And you saw our dear old War Horse General Longstreet. You did not pass your opinion on him but of course you could not <u>see</u> him and, have any but the best opinion of him. But excuse me though I had forgotten you were still tender on that score. Miss Ida is a new string to your beau I had not heard of her before where does she reside? I will not believe that "Maggie" can knock "Nannie dears" nose out of joint. I am so grateful to see how grateful you are for your deliverance from death and destruction.

Ours is one of the few families who have not had a link in the home circle broken. Dear Walter I scarcely knew the difference between you, Alvin and him. I miss him sadly he was always so affectionate and kind to me. I cannot even yet realize that he lies so cold in the graveyard at Water Lick. I dream continually that he has come home on furlough, and always looks as he did the morning he lay so pale and thin in his coffin. Do you ever sit and recall the face of those dear ones who have been taken from us since this cruel war began? Sometimes as I sit thinking of those "bygone hours" I have them so vividly before me that I forget that they "sleep in death" and the awakening of the sad reality oft causes the bitter tears of sorrow to fall, often when awakened from some pleasant dream of having you Alvin, Dick and dear Walter sitting around the hearth in Grandma's room, the war over and all happiness I lay in wonder if we who are left will ever meet together at Old Bel Air. It was a sad disappointment that you did not come home on Christmas. I thought of you, Alvin and Dick whilst enjoying the nice eggnog cake and the balance of Aunt Cattie's _____ things whether you had any and how you were spending the day. New Year's Day I was invited to a dinner party at Mr. Moore's. Went and I had not seen such a table since the war, a plum cake so large that it was handed on a <u>dish</u>, wine and everything nice and good. Spent a pleasant day and rode home on horseback with Mr. Luke for escort. Aunt Cattie sends so much love to you and says she often thinks of you both and pray to the Almighty to shield you in battle and bring you safely home to us. Oh! Irvie she is surely one of the best women I ever knew. there surely is a reward for her in Heaven she has been so kind to our family. She has assisted us so much. And now dear Irvie, if I had anything in the world that would be of interest to you I would write you a great long letter. But as I have some half dozen more to write, I must say goodbye to you till next time.

Now dear Irvie do write to me soon just such a letter as the last and with kind remembrances to each one of the relatives, with you I'll remain ever,
Your Fond sister,
Nellie

I forgot to mention the death of Miss Julia Lane who died of rapid consumption on Friday last. She had been a great sufferer.

Head Quarters Cleburne's Division
Tunnel Hill
January 23, 1864

My Darling Sister,

I wrote you a day or two after New Year's day and was under the impression that the letter had been mailed, until today, I found it hid away among some paper, which I regret much as you should have had it by this time. I will enclose it to you and give you something later. Had almost determined to write no more believing it would be useless, but your letter of the 24th and 30th December, shows that you still occasionally have a mail. Saw a notice in the papers of the burning of Mr. Burst's property, also that a Division from the Army of the Potomac, had been sent to Front Royal on a reconnaissance.

Gen'l. Hardee was married on the 13th and Gen'l. Cleburne went to wait upon him. Has not yet returned, I miss him much wish for his return, Gen'l. Polk is in command during his absence, and is a nice gentleman and good soldier, but still he is not "old Pat".[3] We have moved our HQ from the town about two miles, and are now living in a log house and well fixed for the winter, but don't I dread the coming campaign?

Was disappointed at not being able to go home this winter — leaves of absence are granted liberally — but Roy, Williams and I called a council and decided that it would not do, it cost us something to make this decision, as we were all anxious to see our families before active operations commence. Williams was as much disappointed as either of us, he has a sincere affection for you all. He and I were asked to wait upon one of the Colonels of our Division who is to be married to a girl in the same town where Williams Mississippi sweetheart lives, also my old friend Randall (from whom I have recently had a letter asking me to visit him) but we declined as we wish to go to Front Royal when we ask an indulgence.

I know that I am not nor can ever be sufficiently thankful for the many blessings I have had bestowed upon me, am sure we are not rewarded according to our deeds, it must be the prayers of those at home, which have been heard and answered in this manner, as I have not deserved to be spared more than others who have fallen. How I wish I could lead a new life, my retrospection on New Years day was very unsatisfactory, and led to some bitter reflection. The great danger is not dissipation, as we have little of that, but the want of society to awaken and keep alive the finer feelings and to act as a check when as of this we have none, my female acquaintances in turn were not very refined, and now that we have moved away, will be deprived of this, however it will not be much loss.

Our Commissary Captain Kem, is a Virginian from Hampshire County, and knew a great many of my acquaintances about Winchester, White Post, Berryville, Shepherdstown — he is a very nice gentleman, and I might have known that he was a Virginian. He lives in Raymond, Mississippi, now, and says his wife is well acquainted with Cousin Kate Blakemore he wishes me to go home with him, would not that be nice?

Have not heard from Nannie for a long time she owes me a letter, have concluded that she has dropped me from her "rolls".

I wish the mails with home were more regular, so that we could write more frequently and keep up the _____ but suppose we will have to wait and let my diary do this.

The subject of reenlistment is making some stir in this army, but I believe our Division will all go in again for the war, cheerfully. It is a proud thought to me, that all of our name, as far as I know, between 18 and 45 are in the army. Would it not be a shame to give up our cause now, after fighting as nobly as we have done? I am for holding on to the last, and am not the least discouraged — it is true we were driven from Missionary Ridge, which from an assault, was considered almost impregnable, but then for some unaccountable reason the troops would not fight, I mean a portion of them would not, and losely ran away and caused our centre to be pierced. Thank God our Division was not among the disgraced, but held the ground at night when ordered to retire, which it had occupied during the day, and successfully met and repelled three assaults of the enemy.

I heard a day or two ago that March Blakemore is at Meridian, Mississippi. Marcus Newton is with Alvin in the office at Charleston, I do not know where Dick is.

Am glad to hear that Father and Mr. Richards dined together during the holidays, but supposed that this part of conversationalist was broken up by the death of Mr. Green — by the way, what has become of Miss' Trout, Hayne, and Jacobs?

Feel under many obligations to old Abe, for putting his exemption from the operation of the Amnesty, so high in rank if I am never hanged until I get to be a Brigadier, I will never swing.

Nothing from Alvin for several weeks — I see in the papers a notice of the death of Lieutenant Samuels of the eighth Virginia Cavalry — is this Kattie Boone's husband *(Green Samuels)*?[4]

Much love to all.

Ever your affectionate Brother,
Irving

January 28, 1864
My Dear Irvie,
Nellie left her letters to you and Alvin unopened that we might add a line. It is well she did for I want to send you the enclosed pacquet and did not intend writing you again until I get a letter from you, such a favor I have not enjoyed for five or six months. Indeed your last letter home was dated Christmas Eve. I have written and written you thinking I had letters from you among those lying in the office at Luray. But our back letters have arrived — a great many of them at least — without bringing me a single one from you — if I except one written in August. I excuse you to a great extent on account of the irregularities of the mails - but still Mrs. Roy sends us word that she received letters regularly through Miss Grimes(?) and if Colonel Roy's can come in that way, why can't <u>yours</u> - if you <u>write</u> through the same medium? But

Ma will scold me if she finds that I've been quarreling with you.

I sent you a Virginia home-made Valentine that you can enclose to one of your "Dulcineas" - let me stipulate though that none of those rapid Tennessee lasses get it who "chew" and "smoke" and "snuff" if they are such devotees to the "need" they will not be very apt to appreciate the "flowers" in my little Valentine. I don't know whether or not "Ida" is to be included in this category — though I suppose it does not matter either way as you have forgotten her in this time. You're not a true soldier if you remain true to any one young lady over six months. You can inscribe a little verse on the card before sending it if you choose. Baron or Bryan or _____ for the purpose or write an "impromptu" yourself. We have had some notion of hoisting the "yellow flag" over Bel Air. Last Saturday afternoon Ma went to prayer-meeting - was seized with one of her nervous spells - went over to see about her and when we returned home found Sallie — our cook in bed, Laura the house-maid sick, and Cary and Willie "growling". Ma was better - up and at work with us next day — we had to do all the cooking. Aunt Letitia Buck spent the day with us. You should have seen Laura and I getting dinner. 'Twas not so difficult a task when the cooking-stove was there — but by the fireplace (Sallie had had the stove taken down). 'Twas awful! Liked to have cooked ourselves before the dinner was done. You would have laughed to see Father helping us— we were obliged to have him there to take the pots and kettles down off the hooks - though in truth he could do but little more toward it than we excepting he had more strength - you know he always had the greatest horror of getting a speck of dust in his black cloth and white linen - he has a much greater aversion to seeing me go near the fire with my calico dress on and he actually implored me to go up in the house and let him finish the cooking! — that too when he never put a vessel over the fire before in his life. Next day Monday — we were at it hard. Sallie still sick and Tuesday when Sallie was just able to creep about thirteen of us were on the invalid list. Ma, Grandma, Aunt, Father, the two Lauras, Henry, Eliza, (two little black children), Willie, Evred, Frank, Cary, and Sallie. All suffering from a kid of influenza pervading the neighborhood. Violent colds, fever and head-aches. All except in Evred and Frank and Aunt and I were better yesterday. We were in bed even now my head swims a good deal though. I'm so much better. Poor Aunt Calmes - I'm afraid she is going to be very sick. 'tis the first time since she has been with us that she has been confined to her bed and when she once gives up it will go very bad with her. Poor dear old lady! She has had little to attach her to this life. Uncle Newton is here to see her. Cousin Sue too is spending the day with us and sends much love to you.

We heard from Nellie on Tuesday - she seems to be enjoying herself so much that it seems selfish in me to wish so much to have her home again. I have written this with Frank leaning on my knees shaking me, pulling my pen and ink away from me and asking all sorts of questions which must needs be answered at all hazards. He's the brightest little ray of sunbeam that ever shown over a homestead. You should hear him talk — can count as far as "fiveteen" quite correctly. He thinks he has an exclusive right to me even to the regulations of opening and shutting my eyelids. All send much love. Isn't this charming weather? I'm stupid, perhaps you knew it before I told you. Won't inflict myself on you anymore.

Ever fondly,
Lucie

Ma wrote you last week. Willie has extracted from me the promise that his love shall be sent to you. He's a good boy, indeed.

Head Quarters Cleburne's Division
Tunnel Hill, Georgia
February 9, 1864
(arrived March 1st, 1864)

Lu,

Surely I am the most unfortunate youth in some respects, in the Army, was just congratulating myself, that I had conciliated Nellie, in during which, is seems, you were neglected — well after my word, I do not recollect who I wrote last but think it was yourself. However, if you scolded me Nellie praised me, so it is even.

After returning from a review of our Division by Gen'l. Johnston today, I was made happy by Ma's letter of the third and your of the twenty-eighth January. Had intended writing for several days, but deferred it, feeling confident that letter would reach me from home — just see what my faith did for me!

Gen'l. Cleburne returned from his leave some ten days ago, and was much improved by the trip, says he had a delightful time, Rumor says he lost his heart with a young lady in Mobile. He has been in a heavenly mood, and talks about another leave, already. Gen'l. Hardee has returned and brought his wife and daughters with him, have not seen them with Roy since their arrival, but will endeavor to visit them in a day or two. Am kept very busy now, the greater portion of the Division has re-enlisted and we are furloughing them liberally, causing a great increase in the papers. The troops are as much devoted to General Cleburne, as Stonewall Jackson's men were to him. By the way, did you notice that Congress had passed a resolution of thanks to him?

Cousin Alick Blakemore *(of Morgan's Command)* escaped from Camp Douglass in September and reached Dalton a few days ago. I saw him just as he and George Helm were starting to Virginia. He stated they would go to Front Royal if possible and I think it probable that they will be at Bel Air before this reaches you. It was a great temptation and trial for me to see them starting.

Had a note from Cousin Kate a few days ago — she did not say it, but I learned from other sources that she has another son. It was a very affectionate letter proffering to assist me in any way in her power.

Tell Ma that I am well supplied with clothing, have more than regulations allow me to carry, and enough to last the remainder of the war, the very thing I want is to see you all at home, and I would be happy. There is not an hour in the day, but what you are in my mind — you are constantly called to memory by some little incident, If I have any thing I enjoy, think how some of you would like it — well never mind this is bound to end sometime. I never felt more hopeful or confident since its commencement, and this is the sentiment of an entire Army. I fully believe we will open the spring campaign by giving the Yankees a beating to which Chickamauga will not be a comparison — if this is so, it will end the war. Then the happy time will come, what a glorious reunion it will be! The happiness which I will experience will more than repay me for the hardships suffered.

We are having quite a dull time, the refugees from Ringgold having all left for safer regions — we cannot even get up a dance now. I sit and look back upon the days of Tullahoma, Wartrace and Chattanooga. I have no sweet heart now, so your valentine will not be used.

I sat down with the intention of writing a long letter, but have been interrupted so frequently, that I fear it will be rather an unsatisfactory document.

Enclosed is General Cleburne's photograph with his autograph under it — am sorry it is not better, for it does not do him justice — do not let it fall into the hands of the Yankees, should they make a raid on Bel Air. I wish you to tell me what you think of the General.

Phil Wallace has been up to see us. He sings exquisitely, and has such a choice selection. He promised to write the music of several for me, which I wish to send you, one particularly — "Night" — I am sure you will admire it.

Had several excellent letters from Alvin lately, how well he writes, wish I could enclose you his last, it shows his character to a dot. He is cheerful and happy, not withstanding he has been rather unfortunate in his military life or as he expresses it, "has an India-rubber disposition". Think I will pay him a short visit about the first of March.

Feby 10 Gen'l. C and I went down and took breakfast with Gen'l. Hardee, I think he has shown his usual good sense in his selection of a wife, she appears to be an exceedingly sweet lady. His daughters are very superior girls.[5]

Williams and Roy were both well, but so much engaged with their official duties that I scarcely had a minute's conversation with them — both desired to be remembered.

Love to all — Hope that Aunt may have recovered — My particular love to Cousin E Richardson and family.

Ever your affectionate Brother,
Irving

Charleston, South Carolina
February 10, 1864

My Dear Lu,

I was greatly surprised on yesterday by a sudden opening of my room door and the entrance of our friend Col Newton King. He was immediately stationed in front of the fire and Mack and myself deploying on either side began an assault upon him for news. He was very communicative and we passed off a pleasant hour in a game of interrogatories and answers. He will leave this evening for home and the conveyance for a letter is too tempting to be resisted. I have received yours of the 28th and Nellies of the 3rd January, and hope you are in possession of a couple of missives from Mack and myself dispatched by Lieut. Kearny some three weeks ago. Since that time Charleston appears to have taken an opiate — so dull — so stupid. My correspondents appear, however, to have conspired together to give me a lively time — During the past fifteen days favors from Cous Gen Brook, Jimmie Blakemore, George Williams, Pat Pearre, and last though not least from Cousin Alick — have arrived. The latter gentleman is just out from Chicago. I say just out, but he has been a long time en route. He travelled by the subterranean rail-way — spent several weeks in Kentucky (where he seems to have had a glorious time as he hints in a most mysterious manner that Mack's prospects for matrimony have been utterly ruined by his own appearance on the scene) — and finally arrived at Dalton. He had many "hair-breadth 'scapes" and resorted to numerous Morgan-like dodges into the brush, but for all these hardships he intends to solace himself by a visit to a cousins' at Murrell's blacksmith shop P.O. Nelson C Va — George Helm will accompany him and you may not be surprised if they should make a reconnaissance as far as Front Royal. I am so very glad the dear fellow escaped! He, too, is evidently jubilant, and writes in finer spirits than I've ever before known him to indulge in. He sends much love to all.

By the way, Lu — I have just referred to one of Mack's flames in Ky, and it recalls a laughable little joke which occurred to me last night. M., and I were slumbering side by side, and about one o'clock my dreams led me on a pilgrimage to Kentucky. I had gotten through the lines, halted at a well-known spot, and after a short visit had induced a little fairy to consent, on that very day, to complete my happiness. The aforesaid fairy went out, got into a carriage, and drove off, (I suppose for the purpose of getting some trinket to complete her bridal attire) and I sat down and began a conversation with her sister. The minister was in attendance, the guests had assembled, and nothing was wanted to proceed with the ceremony but the presence of the fairy. The carriage finally dashed up to the door and fairy skipped out; I arose to my feet, and in an instant it seemed that every animated beast on earth had with one accord joined in an angry shout — and I awoke with a spring, to find that Mack had deprived me of a wife by indulging in one of his characteristic nocturnal yells which would awake envy in the breast of a Comanche. My first impulse was to garrote him on the spot, but a little reflection decided me to substitute oral abuse, and this I showered upon him until Morpheus, with his drowsy arms lulled me to sleep.

Pat still speaks of paying me a visit, but he is an uncertain sort of white man, and may not come.

I hardly know, dear Lu, how to meet the implied charge of partiality to Nellie, made in one of your late letters — but feel convinced that the idea originated in the fact of my probably having used some more endearing terms in speaking to Nellie than when addressing you. Indeed <u>I am aware of having done this</u>, but the cause is easily accounted for in that disposition we all have, and which is a part of our nature to address any smaller or younger object of regard in a fond, childish manner. I have long looked upon you as grown — as a woman. Nellie is so diminutive and childlike that I cannot regard her as being a full-grown woman. As to understanding the character and motives of one sister or brother better than another, or feeling the slightest degree of affection for one in preference to any other, <u>it is impossible</u>. I have often called you all in review before my mind, and taking the group one by one, asked myself "If I had to lose one of these, which would I select?" — the answer is invariably the same: "They are equally dear, one as another, they are each and all indispensable to make up the fondly-cherished group, and <u>I cannot love one more than another</u>." I had tried this often <u>before you mentioned it</u>. Your character, Lu, is one of a deep-feeling, silent, loving cast — one willing to make any sacrifice for those around you, and one which a stranger would have to study before giving you full credit for it. Nellie's is no less gentle, kind and affectionate — is fully as affectionate but is more demonstrative. Now, Lu, is not this analysis much more correct than any you thought me capable of making? Be honest — don't let self-abasement influence your answer — and give me a frank reply like a dear good girl — <u>am I not nearly right</u>? If I were to go home tomorrow Orville, Carey and Will would flock around for the luxury of trampling upon my toes and having "a talk" and my affection for them would probably (certainly indeed) be expressive, so far <u>as words and actions were concerned</u> decidedly in favor of Willie — he is younger and he would expect it. Surely, Lu, you would not believe that on this account I cared more for him than for the others — and the same rule holds good in reference to you and Nellie, Nellie and Laura, Laura and Nannie, and so on down to "little ole-uncle-Ben" *(Frank)*; <u>though the latter gentleman did not speak to me when we parted in the winter of '62</u>.

Col King has come — Good bye

Your own Brother
Alvin

My Dear Alvin,

Long and patiently have I waited for the advent of my promised letter. Have you repented that promise, forgotten it, or are the mails and Postmaster after all the real parties to blame for my disappointment? Let the reason be what it may, I'm going to make you the victim of another letter reminding you that I hear in _____ the promise you made and am expecting its fulfillment. I sent you and Irvie a letter from Nellie not long since and added a postscript myself to both of them — would have written again ere this but having just sent a letter to Cousin Marcus N. *(Newton)* concluded you would receive tidings from home through that and would rather have a letter dated somewhat later than his. Father received your long letter to him written on the 20th and seemed very kind to show it to those whom he knew would take an interest in it. He says I must answer it and tell you how much gratified he was at its reception and how glad he is that Cousin Mack is with you. Indeed we are all delighted that you have gained such pleasant, congenial companionship — it must be the next best thing to having Irvie with you.

We have, for the last two or three days, been having the oddest weather I ever felt. How much I've thought of the poor soldiers and the destitute during this time. The children are having a joyous time on the ice. I have been down there with them — nearly half Mrs. Lizzie's school were there and such skating and sledding as we had! Wish you could have enjoyed the fun with us — that is if you still retain a relish for such undignified past times.

The arrival of Dr. Leach's family in town has given quite an impulse to our society — they are sociable and agreeable. Mrs. Lizzie has well on to sixty scholars and Mrs. Mary Simpson twenty-five — so your Front Royal has not had its quota of juvenile inhabitants by this war. Last Friday night Mrs. Lizzie and scholars gave a sett of charades for the benefit of the soldiers. We had a great time preparing for it and 'twas a success too, beyond our most sanguine hopes. We realized over $100 by it and this we intend donating to the purchase of yarn and socks for the poor barefooted "Southern Soldier Boys." I send you a program of the exhibition but you can't imagine how nicely the scenes were performed — how effective some of them were — particularly the Bonnie Blue Flag with eleven young girls dressed in white with red scarfs and the name of the state each represented in white letters on the red. Another girl representing "Maryland" stood in one corner of the stage guarded by a boy in full Yankee uniform with sword in hand and waving the Union flag. Maryland was dressed in deep mourning with a star half hidden by a cloud of black crepe on her bosom, her hair was disheveled, her eyes downcast in proud sorrow, her hands bound with a heavy gold chain. The Bonnie Blue Flag was waved by another boy in the foreground and the song was sung each state coming forward on the stage as her name was called. The last verse "Let the welkin ring with shouts and raise your voice on high, the twelfth bright star in Missouri burns in our Southern sky" and Missouri came out — then "Prepare my southern sisters with a ready heart and hand to welcome to our glorious midst our sister Maryland." And the states turning received her into their midst and "Virginia" broke her fetters and cast them underfoot and the chorus was sung in full by all of them. It was beautiful.

Did you know poor Uncle John was wounded in the battle of Petersburg? He was acting as volunteer aide to General Rosser when the ball struck him in the thigh inflicting painful though only a flesh wound. He sent us word that he was doing very well at the house of a Mr. Spinkle near Harrisonburg. They say he is proud of his wound though you may know how painful and irksome must be the confinement to one of his active, restless temperament. He lost his little "Rosinante" too and I know this distresses him for he had formed, naturally, a great attachment for this dumb friend who has been constantly his companion since she was first presented to him by Miss Gennie Lucas the commencement of the war. We hope Uncle John will be about again in a little while.

Aunt Bettie Ashby has been invalid for more than two months alternately better and worse. For the last few days we have been very uneasy about her. And Grandma has been constantly with her besides Mrs. Bont who is now there. I hope fervently that all will be well yet hope with fear and trembling. She is so good, and so kind to everyone and so universally loved and it seems as if she were the very kind of person ripest and fittest for life in a holier, better world. Uncle Tom is surely harassed with anxiety and cares as such a weight of business on hand and is so uneasy about Aunt Bettie. Annis Buck is boarding there and goes to school at Miss Lizzie Leach.

By the way it is rumored that Molly Buck and Cousin Horace are betrothed. Have no idea how much foundation there is for the story but would not be much surprised if there be some truth in it. Will you be reconciled to yield to him this one of your "quenched torches"? Company E of the seventh regiment has had a week's furlough in consideration of valuable services rendered in the late West Virginia campaign. The boys enjoy their short respite very much. Dick Bayly had company last night. He and Charlie Buck and Richardson waited on me in a deputation yesterday but I declined going feeling so anxious about Aunt Bettie being very unwell and the weather — so cold. Charley Buck has been here every day this week — wonder if he will come today. He's a great comfort to us with his glad, buoyant spirits.

Father received a short time since a letter from Cousin Budd Buck dated Oxford, Minnesota. He wrote making inquiry as to the legacy left by his grandfather and wishing to learn something about his relations in the army. Said he had written both you and Irving without receiving any reply to his letters. Had not heard from his home for two years — knew nothing of his father's decease although he had been dead for six months. Uncle Tom offered to answer the letter in full. Poor boy! I do feel so sorry for him. You ought to write him, Alvin, a good long letter for "auld acquaintances sake" (Frank is standing beside me as I write these last sentences deliberately drew his finger over ink and made the block. This is my chance for writing I always have to hold my inkstand in my hand to prevent accidents.) Nellie had expected to be at home by this time but we were disappointed in sending for her. Aunt Lizzie and Mack Irving are down there now — we expect them home this week — when they come they'll bring us tidings from her. She is enjoying herself very much — more there I know than she could do at home now, yet she wants to see us all and we want her with us again. From all we can learn (<u>not</u> by her <u>own</u> account) she is a great favorite with Uncle Larue and Aunt Cattie and I scarce know how they'll do without her. She's a great girl, Alvin there's no doubt of it.

Have had recent letters from Nannie Taylor. She is well and happy and sends her love to you both — expresses quite a desire to see you. How quiet everything seems in the military world — it seems as if the two contending nations were drawing a huge breath and glaring a quiet yet fierce defiance at each other before commencing the next "bout". Oh! dear, it is with sickening suspense I await the issue of the incoming campaign. I feel as if we were somewhere near the crisis of our national troubles and a reverse or success all important in their influence on the cause.

Remember us all to Cousin Mack. Tell him I answered his letter sometime since though loth to say I'm _____ _____ everytime I think of the _____! _____ hastily written and under such disadvantages I'm afraid he'll be scarcely able to decipher it. Tell him all are well as usual at River Side and have appointed with me a standing fund of love to be sent him in installments every time I write to you. You have also a share in the stock. I'm not going to close my letter yet for there's no knowing when the mail will go out and I may wish to add something to it before an opportunity occurs for mailing it. You and Irvie must not hesitate to write for fear of the letters being captured by the Yankees — they have never gotten more than two of our Luray mails yet and there's no reason to suppose will do any more if old Major Lewis will but attend to his duties as a Postmaster should.

(ending to this letter from Lucie is lost)

February 22, 1864

My Dear Alvin,

It was fortunate that I did not close my letter for now I can tell you all that has transpired during the last few days. On Saturday morning Charley Buck came over to sit some hours — seemed in fine spirits and had me in the parlor singing and playing. We had just come out of Grandma's room when Father entered to tell Charley that he would ride his horse down to Mr. Forney's provided he had no objection. Just then Cary rushed in crying "The Yankees! The Yankees! are in town." Poor Charley started to his feet, threw his rain coat (which had U.S. buttons on it) into my arms, hobbled to the stile and was off toward Green Hill in a twinkling - not however before he was perceived and pursued by the miscreants. He succeeded in baffling them though and we thought him safe in the thickets. Father had started Horace with the horses but they overhauled him and made him dismount the best one — "Old Sam" — our principal dependent for bread and fuel — and carried the inconscious animal to camp followed by the _____ of children and I may say the grown people too. They encamped just across the field this side of Mr. Firth's. Cary ran over to town and the sergeant ("a Jessie Scout" by the way), to return him. Father arrived on the spot just then and the man turned to him saying, "I return your horse provided these two men on yonder hill do not move from their place. I have sent two men to take them and if they leave the hill before they are pursued I shall know you have warned them and will come and take the horse again." As he spoke he pointed to one of these high bare hills just beyond the orchard here and Father saw two figures on horseback quietly stationed there. We at home had perceived the two horsemen by this time just as Father had started for town and would not believe it was Charley till with the aid of the spyglass we saw him in company with another soldier on the very summit of the hill and in bold relief against the sky as if they were there for the purpose of forming a conspicuous feature on the landscape. Immediately Laura and some of the children started off to beg him to leave, but we recollected that to reach him they would have to cross the ploughed fields in full view of all the Yankees and their movements might attract attention to Charley when otherwise he would probably remain unnoticed. Father just then came from town and told us what the Yankees sergeant said about having sent in pursuit of him the words had scarcely left his lips ere we saw the coitiffs stealing out of the thickets in his rear. He dashed off as soon as they came in sight — they followed, shots were heard and they disappeared altogether over the hill. They presently reappeared and we recognized Charley and his companion with them. As they passed the house I ran down the road to speak to Charley and asked him if he had a message home. The poor boy compressed his lips and shook his head while the tears flushed up into his eyes. He is brave and strong and could have born the horrors of captivity with unflinching fortitude had it not involved such painful consequences at home. He knew that he was the stay of his family - that his Father depended on him and looked up to him as if he were the Father instead of the son. He knew that it would be almost a death blow to him and 'twas no wonder he had no voice for even a message to them.

Laura, Cary and I got ready and went over to the camp to see him. Felt very badly threading our way through the regiment where the men were singing and jesting and staring like as many fiends. Miss Lizzie Leach and Miss Gennie Petty were fortunately before me having with a deal of trouble obtained permission of the Col. to speak with the prisoner in <u>presence</u> <u>of</u> <u>the</u> <u>officer</u>. When we came to the group where they stood, there was a _____ of little boys standing around the prisoner abusing the Yankees to all intents and purposes. Poor Charley, when he saw us seemed glad and the weakness came to his eyes again. Of course we could say little or nothing to him as the Yankees encircled us and seemed to be listening with open eyes and ears for something that would offend them apart. As we handed him his overcoat one of them remarked, "He shows the glorious spread eagle." Another cried, "My Boy, you've no right to those buttons if you are not in military service." A third chimed in a jocular tone, "Oh! he's only half and half — Secesh uniform with Yankee buttons. You are not much of a rebel are you my fine fellow?" Charley replied most positively that he <u>was</u> altogether a Rebel. They all then with unanimous voice declared they liked him all the better for not being afraid to declare his sentiments. The Captain who had him in charge seemed something of a gentleman and evidently took an interest in the case rather intimating that he would do what he could toward furthering our object that is, obtaining his release. He then bowing led Charlie off under guard and we went to Dr. Leach's to wait till the Colonel should come in from the picquet post where he had ridden. Miss Lizzie went down to camp with us when he arrived. We found his learship in the centre of the camp standing behind a wagon with some of his officers reading a confidential _____ a letter which he had just _____ from the post office, one that had been left over there. He saw us approaching out of the corner of his eyes and very quietly turned his back to us. Our friend the Captain was standing near him and announced to him that "some ladies were waiting to speak to him." The old bear looked over his shoulder and grunted out, "I told you to speak with the prisoner, why don't you go on?" Then he faced about sharply and Miss Lizzie approaching him told him that the two ladies with her were relatives of the "boy-prisoner" who had come to see him with regard to our cousin. If you can imagine William Jacobs son ten years younger - two inches taller, minus 20 pounds of flesh and sporting an immense show of long red side whiskers you might have a faint idea of the gentleman's (?) appearance. I told him that my cousin was a lame boy who had fled to save his horse, having lost one the last time the Federal forces were in this place. "Well," he said, "He did not behave much like trying to save a horse sitting quietly on the hill in full view of their movements, no he was spying and taking notes." "But," we argued, "admitting he was looking at them, what harm had that done them since there were no Southerners within reach of him to communicate with." He turned about sharply and sneeringly asked, "Do you tell me that when you <u>know</u> better? You <u>know</u> there were 20 rebel soldiers in this town last night." "Yes," turning to his officers near "20 left this very morning and yet you tell me there are none to communicate with?" We declared our ignorance of the fact and I told him truthfully the facts of the case. The old hypocrite - every time he would advance an argument tried to be very facetious turning all into ridicule indeed I was so vexed that I don't believe I could have stood to talk with him but for Miss Lizzie. She was so much accustom to deal with them, so cool and self assessed. At last I said, "Well Colonel, you won't believe anything we say contrary to your assertions, but if you are not molested while you are here you have no right to suppose he has given any information detrimental to you - if he has not informed on you he has not injured you surely will not care to retain the poor boy." "Well," he said, "there's more rebels troops in the place," and paused to mark the effect of his words. We both expressed our surprise by our countenances as well as by our tongues. He then qualified what he said by adding, "If, not in the place but somewhere on the hills around." Looking anguishedly at us and trying his very best to get us to commit ourselves. He then said, "In reference to their disturbing us, I know they <u>will</u> if they can." And he looked uneasy and nervous. I asked him from what direction he apprehended trouble. Thrusting his tongue into his cheek with a knowing look he turned to his colleagues snapping his fingers saying, "I know as well as <u>you</u> do, I've been out to see into the matter myself just now. And you'll know more this time tomorrow than you do now." Coming back to the main subject we asked him if he could not give us a favorable answer. The incident poltroon deliberately turned his back upon us, spit out his quid of tobacco, kept us standing like menials waiting his gracious pleasure, then turning to me in the most contemptible manner he said, "Well, my good woman," (I believe I had my veil down) "I don't think I'll take the boy though of course I can't give a decisive answer till I leave — not knowing what disturbance there may be." Miss Lizzie whispered to me that t'would perhaps be well to invite him to our homes. I never had done such a thing in my life and expressed to her my scruples but she volunteered to do it and at last I looked over my shoulder and told him if he would but come to my home I thought he would be convinced of the truth of what we had told him at the same time pointing out my home. He growled some reply neither affirmative nor negative and we were obliged to be content. You don't know how much humiliated I felt at having to ask a favor of an enemy and such a one. I never had done it before and never would have done it for myself. I can never forget Miss Lizzie for her kindness - she rose from her bed of sickness to do this. By the time we reached home the sergeant who had returned the horse dashed up and announced that he was an agent of the Colonel. Came to talk over the case. He was a cold blooded Yankee as I ever saw said he had been a prisoner himself and knew the sweets of captivity therefore he felt sorry for the young rebel — but there was no hope of his release there was no use trying. Father went over afterwards and saw the Colonel who assured him that he would release Charley after he was safely across the river provided he was not attacked by our troops. By this time, to our great surprise about dusk they saddled up and left. We were sure they intended remaining all night — particularly as they affirmed they were expecting Cole's Battalion from below the ridge to form a junction with them here. To think the poor dear boy was taken off before he had time to see his parents or friends. Aunt Jane and Nannie reached town just after they left and Nannie and Cousin Sue and several others went on down to the river through the night and only reached the bank as the troops crossed to the opposite shore. We could not help hoping all the night and even yesterday morning that the poor boy would come back but he didn't as a matter of course — 'twould have been a violation of all rules of precedence for a Yankee to keep his word. You never saw such universal interest as was manifested for him by the whole community — almost every lady in town appealed for him. Poor Uncle Newton was almost frantic when he heard it and yesterday morning Aunt Jane consulted with her friends and concluded to go on down to Harper's Ferry that she might at least communicate with him and send him clothing. While Mrs. Berry and Mrs. Wheatley went with her. Ma is with Cousin Sue who will remain with Uncle Newton in Aunt Jane's absence. We <u>hope</u> they may be able to do something. Poor Charley! day and night I think of him and dream about him. I feel almost as if he were dead. I shall never forget his expression as he drew us to him and kissed us goodbye. We shall miss him so sadly — he has been a great comfort to us of late taking the place of other dear ones and to think that just as he became so near to us that he should be so cruelly carried off. The ____ twould be a difficult matter but his foot often pains him badly — it hurts him to use it much. Poor Uncle Newton! He says that he never has but once since Charley has been at home neglected going to his bed at night and folding the clothes about and bending over him and saying "God bless you my boy and keep you safely tonight." Now he says the sight of that bed is like a coffin and he has had to have it removed. Oh! I can't begin to tell you of his sorrow. I do earnestly pray the dear boy may be brought safely back to us.

Since commencing this Aunt Lizzie has arrived from Clarke bringing a letter from Nellie. She writes so affectionately, so happily — wish I had the letter to send you but Laura carried it over to Dr. Leach's with her when she went this evening. I think it probable she will return with Aunt Jane as she is going to Uncle Larue's before she comes home. Won't I be glad?

Aunt Bettie, I'm delighted to say, is considered convalescent. Mrs. Borst goes home tomorrow. Mr. Shipe dined with us today. All friends well. Every member of the family unite in love to you and Cousin Mack. God bless you dear brother.

Ever loving,
Lucie

Bel Air, March, 1864

Dear Irvie,

Thinking you may look for a letter before Mr. Wells starts back have concluded to write you this evening by tomorrow's mail.

Grandma, Ma, Lu and I have been and are as busy as bees trying to make a few little articles that may be useful to you such a(s) handkerchiefs, collars, cravats, and gloves to send by Mr. Wells who speaks of starting on the second, wish we could send you some shirts — let us know if you have a sufficiency of cotton socks, we have knitted you some but do not think he would be willing to carry so much.

Lu and I walked all the way to Clover Hill to get the skin to make you gloves on Friday last, but were unsuccessful, and on Saturday while sitting around the fire who should walk in but Dick Buck, who had walked from two miles beyond Burner's Spring before dinner. I think he is not looking so hardy as he did last fall though hope when he returns from Salem he will look better, only has 20 days furlough, 10 of which are consumed coming and going to ____ North Carolina. Hope sincerely that the Yankees will not honor us with a visit whilst he is here. though 'tis reported this evening that 5,000 Yankees are encamped at Markham, if it be so why we may expect them at any time.

I was with Aunt Cattie three months and only arrived here two weeks ago with Aunt Letitia and Jacque who came down after me. my stay there was a pleasant one indeed, all were so kind. I met whilst there Miss Fannie Larue, Christopher Larue's niece and granddaughter of elder Beebe, one of the nicest girls I ever knew, she is only sixteen, taller and as large as Emma Cloud. The brightest black eyes and brownest of ringlets. I have given you to her and am sure you will not disapprove of my choice when you see and know her. She is quite anxious to see you, having heard Jule, Aunt Cattie and Josie Grantham speak of you. By the by Miss Josie was to have been married the 15th of this month to a Mr. John Andre of "My Maryland". I feel quite anxious to hear if she was.

'Tis said that Willie Buck and Miss Tensia's "Charlie Leech" have been exchanged and are in Richmond, hope it may be so, but fear it is too good news to be true, would it be singular if a <u>wedding</u> was the result of "Charlie's come home." I shouldn't wonder.

Mrs. Childs with the children from school have come in with their budgets of news, and all is "confusion of tongues." Laura, Orville, Cary, the Leeches, Nannie, Bob, Jacque, Allie and some others are planning a raid upon Clover Hill tomorrow to spend the Easter holidays, all them anticipating a delightful time of it.

Mack Irwin started to join Captain Buck's company some two weeks ago, poor fellow, he is so delicate, I fear he will not be able to stand it any length of time however I believe he will make a good soldier otherwise. I did not tell you that Fannie and I rode over one day with Mack and spent the day with Cousin George Carter and passed the time very pleasantly indeed, both gentlemen exerted themselves very much to make us enjoy ourselves. Just to think of living year after year in that great house all alone not another white person to speak to. Ugh!

Did we write you that John Smith had been seen and recognized by someone who knew him, in the Yankee army in Strasburg this Winter? I can scarcely think of him as being so bare hearted though he may be an example of "evil communications."

Giles Cook returned from the army with Dick and expects to join Captain

Buck as soon as his limb becomes stronger poor fellow! The surgeon says he will never recover from the lameness and will always have to walk with a cane is it not sad to think of our <u>school boys</u> becoming old men before they are grown? Poor Dick and Scott, they have escaped wonderfully think how long they and Gus Tyler have been in active and hard service and not a scratch have they to show but good soldiers have they been.

We have received long and satisfactory letters from Cousin Mary Cunningham, Cousin Libbie, Cousin Cat and Cousin Rebecca Williams. Cousin M. writes that she had sent Willie clothing and money and that he was doing well, also that she had heard from Cousin Lucy and Aunt Betsy who are well but did not say where they were. Cousin Libbie writes that she had contributed to Willie's comforts as far as she was allowed. her long letter was filled almost written about her little Josie upon whom ever thought and wish seem to center. She must be a remarkable, intelligent, sprightly child, just think of her being only five years old and asking questions that would stump a sage. she told her mother that she never saw her father while he was upon earth but when her Savior takes her to Heaven she will see and know him there and wonder if he will love her there like he would have done here. Whenever she is sick she asks her Ma if Christ is going to take her away like he did Belee (a little friend who died) and prays that God won't take her away till he takes Ma too, as she is the only little girl she has, and she would be lonely without her.

Cousin Rebecca writes that they are all *[well]* and Robert has a large school. Don't you think he is a young teacher? Cousin Mary said she had heard from Mrs. Porter (Mary Lane) and that her house near Columbus had been burned to the ground. I suppose by the Yankees of course. Several houses were burned in Clark whilst I was there and known to be incendiary.

From having been the most unimpossible I think you have been the most susceptible young gentlemen I know of. And that reminds me that piquant little missive you sent in your last, what is the meaning of it? I hope I judge you wrongfully and that you have not been treating that poor little girl amiss if you have I hope someone will trounce you soundly for it. indeed I shouldn't mind giving you a lick myself. however I admire her spirit though <u>I</u> would not have done as she did for a kingdom. I don't think you would act so mean.

The conscript officers are sweeping the country thank Jeff Davis for those who have been resting their lazy bones enjoying the of home whilst others who were physically not fitted to endure the hardships of the march and camp life — among those whom Lt. Broadus has captured are Stintson Smith and John Peyton, the latter of whom a greater coward does not exist, he has behaved most disgracefully since the first three months of the war dodging and hiding around home not assisting in making the bread or salt he ate. Says 'tis no use for him to fight that the Confederacy is played out and we are whipped. It is very mortifying to his poor wife and justly so too. Was not hers a sad mistake though?

Macks Bayly and Richardson have not been heard from lately, at last _____ the former had been supplied with everything needful to his comfort by his Uncle Thomas. It seems to me I would have endured almost any amount of suffering before I would have accepted a fawn from him a traitor to his blood and country.

All are quite well and each one desires to be affectionately remembered to you and the relations generally. Write. Tell us of your trip to Charleston, and always tell us of Alvin we hear from him so seldom.

Ever your devoted sister,
Nellie

Head Quarters Cleburne's Division
Near Dalton, Georgia
March 3, 1864

My Dear Lucie,

Yours of the 14th and 17th has just been received, and I will reply immediately, as Geo Williams has just informed me that Mr. Wells will start to Front Royal in the morning, and I know it would be a great disappointment if he were to arrive without a letter from me.

I wrote you on the 21st Feby that our Division was ordered from this point; we had proceeded only a portion of the way, when we were hastily recalled by a telegram, to assist in repelling an advance of the enemy. We returned with all speed, expecting to be thrown into a battle, but the enemy wisely concluded to retire — only a small fraction of our Division was engaged. We are now perfectly quiet. We had such a delightful time while we were gone it was too bad to call us back. Had gotten to a little town *(West Point, Georgia)*, and made the acquaintance of all the ladies — (while laying over from one train to another) had the room engaged and every thing ready for a dance, when the order came ticking over the wire — which of course broke it up. Confound all telegraphs! We were much disappointed and I think the girls were even more so than ourselves. The trip did the troops more good than a furlough, they are in better fighting trim now than I have ever before seen them. They had jokes of every description on the citizens. Some of them went into the practical and numbers of luckless civilians lost their hats by idle curiosity in getting too near the train.

Would like much to have intrussed your tableaux, I know it was good, I read the portion of it relating to Maryland, to Capt. Hill (Nannie's "Cousin Charlie") of our staff, who is a Marylander, and he appeared to be much pleased. The ladies of the west are emulating the ladies of Virginia, our Division constantly receives donations of clothing etc. from the ladies of Georgia, we receive more than any other from the fact that it is composed mostly of soldiers whose homes are in the enemy's lines, and then they know we saved them at the battle of Ringgold Gap.

George Williams had a letter from Marsh Blakemore a few days ago, and Roy saw him at Demopolis. He writes in fine spirits and like a good soldier, as I have no doubt he is, spoke of having letters from
_____ , of recent date.

I must apologize for using the words "holding on to the last" in one of my former letters — and acknowledge that for the moment I had forgotten that I was speaking to a Virginia girl instead of a North Georgian. You must remember that I have for the last few months been in a section where every one is whipped except the Army. Feel prouder and prouder of old Virginia every day of my life. Col Granberry of one of our Texas Rgts, has just returned from Richmond, and remarked to me, that he never before understood why the Virginians had such an amount of state pride, but that this trip satisfied him they were pretty entitled to all they had that he found elegance and refinement, the moment he entered the state.

General Cleburne expects to start on a twelve day leave this evening to visit his sweetheart, he has scarcely been back a month, this is very suggestive, is it not? Would not be surprised at another wedding soon. When he returns I shall take a short trip to Charleston, to see Alvin. I pledge myself to pay you a visit next Christmas, provided I am alive, and the place is practicable. We did not come this year from the fact that the place was disputed ground and we thought we might get to Virginia and then not be able to get home.

I have bought me a new horse, my old one was completely worn out and I sold him for more than the new one cost me. Have not named him yet, but will call him after the first battle I ride him through.

So sorry I have nothing to send you, this is such a splendid opportunity — but know of nothing you would prize except a ring, which I am so superstitious about, that I do not like it to go out of my possession.

Am in hopes your fears in regard to Aunt Bettie may be groundless. I agree with you when you say she "is one of the very best women who ever lived" — and I love her dearly, and will hope for the best. Poor Uncle Tom, he would indeed be lonely without her.

Have no doubt Uncle John is proud of his wound, as he may well be. Is he not in danger where he is? Pretty young lady, wound, sympathy, etc., very apt to make work for a parson.

From the enclosed note you will see that I had to use some diplomacy to get out of a scrape with one of my lady friends — but I did it beautifully.

Love to all, will write again in course of a week.

Ever your affectionate Brother,
Irving

China Villa Feb. 22nd (1864)

My Dear Friend: *(see last paragraph of letter dated March 3, 1864)*

I write only a few lines on note paper to ask what is the matter you have not written me in more than a month and if I thought it was intentionally done as you were tired of the tedious correspondent. I would and for a confectionery yield and write a line to you, but I feared you were sick or off on a leave and had forgotten to write to Box Springs. I then have an opportunity to send this as a friend from Hardee's Staff has been visiting us and kindly offered to carry this to Tenn. Army for me.

For fear I am taxing time and patience I will bid you good night and sweet dreams.

Your Affectionate friend,
Laura

N.B. If you say let's wind up the correspondence. Please mail me my letters if you have them. L.G.M.

Bel Air
Sunday, April 10, 1864

My Dear Child *(Alvin)*,

The weather being too unfavorable to think of going to church. I have concluded to devote at least a part of the day in writing to you. your letter of the 10th of March to Lucy reached us a week ago — she was from home and I should have answered sooner but your Uncle Tom expected to go to Richmond and I intended sending my letter by him thinking it would reach you sooner but he has declined going till after court so I will send this by the first mail out and Lucy will write by him. I have succeeded in getting both of you pants but not such as you wanted. material of almost every kind is impossible to get and so I do not suppose gray cloth could be had in the county unless in the homes of some speculator that I know nothing about but your Uncle Tom happened to have a piece he had made for himself and finding I wanted he makes you a <u>present</u> of it — and you esteem it a great favor. he could have gotten sixty dollars a yard for it. it is <u>all wool</u> is black but I thought you might exchange it for gray either at some of the shops or with individuals as many citizens would prefer that color. it is the best I could do — but for your Uncle Tom's kindness to us I know not what we should have done during these hard times. he has given us over 100 yards of calico at one time besides <u>many</u> other such favors in fact he is a public benefactor — the only disinterested energetic person in the whole county. through him all the salt and cotton for the county has been gotten and he has done it at the greatest trouble and fatigue. he has carried nearly all

219

of the money that has been funded. the last time he was down he carried $71,000. he has never made the first cent by the war and has fed hundreds. he expects to go to Richmond and North Carolina in short time to buy cotton for the county and I will send the pants by him and he will have them sent by express to you — and I hope you'll get them safely. I know you must need them. do not see how you have managed to get along on your salary. I wish you to write to your Uncle Tom and thank him for the pants and also for the boots he sent you some time ago. I know he would appreciate it. you can hardly form an idea of the scarcity of almost everything in this neighborhood. your Uncle Mack has about 100 head of stock and he said the other day he had but 5 shocks of fodder. he is one of the few who has made money since the war. he is all the time increasing. there is but little meat or corn in the county and flour is scarce and very high. there is an effort being made to raise a large crop of corn this year — if the Yankees would let us. there is more land plowed than has been for years. we will be able to put out but little having only two horses and Horace and old Gilbert and they are as trifling as they can be or under no control and do as they please. your Father is afraid to cross them the least or take any authority over any of them. Horace is drinking very hard and I believe with all his indulgences would have left but for fear of being put in the army. I think while we have them they ought to be managed and made to know their places and I do not believe they are as apt to leave. Lucy went to Clover Hill two weeks ago to spend two or three days and it has been raining or snowing ever since and the river has been so high she cannot cross and there is no telling now when she will get home and the river is still rising. it will seem strange to you but this week we have had the deepest snow of the Winter and although it has been raining hard for two nights and a day it is now lying white on the mountains. I know Lucy's anxious enough to get home as she did not go prepared to stay so long. Dick Buck left last week to join his regiment in North Carolina. he had a 20-day's furlough but found time to visit his "black-eyed Sue." he was looking well but was I think unusually serious, does not like North Carolina indeed, they all seem to prefer fighting in the "old dominion." Giles Cook left a few days ago to join Company E. Seventh Regiment (Cousin Horace Buck's Company). he is still lame and it is thought will be for some time. Wythe will have to go very soon. he is anxious to join the cavalry but it is very difficult to get a horse. Ed Brown and several others from here will go under the last call. young men are very scarce in these parts now. the conscript officer has taken 70-odd in this county. John Payton who married Fannie Kendrick among them. Willie Green is in town now he is a very handsome fellow. he belongs to Lee's body guard. we have seen by the papers that General D.H. Hill was in Charleston. have you ever met him? when he was stationed near Rose Hill last fall a year ago he sent for your Father about nine o'clock one night to consult him about the roads around here. he was hourly expecting an attack from the Yankees and was entirely unacquainted with the country. he went and staid until twelve o'clock with him.— should you meet him you could tell him it was your <u>Father</u>. Irvie I think has met with him. I can imagine how unpleasant the heat, dust and mosquitoes must be to you and fear it will be worse before the summer is over. I suppose ere this you have had Irvie with you. the meeting will be most pleasant after being separated as you have been. it seems we are all to be separated for awhile. Irvie writes that he will certainly try and get home next Christmas. poor fellow we do not know how many of us may rest under the sod before then. I dread the next campaign — but know I need give myself unnecessary concern about anything all things will be right and work together for good to those who love God — may we all be of that number.

Saturday 16th — I commenced this a week ago. I left unexpectedly and went to see Cousin Sam Buck. I had a pleasant visit for four or five days and returned yesterday. I forgot to tell the girls to mail it for me. Lucy has returned. the rivers are still high and it is raining again. Henry Buck is at home on leave. it seems but little trouble for the boys of that company to get home — some of them are always around here. Tom Buck is improving and I hope will entirely recover in time but they have never been able to find the ball. he is as full of life as ever and his stories of prison life are very amusing. all as well as usual at Mr. Hope's — have not heard from Cousin Bet for some days. our love to Marcus N. it must be very pleasant for you to be together as you are. all join in love to you — God bless you my boy.

Your mother,
E.A.B. *(Elizabeth Ashby Buck)*

Don't be discouraged I hope you may be able to hear from Kentucky soon. You will have to exercise patience in this as every thing else.

Home
April 19, 1864

My Dear Alvin,
You need not think this short letter is intended as an answer to your long and most warmly welcome letter of the 10th of March. Ma has just started a letter to you and has I know given you all the news. I only write because of a natural aversion to neglecting opportunities for sending a letter such the present one offers. Uncle Tom starts for Richmond tomorrow on that everlasting cotton question. Well we have succeeded in getting you a pair of pants. Uncle Tom sends you a pair of his. Father says he has tried everywhere to get the jeans but could hear of but one single piece and that was not dressed and entirely unsuited for the purpose. Uncle Tom is so very kind to us — you don't know how much indebted we are to him and Aunt Bettie. They're both the best humanity not faultless but still good.

And now as to your query with regard to the promise which Father made to that Yankee with the regard to the horse when Charley was captured. The Yankee did not <u>ask</u> Father to make the promise — he merely told him in giving up the horse that "in case the rebel on the hill disappeared he would return and reclaim the horse" at the same time informing Father that he had sent a detachment around to take him, and Father had not more than reached the house when we saw Charley leave pursued by the captors. So you need not think there was any ungenerous dealings with the poor fellow. It would have been mean indeed to have made such an agreement as my bungling account of the affair led you to believe Father guilty of. We would have sent to Charley when we first saw him and Laura and Orville even started to him but they would have had to cross the orchard and another hillside field to reach him in full view of the Yankees and we feared that going to him would attract their notice when otherwise he would escape detection.

We are having lovely weather — it's high time for it as the past three weeks were perfect seasons of strife with the elements. We are beginning to rejoice in the sight of a few fields of green wheat and the farmers are straining every nerve to cultivate every possible acre of land they've learned from sad experience that 'tis a necessity with them. Father is putting in a good deal of sorghum. Has a few acres of corn and wheat in the orchard field and some potatoes in the garden. I used to take no interest whatever in these practical details but you don't know how I've learned to watch the springing grains and the progress of the plowing and sowing and reaping. If we only could keep what we raise! but, from present prospects this is impossible. Everything seems to portend in advance of the Yankee army upon Staunton and 'tis most generally thought the main column will move from Martinsburg on through the Valley and we shall be again "swept with the bosom of destruction." I can't tell you how we dread it. Write us often while you can for when the place is once more occupied by the enemy we may say adieu to mails and letters. Don't you envy us the prospects? I'm so glad you have occasional communications with Kentucky. I can't exactly say I sympathize with you experimentally not having any "bright particular star" whose radiance to be deprived, but I can imagine that 'tis anything but exhilarating to be denied all intercourse with one to whom our thoughts and hopes seem constantly recurring. You <u>do</u> bear it bravely and I feel assured your patience and endurance will receive their just reward and then !— oh! who shall paint the charms of that far off period "after the war!" I suppose Irvie has spent his furlough with you and hope you enjoyed it as much as I have thought you would. Lazy boy! He has not written us for more than a month and we are entirely in the dark as to his movements.

Don't you think that Ma dreamed last night that she met General Beauregard and he told her he had to reprimand you for your inordinate use of tobacco! So look out for squalls. Tell Cousin Mack that I had to acknowledge the reception of a joint letter to Nellie and I from him and that I will do so very soon to the best of "epistolar ability." The River Side have all been quite sick but are better now — well indeed. Give a great deal of love to him from us all.

You speak of George Williams having lost his lady love as if it were an irreparable misfortune — as if a soldier hadn't so many strings to his bow that he could afford to break one and never miss it either. Why Dame Rumor says he has already ____ with balmy smiles the wounded inflicted by the last pair of eyes. Heigh-ho! So wags the world. If I had an interpreter I would send him with my letter to assist you in reading it, as I have not you must endeavor to decipher it yourself and excuse the execution on the plea of great haste and a most villainous pen. All well and send oceans of love.

Fondly,
Lucie

I send you and Cousin Mack each a cravat — poor specimen but the best I could do. Do you want a tobacco bag? There are also three pairs of socks for you.

Atlanta
May 9, 1864

My used to be friend: *(see last paragraph of letter dated March 3, 1864)*

Will you please tell me how I have offended you? I have been in this City three weeks and not one word from you. Don't lets parley this way, but either write as true friends or quit. I __ when you treated me with silence before, I never would be so foolish as to write and enquire this course, but woman like its the same thing again _____.

According to promise I had the photograph taken for you and must conclude you dont want it.

Good bye and the prayers of Laura is you _____ come safely through the impending battle unharmed and your Crowns may be of the brightest laurels.
God bless
Laura

(First Page Missing — to Colonel Benton Roy)

May 1864

breeze would waft you with mingled odors of sweetbriar and locust bloom — or all together we cast over your senses in such another dreamy languor as incapacitates one any other employment than _____ air -castles. However, if I write as my mood inclines me and go to building these baseless fal__ on paper you may call me "sentimental" and I'll take care not to lay myself liable to such epitaphs.

You know ere this of a new tide of glory which is shed upon our little army on the Rappahannock, — "<u>little</u>," I speak in comparison with the host opposed to them has not God been good to us beyond all we could have hoped in upholding our cause, through the fierce ordeal and strengthening the arms of our warriors against the myriads of foes that come like a strong wave to overwhelm us. Truly, "the battle is not to the strong" in <u>human</u> "strength". Siegel's advance up the valley severed our line of communication for a while, and all the time that this terrible conflict raged we were in utter ignorance as to its result. Our only means of obtaining information was through errant cavalrymen from whom we've learned to place but little reliance. It was a sad, anxious time and for days nature herself seemed inflicted with the general gloom and solemnity that filled our hearts. I at times could almost fancy the air filled with the smoke of battle and heavy groans and gulps of the wounded and dying. In proportion to this depression has been the elation of Spirits since the glorious tidings of victory reached us. I write as if the whole thing was settled, as if our success were a most decisive one although at last advices the army were actively engaged. Such is our confidence in our perilous Lee under an over ruling Providence that not a cloud of doubt rests on our minds as to the issue. Yet our successes have been dearly bought ones too. Some bright stars have been stricken from our galaxy of noble spirits. The guiding Star of our sheval cavaliers the brave Stuart is gone from our view like a brilliant meteor but he leaves a train of light behind that will not vanish into darkness ever. May he find peace beyond the grave — peace surpassing that for which he so nobly contended here.

Of our personal friends I *(I'm)* very happy to say none have fallen so far as heard from. In the Seventh Cavalry Lt. Wells was wounded and Alfred McKay. You have perhaps noticed in the papers the complimentary notice of our little Company B of the Seventeenth the little hand full of brave boys repulsed some regiments of yankees. Aren't you proud of them? Major Simpson and Mr. James Miller were wounded though I believe not seriously. Scott, I presume was not in the engagement as he has been so long in detached service. There are conflicting rumors of a battle in North Georgia — but we need confirmation of every report before we allow ourselves to credit them. If there <u>has</u> been one I've an abiding confidence that you are all safe and are looking forward to your helping to burn the yule-log at your home by Christmas. Everyone seems impressed with the belief that at "_____ _____ _____" would have "smothered his wrinkled front" by this time. Do you know I look forward to the "after the war" with a mingling of pain and pleasure! I fancy when the first enthusiasm has died away after our independence shall have been established, when the excitement subsides and we shall view things in the sober great light of common place every day life — there will be a rebuilding, the lost feeling — such as one experiences upon emerging from a brilliantly lighted theater into a dismal, rainy night. The old flowers of feeling and habit which have been self-sustaining during the while of events will then sink back to the old accustomed places and seek for the supports to which they clung and seek vainly alas! in many cases. But there will be such a demand for the exercise of every talent and energy that we shall not have time for brooding over these things and 'tis best we should not.

The past week has been one of great excitement in our little community. Siegel's advance upon Staunton was foreshadowed by a "grand reconnaissance" in force from the direction of Luray. We had unwelcome guests for the whole of last Thursday. They made war upon poultry-yards and granaries but did no serious mischief otherwise. One of the Colonels made your Father's house his quarters and he and his compeers behaved with tolerably propriety. Father just opened the door to say that the yankees are reported crossing the river en route for town. Thus we've kept constantly in the _____ _____ — I don't believe the report though. You have most probably heard of Dr. Leach's marriage to Mrs. Armstead. Tis a most painful affair and I feel deeply for his daughters. They all had to leave home. Miss Menie has for the present a situation as governess at Mr. Barbee's — Miss Lizzie has applied for a situation in Luray and Sallie will obtain one as near her sister's as she can. To think of a family of young girls being thus scattered to the four winds. Poor Miss Lizzie has sadly changed since you knew her. Sorrow has wrought more than time. It would have given me great pleasure to have contributed to the stock of neckties sent from Front Royal to my friend the Colonel. But I knew he had so many friends that he was kept abundantly, supplied with everything of the kind and I really thought it be greater charity to send those who were not equally as fortunate. _____ materials for needle work — <u>fancy</u> needle work — then accessible however I should have returned a little memento of home made manufacture at any rate. As it is he will I'm assured accept the "will for the deed". I would have been in Clark ere this I suppose but for the unsure impoliteness of the yankees who would not change their program of operations to suit my convenience. "Mr. Seigel" has hope learned better "manners" since. General Breckenridge administered such wholesome correction. Now I shall have to wait for further developments of the military plans at Martinsburg and also for a subsidence of the waters that have become much swollen in the late rains. It will certainly not be my fault if my line of communication is not kept open but 'twill be most difficult to do as I know from experience. Was at your Father's two evenings since all well and cheerful your Sister was there with little Walter — very like the first little Walter. The yard looks beautiful now, you should see it. Nellie is sitting by me chattering. She says in reply to my query, "What message." "Tell Colonel Roy if he comes home I shall have an opportunity of proving whether I've forgotten the use of my tongue — if he has not heard me open my lips for <u>three</u> years I shall make him to wish never to hear me again for <u>six</u>." She has not changed greatly — is grown perhaps more womanly and thoughtful, but is still the same merry saucy child that ever she was in manner.

I do not know what poor Miss Tensie Tyler will do now that old Mrs. Turner is gone. The situations is a sad, lonely one, poor thing. I'm going into the mountain tomorrow to get some flowers, expect to have a pleasant jaunt.

Do you find it possible to decipher my letter when I write in this careless manner? I am very often puzzled to read my own handwriting and wonder if my correspondents are any better acquainted with it. I've gotten into the habit of writing hurriedly and find it difficult to do otherwise even when I wish to. All unite in cordial remembrances.

Ever truly,

Lucie

Head Quarters Cleburne's Divs
Pumpkin Vine Creek
May 21, 1864

Miss Laura,

You have doubtless ere this learned the injustice done me in your notes of the 9th Instance, by the reception of my letter of 24th April, which I trust explained satisfactorily my silence. If my memory serves me correctly, your letter was ten days or two weeks en route. I answered the day week it was received, and directed it to Box Springs. Your absence necessarily delayed its receipt. Hence the delay. I think you are inclined to be too exacting; and do not make due allowances for circumstances.

Your note contained the second proposition from you for a discontinuance of the correspondence. In reply, I can only reiterate what I wrote on a former occasion.

For fourteen consecutive days we have been marching, skirmishing and fortifying[6]. To day is the first rest we have had, I am a mere shadow of my former self, you would scarcely know me. Through the kindness of the good God, I have so far passed unharmed through the several skirmishes. I am happy to say that our Army is not at all demoralized, and confidence is unshaken in Gen'l. Johnston. All fully believe that he will yet win for us a great victory — God grant it.

I see Capt. Johnson, frequently. By the way, I have some news for you — a gentleman and entire stranger to me, from the vicinity of Thomaston, Ga., told a friend of mine that it was currently reported that you had rejected me. Was any thing ever so absurd? We are mighty good friends, not that either sweethearts, but we are not half foolish enough for any thing of this kind. I did not even take the trouble of contradicting this report.

I think I have every right to your photograph and accordingly claim it — please endure it.

If you conclude to continue the correspondence, write and direct to "Army of Tenn" and I will get it. Be sure to enclose the photograph at once.

Regards to your sister,

Hastily and your friend
I.A.B.

Brother Mine *(Alvin)*,

Where <u>are</u> you, and how have we sinned against you to deserve a sentence of perpetual silence on your part? I have been most anxiously awaiting tidings of you since Beauregard was appointed his new field of operations so that I might know where to direct a letter which I've been most anxious to write you. Patience has worn threadbare and tattered and as a "_____ resorte" I'm going to send this to Charleston trusting that in case of your having left there you have given directions to have your letters forwarded to you wherever you may be. You should take it as a compliment my writing this afternoon, for I'm very stupid and so unwell as scarce to be able to hold my head up — have had a boil or felon or something of that description on my finger and it makes me so nervous and feverish. Isn't it well that I'm not a soldier to have my hand or arm amputated when such a trifle gives so much trouble?

We are discontented about our mails again. The destruction of the Central Railroad by the Yankee raiders will interrupt communications — we have no idea of the extent of the damage or the time that it will probably take to repair it but of this we are certain, when an interruption of this kind occurs it's influence is twice as lasting as need be. Not a single line have we had from you of later date than March 10. Mrs. Moffat is here now has just come up to say they have a paper of the 4th from George in which he acknowledges the reception of the articles expressed to him in the same package with your pants, so I suppose you've gotten them and have also received the letters we sent you at the same time. Tell George Mrs. M. sends her love and says all are well as usual at home save for Ma who is suffering from a cold. We occasionally have the Yankees with us since Seigel's advance up the Valley. There was a body of 600 in town about two weeks ago — saucy creatures who confined their "rebellion crushing" proceedings to massacring the innocent denizens of the poultry yard and pig-pens and stealing grain. They were frightened off by a warning of the approach of Mosby's troop and the greater number of them were said to have been nearly captured after having left here. We had a squad of "rebs" to tea in a few minutes after the "blue birds" flitted, and an alarm came that the enemy were returning. You never saw a room give up its occupants as that dining room did, and such "mounting in hot haste and steed." Major Turner came home last Friday and took the precaution to spend his nights with some country neighbors. Mrs. Turner was absent on a visit to her Fathers so there was no one at home but little Lucy and one of the Misses Roberts who was staying with her. On Saturday night the Yankees — 15 in number — went to the house and demanded admittance which was at first refused but finally they were allowed to enter and finding their bird flown proceeded to take possession of his watch and boots which he had left at home. They lingered about the premises till dawn when they concluded that "discretion" was "the better part of valor" and retired across the river. Major Turner's return home was a sad one. He entered his house and found Lucy putting on her bonnet. He asked her where she was going — she replied, "To her grandmother's funeral." It was the first intimation he had of his mother's death. Poor old lady! She was not sick quite a week and had but one child to witness the close of her useful, good life. She was a nice old lady — one of the most self-sacrificing, earnest human being I ever knew. Miss Tensia Tyler with little Robbie Turner have gone to Clover Hill to live and poor Dr. Turner is left desolate indeed. First his wife, then Miss Julia Lane, Robbie's second mother and lastly his mother in less than two years time. I believe he intends getting a housekeeper and have Mr. Berry live with him. I do feel so sorry for him. I suppose when "Charley comes home" Miss Tensia will go to house keeping on her own account.

Julia Buck spent some time with us a fortnight since. Alvin she's a dear girl and I wish you knew her better. She was speaking of you and Irvie when here and said, "You don't know how near those boys are to me, Lu. I sometimes wish so much they would write to me." She would not like it if she knew I had repeated what was uttered in a moment of unrestrained interchange of thought and feeling — it was a good deal for her to say and more than I ever heard her venture before. Laura has just come in from school and says she heard today that the Yankees had been to Cousin Eliza Buck's and forced off two of her negro men, taken her horses and carried little Tom off with them. Isn't it shameful? 'Tis said that Hunter the Hateful has been appointed successor to Seigel, if so we who are so unfortunate as ever to be in his power will suffer for the change. We have been peculiarly favored with the most villainous ringleaders of the Union armies always. Geary, Blenker, Banks, Milroy and now Hunter and next possibly Butler or Mitchell. I think if either of the latter named gentlemen were to grace our town with their presence I should be tempted to play Charlotte Conday to their Marot. It may seem strange to you my saying that we know little or nothing of the definite results of the battles of the Rappahannock but 'tis true nevertheless. We know that we've repulsed the enemy in every attempt he has made with heavy losses — we know that so long as we hold our ground we are gaining while the Yankees who gain nothing are losing greatly. But we know too that at the latest advises the armies were still confronting each other and we had not been able to put the foe to flight as hitherfore. We know that our noble warriors have reaped fresher and greener laurels than ever before — officers and soldiers — and alas we know that many, many brave ones will only view the immortals of the angels instead of the boys with which a nation's gratitude would deck their brows. Still, with all our losses how much have we to thank our good Father for! God is our strength and our trust. 'Tis to him alone we owe all that we are and all that we have. There are rumors to the effect that not only Beauregard, but Johnston himself has come on to unite with Lee against Sherman, Thomas and Grant. If this be so I shall have a deep interest in the contest and there has been a thought or prayer for you and Irvie and all our dear ones with every throb of my heart since I heard it. I was asleep a little while ago and dreamed that you were both at home — thought Irvie had run up to my room to tell me you had come and, with our arms around about each other we were seeking you when the scene shifted and I was walking over an immense white linen sheet clotted with gore upon which a poor wounded soldier had just died. Oh is it not hard to be cut off from communications with you all just now when we are more deeply concerned for you than ever before. I sometimes feel as if the suspense will almost craze me — and yet I try to commit you and ourselves to the care of an all wise, all powerful God and not let my mind dwell on the dark side of the picture. Of friends lost in the late engagements I have heard of none. Mack Roberts was killed in the 17th. Major Simpson and Joe Miller painfully wounded. I'm so sorry for Major Simpson and his family. He is their stay and support, their idol — his limb has been amputated and will greatly decrease his ability for doing anything besides the source of mortification it will be to him — though I don't think it <u>ought</u>. He should be proud of it. If anyone I love should lose a limb in their country's service I think they would become doubly dear to me. Major Simpson is said to be in Richmond doing well. Sam Buck was slightly wounded and is at Mr. Pittman's playing the interesting invalid for the benefits of his fair nurses. Alford McKay was slightly hurt too and Lt. Wells very seriously wounded while leading a gallant charge made by Company D in his regiment. We hear too that Scott Roy was captured at _____ not long since and I almost hope it may be so as it might be the means of preserving him from imminent danger in these deathly contests. Poor boy, he is so associated in my mind with dear Willie and Walter that I tremble lest his fate be as theirs — and yet it does not seem either as if <u>all</u> our noblest and best would be permitted to be snatched from us. Scott is such a good brave boy and we have all learned to love him very much.

My dear Alvin I had not intended writing such a miserable "Jeremiah" but my heart is so full of fears and anxieties that 'tis difficult to write of anything else and I am really nervous and unwell. Poor Ma is suffering in mind as in body. That is one reason why I've been more than usually depressed. She has occasionally recurrences of those violent nervous spells and they always leave her weak and sick — she has just had one and the suspense and uneasiness which everyone feels more or less would of course be more deeply felt by her. However, it will wear off in a little while unless there is really some more dreadful grounds for our fears than we know of. Don't let what I say make you uneasy. There is nothing more the matter with her than has been the case for several years. She is going about as usual sewing and attending her flowers, but she looks thin and pale and I'm so silly as to be fearful of everything that threatens harm to anyone I love. Never mind, when this battle is over and if you and Irvie <u>are</u> there and all should be well as I sincerely hope it will — then you will come to see us before Autumn and we will have one sweet season of domestic happiness, won't we?

Everything is looking beautiful about the old place now. We have a good garden and Father's little lots of sorghum, wheat and corn <u>ought</u> to yield well for they are nursed most faithfully. It makes me feel so sad to see Father laboring day after day like a common field hand to cultivate the ground when 'tis impossible to obtain a hand for love or money. Yet his health was never better and he feels better satisfied than he could be were he idle. Horace, to our great surprise is still with us — nothing but his fears of being conscripted in the Yankee army has ever detained him here I'm sure. When the Yankees were last in they endeavored to persuade him off and he used this as an objection. They told him they intended sending a regiment of his own color into the county for conscripts that he would <u>have</u> to go <u>then</u> and 'twould be better for him to go at once voluntarily. He very wisely decided that 'twould be better to "endure the ills" he <u>had</u> than to "fly to those" he "knew not of." While the Yankees were probing around here last week Father used to tether the horses in the pine thickets at night and work them in the harrow during the day. He and I took a walk yesterday evening to look up our gallant steeds that had strayed off into the fields. I hear Grandma sitting in the door and singing some ___ old hymn, Aunt is taking her afternoon siesta, Nellie is fingering the keys of the piano. I think she looks so well with her ringlets over her neck and crimson roses twined in them. My pet Frank has just come in to enter a complaint against Everd whom he says has "climbed into his bed" and won't "let" him "go to sleep." There how sad that sounds.

"Billiows hark to billiows calling — on my heart their fury play.

Faith decries no pleasing object-far far away." Grandma is singing Cousin William C. Buck's hymn. You remember it. Have you heard of Mr. Joseph Major's death? We learned it through a letter from Cousin Lucy A. Blakemore to Cousin Bettie Richards sent through a flag of truce. I think it was of typhoid fever of which he died. Don't know when it occurred. Poor Ret must feel sad and desolate both parents within so short a time of each other. Alvin, did I ever propose your sending your letters through Martinsburg? Cousin Sue Buck corresponds regularly with Cousin Mary and writes just as much as she pleases . Mrs. Finney is her agent — she has so many friends in Martinsburg and has all the letters sent directly under cover to a relative of hers there and he sends them by private conveyance to Winchester and thence to Mrs. F. There would be no harm in trying this mode as an experiment. I wish it were only right and proper for us to correspond with her as we have facilities for it which you have not.

Aunt L. Buck spent the day with us during the week — seems more cheerful than for a long time before and had a hearty laugh over your story of the "optical illusion." All friends and relatives well. Mr. Richards was here this morning. The Yankees of course treated him badly as they never fail to do. Cousin Bet had a letter from Mack a few days since — not a very recent one — but he was well and doing as well as could be expected. I had a little letter from Dick Bayly the other day — since the severe fight in which his Brigade was engaged — he was well and cheerful. Ninian Leache will leave tomorrow or this afternoon for his regiment and has promised to take this with him to have mailed. Laura is waiting to take it over to him. All unite in more love to you than I can express. May God keep you my precious brother. Ever fervent prayer of your devoted sister

Lucie

Alvin Dear Brother,

I cannot tell you all I want. I cannot say what I hope and wish for you — but you must read my heart by yours and see all the depths of a sister's affection for you. You can't imagine it <u>all</u> I know. I have been wanting to have a long private conversation with you ever since your arrival but have been disappointed in my wish. Think of all who love you so much and who are watching your course with anxious eyes and hearts.

God bless you and protect you. Your little sister will try to pray for you.
Fondly,
Lucie

Bel Air, June 21, 1864

(To Alvin)

Once more my darling brother we have been compelled to <u>take up our abode in the kitchen</u> for awhile (Grandma, Laura and I) owing to the indisposition of our cook and the departure of our <u>last help</u>. It has been sometime since we wrote to you last but we have been entirely cut off from all mail communication for some weeks and all the news we poor Rebels get now is from a few papers which passing Cavalrymen bring us and most of them are a week or so old. Such a dearth of rumors we have never known here. Ma and Lu started for Clarke today, two weeks ago the former to remain four weeks the latter to remain till fall just to think how I must miss my other and better self. I feel already as if she had been gone six months. Mr. Yates from General Beauregard's headquarters is staying at Mr. Hope's where he expects to meet his mother, and he told Father yesterday that he left you, Cousin Mack and George well ten days since on the south side of Richmond, the first intelligence we had of you since Cousin Mack's letter to Aunt Letitia from Weldon. Dick Bayly, Giles Cook and Mack Irwin are at their respective homes on furlough which expires tomorrow. Dick promised to enclose this in one to Cousin Mack and as our chances of getting letters to you are so uncertain have seated myself by the kitchen table under the window to write you between furnishing wood and water for the dinner. I'm helping Grandma to cook. We received letters from Ma and Lu by Neville on Wednesday last, the latter writing quite like she was homesick, we were quite uneasy about her health and urged her to go which she did, much against her wishes, but four years confinement at home for one of her disposition! It's enough to make her feel permanently old. She feels as much responsibility about the children housekeeping as Ma and I believe <u>more</u>. This day one year ago our poor Walter fell, I wonder if you will think of it. Oh! my heart and head have been so full of him the last few days. I can scarcely believe that he has been dead so long, how I have missed him none can ever know. It grieves me so to think that not a flower has been planted over his grave, it seems so like we have forgotten him already. Had it not been that Sallie's indisposition I had intended walking up there tomorrow for that purpose with Jule or Jacque. I wish you could see the latter; his resemblance to dear Walter is so remarkable that not only his own family sees it, but he is known to be his brother by strangers who never before saw him. Were you not pained to hear the death of Major Simpson, he died on the 9th in Richmond at Mrs. Luisner's, (Cora Pritchard) residence. Victor Brown was with him in his last moments, said he was doing very well till within two days of his death, mortification set in. he seemed perfectly resigned and died happily. Poor fellow! He leaves a distressed and helpless family. He was a good son, brother and patriot. We feel so thankful when we think of the many many such who have fallen victims to this cruel war, that our only two soldier boys are still preserved to us, and we earnestly pray that we may live to meet after the war. You don't know how we have looked for you home since we heard of General Beauregard's removal to Richmond. Lu and Laura took it into their heads a few evenings before the latter left that you would certainly be here that evening. The impression was so strong that we sat up later than our custom watching for you; about 11 o'clock Lu awakened me starting to the window declaring she fancied she heard and recognized your footsteps. I think of it so much that when you do come it won't surprise me much. The children have an idea that you are something rather above "the common herd" and it has become a byword with them "never mind if you don't behave I'll tell brother Alvin when he comes home and he won't love you." They have even prepared what they will wear, say and do upon your arrival. I wish I could recollect a conversation I heard between Nannie and Willie in the garret not long since, however Willie concluded the long discussion with "Well, Annie, I'll bet you $50,000 if General Marion had been living he would have come South and made 'poor brother Alvin' Brigadier General on his staff." You and the sorghum crop are the last themes discussed by them at night. Frank talks so much of you as if he had been raised in the same cradle with you he is such a good sprightly boy, and Lu thinks him much prettier than Evred, but I think not, the latter is just the age to "sauce and be kicked" by you and Irvine. the age you like them, he's a real yankee boy though, his pronunciation is as broad as if he had been born and bred in Massachusetts.

We heard yesterday through Tom Petty and Nick Lake who just arrived from up the Valley of a great victory at Petersburg and North Georgia, also the capture of "Beast Hunter," however it will be days before we can have any confirmation of them. Cousin Tom Buck was down on Saturday and spent the day with us, what a rare one he is, kept us laughing from the time he took his seat till he left. I like him so much because he is so good hearted and so funny. He says he is coming down for me just as soon as he hears Ma has come and take me up home with him. rumor says he is not insensible to Cousin Emma's charms and I have an opinion founded upon my own observations that it 'tis not altogether untrue. I'd love to ask him "when he saw Cousin Mary, Elizabeth, and Emma last." Father had three letters from Uncle John lately. He was well and very busy attending to the sick and wounded of the

Brigade and getting up something to make soup, a soldier supped with us a few evenings since and told Father that Uncle John, himself, and his companion had carried a large bag of turnip seeds about with them. I had forgotten the distance and time each one of them carried it; finally one of them left it on their campground having used it the night before for a pillow. Uncle Gilbert, Horace, Father, Orville, Carey and Willie have made regular and the only hands in the corn and sorghum fields. So far our prospect for cornbread and molasses is flattering, though our wheat is not looking so well. Laura and I are so near of a size as to be able to wear each other's clothes tho she looks the taller of the two. She is certainly one of the quiescent girls you ever saw. Lu and I tell her she is just as cynical as any disappointed old maid, has none whom she calls friends, companions, but Nannie, Bob and, Jacque Buck, and Sallie Leache, feels a contempt, and disgust for all the rest. She and Dick Bayly put their heads together yesterday for the purpose of sending Lu a quiz and 'tis admirably planned. Tell Cousin Mack, Dick has raised quite a tender crop of chin whiskers and mustache is "soft as the down on a baby's chicken wing" (an inch long). Looks handsomer than I ever saw him. Cousin Mary P. Cloud has been staying with me mostly since Lu left is more cheerful than I have seen her since last summer. Cousin Mount has come back to Company E. I am so glad he has the fortitude to come back and live down, what in moment of error he committed. It is a great satisfaction to his family and friends to think that even whilst in the Yankee lines he accomplished so much for the government at Richmond. Mack Irwin was down to see us a day or two ago, I don't think camp life agrees with him. The boys saw Dick Buck a few days before they left camp, said he looked well. I wanted to write to him but shall not have time before Dick comes. Have heard nothing from Willie or Charlie since Mrs. Kiger came in. Poor Charlie, I missed him so much when I came home, he was so sociable and cheerful. Laura and all the children join me in love to you. Grandma is at Uncle Tom's or she would send you a message. You would excuse this letter, both writing and style, did you know the fifty interruptions as well as inclination of my pen to proper it's function, and now I must write Irvie a note to enclose in one Lucie left me to send him. Do write us often, the mails are so irregular we may possibly get some of them.

Hastily and Fondly,
Your Sister (Nellie)

Father has gone to spend the day at Bel Mont with Mr. Shipe, a wonderful feat for him. Uncle Tom left for Staunton to see about his cotton. We have a fine garden. Wish you were here to enjoy the cherries, currants, gooseberries, strawberries were so plentiful. When you write direct in care of Mrs. Borst—Luray and we will be more likely to receive.

My Dear Alvin,

'Tis impossible for me to know when I will have an opportunity of sending you a letter, but I mean to write and trust to fate for furnishing the means of getting it off. I've been with Aunt Cattie nearly six weeks now, Ma only left me last Wednesday. I can't say whether or not there is any prospect of my becoming a victim to homesickness — am rather afraid I have a slight tendency that way. They are all so kind as can be to me and I'm afraid I shall be ruined by indulgence if my sojourn here be of long duration. Cousin William is living here with his wife whom I like very much, and Cousin James has just brought his bride home for the first time. They've been in Albermarle Co. since last August and were married there last December. You know she was formerly Miss Kate Grantham. At present she is with her mother and he _____ between here and there. I never saw anyone more improved than he is by marriage from being a cynical, pranking sort of tease he's grown one of the most cordial whole — souled fellow you ever saw. He and I are _____ friends and though we were never partial to each other of yore. Cousin Kate, as I call her, is a fine woman but at present is grieving herself to death over the prospect of Cousin James having to go into the service. His health is really bad and I do not think he will be able to stand the hardships incident to military life very long. Cousin Mary Cloud is here with me and is a great comfort when I begin to feel symptoms of homesickness. 'Tis such a lovely afternoon and I'm sitting in a low chair out of the broad front porch, where the evening sun is laying a <u>fluor</u> of mosaics out of the shadows of leaves and flecks of sunbeams. There's an oleander in bloom on the step here just in front of me and the breeze ever and anon comes hurling the delicious vanilla perfume from the blossoms into my fancier. I've been sick all day and I suppose enjoyed it more from having been debarred from out of door sights and sounds for two days. There's a lonely brier of clematis in the yard to my right and the poor vine has been trying it's best to bloom out in it's white summer dress, but this terrible drought is a great detriment to blossom and leaf. It it becoming really fearful, the foliage of trees is dropping off as if it were October instead of July while the grass all looks as if a seething iron has been passed over it leaving it nasty and brown. I trust it will not prove the forerunner of a famine the usual concomitant of war and pestilence. I'm writing in fear and trembling here for ten chances to one a horseman will appear at the gate just about the time I feel comfortably settled and there's nothing for me to do but beat a hasty retreat. This is my great trial here — company — unmitigated, untiring company morning noon and night, they're coming in and Aunt Cattie is miserable if I don't undertake to entertain all who come. 'Tis true they are very nice, well bred people, many of them the "FFC" but they are so stupid and uninteresting to anyone as shy of strangers as I have always been. Last Monday we were all invited to dine at Mrs. Lukes. Aunt Cattie, Uncle L., Ma, Neville, (who had come down for her) Walker and I went from here and we met there Cousin George Carter, Mr. Allen, Mr. Shirley, Colonel Grantham, Mr. and Mrs. Enders, Miss Moore and her brother, old Mr. Page and his three daughters, and oh! lots of others. You would never have thought of war prices to have glanced down Mrs. L's abundantly spread board and frozen creams, custards, lemonades and cakes greeted us like old familiar faces. We dined at Mrs. Davis' a few days before and she too had fruit and cake. And now we have an invitation to Mrs. Moore's. Persons here live apparently in precisely the same style as before the war — with these exceptions — there are fewer servants and horses and carriages and more work and walking done than ever before.

I started down to Harper's Ferry last week but only got within three miles of the place for we met soldiers who constantly warned us back telling us how the Yankees were shelling our forces in there from the Maryland Heights and had killed several ladies and tore the arms off a little infant in the cradle. Indeed they had that morning thrown shells beyond the point where we turned back — a distance of four miles. It was a disappointment my not being able to get into the Ferry but I enjoyed very much the view of the Heights which we had from the road. The Yankees were fortified near the summit — and we could see their encampments very distinctly the white tents looking like big flowers that had burst into snowy bloom on the mountain. Then they had cut winding roads all along the sides and they looked like silver threads woven into the green background.

The movements of Early have puzzled us a good deal, but late developments rather induced the impression that his Maryland campaign was but a ruse to draw Grant from Richmond and now he has effected that, he has recrossed the Potomac at Leesburg and gotten Grant between him and Lee and from the cannonading heard from that direction today I hope they are giving him some stern lessons in good behavior. We were so much in hopes the seat of war was about being transferred to the enemy's soil and that when the Yankee exodus took place this time that was the last we should see them. But I can't help thinking the "beginning of the end" is at hand and we can quietly trust to Davis, Lee, Longstreet and company for disposing of them (our torments) in best possible manner.

I have learned through letters from home that you have been with Beauregard in Petersburg and I could not help hoping the army in passing would bring you within our reach. Indeed I've been silly enough to allow it to make me right nervous and I never heard the gate clang and the rattle of spurs on the porch but I think — "Suppose that's a messenger come to tell me Alvin's at home or suppose it is himself." I have given them strict instructions at home to send for me in case you should be able to get home. If our army had remained in Maryland I should certainly have expected to have seen you sometime this summer. Don't know when I shall get home — not for six weeks I guess. Have just read "Macana" — have you seen it? 'Tis one of the best things of the kind I ever read. I think the authoress is rather ostentatious in her display of learning and sometimes she repeats herself but the fact is my feelings were so enlisted in the work I could enter so entirely into the whole thing that half my time I lost my own identity, forget to notice the style, forgot I was reading a romance, forgot everything but my sympathy with what seemed real, tangible joys and sorrows of real living personages in real earnest life. Read it by all means if you have not already done so.

I have not thanked you for that long letter to Nellie and myself but you didn't know how I do appreciate it, only wish I felt well enough to try and make you a proper return for it. There! Didn't I tell you so? Here come Oren and Edgar Allen up the walk and I must make my exit from the porch — wish they had waited till anther day. Poor Cousin Willie, I feel uneasy about him, they tell me that the majority of amputations have proved fatal this summer and I'm so fearful lest another one we love may "Fold the white tent of his life, For the pale army of the tomb." Wish I had it within my power to do something for him to render the afflictions more endurable but I don't know how that could be. Perhaps it all "will work together for good" to him. I trust so indeed and then his misfortune will prove rather his blessing. I suppose George Hope has by this time united another destiny with his. Poor boy! And poor girl! I wonder if either of them has any conception of the importance of the responsibility which they've assumed.

I quite sympathize with you in your failure to receive tidings from your "kin lassie" — but never distrust her, always remember the difficulty attending all earthly correspondence these uncertain times and scold the Yankees and abuse Fate and shake your fist as much as you please at the "underground railroad" but never doubt her constancy and truth.

'Twill all be the more welcome when you are here again.

I'm so glad you are emancipated from the throeldom of "Riciopolis". Perhaps now that you've touched Virginia soil you feel stronger and refreshed every way just as the son of the Earth in one of the old mythological fables. As long as he stood in his Mother Earth his foe could not subdue him because she imparted to him strength and vigor by contact, but as soon as he was lifted from her breast he became an easy prey. Do wish I knew where you are and what you are doing. Hope you will find Petersburg a more hospitable, social place than Charleston. Never omit an opportunity of forming acquaintances that may prove pleasant to you — one can never have too many friends and I think you may find one friend in every hundred acquaintances you make. I'm going off in the garden to hide under the snowballs for Aunt Cattie will want me to go out and help entertain those gentlemen and I don't want to do it. Don't think it will "pay", there's no chance in me finding a friend in either of them so you needn't say I do not practice my own theory. One is a quiet, unoffending, courteous, stupid bachelor, the other his nephew. I can best describe in the language of the immortal bard as, "The toad who dressed in soldiers clothes and went in the field to shoot some crows." I oughten not to talk so about him for he's been wounded and is I expect brave and can't help being dimenutive and insipid any more than I

236

can being spiteful and ugly. Good night dear Alvin and more anon.

July 19, Tuesday (1864)

Well my dear Alvin, events have been on the wing since I laid aside the letter commenced for you last Saturday. Sunday I came down to the dining room expecting to find only the family at the table instead there were six soldiers confronting me at the door and this was the first we knew of Early's having "fallen back" in this direction. By sunset we had given dinner and supper to sixty-odd men, and were almost "run off our feet." Our forces went in the direction of the river. They've had several stiff skirmishes in which we were the best men but it seems that the Yankee force has been so much increased that Early will be compelled to fall back before the overwhelming forces. I dread to see the Yankees in here again for we "Border Rebs" will certainly have to pay the penalty for all the Confederate ravages in Maryland. Hunter burnt Letcher's house is pure diabolical malice. Early burns Blairs in retaliation, then as a kind of reportee Hunter comes over to Charlestown last Sunday and burns Andrew Hunter's residence. Isn't it horrid? Whither are we tending I wonder? How momentous is the present crisis and what would not I give for the Scottish gift of second sight for only one month ahead. Perhaps — nay, I <u>know</u> tis better as it is. Have heard nothing from home since Neville came down for Ma nearly two weeks ago, have been looking for some of our Warren friends down but in vain. All was well when I heard save Frank and Evred who were just recovering from a spell of sickness and Uncle Tom who was quite unwell. Presume they're all right by this time. Cousin Mary and I were in bed just now when we heard Cousin James come up the steps to go to bed and then Cousin Kate said something about the army falling back tonight and Cousin James must go with it before sunrise. So up we jumped. I ran over and begged a light from Cousin Kate and Cousin Mary and I are sitting on the floor with a candle between us writing away as if for dear life to finish our letters to send out to Front Royal by him. I'll send this to Ma and she'll have it mailed for me. Just think, we had two nice surgeons taking tea with us and spending the evening and now just as we're making pleasant acquaintances they have to leave. "Oh! twas ever thus from childhood's hour, etc." Boo-hoo! As well make sport of it as cry.

I shall dream of you tonight most likely for I do so often. If I could only dream you well and happy and home again in reality I would be willing to dream always. Good night brother dear and God bless and keep you.

Fondly,
Lucie

Cousin Mary sends her love to you. Remember me most warmly to Cousin Mack.

My dear Cousin: *(Lucy)*

I rely on the kindness of your nature to pardon me for a delay somewhat longer than was absolutely necessary in replying to your last letter, which, however, I may say, was "enhapant" a good while on the route, as it had to go the rounds from Charleston to Welden and Petersburg. I should have replied to it immediately, but that, at the time, our mail communications were cut off with Richmond, and shortly after they were reestablished, Gen'l. Lee's movements from Spottsylvania to Richmond, and the cutting off the Central Road by the Enemy cut off communications between Richmond and Front Royal. Since these communications were reopened I must confess that the continued state of excitement incident to active operations here and elsewhere, have rendered me unfit for a correspondent. My mind craves for news to such an extent that nothing but a sense of stern duty can keep me down at my desk. So much by way of apology.

You will no doubt, ere this reaches you, have received tidings of Gen'l. Hood's victory near Atlanta on the 22nd.[7] This news has relieved every one here of an immense load of anxiety; for only in that quarter was there any apprehension of disaster to our armies in this campaign which has been so universally successful to us in every other quarter. It is true that the accounts which we have from there so far are quite meager; but enough is known to satisfy us that Sherman can go no further, and if he is not already retreating he will most certainly have to do so before many days, if, as I judge he will, the dashing, glorious Forrest should fall on his rear — I suppose, of course, you have seen the accounts of Forrest's last two battles in Mississippi — one at Tishamingo Creek, in which, with 3,000 Cavalry and two Batteries of Artillery he completely routed 10,000 of the Yankees. I enclose his congratulatory address to his troops after that battle. Since that he has defeated and driven back to a still larger force, under the Yankee Gen'l. A.J. Smith. Richard *(Blakemore)* wrote me quite an interesting letter, giving many details of the Battle of Tishamingo Creek. He is now adjutant of the Artillery of Forrest's Command.

Alvin received a telegram today from Benton Roy, stating that he, Irving and George Williams are unhurt.

Dick Buck came down yesterday to see us. He is a noble fellow. He is stationed on the lines originally established by Gen'l. Beauregard, after the Battle of Dreury's Bluff, in front of Bermuda Hundred's Neck. It is only about seven or eight miles from here.[8] Dick Bayly was here also, about ten days ago. You can scarcely imagine how delighted I was to see him. You may be sure that, during the two days he was here, we did not fail so speak frequently of our ever memorable visit to the Valley in the Autumn of '62. Oh! how I wish I could be there again this Fall. You of the Valley must be enjoying unusual immunity from the troubles of War, now that our forces are again between you and the Maryland line. I hope they may remain there till the campaign can again be transferred from the James and Appomattox to the Potomac and Susquehanna. In that event, General Beauregard might be ordered there, and Alvin and I would then have our much coveted opportunity of visiting home.

Jimmie Blakemore is stationed only about two miles from us. He has been to see us several times. Isn't he a sprightly boy? I feel a great affection for him, enhanced no doubt, by the fact that I believe he loves Sister almost as much as if she were his mother.

Alvin is enjoying his usual good health and spirits. I have not known him to have the blues but once since we have been out on this campaign; and that was the result of his too frequent and earnest meditations upon his "old Kentucky home" and his fair enslaver.

We occupy our time mostly at work. I rarely have leisure nowadays to devote to reading, except, of course, the daily papers, without which I would feel at a loss. The little spare time I have had recently, though, I have dedicated to the perusal of two or three novels, among which was *Macaria*. Have you read it yet? It is by Miss Evans. It is written in an extremely vigorous style. In fact, if the author's name had never been announced, I should have pronounced it the work of a man. (No disparagement meant to the Fair sex, dear Coz). She evidently attempts, though, to make a great display of her classical love, and lugs it in rather too often. Some of her characters are over strained; but upon the whole, the work is very interesting, and presents some excellent views in connection with our present struggle for independence, and partakes, toward the last, of the character of an historical romance — the closing scene being on the battlefield of Malvern Hill.

So Nellie won't write to me any more. I suppose I ought to be angry with her for it; but when I recollect what a poor correspondent I am, I can't blame her much, and therefore won't scold her about it, but will only thank you the more for your patience in continuing to correspond with such a lazy fellow.

I presume the Richmond papers reach you now with tolerable regularity. It is therefore unnecessary to give you any news of events in this immediate vicinity, as they will keep you thoroughly posted. One thing, however, I may say, in this connection; and that is, that you need have no apprehensions whatever, of the result of the campaign in Virginia. Grant can no more take Petersburg or Richmond than he can fly. He is at the end of his cord. He cannot advance, and he does not give up the campaign, for fear of his own people and government. So he lies in idleness in the swamps of the Appomattox and James, and disease will work on his army as effectively as Confederate bullets.

Give my love to all at Bel Air and at Riverside. Hoping to hear from you soon, my dear Cousin, I am, as ever
Yours affectionately
Newt *(Marcus Newton Blakemore)*

My Darling Brother, *(Alvin)*

A great desire to see and talk to you this beautiful morning has seized me! and being deprived of such a pleasure, have concluded to write you instead. I wrote to you and Irvie, by Dick Bayly, some two weeks ago! but as it was directed to Charleston I fear it may never reach you. I told you of ma's and Lu's visit to Clarke Co., we sent down for the former on Thursday last. Nev *(Linton Neville Buck, age 17, of Clover Hill)* drove the Witherspring wagon down with Cousin Mary. B. Cloud, who expects to go from Aunt Cattie's *(Catharine Elizabeth Buck Larue of Bloomfield, near Berryville)* to Baltimore where she expects to remain for some time. Two letters from Irvie of May 30th and June 5th, and one from you of May 6th and 28th, reached us only last week! Just to think of it after such patient or impatient waiting to get them a month and month and half old — tis vexatious truly. I ought not to quarrel either since we were too glad to get them, even with their antiquity. A letter from George Hope last night says you had gone to Petersburg to General Beauregard. I know how delighted you must be, to have your foot on Va. soil again, and breathe Va. air. Don't you feel as if you were almost home? When I think of the shortened distance between us I feel as if "Alvin can come home at any time now". Can't you now? It would be such a gratification to have you with us now. And whilst our army is in Md. I would like to have you, when we have no fears of the Yankee Cavalry raids, and then you could visit Aunt Cattie and bring Lu home with you. Irvie writes he received George's wedding card for June 16th so I suppose the honeymoon is almost past. I should not be surprised if from force of example you took a notion to go and do likewise. I am crazy to see this cousin "sister of mine that is to be". I have such confidence in your taste and do not fear that I won't love her very dearly when I shall know her. I have heard so much of her firmness of principle and kindness of heart withal her innocence and frankness of manners, free from all affectation that I am crazy to see such a combination of virtues, such a rarity from the generality of girls. She must indeed be a gem of the first water. I hope Irvie may be equally as fortunate but the mischief of it is he don't seem to care a fig for any one girl after two weeks flirtation with her. He is such a scamp, enclosed Lu a letter from one "Laura" and his answer. Take it for granted he keeps you posted as to his "Affaire de Couer" and has told you of it. I judge from the two epistles they are pretty equally matched. Poor fellow from his account of rations, clothing, etc. of the army they must be having quite a different time from last year's dancing and frolicking. The service too seems much harder being in the saddle from forty to sixty hours is something new to the Western Army, though not uncommon in our Va. Cavalry. How it does worry him to make any comparison between the two armies, East and West. Lu takes delight in writing him of a success in Va. — of a drawn battle in Tenn., etc. She is sure to get a tart reply. I suppose ere this Dick *(Buck)* has been to see you and you know more about him than I can tell you. He wrote on Friday a week ago that you were in

Petersburg and he was going to see you. The four younger children are clamorous who I am writing to and if I won't "give my love to Brother Alvin", I can't tell the number of messages I have promised to deliver, not one of which I can remember. We have for the last two summers been in the habit of taking the four down in the race every evening to bathe and after they are put to bed Lu, Laura and I going in. Since the dam has been repaired and refilled with large rocks, tan barke and sand, it is a delightful bathing place. Last evening Laura and I took them down put them in up to their necks in the dam and were watching their gambols when we heard a tremendous splash and a burst of laughter and upon looking up saw Allie, Orville and Carey plunging and diving in the water. They had put on dirty clothes come down and jumped off the big rock. Laura had expressed a great desire to learn to swim and they took the occasion to instruct her. I knew ducks water fowls not animals could perform such evolutions as they did. They stood on their heads in water so deep that nothing save their heels could be seen, swam on their backs, sides, and dived under each others legs coming up behind them and throwing the one under which they dived head foremost in the water by catching their heels as they rose. It frightened me to see them fall backwards off the bank into the water as if they expected to fall on a feather bed, and they could stay under the water several minutes at a time. I don't know when I have laughed so heartily.

Allie is almost as tall and quiet as you, and to see him floundering and panting like a grampus twas too ludicrous. Grandma and Aunt Betsy have gone over to hear Dr. Thompson preach. Father ate his breakfast at five thirty and rode up to Clover Hill to spend the day with Uncle Fayette — a most unusual feat for him. Laura is up stairs joining Frank in a nap and with an occasional invasion of the children, chickens and turkeys and Aunt Calmes quiet companionship I have been uninterrupted. Laura said "tell the boys I am raising some twenty odd chickens which I hope they will help to consume this summer and in case they should not I have an equal number of turkeys for next winter for the same purpose". I wish you knew that girl better, there is something so quaint and original about her. My love to Cousin Mack and tell him Cousin Bet and family have gone to Winchester to see old Mrs. Richards who is quite feeble. Aunt Letitia is at home alone. Mr. Richards passed here yesterday and said she was well. Tom Brown is in town — his wound is almost healed. Mr. Cook has gone to Richmond for Wythe *(Cook)* who was wounded through both legs, not seriously but severely. Do write us very soon as we are so anxious to hear from you. I forgot to tell you that Lucy wrote us that she had been down to Harpers Ferry. Had a fine view of Maryland Heights and was delighted having been there whilst the Yankees were shelling the place.

Ever your devoted,

Nell

P.S. I expect you know more about the movements of Ewell and Hill than we do. Mrs. Hope is quite complaining. The heat prostrates her so I fear her days are numbered.

Near Petersburg, Virginia
Tuesday, July 26, 1864

My Dear Nellie,

I know you will be disappointed at seeing Mack *(Blakemore)* unaccompanied by me, but the fact is only one of us can leave at a time and I have decided to wait until Pat can leave his command and bear me company. He made a proposition in a late letter that we should go on together this winter and if Providence wills everything favorable for us, you, Lu and Laura may test your culinary powers upon one of Laura's pet turkeys on the 24th of December, with the assurance that we will endeavor to appear with you at the family board the next day. Benton Roy telegraphed me on the 24th that he, Williams and Pat escaped unhurt in the battle of the 22nd at Atlanta. The enemy got decidedly the worst of it. Today we hear that Early has threshed the Yankees terribly at Kearnstown. Hurrah for Secesh!

Dick Buck[9] came down on Sunday last, with Billy Rust[10], took dinner and stayed until late in the evening. I had a long confidential talk with the dear fellow, each of us unbosoming the pent-up feelings of two years — our past experience and future prospects. He spoke touchingly of poor Walter *(Dick's brother)*, and though I am not given to displaying emotion of that kind, an unbidden tear trembled in my eye and my voice was unsteady as we conversed about him. Dick Bayly stayed with us a couple of days, a week or so ago. He is a noble little fellow. The two Dicks are a matchless pair of boys, of whom their relatives may well be proud.

Nelly, you must take good care of Mack. He is my shadow. I am his. He tried hard to induce me to take the furlough and let him remain, and a more generous-hearted true friend I cannot claim than Mack. He can give you a description of our lodging like kittens when the Yankees were shelling our camp some days ago. We had to leave the tents and hug the trees, and finally to take position about 300 yards from both.

Grant is effecting nothing here. He may shell and sharp-shoot to his heart's content, but that will not take Petersburg. There is almost incessant picket skirmish on the lines, sounding like wood-chopping, and at night the mortars join in and bellow villainously.

I send by Mack for Father, a rough sketch of a "Monitor", and enclosed in it is a duplicate or triplicate of a letter signed by "Old Beaury" himself — it may serve to satisfy him that our gallant little hero doesn't regard the "Old Court" as altogether useless, and that he has exerted himself to start me up the ladder of promotion. I never mentioned it before, because there was a faint hope that I might get the position and give you a surprise; but now I have a good opportunity for sending it home for safe-keeping, and here it is. Ask Father to keep it in the scroll form and not to fold it, as the creases would injure it. I am not unwilling to acknowledge that I am proud of this mark of approbation from the hands of one of the very greatest men of our day, and this is not the only attempt he has made to advance me.

I hope Lu has returned *[from Clark County]* and will be with you when Mack arrives. She would relish his company — he is <u>so</u> lively and cheerful.

Well, Nellie, this war will hardly last more than eight or ten months longer, and we boys are already discussing plans for the future. I cannot resist the idea that there is a better time in store for our clan. The wheel of fortune turns regularly, and we must try to be brought to the top once in a lifetime. Uncle John is expected to visit us daily, but he is very, very slow moving. I want to have a long chat with him. Has Uncle Tom received a long letter I wrote him several days ago? Hope he has recovered.

Love to all — Must write to Lu next.

Truly your own Brother,
Alvin

Bel Air, Tuesday, August 30, 1864

My Dear Irvie,

No letter from you since the 12th of July. why I cannot tell as the mail communication seems to be open. we feel all the time anxious about you. that appears to be the most important point now and we know where there is anything to be done your division is almost sure to have a hand in it. I was at Mrs. Roy's yesterday and she told me that Mary Carson had a letter from the Colonel of 12 August and that all were well. from what we learned our letters from here do not reach their destination. Nellie and I wrote to you a short time ago and Lucy also wrote from Clarke. we have had quite stirring times here within the last few weeks of which you no doubt have heard something. the army in passing staid several days and we had Gen. Anderson and staff with us. (You know it is Gen. Longstreet's old staff) so we had the pleasure of meeting a number of acquaintances. Major Latrobe, Colonel Manning, Major Walton and others. they are the nicest gentlemen I have met. the battle was fought from Guard Hill to Mr. Painter's. they had every advantage of us and the wonder is that any of our men escaped but their losses of killed and wounded was much larger than ours. but oweing to bad management we lost about 200 prisoners. had our officers obeyed orders our loss would have been very slight. we have about 50 wounded in town most of them doing well — two died day before yesterday. the citizens are not in a condition to do for them all they need but it is wonderful how they can do as much as they do. you will be surprised to here that Alvin is at home — he took us greatly by surprise as he had written by Mack that he would not come til Christmas — but he got sick and so concluded that he had as well be home. he walked from Culpepper Court House and was pretty much used up when he got here and was looking very badly. but has improved much and looks like himself again but misses you so. it does not seem natural for him to be here without you. we have not half enjoyed his company. we are constantly reminded that there is "a vacant chair." and then Lucy was not at home. I had been trying to go down for her but the involvement of the army prevented me. but as soon as our army got possession of Berryville I went down. I found Lucy quite unwell and the next day she was confined to her bed and during the two days that I staid she had three chills but insisted on coming home. I was doubtful when started about being able to get her home that day — she stood the ride better than I expected — but has been confined to her bed ever since. she has a dreadful cough and I feared Pneumonia but she is better this morning and I hope will soon be up. she dislikes being sick so much while Alvin is here. I do not think her trip did her any good — she says she was not well two days while she was gone — Alvin went to Mr. Richards' yesterday and will be back this morning. he says he is not going to give up his trip home with you next Winter. J. T. Petty is home also he spent the day here on Friday. Alvin is so fond of him. we are anxious about our army in the valley, fear they will have to fall back. the Yankees burnt every stack yard and many cows from Mr. Painter's to Berryville. there is not a hand full of anything to feed a horse on between here and there. in Clarke and Jefferson they took all the meat stock and fowls in many places did not leave families a cow to give them milk. at Colonel Larue's they searched for money and jewelry and Fannie Larue had a regular fist fight with one over a box of your Aunt Amelia's jewelry she struck him on the nose with her fist and nearly knocked him down and he snapped his pistol at her but he did not get the box. she struck another with a rock, they took all of their meat that they could find, all their horses but one they hid in the cellar, their preserves and nearly all their fowls but did not take his stock as they did most places — Lucy intended writing to you but is not able. will do so as soon as she can — We are all well — Your Aunt Bettie and the little boy are doing well — it is the greatest pet you ever saw. they call it William Richardson — do write often, we are so anxious to hear — Remember us to all friends and relatives — and now I commend you to God and pray he may keep you safe and that we may soon meet again.

Your mother,
E.A.B. *(Elizabeth Ashby Buck)*

Home, September, 1864

My Own Dear Irvie,

    With a heavy heart I have seated myself by my favorite window to pen you the first messages of love I've been able to send you for a long time. Our dear Alvin and Cousin Mack have just left after their 30 days furlough and we feel as if a corpse had been carried over the old threshold. Tomorrow our Luray mail comes in and we long yet dread to learn the tidings it will bring. We have none of the particulars of the fall of Atlanta only 'tis said Hardee's Corps was cut off from the main command and bore the brunt of the struggle. That Cleburne was in the melee I do not doubt and oh! what would not I give to know you were safe. Just at this time last year after the battle of Chickamauga we were suffering the same anxiety on your account. I'm afraid it's very selfish of me, but I take little interest in the newspaper accounts of the Western Campaigns, if they only speak of the safety of "Major General Cleburne and Staff" it is much more than all the descriptions they could contain. Well "wait and trust" is my motto, it has been a good one thus far and I will not abandon it now.

If it be possible I want to give you a detailed account of all that transpired with us since you last heard from us.

I was in Clarke nearly months and wrote you but once while there because I did not know your address. The last fortnight of my stay was a most exciting one. First we had Sheridan's and Averill's like wolves let loose upon us and such a time as we had! Fannie LaRue was staying at Aunt Cattie's and she frightened us almost in her encounters with those double-dyed demons. Once as they were carrying off Cousin Will's pet horse she ran out and tried to wrench the reins from his hands, he tried to ride over her and she seized a rock and flung at him. He drew his pistol but did not shoot. Again, while searching Aunt C's drawers Fannie tried to conceal and casket of jewelry which had belonged to Aunt Millie and was left carelessly in the drawer. The little viper who was conducting the search saw her and ordered her to surrender it she refused, and tried to get upstairs with it but was stopped by him in the hall. He threatened to shoot her, she dared him and he laid the muzzle to her head and fired. 'Twas a blank cartridge with which it was loaded but she didn't know this and stood it without flinching. The Yankees caught the hand containing the casket and with the unoccupied fist she dealt him a blow — true Sayers-style — that sent him reeling 10 feet from her. We all rushed forward at this dreadfully alarmed for her but another of the "detectives" came forward and interfered. Once they were very near killing Uncle LaRue and I was fully convinced the house would be burnt over our heads. They killed the sheep, stole all the available horses, broke into the pantry and with impious hands seized the jams and preserves I had taken so much pains to make just the day before. I tried to hold onto one jar but the wretch pulled it out of my hands and pushed me rudely away. All day the yard was filled with the cries of the murdered fowls and the oaths of their assassins. It was raining and cold and we had to stand picket on the different porches from 9:00 in the morning until 5:00 in the afternoon. Sometimes they would try to frighten us away by loading their guns and pretending to fire. Then they would swear horribly. I couldn't help but be amused at Fannie. They found out she was from New York and delighted in provoking her to quarrel with them. One of them was telling her of his chase after an old hen. She retorted by remarking that if he would only display as much perseverance in the pursuit of rebels he "might occasionally" succeed in catching one. The Yankee said he had seen the Rebels run a great deal faster than the hen. "Well," said Fannie, "If you did 'twas when you looked over your shoulder." She told one of Averill's cubs that when our boys charged your Brigade their war cry should be "BAAH." The gentleman with some of his conferees had been sheep stealing. They searched the servants clothes and stole money and other little trifles from them and indeed did everything that was mean. I would not condescend to bandy words with them, when forced to exchange words my sentences were as short and sharp as possible — sometimes they would force an angry expression from me, but as for using anything like force with them I know it is utterly absurd, the physical strength is all on their side and I will not provoke them to a test of it. If they take a fancy to have anything and decline listening to sober reasoning and the voices of justice and mercy I should never attempt to resist them further, for 'twould involve too much condescension on my part all to no purpose.

After the Yankees left as our forces came into Berryville shelling the Yankees out of their fortifications there and taking quiet possession. Ma wrote you of the sad desolation that marked the footsteps of the retreating foe. Not a barn, not a stable, straw or wheat stack from Nineveh to Berryville. Even the fields of grain and grass burnt. Met some old friends in the army. The next day after our army came in — Tuesday — I was taken with a chill and was just worn out with nervous excitement. That evening Ma and Orville came down for me and told me Alvin had been at home a week. I felt so impatient to get back that I believe it made me worse and we did not start home till Friday. Was confined to my room nearly a week losing so much of Alvin's society and grieving so about it. After I got well there were constant reports of Yankees coming into town from various directions and we were afraid for the dear fellow to remain many nights at home, so I saw, comparatively speaking, but little of him, but that little Irvie it has done me more good than anything that has happened for nearly three years. I felt younger and more intensely happy than I believed possible a short time since. He has improved so much and although ever affectionate and kind there was a deeper tenderness in his manner something I cannot explain but which made me feel like I wanted to cry every time he put his arm around me and laid his head on my shoulder. Our happiness was not complete though, when his footsteps made music to our ears the melody was imperfect for the want of another triad that used to sound in unison with his, when we sang at the piano there was a "chord in music we missed for your voice was away" and a "chord in each heart that re-echoed regret at your meansome stay." How often he spoke of "Pat" and wished he could have him with him to enjoy the comforts of home. how often we all sent thoughts of longing and regret to the distant battlefield and with swelling hearts wondered "when shall we all meet again?" Irvie, Alvin is such a dear good boy. I know, for he has told us, that his acts are not all consistent with his profession that he has made, he is so impulsive, so full of fun and glee that he is often carried beyond the limits of staid propriety, yet in his inmost soul I believe him to be a Christian an earnest and humble one.

Dear boy! dear brothers! I sometimes tremble when I think we making too much of our idols. You are keeping our thoughts too much from other things, binding us too strongly to things of earth and our punishment might be the removal of those objects so dear to us — and yet if I ever have lifted my heart to God in sincere supplication, if I ever have made a prayer it has been for you since you have been in the army. Sometimes I feel as if I would give anything just to take your place and endure your trials and hardships for a time and give you a long season of rest which you need, again I would make my love a mantle to envelop you in and save you from all danger and suffering, but how impotent I am to do ought for you, how surely I know that no other hands can we commit you than God's. that He alone is able to do that for you of which we are incapable. I fear I'm writing very incoherently — but you must know that Cary is singing on one side of me and Ma reading aloud a political letter on the other so that in the confusion I scarce know what I say.

Alvin and Cousin Mack with Ma, Nellie, myself and some few persons from town were invited to spend the evening at Mrs. Hope's this day week ago. We had a quite pleasant time and had just risen from the tea-table when the alarm came that the Yankees were entering town. The surgeon from the hospital with one of his patients were there and they with Cousin M. and A. were hustled out of the house minus their hats and started through the orchard cornfield in the greatest hurry you ever saw in your life. They thought the Yankees were so near that they expected to be fired into every moment and this haste was most amusing to behold badly frightened as we were. Alvin laughed himself as he clambered up the hill. Our party was broken up and we showered immemorable inverted blessing on the Yankees. 'Twas a false alarm after all and the boys were so provoked about it. They were forced to flee several times afterwards in just the same way. You don't know how vexatious it is unless you could be here to participate in such scenes. When you come next December I hope there will be no cause for such excitement and we may enjoy peace and quiet with "none to vex us or make us afraid." Alvin's furlough was not quite expired but Cousin Mack's had and he denied himself a few days more of enjoyment for the sake of having company back. Besides he thought if prompt in his return now there would be more chance of his obtaining a furlough for next December and he is fully resolved to come if he can. This hope makes the parting less bitter yet we already begin to miss him sadly and feel lost without him. He goes back much more comfortably than he came though. We've repaired his clothes and given him a new outfit from shoes to cravat and tobacco-bag. He needed it poor boy. His health is much improved by his sojourn too and he looks scarcely the same boy that he did even when I saw him first two weeks ago. You don't know what a comfort he seemed to be to Father and what a mutual gratification it seemed to be to both of them that they understood each other better than they used to. Father is in better spirits anyway than usual — he's always a philosopher — a real stoic in bearing his troubles though. We had Lt. Crittenden to spend a night and day with us a week since. Why did he leave the Staff and what kind of a ___ ___ is he? We were prepared to think everything kind and charitable of him because he had been with you and came up late in the evening while we all sat on the porch, and inquired of Irvie's Father. We felt as if he were a connecting link between us and you, but there is something queer about him. He seems gentlemanly, refined and intelligent enough and I felt sorry for him, yet he impressed me with the idea that he wanted us to think him eccentric and such an assumption always makes one ridiculous. Tell me, is he an misanthrope, is he an universalist and has he a mania for becoming an American Bonaparte? This is all I could make of him. There was also an old acquaintance of yours at Uncle Tom's a few nights since young Clark of Baltimore. He said he knew you when you lived with Dan Holliday and also saw you last April while with the Western Army. Mr. Shipe who was here the other day says he knows him well. By the way he is a genuine fellow, Mr. S. I mean — seems to regard us more as relatives as anything else. He inquired for you when he came in and remarked that he felt always afraid to ask the question lest there should be bad news for him. Old Mr. Almond's house was burned in Luray a short time since. There was a quantity of salt stored away in the old ware-room. Some man applied for it and was refused and 'twas supposed he burnt the house in revenge. Wasn't it too bad? Mr. Pittman's family are turned out of house and home and I don't know what they'll do. Ma wrote you of the second "battle of Front Royal" which took place near Guard Hill. The old place will become classic-ground after awhile. General Anderson and his Staff, Longstreet's old one — quartered here when the army passed down and I missed seeing the Major. Perhaps 'twas as well though for they say he mistook Laura for me and I feel so chagrined at his having so utterly forgotten me that the disappointment was not half so bitter as it would otherwise have been. Laura is nearly as tall as I am and we are not unlike in appearance with the exception of my wrinkles and crow feet — so there is some excuse for him — they say he inquired very particularly after my health too and this mollifies me. Irvie you must not think anything of my jesting in this way — 'tis not very delicate in a lady to make so many professions of admiration for a gentleman of whom she knows so little and who cares nothing for her, and I only make all this time over Major Lathrop to quiz you — guess you knew that though.

What do you all think of the prospects of peace, there's a great stir here in consequence of McClellan's nomination — there's a variety of opinions respecting the affect which his possible election will have upon the war. For my part I expect nothing from any of the Northern politicians, they're not to be trusted with anything save their own interests. We will have to end this thing by our own exertions and the sooner we do it the better. There you have a sage's opinion and you must feel it's weight. All friends and relatives well. Ma, Nellie and Laura send love and say you must write whenever you can. We have not heard from you since the 12th of July. Think of it! Grandma is spending the day in town and Father is away about the farm somewhere. I shall not read this over for I have not time to rewrite it and I know it will disgust me if I do venture a perusal. Please excuse manners in matter of writing.

Everett has just run in to say Uncle John has come. I must hasten out to meet him.

Farewell my own darling Irvie and may God bless you.

Lovingly,

Lucie

Our best love to all friends, say to Colonel R. *(Roy)* if he is with you that I will write by next mail. Cousin Will Cloud was wounded at Ream's Station, not seriously — is at Dinwiddy Court House doing well.

Bel Air, September 12, 1864
(To Colonel Benton Roy)

Really my good Socrates I had not imagined you possessed so much of the xantippe element. What a rebuke of a negligent correspondent you administered! and how unjust it was! Listen, and I will convince you that it was unmerited. There came a letter from you in April which met with an immediate response from me, this was the last intimation I had of your existence till late in August when yours of July 16 is received <u>30 days after date</u>. Thus it seems there are two of us in league with the mails. My sojourn in Clarke made no difference in this respect because my lines of communication were open all the while and letters did not fail to reach me. You asked me how many letters I have written this year. I <u>think</u> this is the <u>third</u> and as you have written me three we're even <u>there</u>. Some of your correspondents has evidently been spoiling you, but you must not expect me to do so too for I'm conscientious on this case. It was my intention to have written you upon my return home a fortnight since, but I was sick when I got here and for a week after enjoying Alvin's visit to us only heart friends separated by dreary years of suffering and trials permitted to meet again unexpectedly can imagine the heartfelt pleasure we enjoyed in having him with us — indeed I didn't know I <u>could</u> be as happy. I feel as if he had administered a drought of healing and strength to me so much brighter and better do I feel for having had a few quiet unreserved talks with him. There was so much to tell — we had so many questions to ask. I did not finish all before he left. Only two circumstances marred our presence, the absence of Irvie from our circle and the constant rumors of a yankee raid keeping us uneasy for Alvin's safety. We made the best of what we had though, and now that he is gone we hug to our hearts the hope inspired by his last words to me. "Never mind Lu! Cheer up and take care of yourself and I'll be home again with Irving in December." If you <u>should</u> all really come then, do try and leave your grave, dignified, official selves with the army and bring back to us the cheerful boyish friends who left us long ago. There have been losses enough and changes enough wrought by death, til we feel that the living are left to us unchanged.

It is a frequent and sad though with me — the number of bright and brave young spirits—

"Those we've loved grown faint with strife
As droped and died the tender womb
Folded the white tents of their life
For the pale army of the tomb."

Major Simpson's death was a shock to us all. I felt it deeply owing to the misunderstanding existing between us. I felt no unkindness toward him although there was a change from the old friendly feeling, still I have reason to believe thinking me unkind. Heaven knows how sincerely I regret it.

We feel troubled about Irvie since hearing of the fall of Atlanta — and you all. I trust all is well. If this be the case 'tis only once instance added to many others in which a kind Providence has shielded from the death that swept from your side as strong and brave and valued lives as your own. Have this same kind care has been with you through these years of danger and blight, have that same kind Hand has ministered to you and guided you! Every day has brought increased indebtedness to the love of your Heavenly Father has it brought an increase of gratitude as well! My dear friend do not deem these considerations unworthy or soldiers thoughts — they of all others must need super natural Strength and aid — they of all others should seek it and feel grateful for it. I can not understand how a soldier can be brave, when he faces death hazards not only his hopes in the present life but all prospects for eternity.

We had several letters from Irvie a few days since but none of a later date than the 15th of August. Alvin has promised to telegraph him from Petersburg and will let us know, I hope, by Saturday's mail the result.

You don't know how happy I am to be at home once more. My three month's visit <u>ought</u> to have been a charming one there was everything to make it so, but like a spoiled I cried for home. Nellie is the cause of this, because I'm excitable and rather nervous in temperament, she makes it her duty to protect me from every unpleasant contact and of course when away from her I miss her vigilant care. You see there's selfishness in our curious affections. I can tell you little or nothing of the good citizens of this borough have not been in tune since my return. Your Ma I heard from yesterday, she is well as usual. I think your sister is with her. Misses. Mary and Jennie Cloud are playing the part of ministering angels at the hospital. I believe they have been instrumental in saving the lives of many a valuable valiant soldier. You speak of the atmosphere of the border counties being detrimental to ones temper. It is not to be wondered at I'm sure I enjoyed to the fullest extent the advantages of proximity to the Enemies Country. I never before confessed being afraid of the yankees but do so now frankly after witnessing so much of their fiendish behavior. After their first descent upon us I that night had a high fever and was delirious all night. I pray heaven they may never come in here again. And Mr. Davis has declined adding another star to your constellation? 'Tis too bad of him and I refuse him my support should he ever again become candidate for office. But these stars are after all mere toys and as for titles, don't you think "Lieutenant Colonel" quite as imposing as simple "Colonel Roy."

Heard a few days ago that the Seventeenth were all well and happy as soldiers usually are.

Are we not having charming nights now? There is something peculiar sad and sweet in this month to me I think somewhat from association and also because there is so much of subdued _____ in it. Sometimes I come up to my room and leaning out of the window sit for hours scarce conscious of anything save of being enveloped in an atmosphere of tranquil, holy views. There are aspen trees just in front of my window and every night the moonbeams gleam on the polished leaves and light them up in myriads of starry splendors; and they twinkle and whisper with such life-like notions that I find companionship in them unlike what one finds in most inanimate objects. The stars never are so beautiful as at this season, they shine with such a tender radiance. When the least ruffled or out of tune if I can steal away by myself and have a few moments quiet _____ with them it calms and subdues my _____ — feelings sooner than anything in the world. I fancy there are numberless holy eyes that look deep, deep down into my heart and seeing all the wild turmoil and darkness there approach me with their gaze. They always leave gleanings of their silvery silence behind them. Nellie says she does not wonder you were unable to find the "key of her affections" when it has sailed away to Europe on board one of our ironclads. She is somewhat apprehensive that it may be lost at sea. All write in kind remembrances and good wishes as ever with warm regards.

Lucie

Petersburg, Virginia
September 12, 1864
Monday 12:30 P.M.

My Dear Lu

Van D., and myself arrived in camp some three hours ago, and having shaken hands around and unpacked our baggage, I'll try to give you an account of our trip.

After parting with Father and having taken a "last, long, lingering look" at the group on the house-top, we met Uncle Mack near Scroggins' mill, had a short conversation and moved on in the direction of Black-Rock, which point was said to be in possession of the Yanks — but this rumor proving untrue, no interruption was experienced. About nine miles from home we met Uncle John, and tried to induce him to go in to the house of a Mr. Johnson hard by. He was in too great a hurry to do so, and we drove up to the door and made a successful application for shelter and supper for man and beast. Mine host was a Scotchman, who still bore fully to the old British Lion and from his conversation appeared to be a strick neutral — mentioned having once owned some very superior Scotch whiskey, but didn't hint that there was any on hand at that time, although Van D., and myself assumed thirsty countenances and paid some delicate tributes to the excellence of the aforesaid beverage.

Making an early start next morning, we jogged along some three miles further, when a rain came up, compelling a halt at a hut on the roadside. By this time we were convinced that our beast was either idiotic or very unsophisticated. She seemed determined to occupy both sides of the road at the same time — staggering like a loped without any apparent cause — now trying to run us down some steep bank and presently steering straight for a hill on the opposite side. This perverse course nearly exhausted the whole stock of genteel abuse in our party; and poor Ed, who was at the helm, was particularly liberal with his lefthanded compliments. When the rain cleared off we struck out for "Little Washington," via Flint Hill, over one of the worst roads that ever was made. Arriving at W., we went to Mr. Bowens, had our beast fed and got a good dinner. After talking awhile to the Miss Happer we arose and went out to pay our bill; but Mr. B refused to receive a cent. We found the Misses H. very intelligent, nice girls, and regretted the necessity which compelled our departure at an early hour in the afternoon. Mr. Griffins, eight miles from Culpepper, was the halting place for the night. Here Van D., who was suffering from neuralgia, was kindly nursed by one of the fair occupants; and at 7 o'clock on Sunday morning we drew up at the depot in Culpepper. From there to Richmond nothing of note occurred. Van D., came very near being arrested there on account of his furlough having expired — or at least appearances indicated than an official was laying a trap for him — but V.D., "smelt a mice" and outwitted the kindly-disposed functionary. Upon getting off the cars here, I either jostled my straw hat off while going through the crowd, or some Confed stole it. As it was upon my head fitting lightly upon the old felt one, I didn't miss it until having gone some thirty yards from the train, when upon turning back and making inquiry, it was too late to recover it. As the weather is very cool, I'll not need it, but regret its loss on account of its having been a present from Orville.

Jn Latham informed me that Gen'l. Govan was captured in the melee at Atlanta and I fear Geo Williams went with him. Before closing this I hope to get a dispatch from Roy. Latham returns his thanks for the tobacco bag, and says he trusts to be able to express obligations in person at some day. He is very much delighted with it.

McClellan's letter of acceptance is "Union" to the core, and if it foreshadows truly his policy in the event of his election, it is equivalent to a declaration of an intention to prosecute the war, for the South will not accept his Union terms. But

Mr. Mac will no doubt trim his sails to suit the popular current and besides, I think his election extremely improbably. Lincoln has decided not to enforce the draft, fearing no doubt that it would injure his prospects with all the people. Opinion is very much divided in the army as to the duration of the war, some thinking it will be closed up in two or three months, while others can see no termination to it. The fighting will need be confined almost entirely to Virginia. Sherman, it seems, is in no hurry to move from Atlanta, and, indeed, may winter there, while Grant will probably seek to rival the capture of Atlanta by making a desperate attempt upon Petersburg and Richmond, which, if successful would contribute vastly towards the reelection of Abe, and at the same time add a lustrous laurel to the wreath of Butcher Ulysses. We must make a sturdy effort this fall and winter and trust in God to reward our sacrifices and patriotic earnestness with victory. I believe He will crown our struggle with success and secure us a happy independence yet.

Tuesday Sept 13th — Poor Van has recovered from his neuralgia, but is now a victim to "home-sickness." Scott Roy came in this morning and breakfasted with us — he intends going to the Valley and I may send this by him. Jimmy Blakemore has also been in, and sends his love to all. The enemy have put a large fifteen inch Mortar in position, and last night it opened on the city, the shells crashing in among the buildings with a genuine Charleston style. It is mounted upon a car which runs up on the Rail Road, and when the Yanks get tired of the amusement of house-smashing, they roll it off.

The weather is very bracing and we are surprised to find it so much cooler here than in the Valley. Fortunately, Van and myself are well fortified with clothing, and, if rations don't get short, can winter comfortably. It has been four or five years since we have had an opportunity to skate any, and in the event of our remaining in this vicinity, the Appomattox will offer good facilities for the indulgence of my favorite sport.

Well, my dear Lu, my thirty days' furlough appears like a pleasant dream, and it is a real treat to think calmly and quietly of the many happy little episodes that occurred daily at dear old Home. Little incidents almost overlooked at the time, and trifling in themselves, are now recalled and held in precious memory, for by them were shown the deep affection and tender solicitude you all bore towards as unworthy an object as myself. I think Father understands me better than formerly, and is disposed to forget my former follies. God bless him — he can never know how I love and revere him! But few persons are blessed with such a father, and that I ever gave him pain by a wayward course, grieves me. It was the result of an impulsive nature, too much prone to act first and think afterwards; (for this is one of my pet sins — hard to shake off — and one of the most dangerous that a man can contract). Did you ever think, Lu, that when the Devil wants to set a delicate little trap, he baits it with a nice little peccadillo and increases it with the capacity of his game? A disposition to find something ludicrous in every occurrence is another one of my failures, and I recollect having once laughed very heartily when a horse threw an old gentleman upon a spot of particularly hard ground in the street — not from want of sympathy for the unfortunate man, but because he happened to select a unique way of landing on the ground.

Sept. 14th — Well Roy has not yet replied to my dispatch, and as I want this to reach you by Saturday's mail, I'll have to close it. I think we may hope for the best, as he would probably have telegraphed me immediately after the retreat if anything had occurred; and Pat may not have had time to write until two or three days after the affair occurred. In addition to this the mails have to be sent around by the Danville route which is much longer. Besides, my dispatch may be 24 hours in reaching Roy, and his answer equally as long in coming here — sometimes dispatches are several days <u>en route</u>. Immediately upon receipt of one I will enclose it.

Give Van's and my love to <u>all</u> at home and all our relatives. Tell Uncle Newton, his letter to Charley will go by next Flag of Truce Boat, as it will be mailed tomorrow.

Dick Buck is well, but I've not yet seen him.

Truly your Own Brother
Alvin

Van's dulcined*(?)* has a "V: as the middle initial — a fact I've ascertained since arriving here — Don't it foreshadow an intention to become
<u>Mrs.</u>   <u>Van Dorn</u>?

14th - Since closing up I received the enclosed letter from Cou Geor B — <u>Thank God it's no worse</u> — I think Jack Latham mailed the letter to me from Irving which Cous G., speaks of — but I did not mention it because it came to this place some ten or twelve days ago and I didn't suppose one could have arrived here so early conveying intelligence from the fight of the first. If this should not have been the letter Cous G. refers to,it is still en route somewhere and the one mailed from here for Front Royal is of a date prior to the time he was wounded. Poor Geo has indeed been picked up and I would much prefer Pat's *(Irving)* condition to his. Will write to P., immediately —
Affectionately
A *(Alvin)*

Latham says the ladies in Columbus were very kind, and Pat will no doubt get good quarters at a private house.

The Yanks have just ceased a heavy bombardment of the city.

(Letter enclosed in letter to Lucy from Alvin on September 12, 1864.)

In the woods near Griffin

September 7, 1864

Dear Alvin

I am sorry that this return for your letter of May last is occasioned by a circumstance so similar to the one which prompted you to write me then. Our correspondence has degenerated into <u>Bulletins</u> simply.

Irving told me he had several days ago written to you giving you the particulars about his being wounded in the calf of his leg on the first inst. I was then at Atlanta which we evacuated that night and our Corps only reached here by a very circuitous route on the fifth. Learning through the papers that a Capt. Buck was admitted on the second into hospital here I rode down to find him and had no trouble in locating his ward tc. Found him sitting up in bed overhauling his "portable property" with a dozen or two of apples stowed away as <u>reserve rations</u>. He is much fleshier than when I last saw him and says his wound has not pained him in the least so that he considers this a mere resting spell in which he can make up in sleep for lost time during this campaign. He left yesterday for Columbus, Georgia where he expects to remain the balance of this month when he says he will be again ready for duty.[11]

Well old Sherman flanked us out of Atlanta most beautifully and scientifically. I don't know who is to blame but the counter movement on our side was very bunglingly executed. We were scattered every direction and every one seemed to be going it on his own account. I think the Yanks might have damaged us greatly if they had known of our condition or been in a situation to have taken advantage of our loose order.

I suppose Irving wrote to you of the Capture of George Williams with Gen'l. Govan in the first. I am glad the boy is safe but wish they had somebody else as we shall all miss him very much.

Have you seen Billy lately? I received a telegram from him at Richmond en route for old Bush's Head Quarters and presume he is now again on duty. Tell him I have written to him twice since receipt of his last. Have had nothing later from home than July 19th. <u>Cad</u> was or had been quite sick with <u>billing</u> fever. I am very anxious to hear from her again as I see they have had several severe fights with Woodward in the town since, and in one of which he was killed. Alick passed through this place two weeks ago on his way to Kentucky recruiting for his command. He was looking hearty and was in fine spirits. Mac Catlett went with him. Sorry to see by this days paper that General Morgan[12] is killed. Hope Duke may succeed him as I think he is perhaps a better officer than Morgan was.

Remember me to Mac, Newton and Billy and any other of our relatives with you. Write to me

Your affectionate

G.B.B. *(George Brooke Blakemore)*

Hospital
Americas, Georgia

Dear Cousin Lucy,

I arrived here today for the purpose of seeing Irving and am gratified to be able to write you that I find him much improved. I have just had a long talk with him about the events of the day upon which he was wounded and I captured, and we recalled many incidents which provoked from him hearty laughs. He was quite sick six or eight days ago, his wound having gangrened and he being further a sufferer from fever; but now all is better, the gangrene has been arrested and suppressed and his system is free from fever. I hope that his recovery will now be rapid and that he can soon leave his couch. I regret very much that I could not be with him during the worst of his illness, but I arrived from my Northern trip only on the 21st, and was not informed of it until the 27th. He has borne the pain caused by the wound with the greatest resignation, and by his patience and good temper has won the affection of his surgeon, Dr. Cross who takes the greatest interest in his welfare. He has good nurses, is in a cleanly quiet room, and is frequently visited by ladies, who vie in their attempts to please him and comfort him. He speaks most frequently of these kindnesses, and you may be satisfied that all is done for him that is possible, except to a sister or mother, but as it is impossible for you to be with him as you so much desire, I hope you will be content to know that every care is given him. The reputation of his command was sufficient to procure for him marked attention, but his own popularity with all who approach him ensures him all assistance that he needs.

I will write you again tomorrow more fully concerning him, and meanwhile, if I have not given that impression above let me assure you that you need not be uneasy about him at all. He has been gradually improving for five or six days, and is better now than at any time for two weeks.

Knowing the desire which all the family will have to know everything concerning him, I must ask from lack of time, that you will allow me to defer a fuller account until tomorrow, when I will try to be more satisfactory.

His love to all — and mine, I am Cousin Lucy,

Respectfully yours,
George A. Williams

Americas, Georgia
October 3, 1864

Dear Cousin Lucy,

I am compelled to resort to pencil in consequence of _____ pen and ink — but I hope the tracings will remain sufficiently distinct to convey to you some account of your dear brother. I promised to write yesterday, but circumstances prevented, and as the mails are so irregular at any rate, I hope you have not been disappointed in not hearing from him so soon as you may have expected. Since I wrote you there has been continued improvement. His system is in better condition and his face is brighter. He rested well last night, and he is easy today. He thinks his wound does not look so well this morning but the surgeon says it does. We succeeded in getting him to consent to be removed into a tent, to which he had objected, fearing he would not receive such good and constant attention. The change was made yesterday morning, and he now expresses himself much pleased that it was done. Of course he is as well cared for there, and has the benefit of free and pure air, and a change of scene, which I know grateful to the sick. He is also in a more quiet place, there being no other patient near him. He has a negro boy in the tent with him constantly, who is very faithful and gentle with him. Several attendants are even at hand, and the surgeons do not restrict the number of their visits, or confine them to the prescribed hours. Ladies came in at all hours on their errands of mercy, and take especial pleasure in providing for him, a member of Gen'l. Cleburne's staff, and the favored one with that warrior. He reads considerably and has just finished *Pevine of the Peak* and sent to a young lad for *The Fair Maid of Perth*, which I have recommended to him, I am glad that he has seemed gratified at my visit. We have talked over the events of the 1st Sept and 31st Aug, and compared notes, and have made ourselves mutually acquainted each with the other's adventures after our misfortunes upon the first named day. We had often before congratulated ourselves upon our favored lot in escaping from so many hard fought fields; and upon our having never lost a day from duty. But that affair of Jonesboro terminated that period of Providential protection. We have now entered upon another era in which I trust we may be similarly blessed again. Irving at least will be safe from the dangers of the field during the remainder of this campaign which now promises to be vigorously renewed, as his wound will not heal sufficiently early to allow of his returning to duty before it must end. If he can only continue to improve as I hope he will, he will soon be able to sit and then to move about, and partake of the hospitality of the well-to-do persons who live in the spacious surroundings of this little place, and who, from the short reign of hospitals among them, are yet more eager than their countrymen elsewhere to comfort those who have suffered in their defense. Then I hope he will get sixty or ninety days' leave and visit the dear ones at home, to which event he has so long been looking forward with delighted anticipation. Such a reward will readily be granted him by those who dispense indulgences, and who well know it deserved by long and close attention to duty. But when he wishes he will advise you of his intentions. He has received your letter of _____ and one from Alvin of the 14th, I know you always write him regularly and often, but I would suggest that you write even more frequently whilst he is off duty, as there is nothing to engage his mind and he grows wearied without diversion — and then the gratification of hearing from home will be heightened too. I have answered Alvin's letter; but have to regret that I can so illy fill the place of him for whom I speak. A letter from him could be more gratifying and assuring than all I can write; but you know it is difficult for him to sit up long enough to pen a letter. He still keeps up his diary however, and I have just copied the military items of the month of August for his chief.

Irving's tent is pitched apart, in the Court House yard. A large oak tree shades it pleasantly during most of the day, and the kind surgeon is having an arbor constructed to keep off the other rays that would strike it.

The yard is beautifully upgrown with grass, and is kept scrupulously clean. The tent is of the most commodious size, and its uplifted walls admit every breeze to fan his brow. He is freed from all annoying disturbances, and is altogether so pleasantly situated that I <u>augur</u> good results from the change.

I greatly regret that the activity of the campaign will not admit of my being with him until he is entirely recovered. Were we in camp, I <u>would</u> stay. But on the evening of my departure from the Army (20 Oct) it was announced that our Corps would move next day. Important operations are now in progress, and I have already stretched my leave of six days so that I get back before any engagement, it will be all well. Nothing but my anxiety for one I love so well would have reconciled me to be absent.

Irving and I are again called upon to lament our separation from Col Roy, and the loss of his chief, the pride of our Corps, and the right arm of the Army. Some time since he applied to be relieved, but the President wished him to await the termination of this campaign. For the battle of Jonesboro Gen'l. Hood blamed him, saying it caused the fall of Atlanta; while the Corps and its commander have in no engagement made more character than at that affair, where six corps were opposed to ours alone, while the Comdr in Chief was returning from Atlanta with Stewart, and calling Lee whither he was not needed. The enemy hurled six against one, while he kept one idle and we two. That strategy was not Gen'l. Hardee's. I am told that Gen'l. H. was flattered the night before his departure with the most touching ovation that has been given any officer. The whole corps quitted quarters and besieged his encampment in a forest of pines. Scarcely enough men were left for guards, officers and men were moved to tears at parting with the noble old hero — and he was equally pained to leave them. Roy was very anxious to visit Irving and had gone to the cars to come when he was advised of Gen'l. Hardee's orders, and compelled to forego what he considered a pleasure and a duty. We will miss him very much. Such a long association can only be broken with pain. To me it has been peculiarly beneficial as I had a warm friend at each Hd. Qrs. in the ascending scale, to whom I could look with confidence for many favors that would otherwise have been unsought, and although I had no use for personal indulgences, it was often a source from which I obtained them for friends.

11 P.M. - I have just come from a long talk with Irving in which he has spoken very freely and feelingly and given expression to the good and noble qualities which actuate him. We have reviewed personal and military affairs, and have laid aside the restraint which office imposes upon us whilst in the field. He is not fatigued by any amount of talking, and regretted for me to leave even at this late hour. At the dressing of his wound this evening four surgeons including Dr. Cross and Dr. Gore the surgeon in charge, were present and all agreed that the symptoms were more favorable and assured him he had no cause for uneasiness. He wishes me to tell you that it is much better. I will be glad to know that I leave him under such favorable circumstances. I shall leave him at ten tomorrow morn, sorry that I cannot remain with him till he's able to go about. I think you may expect the next letter from his own dear hand. I regret that a sterner duty calls me away — but nothing will excuse a longer delay, especially as I feel that our Army will ere many days again measure weapons with the enemy on the far side of the Chattahoochie. We will doubtless have a very active season until Sherman is expelled from Atlanta or Hood departed. I hope I shall not have lost a skirmish.

Unless he advises you otherwise address Irving, "Bragg Hospital, Americus, Sumpter Co. Ga" — ("Staff of Maj. Gen'l. Cleburne"). Should our movements cease soon, I will try to see him again. I will not close before tomorrow as the mail leaves on my train. He wishes me to say this is in answer of your last. I will not attempt the transmittal of messages of love, which will lose their force thereby, and as I could so _illy_ speak what you can well imagine. I leave him feeling assured that no kindness will be denied him, and that the humane gentlemen who care for him will watch and work for his good and comfort. I have made arrangements to hear frequently from him.

Overlook the unsightliness of my scrawl, if you please, Cous Lucy. It is unmeet for lady's eye, but all I can do under the circumstances.

Morn. 4th — I leave in a few minutes, and am glad to report Irving doing very well — rested comfortably and looks bright and cheerful. Wound getting on finely.

Excuse my hasty closing, Cous. Lucy, and believe me

Yours sincerely
George A. Williams

My Dear Irvie,

We have had no regular mail since the Yankees passed up the Valley and it was a mere chance your letter announcing your wound reached us Scott Roy brought it from Gordonsville and we got it the evening before the Yankees came in. just to think how uneasy we had been about you and but for that letter would still have been in suspense not knowing what your fate might have been — and Mrs. Roy too has not had a line from Benton. we know it is all owing the non arrival of the mails. but I believe the Culpepper mail is running again and we hope soon to hear from you. Lucy wrote to you last week and sent to Alvin by private hand for him to forward to you. we have since heard that Beauregard has gone south. do not know the truth or if the boys have gone with him. have had no letter from Alvin since he left but know he has written. wish we knew where he is. would not be strange if you should all meet in the same army again? the last paper we had contained a notice of Hardee's having been relieved of his command by his own request. I fear you and Benton will be separated as he of course will remain with the General — you would feel almost lost without him or George. poor George, we were so sorry to hear of his being captured it will go hard with him he is so spirited but hope they may effect an exchange as we noticed by the papers that the officers were trying to do so by the way Lucy had a letter today from Mack Bayly written some time ago. he is still at Fort Delaware. Lucy wrote to you of the terrible times we have had with the Yankees but we fared better than we expected. they troubled us but little but we do dread their return. we heard today that they were in Luray with a large force supposed to be retreating if so we may well dread them. they will be desperate. they nearly ruined Uncle N. *(Newton)* and Mr. R. *(Richards)* when they went up. broke his mill so it will take a year to repair it in some instances they stripped families of even their clothing. they behaved very badly on Capt. Roy's farm. they camped there and destroyed most of his stock. we had a letter from Colonel Larue today. they did not leave him wheat enough for bread and seed destroyed all his corn killed his hogs and poultry and I do not know how the people there are to live many farms have not a panel of fence left. if we can only keep our houses and what is in them we will feel that we are fortunate tis said that they have issued an order to arrest every man from 17 to 50. we are uneasy about your Uncle Tom and Allie. we have been making some molasses but the cane is hardly ripe enough we have a tolerable crop if we can only keep it. Lucy wrote to you about Evred's breaking his leg. he is doing very well and we hope he will soon be well. Lucy had a letter from Nannie lately she as usual inquires after you — wish you would write to her. you do not know how thankful I try to feel that you escaped as you did it is a thousand mercies that you were spared and I hope you are grateful to God for thus preserving you. do not be in a hurry to get back to service — but take care of yourself and do not let the Yankees get you— . write when you can and we will do the same — we will get them some time. I have written hastily to send in the morning by Victor Brown. kind regards to all friends if you have an opportunity say to Colonel Roy all are well at <u>home</u> though I have no doubt they will continue him letters. all friends well. how I wish it was so we could have you with us to nurse you but would not have you here now. all join in much love to you. I commit you to God's care, may He shield you and keep you is my prayer.

E.A.B. *(Elizabeth Ashby Buck)*

Bel Air
October 23, 1864

"Hold um tuddy Itchie," *(Dick Buck)*

And don't look too doleful when you open the envelope to find one of my "four storys" as Irvie calls them, I am only going to answer in this one the five of yours, dates of which are in my letter case but have slipped my memory. My only excuse for long silence is, in the first place, when Alvin came home (those thirty days are among the happiest of my life), I had just as much as I could do to look at and to talk to him; in the second place, ever since then we have been subjugated and I have not had the heart to write.

I do wish my dear Cousin I could recollect and tell you all we have passed through since Alvin left us; purgatory I might say is a circumstance to these last forty days and nights. You remember I wrote you about Gen'l. Anderson and Gen'l. Longstreet's old staff having dined with us when our army went down the Valley, after Early's retreat from Winchester. Gen'l. Wickham attempted to hold a large force of yankees in check at Weston's and would have done so had not the yankees out numbered him ten to one; his men fought gallantly, sustaining but a small loss in their retreat. I can never forget that morning. I rose early and was in the kitchen assisting Sallie in baking bread for a little Confed, (which he never got, poor fellow), when the firing commenced. We heard the Yankees' cheer and charge across the river, and knew what we might then expect. In less than ten minutes the whole face of the country seemed covered with blue coats and the air was rent by the most hideous yelps that only a yankee can make. For three days the cavalry wagons and artillery were passing through toward Luray. We fought them all along the road to Bentonville where we made a stand till morning and then fell back to Luray and so on to Port Republic. Then we gave them their desserts and they came back, burning, destroying and stealing in the most heathenish manner. They burned all mills and barns as far as Clover Hill, excepting Hazard's mill. A negro and white yankee burned the Clover Hill barn, then rode up to the house and said they had orders to burn it too, but if Uncle Fayette would give them forty dollars in gold they would not do so; if he did not they would shoot him. Jule had some money concealed on her person and becoming alarmed for her father, threw it to them. We have not heard the extent of the mischief they did there but understand they burned even all Uncle Fayette's farming implements.[13] Some two weeks ago Aunt Susan *(servant at Clover Hill)* and her three children went off one night to the yankees, saying she was going to look for her husband. The last I heard from there, Aunt Lizzie had just finished churning and said it was the hardest days work she ever did. Did you ever dream of her coming to that? Mrs. Miller's, Mrs. Green's, Capt Gardner's, Capt Roy's *(servants)* and Horace have all gone to taste the sweets of freedom. Some twenty or thirty white families have also gone, a happy riddance indeed. Copp and family started last Saturday evening and there is a rumor that he was captured by McCauslin's men next day and forwarded to "Camp Lee"; I can't vouch for the truth of it. Horace left us in the day, Friday to see what he could pick up off the camp ground, returned at midnight and took his clothes which he had packed previously. We all saw from his movement several days before that he intended it. It was last night, two weeks ago we went on top of the house and witnessed the burning of Mr. Weston's mill and house; had it been the funeral pyre of Lincoln and Cabinet, Grant and his hirelings, I should have thought it the grandest, most beautiful fireworks ever seen; as it was, when I saw those terrible flames licking upward, illuminating the whole face of the county and sky and thought of the fiendish cowards who could not compete with our brave southerners in the field and were waging a cruel war against their helpless wives, mothers, sisters and children at home, I felt strong enough to consume the whole of Yankeedom. Starvation is now their declared purpose in the Valley, and tho' they may partially succeed, we are not more yankees now than we were when the first call of Virginia summoned them to the field. They can't burn all the dry leaves, tree branches and water. You can't imagine, my dear Cousin, what a trial it was to have them dash up and ask for bread, when they had burned our mills, taken our grain and to have to feed them and not open our lips to tell them what we thought of them. The 77th New York (commanded by Col French of the 6th Corps) camped for three days on their return from up the Valley, in the field to the right of Uncle Toms and between Mr. Glasscock's and the woods. Col French was an old friend of Uncle Marcus in the old war and I give him the credit of having the best behaved men I've seen during the war. Your Pa and Jacque were obliged to leave home with the horses and for fear of their conscription, which, I am happy to say, was not put into execution. The servants betrayed your Pa; told where all the things were hid and they took every grain of tea, coffee, sugar, all Aunt Letitia's preserves, some of the best clothing and Jacque's clothes, knives, forks and oh! Dick, the grapes were ready to gather and they took the last one of them. Just to think of it, and I don't expect my poor Coz has tasted one this season. Your Ma was very much alarmed, but Gussie fought and matched them to the last. When you come she will tell you how she cut one with a knife and kicked another from the top of the steps to the bottom, and saved a good deal by the way she managed them. I tell you she is just as spunky as she can be with them. Miss Caroline Willis and Gussie jerked

Uncle Mack's overcoat off a yankee's back and pummeled him well. All Aunt Letitia's goods she got in Clarke last winter they took. They left Uncle Newton the house and out houses and four sheep not a grain of any thing. The last we heard from Mr. Richards, his servants, two pigs, a few potatoes, a barrel of corn and three cows was all he had. And don't you think his Confederate bonds and every piece of meat were burned in the mill? He, like many others is completely ruined. Dr. Dorsey had half barrel of flour and one piece of meat; he, Mrs. Dorsey nor the children have a single rag of clothes but the ones on their backs, and only enough cover for one bed. He was here and said they even took her stockings, his little dead girl's clothes, and said he would have to borrow a shirt when he had his washed. Scott was here in the intervals of their invasions and can tell you of the six men of Mosby's they shot after they had surrendered, one of whom was poor Henry Rhodes whom they caught at Mrs. Jones' toll gate, tied him between two horses and dragged him past his mother's door to the field just opposite Cousin Elizabeth Richardson's, where they shot him three times. Mrs. Rhodes and Emma had extracted a solemn promise from old Custer that he should be treated as a Confederate prisoner and whilst the former had taken his hand in gratitude for having saved the life of her son, he lay a corpse. Two men, a Georgian and a Virginian were hung in the woods beyond Cousin Elizabeth's. It was a horrible day to us.[14] Jim Anderson and Ed Saffle were in the mountain with their horses. Ed was up a chestnut tree when the yankees came up and made him mount Jim Anderson's horse bare backed and trotted him all the way to Guard Hill where they pleaded "citizen" so hard they let them off. Jim started for the mountain instanter.

Cousin Elizabeth fared like all others; badly. They suffer as much from their insolence as any thing else. So far we have fared better than many of our neighbors. They killed two of our hogs, took nearly all of our corn, killed fifteen turkeys (we thought to keep them for our poor boys Christmas), tore down our fence from the wood pile to the corner, and even burned the little gate up. Tore off the carriage house door and the weather boarding off of it and the mill; but I feel so thankful that we came off so well. A drunken Irishman was all that came in the house. One night they camped in the meadow next Mr. Petty's shop and half past eleven we were aroused by hearing them breaking open the smoke house door. When we got up the yard was full of them. They were in the garden digging potatoes, stealing every thing they could lay their hands on. We have not for five weeks laid down without all of our clothing on. We hear this evening that Gen'l. Sheridan with thirty thousand men will pass through tomorrow on their way to Culpepper; what we may suffer the next three days the Good Being only knows.

I suppose you have heard ere this of the death of poor Eddie Brown, Joe Painter and Joe Johnston; Mack Irwin and Alfred McKay were wounded. Early captured in the fight on Tuesday over two thousand prisoners, a hundred wagons and twenty three cannon; it was quite a surprise to the yankees, as to us. We were awakened at five o'clock by the sound of cannon, and I'll tell you it was the most pleasant music that we've heard for many a long day. Our men were passing through all day and we had quite a day of rest. We laid down slept soundly, to wake on the morrow and find our army all gone. Early at Fishers Hill and the Yankees at Guard Hill again. The battle was ours up to four o'clock when our men straggled to plunder yankee camp ground and the Yankees received heavy reinforcements. Rosser pitched into their rear and played the wiles with them; we have heard nothing from our friends with him, since we drove the Yankees nearly to Winchester. Cousin Mount, Willie Buck, Willie Cline and Giles Cook were on the mountain all the while and worried them not a little; and don't you think they rode into town one evening just as a squad rode out?

Scott Roy is still sick with chills and fevers at Mrs. Millers when we heard last but suppose he has left ere this. Do you know that 'tis said Dod Foster and John Shipe are leading the Yankees through the mountains? I hope they will yet catch it. This day two weeks ago Eliza Hope came up almost carrying her mother in her arms and said they were going to burn the mill, and we all started in great haste to try to save what we could for them, and in less time than you could imagine we had every thing moved out and in the west end of our house, but fortunately they changed their minds. Mr. Hockman's and Petty's mill and house (Water Side) were burned. Mr. Hope's and Father's are the only ones left for miles around. They even burned Uncle Tom's saw mill because a bomb shell picked up from the battle field had been laid in there and they said there was ammunition concealed in it. To think that September grapes, hardy chokes, water melons and beans have all passed and you were not here to enjoy them with us. You don't know how much I thought of, and wished for you, especially whilst Alvin was at home. Have you seen him and Cousin Mack since their return?

Cousin Mack met with a Miss Alice Williams on his way up; rode in the wagon with her several miles; fell in love with her eyes and went to Fauquier to see her; quite a romance wasn't it? You should hear Alvin tell how one evening we were invited to spend the evening at Mr. Hope's, and the cry of "yankees are coming" started them over the hill through the cornfield to Johnston Lake's bare headed, and spoiled all our fun for it was a false alarm. Mrs. Wheatly's darkies all picked themselves up a night or so since and left.

Nov 6th

Two weeks since I commenced this and we are still in Yankeedom! but faring far better than at first. Orville and I walked up to Belmont this morning, the first time I have left home since Evred broke his leg some eight or nine weeks ago, and you don't know what a treat it was to breathe pure fresh mountain air once more; and oh! the woods; what would not you have given to have been in my stead. Surely fall is the most beautiful season of the year, more especially in this beautiful little valley. I spent such a quiet pleasant day with Aunt Letitia and Uncle Mack and of course you were duly thought of, wished for and spoken of frequently during the day. Jacque, Gussie and Eltie walked as far as Mr. Criser's with us; was quite night when we arrived. Some two weeks ago Uncle Mack returned from his "home in the woods" and when he got up next morning found that William, Bernard, ____ Jim and Eveline had decamped; are you not surprised at the two last? We thought them so faithful. Margaret is in Luray and Horace was off with the horses; to think of parents leaving the only two children they had in that way.

For two weeks past we have had a guard of ten yankees in town who are very faithful and have protected us well. Our men have promised not to disturb them night or day; and don't you think last night one of our men walked in the Hotel dining room which they occupy, took his seat amongst them, conversed with them sometime and walked out and left them. The guards have orders not to fire on them and they come in every day, some of them. We feel quite a sense of protection now, knowing that Co E and Mosby's men are all through the mountains. We can not find out whose troops occupy Milford now, but it seems to be generally understood that we have been largely reinforced and some even say by Pickett's division, but it's too good news to be true; and don't you think 'twas even told your Ma that you had been seen there and she said she could not help looking for you a day or two. Don't you think I had some grapes yesterday, wish it had been you. Gen'l. Lomax sent a flag of truce over to Guard Hill, on Thursday evening they returned at night fall and serenaded the ladies in Front Royal with bugles, tunes so sweet, we all sat out on the West End steps and listened to them a long while. Not one word have we heard from Alvin since Scott was here; A letter from Benton to his Ma of Oct 11th, says he had just received a letter from "Pat" who was in Americus, Ga., doing well and said he would soon be winding his way homeward. Just suppose for one instant if it could be so; I should almost go deranged with joy!

I know how anxiously you have been wading through these pages for the following, which will be worth all the balance of the letter to you. I received a short note from Sue a month or so ago, saying that her mother was quite ill, not expected to live, and begging if I possibly could write to you and tell you; but you know I've had no opportunity for so doing. I have heard nothing from there since, excepting that one of Mosby's men said he left there the latter part of last month and Mrs. Bayly's physicians had all given up all hopes of her recovery. I suppose she has consumption. How sorry I feel if poor Sue should again be left motherless. Some in from Fauquier said that while the Yankees were running the cars on the rail road down there, they took Mr. Sampson Bayly and one other prominent citizen and carried them backward and forward on the cars with them to prevent Mosby's men from firing into their trains. Did you ever hear such villainy? I wish I had something new to write you about her but I suppose she manages to get a letter or two out to you now and then through Mosby's men. About a fortnight since, the Yankees went to Mr. Peter Bell's near Cousin John Buck's and found one of their men who had been killed by some of our men, and took Mr. Bell and his partner Mr. Trester with his little son out a mile from the house and shot them both in the presence of little Trester whom they tied to a tree, telling him they wished him to see his father die. After this they went back and burned Mr. Bell's house. Old Mr. John Bell has taken Mrs. Bell and her children to live with him. We have still a few hogs and flour left to live upon, and should these hateful wretches be driven from here to enable you, Alvin and Irvie to come home at Christmas, we can give you a hearty welcome and something to eat. Gussie has some grapes hung away for you. I forgot to tell you that Uncle Mack thinks Horace has gone. He came down to town this morning with Jessie and this evening we met the latter going home alone. If I just had two days conversation with you I could tell you enough to make you laugh and cry yourself sick; but dear me, when can we ever have that pleasure? It seems to me that they never intend going. Guard Hill this morning was covered with Head Quarter tents.

You see Frank has added a post script to my letter, not only with the pen but his finger marks, the little scamp. Aunt Letitia says Mamie was so alarmed when the Yankees were around she had to send her to Mrs. Smedley's and Mrs. Simpson's. I know you are tired but I dislike to say good bye so much. Lucie, Laura and all say "give my love to Dick". Lu says be a good boy. Now won't you write me soon and tell what you have been doing with yourself all this long while.

Wishing you a good night's rest, I am as ever your affectionate,

Cousin Nell

P.S. I did not tell you that for three nights while the Yankees were here we had regular corn shuckings in the smoke house and invited the Hopes up to help us and we had a merry time of it, I can tell you; and when the Yankees came to dig our potatoes, we every one of us turned out and dug in one patch while the Yankees were digging in the other, a negro with them at that and as saucy as he could be. I got three red ears, Laura two, Ma two and Mr. Hope one, and Lucie one.

Home
November 1, 1864

My Dear Boy, *(I.A. Buck)*

It has been a long time since I had the opportunity of writing to you but you are doubtless aware that we are and have been entirely cut off from the outer world for the last six weeks. have heard nothing from you since your letter of the 2nd September except through Benton who said he had not heard from you since the 5th and that you were then suffering much with your wound, that he had written constantly to you but could not get a letter from you. we felt quite uneasy about it at first but comfort ourselves that his not getting your letters was owing to his moving about so much. we have heard nothing from Alvin since he left us and are anxious to know where he is. I cannot give you an idea of the state of things here and all that has transpired around here in the last two months. the Yankee army has been stationed here in large force. their camps are mostly at Guard hill and at the river of their depredations you know some things from the papers. tis enough for me to say that the once beautiful and flourishing Valley is now almost a waste. mills, barns and houses burnt, crops destroyed and all kinds of stock driven off and many houses stripped of everything and families left destitute of necessities and are drawing rations from the Yankees. there are but few negroes left old or young. Horace and all of Captain Roy's left together. your Uncle Mack's Eveline and Jim. Uncle Fayette's Susan and her children, one of Cousin E. Richardson's boys and nearly all in the neighborhood but your Uncle Newton's and Uncle Tom's. Sam Gardner has not one left. but I think they are a good riddance. we are better without them unless they were under better control we can live without them. if they will only let us alone. Old Mr. Marshall's family have been driven from their home and their house and furniture rendered unfit for use — every window in the house broken. Dr. Dorsey has nothing left but his house and furniture even his clothing and bedclothes — did not leave him or his children a change. Uncle N. is nearly broken up — they annoyed your Uncle Mack a great deal but he has escaped better than could have been expected. your Uncle Fayette has lost his barn and all his milch cows and a great many other things — took $40 in gold from Jule. it has indeed been a reign of terror with us. but individually we have fared better than almost anyone else lost most of our corn some hogs and calves and a good deal out of the garden but have not had them to come in the house and as yet have our horses and cows which is a great blessing indeed we have much to be thankful for. have found some of the officers very gentlemanly and apparently disposed to do all they could for us. Lucy wrote to you sometime ago of Lt. Crittenden having been to see us. it was while Alvin and Mack were here and they took a great dislike to him but for some cause I felt a great sympathy for him his coat and hat were in a delapidated condition and we took them and mended them for him — Soon after he left here he and another soldier were captured in Luray — they were put in a pen and kept a day and a night and then were shot for two of their soldiers that they found with their throats cut. Captain Pendingest captured them and he was here yesterday much disturbed by seeing an extract in the papers of his having done it. he says he knew nothing of it—he has been a great friend to them at Rose Hill goes to see them almost every day. I do not know what they would do without him. he has also been kind to us and your Uncle Mack—he seems to be much of a gentleman — he is on General Powell's staff — and has a brother a Colonel in General Early's command — It is a great misfortune that Early ever came into the Valley he has far as we can judge has done nothing to benefit the cause and done much to injure us. he has several times gained _____ and victories and then lose all he gained and more until he has nearly ruined one of the finest armies in the Confederacy — for I fear it is too true that his army is dreadfully demoralised. a man that will get drunk on the eve of an important battle should not be permitted to retain his position an hour — but for such things we should not now be surrounded by an immense army and the people deprived almost entirely of substance and we cut off from every privilege. if it was any advantage to the Confederacy we would be willing to bear it but such is not the case. poor Eddy Brown was killed at Fisher's Hill. Mack Irwin and Alfred McKay were wounded and several others of the company killed. Dick Bayly was wounded in the shoulder by a fragment of a shell in the shoulder on the 17th near Winchester. he is in Page. Will Cloud was wounded sometime ago but has nearly recovered. Willie Buck has been exchanged and has been within a few miles of home for several weeks. but could not get there he is now in Luray. it is hard after being gone so long that he cannot see his family. tis said they are going to rebuild the railroad to Strasburg if so I suppose we may content ourselves to remain under Lincoln government for some time indeed they tell us all the time that they are going to stay here all Winter — but I trust there is something better in store for us. and that this state of things will not last much longer. but if it does we will try and make the best of it. last week the girls and myself dug potatoes and the garden during the day and shucked corn til midnight — the boys, your Father, and the girls carrying it in bags on their backs to someplace of safety — and all done with the greatest of cheerfulness. we would be in one part of the garden digging potatoes and the Yankees niggers and whites in the other part doing the same. we find it necessary to do everything to live through the Winter — expect Horace took John Henry but have not heard. what an ungrateful creature he is. if you know where Alvin is try and let him hear from us — we cannot write and if we could do not know where to direct it to him — this we will try and slip out by some private hand — congratulate George Williams in his good fortune. hope some thing may yet turn up by which you can get home this Winter — it is too bad — it has been so long since we saw you — hope you may be recovered from your wound but do not care about your being in a hurry to get into service. all join in much love to you. Evred has entirely recovered. may God Bless you my dear boy—asks your Dear Mother,

E.A.B. *(Elizabeth Ashby Buck)*

Lucy and Laura have gone to the pickets to try to get your Uncle Fayette's milk cows from them.

Tuscumbia, Alabama
November 5, 1864

My Dear Mordecai: *[M.C. Hopewell of Staunton, Va.]*

It has been a long time since I wrote you, and a long time since I got your last, for which this is an answer. It is a source of regret to me that this has been the case, but the matter was one of necessity, as you will see when I tell you something of my career during the period that has elapsed since I last wrote you. The fears which you expressed in reference to the result of the fighting about Atlanta in connection with myself had some realization. I was captured at Jonesboro on the 1st Sept. along with my General and nearly one-half our brigade. I will not occupy you with an account of my "Northern tour," Further than to say that the only part of it which I at all enjoyed was its brevity. After a week's confinement in Chattanooga, which a fellow prisoner facetiously termed a "playing checkers with our noses," we were sent to Nashville, where we were favored with quarters in that time-honored institution, the Penitentiary. Fortunately our stay there was very short, only about 8 hours, after which we were again shipped to Atlanta, and exchanged at Rough & Ready on the 19th of the same month. I am sure you did not know that your old friend was one liberated by the truce which you regretted as fearing that Gen. Hood would allow himself to be taken in by it. While a prisoner, I took occasion to write many letters home, but saw no persons whom I knew save some friends acquired during the campaign of '63 in Tennessee. One of these was a young lady whom I cultivated assiduously during that halcyon period of war and who came, upon learning of my coming, to the train, welcoming me, prisoner though I was, with smiles and favors which wellnigh made me forget my situation. She it was who knowing my lack of Yankee funds, snugly slipped greenbacks into my breast pocket — what if the cunning, curious Yankees did gloat with their eyes, and take her name in their memoranda. A favor for which I hope soon to be able to repay her, but in different currency. All this whilst the train stopped at Wartrace, and I went off remembering the fairy form and beautiful face and carrying in my pocket a touching souvenir — not the greenbacks —

Upon being exchanged, I reported for duty immediately, but was called in a few days to visit Irving Buck at Americus, Ga. Him I found very ill from the effects of bilious fever in conjunction with gangrene in a wound received in the same engagement to which I owed my capture. I remained with him a few days, leaving him improved and reached by brigade just in time for the march in Sherman's rear. Since then we have been marching every day, except 6 or 8 and during those short halts you know I always have a press of business; everyone having something to rush through to the A.A.G.'s office. My brigade had been left in rear of the Army, on the Chattahoochie, guarding a pontoon. We marched on Oct. 8 taking this bridge and a large supply train, joined our Div. at Lafayette, Ga., went thence to Gadsden, Ala., and came here via Decatur. The last named place we invested and expected to be called upon to assault, but it seems not to have been Gen. Hood's plan to take it. We expected to have left here several days ago for Middle Tenn. but there has been a delay which the _____ are unable to account for. We have done very hard marching, and our stock is already much impaired by heavy roads. A further march into Tenn. so late in the season will cause much suffering and hardship and now that

Sherman seems to have got his force pretty well shifted to the new field, it may be that our move into Tenn. is blocked. If so, the result anticipated is not accomplished; for Sherman still holds him to fight with a force weakened by the garrisons he has been compelled to leave in Georgia.

I have no calculations but await developments of which you will be advised by the press. Since writing the above the grapevine dispatch is that we have been awaiting the arrival of a supply train; that we move day after tomorrow across the Tennessee, which has already been bridged for several days by our pontoons. A part of Lee's corps has been at Florence for nearly a week. So I think we will take the warpath soon. Gen. Beauregard is here. I am glad of his return, especially as he has Col. Brent with him & will bring Col. Otey, Alvin Buck & Mack Blakemore. I am glad to have these old friends again at Dept. Hd. Qrs. My Channel had been seriously interrupted by Buck's absence, Roy's transfer with his chief to Chas.ton, and the absence from Army Hd. Qrs. of my friend, Maj. Falconer, who was wounded lately. With them I had a friend at each Hd. Qrs. above me & could get many little favors for friends.

You are very just in chiding me for not writing to my Capon cousins. But I found myself engaged with so many correspondents when I came west and so little facility was there for communicating with their remove home, that I have not written them for a long time. I will try to send a letter through you. Be good enough to remember my love to them, when you write home, and speak of my solicitude for their welfare. I have letters from home up to Sept. 6. All were well. Robert was in St. Louis trying to get into business. My Father was there also, having left home on account of some excitement caused by his having visited professionally a wounded bushwhacker. My sister spoke as if she apprehended no danger for him and thought he would soon return. It is a mistake that my sister has married — one which the people about Moorefield seem to believe a fact indisputable, however, as I have heard of thence several times. I fear this may not reach you on account of the late perturbations in the Valley. Oh! That unfortunate district! How the faithful and loyal people have suffered. Army after army has pursued its opposing host across its once fertile fields, until all must be a lonely waste. Roy wrote me that he really feared our people would <u>starve</u>. Is it so bad? I feel deeply for those noble people, from among whom I am proud to have come. Give me a true statement of affairs in Hardy and in Warren mentioning individuals. I have nothing thence since your last. We have confused rumors of a disaster to Early, nothing reliable; no paper since 21st ult. The Army P.O. has just arrived at Cherokee, 16 m. west of here and I hope we will get some news and letters.

Do you remember Tom Bartlett, who went to Sicker's school & was a chum of Garrisons? He is a Capt. in a Regt. of my brigade, having come out from St. Louis in the beginning.

I have letters from Fritz Bierkamp & <u>Oscar Marshall</u>, both in Richmond.

Nothing from Mack Gamble for two mos. Was then with Morgan's command in E. Tenn. Pardon me that I have written in so businesslike a style. There have been so many about me talking that I have been unable to get down into my better feelings, which require some warming and time to be coaxed into action. I hope you will write me again very soon. Your letters are so full and satisfactory, the best exponents of affairs about my old home that I am fortunate enough to get.

Make my highest regards to your Pa & Ma, the latter I shall always remember as an old friend of my own dear mother.
Again, write soon, as ever, and truly, Your friend,
G. A. Williams *[Capt. Geo. A. Williams]*

P.S. I forgot to say that poor Mack Blakemore fell at Altoona, 5th Oct. within 50 yards of the enemy's fort, among the very foremost in that unsuccessful charge. The fourth first cousin this war has cost me — and all of them those whom I knew & loved best of my relatives. G.A.W.

Bragg Hospital
Americas, Ga
November 12, 1864

My Darling Sister,

Your letter of the 20th of September reached me a few days ago, much to my gratification, but I was disappointed at your not having received some one of the numerous letters I have written since the one at Griffin on the 2nd of September. Had you done so they would have kept you informed of the progress of my wound. I made my debut on my crutches at the Baptist church two weeks ago. Was very awkward at first and fell down a pair of steps — happily not injuring my wound thereby. I am now staying at a private house — Mr. Farlow's — and am treated with every attention. Am revelling in sausages, eggs, hominy, spring mattresses, rosewood, and marble. I have just returned from the plantation of a brother of the gentleman with whom I am staying. Five young ladies were in the party. We went down on Tuesday and stayed until this morning. We had a royal time. Had rides (I in a buggy, as I cannot ride on horseback), ate sugar cane, walnuts, chufas, candy etc. Two of the ladies have splendid voices and we had magnificent music. Consequence is I am over head and ear in love (who could help it?). My adored is of course perfect, but I will defer particularizing until I see you — by which time I will know my fate.

My wound is doing finely, but there is still a piece as large as my hand yet to heal, but it gives me no pain and Mrs. Farlow will not allow me to be imprudent. She is a Baptist and of course a good Christian as all pensioners are (Ala Burton).

Was so glad to hear that you escaped so easily from the Yankees, but fear that you suffered after Early's last defeat, which as far as I can judge was a most disgraceful affair.

Had a letter from Alvin after the 31st of October. General Beauregard was on the point of removing his Head Quarters to Selma, Ala., where I suppose he is at present.

I will start home as soon as my leave of absence comes back from Army Head Quarters, but we have no idea as to where General Hood now is. We receive no mail at all from the Army. Have doubts about my being able to reach you all, but will make the attempts, and when I get to Culpepper, if the Yankee's occupy Front Royal will turn back. Am so anxious to see you all that I will run almost any risks to do so.

Am going to Columbus next week to visit a lady friend who has been inviting me to come and let her nurse me ever since I have been wounded. Will probably be absent a week.

The gentleman at whose house I am staying has two sons in Early's Army. The fortunes of war may throw them into Front Royal sometimes and if so I am going to ask them to call at Bel Air. They belong to the 4th Ga. Regiment.

Had a letter from Col Roy dated the 8th of September. He had been suffering from the chills but had recovered.

The weather here is as balmy as Spring, and we have roses and other flowers. Think I would like to settle in this vicinity.

My love to all — Hoping to be with you soon, I am your affectionate Brother,

Irving

Home *(Bel Air)*, November 24, 1864

My Dear twenty four year old Irvie,

Drooping eye lids and weary eyes admonish me that 'tis bedtime. Yet I must steal a half hour from customary slumber in which I assure you we have not been unmindful of your birthday. I should not have postponed writing till this late hour but I spent the day at Rose Hill and have not before had an opportunity — it seems useless too, for you most probably have started for home ere this and I don't know where to direct to you. Still we never neglect you on this day and I should not sleep so soundly tonight if I did not write you.

And what have I to tell you? 'Tis nothing but a resume of the old story of wrong and outrage of which you must be weary.

I sent you a long letter a week or two ago written in quite a Jeremiah style giving you all the items of interest up to the time of writing. We had just then received our last letter from you bearing date of Oct. 19 when you were only just able to sit up. You don't know how great a solitude we feel to hear from you again, and to know if you are really getting well and all about you, but this is impossible in the present state of affairs when our mails are semi-occasionally smuggled in by stealth as they have been for the past 2 months. I try to collect my thoughts sufficiently to give you a definite account of the past fortnight, but it seems so like a confused dream that it seems impossible to remember all clearly. One sad fact is distinct enough — poor Lizzie Buck's death — a dear good aunt we have lost in her. I wrote you in a former letter of Henry's miserable desertion (that ever I should live to write it!). It may seem a hard thing, but everyone thinks his conduct was the indirect cause of his Ma's death. You know how high minded and noble Aunt Lizzie was and it was more than she could brook to know one so near to her could be guilty of so dishonorable a part. Poor Henry! I do pity him from my heart's depth. What must be his anguish when the tidings reach him! The offense is a grave one and I could have much more readily given a brother of mine up in an honorable death than he should seek safety in a dishonorable life, but the hapless boy's cowardice was constitutional, he couldn't help it and is to be pitied rather than blamed for it, but oh the shame!

Aunt Lizzie never was quite herself after the burning of the barn and the fright she received from those miserable Yankees. Then came the blow Henry dealt her. She seemed rather more cheerful on Tuesday and had Cousin E. Cloud to dine with her and remarked upon the hearty dinner she'd eaten. That night she was taken with cramp colic and suffered much but no one of the family thought it anything serious. Wednesday, Thursday and Friday she suffered intensely, was delirious all day Friday and that night she died in convulsions.

Cousin Elizabeth Cloud was with poor Jule or I don't know what the poor child would have done. We knew nothing of her illness till the night she died and only heard of her death at noon on Saturday.

Ma, Cary and I went up to Clover Hill that afternoon. Poor Uncle Fayette met us looking as if years instead of months had bowed his form and whitened his head since we saw him last. Emma was with Jule and Irvie I can't tell you how much I loved and admired the dear good girl — for the courage and fortitude with which she bore this sore trial. Deeply grieved, she was, no one could doubt who saw her pale sad face, but there was no outward demonstration and I felt that, as she said, it was God given strength. Think what a life of ease and luxury she has led and now all her trials have fallen at once. She says she feels that such a solemn responsibility rests upon her in the care of her little brothers and sisters, and besides they have now no servant to do for them, but old Aunt Harriet who is crippled from rheumatism and her duties are laborious enough of themselves without anything more.

She is such a noble, true girl and I believe such an humble good Christian and is better adapted to bear her cross than any one I know of. She spoke of Henry, "my poor brother," as she called him and asked — "Oh Lou! were you not surprised?" She had heard all that we had of his going to Kentucky and knows nothing more than we do further than that. Mack Irwin was with them having just recovered from

273

his wound and took Henry's place more completely than Henry himself could have done.

You never saw such thoughtful affectionate attention as he lavished on Uncle Fayette and poor Jule. I shall always love him for it. He was as much distressed as if at the loss of his own mother and indeed Aunt Lizzie was the truest and best friend he ever had. You should have seen Aunt L. in her last placid slumber. She seemed just to have fallen sweetly asleep with a breathing smile on her lips and I could scarcely believe that her eye lashes were not quivering on the rise so life-like did she look.

We buried her in the orchard by the side of Eugene and Willie. She made no request, left no message not being able to speak. And it would have been next to impossible to carry her to Waterlick.

I know it is usual to speak of the dead in exalted terms, but our hearts as well as our lips testify to the love and respect we bore her in life.

She was the most earnest sincere friend — "a perfect woman nobly planned to man, to comfort and command." For sure her own family circle knew her well — those who knew her best loved her most and trusted her. She ever made me feel like her own child when an inmate of the family and I loved her like a second mother.

Many thought her haughty because dignified and stately. I never felt or saw any evidence of hauteur in her. She was ever one thing kind and good. What a loss she is to her family! I think Jule will send for Annie Ford to come live with her. Emma is with her at present and will remain till Annie comes, or if Emma leaves I will go to her. Miss Tensia has a maiden Cousin living at Dr. Turner's with her and this prevents her staying at Clover Hill.

In the battle of Cedar Creek on the 12th, Cousin Sam's son, Willie, was killed — shot through the head while gallantly holding his position as vidette at an exposed point. He is said to have been a brave soldier and I know he was an amiable good boy. Whose fate would you choose Irvie — his or poor Henry's?

Willie's Father has an honorable grave to look on when he thinks of his boy. Uncle Fayette has an aching void in his heart, a tale of shame for his thoughts.

We have just had another visitation from the Yankees — the most trying of all. Merritt's Division came in unexpectedly and encamped on the pike from above Rose Hill to town on Monday night last. They were on a reconnaissance to Millford. One regiment was left to hold this place. Such savages! We had them coming in all day demanding everything we had in the way of edibles or threatened to search and burn if refused. Some enemy (we had our suspicion of the individual) had informed them of Father having molasses and <u>where</u> it was. One wretch with his negro conferee came and stole every morsel of bread we had in the house and a five gallon keg of molasses, at one time leaving one of his comrades in the basement drawing his pail of it from the barrel. I took his pail away and stopped the spile and Nellie pitched down to Rose Hill with Cary to get an officer or a guard.

The Commander General Devin's was quartered with Cousin E. Richardson. There was a mistake made in his name — of that I am in morally certain — the "L" should have substituted the "N" and 'twould have been altogether appropriate.

In the most surly manner he denied a guard asserting that 'twas entirely unnecessary. She went on up to the camp to see Major Berge. He seemed to feel sorry for her and wanted to send protection but the old block headed of a general would not let him. She tarried several hours thinking the matter would be reconsidered but in vain. Meantime we were under going tortures. Squad after squad came and swore and threatened and stole. Broke into the cache where the potatoes which we had dug with our own hands were concealed and carried off several bags full. There was an old U.S. blanket of Horace's over them to protect them from the cold. This they seized saying it should be carried to Gen. Merritt that officer having given orders that all houses should burnt in which U.S. property was found. One little white headed boy came to buy butter, we let him have a little for which he paid with a "grab" of ground coffee — we told him we hadn't it to share but for that he cared not a _____. I threatened them with guards but they laughed in my face and swore they were not afraid of guards.

Nellie came back unsuccessful and then Ma started out with Cary. She came back minus guard. Just then the white headed scoundrel returned and whined for more butter. Being presumptuously refused he went off and brought back 8 men — 3 negroes among them and commenced to systematic pillage. I determined in my desperation raise a protestation or a row on my own account, donning shawl and bonnet I took Orville for escort and <u>flew</u> down to Rose Hill and invited myself into the General's apartment. He turned his back and marched to the window, I followed and inquired if "this was General Devin's?" Scowling over his shoulder he growled back "that's my name." I stated I must apply for a guard the <u>third</u> time and told him how we were situated. He said 'twas not his business to give protection. I must see the Provost, the Provost, Captain Bean made his appearance, I made application and received as reply, "No, I will give no guards, 'tis not necessary" — tossed at me from over his shoulder with a rude frown. However Gen. D. stepped to the porch and ordered the Provost guard to "go over to that white house on the hill and arrest and hang every man seen coming from there."

I followed on after the guard and had the pleasure of meeting them upon their return to the quarters with every rogue riding between their file under arrest — the white haired gentleman prominent. One of the sergeants was at the house when I got there with two of his men sitting quietly before the fire in Grandma's room. He was a polite accommodating fellow and against orders and at the risk of being punished for disobedience left us a guard for 2 hours.

I may here remark en passant that this obliging disposition may have been attributable to the fancy which he took to <u>Laura</u>. They had had a time of it while I was gone every room in the house was searched. They made a raid upon our sausage,

275

but Nellie kept them at bay with a <u>carving knife</u> while she dispensed just what she pleased to them.

I wish I could tell you how she and Laura managed them when they searched the drawers where the baby's clothes are kept, snatching stolen chattels from their hands and taunting them with not finding what they sought. They did not find a morsel of butter. Nellie would not let more than one of the wretches go into the garret where our corn and little turkeys were.

While the whites were stealing in the house, the blacks were in the porches and entries stealing all our candle sticks. We didn't really lose a great deal, six gallons of molasses, 3 table napkins, 2 bags of potatoes, 2 of corn, all the fodder, hay, two loaves of bread, a beautiful little jappaned spice chest, candles and candle sticks, 8 jars of milk, a duck, sausage and liver puddings and an ironing handled table knife and a lot of ginger cakes, besides vegetables from the garden and father's beer. No doubt they could have done more serious damage but for fear of the guards coming. We have the pleasure of knowing that every Satan's son of them were punished gloriously! 'Twas a bitter cold night and they were kept for 4 hours in front of Cousin E. Richardson's door, carrying barrels and boxes on their heads and riding each other around in the circle on a rail, the officer standing by, salve in hand to see it well done. They were not allowed to eat supper, were deprived of all their spoils and sent off on picket. Wasn't that glorious. The fellow left with us for guard proved faithful to his trust but we loathed him when he told us he helped hang those two poor dear boys of Mosby's. I shamed him for it and he coolly pleaded obedience to orders. They all left very early Wed. morning much to our delight. Cousin E. Richardson was as usually treated shamefully — her pictures torn down in the parlor. Eltie's music all torn and the yard and garden fences destroyed — her carriage used as a stable, her hogs and cows killed, all her rails burnt and both of her kitchens taken from her while they staid there. She had to do the cooking for the family by her chamber fire place burning bits of wood as they could beg it from the negro cook belonging to the officers.

You never heard of such an insolent set as they were. And don't you think Dick Bayly who is suffering from his wound was concealed in the house all the while. He had started to go home but was weak and had to stop there — the Yankees came in and caught him there. He is going to Luray tomorrow. Poor fellow, I'm uneasy about his wound. No one suffered as Mr. Richards, Cousin E. and ourselves.

Mr. Jackson brought his bride — Miss Keerfort home yesterday, have not see her yet.

Dear Irvie, what shall I say to your coming home. Judgement tells me 'tis imprudent for you to come while the Yankees still have possession of the Valley, but my heart pleads so for a sight of you once more. I ____ ____ ____ can not tell you you will be unsafe, you must use your own discretion. The fact is I hope you've started home ere this.

'Tis late — I must close.

All unite in loving messages. Aunt C. sends love and says, she wishes "this cruel war" was "over."

God bless my own brother and restore him to us soon in safety.

Very hastily but fondly,
Lucie

Americus, Ga.
December 27, 1864

My Darling Lucie,

Yours of the 24th of November reached me a few days ago, and I concluded to wait until after Christmas in order that I could tell you how I passed it. The morning was dark and rainy — at 11 o'clock went to the Episcopal church after which I dined at <u>home</u> with several friends. Had a most excellent dinner, and many times during it my thoughts wandered how you all were spending the day. How willingly would I have exchanged my fine repast for one of the most humble character's provided it could have been shared with the loved ones at home. It rained incessantly during the afternoon and I was in the parlor all the evening thinking of you all. The next day was spent in rehearsing for a tableaux that came off last night. The ladies requested me to take a part — the proceeds were appropriated to use for the poor. I think it was a success. I acted a part in the "Guardian Angel" — "Marmian's death scene" and was the drunken surgeon in a conscript medical board. The latter I am sure to have acted to perfection. Today I am to dine at Col. Tim Farlow's (a brother of the gentleman with whom I am staying). And then to a candy pulling at the same house tonight. I laid awake a long while the night before Christmas thinking of all the little ones at home. Wondering if they would hang up their little stockings as we used to do and wondering what old Santa Claus would contribute.

You have doubtless learned from the papers the death of my General.[15] Poor fellow, I mourn his death. I perhaps knew him and loved him better than anyone in the Confederacy. He was a true and good friend of mine, and was a great help to me. Have learned nothing of the particulars, but feel assured that he died at the post of honor. He left a reputation much to be envied. Do not know who will succeed him, but think it will be Brig. Gen'l. Polk or Smith. Both of whom will be pleasant gentlemen to serve with. Of course the General's death does not affect my position at all. Have not heard from George Williams since the fight and feel some uneasiness on his account.

Your last letter was quite a sad one. Was so much disturbed to hear of Aunt L's death. She was a favorite of mine. And then you allude to Henry's having deserted. This was the first I had heard of it, as your former letter has not yet reached me, so I know nothing of the particulars, but what a disgrace. What could have induced him to such a dishonorable step? Indeed, my dear Lucy, I had ten thousand times rather fill an honorable grave than to stand in his place. Just to think he has forever severed himself from his family and stained the hitherto fair reputation of the name. I pity him from my soul.

I am still at Mr. Farlow's and have been treated with the utmost kindness. His wife has been a mother to me, and she has laid the family under lasting obligations. I wish, Lou, you would write her a nice letter of thanks. I think it is due her for I am considerably indebted to her for my life. Direct your letter to Mrs. James Farlow. She was much pleased with Alvin, and is very anxious that he should call upon his return from Savannah. My sojourn in Americus has been most pleasant and un-marred by a single disagreeable incident. I have many true and valuable friends both male and female. My wound is nearly healed up. Have thrown away my crutches and am now walking with a cane though I am quite lame. I shall report for duty about the 1st of February. Mrs. Calloway (a daughter of Col. Farlow who married after I came here) has invited me to go to her home some 60 miles south of here and we will go about the 1st of January. She is such a charming lady that I know I shall have a pleasant time.

Received a letter from "Nannie Dear" a day or two ago. Much to my surprise, she informed me that Miss Clara was to be married on the 20th of January to a Mr. Warren from Fredericksburg. It was with a sad heart that I abandoned my intention to come home, but Alvin advised me not to attempt it and I knew you would all be uneasy about me the whole time I would be in F.R. And lastly, the roads between this point and Augusta are out and I would have to walk 40 miles which would be an impossibility. You do not regret this more than I. My heart has been set upon it the whole year. I have been most comfortably situated, and treated with the greatest kindness. Mrs. Farlow sits by me as I write and says I must give her love to you all. She is a gem of a woman. Her husband is a noble man. He has a son at home now about my age, who belongs to the 4th G. Regt. of Early's Army and will return to it next week. He has promised to make you a visit if he should ever again be in the vicinity of Front Royal. Have heard nothing from Alvin since he left here for Savannah six weeks ago, but suppose his letters have been lost, the mails are so irregular. Wish he would make haste and return. He made such a favorable impression upon all who met him here. When you write again, direct your letters to me "care Maj. Gen'l. Cleburne, Army of Tennessee".

My love to all.

Ever your loving Brother,
Irving

Since writing the foregoing, I have received a letter from Alvin dated the 8th of Dec. He was then in Charleston but expected to return to Selma about the last of this month, when he will call to see me. I will go with him from here to Gen'l. Beauregard's Head Quarters, where I will remain until fit for duty.

Your own Bro.
Irvie

---

[1] General Rosecrans, U.S.A., moved his army through the mountain passes south of Chattanooga. General Bragg, C.S.A., was forced to evacuate Chattanooga September 8, 1863, to prevent being cut off from his supply lines. Bragg saw a chance to turn the Yankees' left flank and moved his troops across the Chickamauga Creek on September 19, 1863.

Longstreet, with his I Corps, arrived from the Army of Northern Virginia on the night of September 19, 1863. The Confederate attack on the twentieth got off to a late start and General Thomas, U.S.A. held on the Union left, but he needed assistance. General T.J. Wood's division was sent to his aid from the Union center. Longstreet on the Confederate left, noted the gap in the Union lines, and struck driving the Federals back into Chattanooga.

U.S.A.		C.S.A.	
Effectives	58,222	Effectives	66,326
Killed	1,657	Killed	2,301
Wounded	9,756	Wounded	14,674
Missing	4,757	Missing	1,468

Thomas held long enough on the Union left to save the army, but as it retreated into Chattanooga it was beaten and surrounded. Bragg, much to the dissatisfaction of all his generals, elected to lay siege to the city.

Rosecrans, U.S.A., needed help, so Hooker was sent from the Army of the Potomac with the Union XI and XII Corps on September 24, 1863. This force arrived at Brown's Ferry below Chattanooga on the twenty-eighth of October.

Sherman, from Grant's army in Mississippi, was ordered to Chattanooga. Bragg still waited.

On October 17, 1863, General Grant was given command of the Union Armies of the Tennessee, Cumberland, and Ohio. Thomas replaced Rosecrans as commander of the Union Army of the Cumberland. Grant arrived in Chattanooga on the twenty-third of October. Supplies and reinforcements began to arrive via a pontoon bridge across the river and the city was relieved of siege. Bragg had waited too long. He had even detached Longstreet's I Corps on November 5 and 6 to Knoxville to fight Burnside, U.S.A. Thus, Bragg weakened his army by 12,000 men. Sherman's army arrived at Chattanooga in mid-November and formed the Union left flank. Thomas was in the center, and Hooker assaulted Lookout Mountain on the twenty-fifth. Sherman struck the northern end of Missionary Ridge, only to be repelled by Confederate General Pat Cleburne's division.

Thomas's forces on November 25 were ordered to advance on the rifle pits below Missionary Ridge. This was more of a diversion for the action on the right and left flanks, but without orders, and to the astonishment of Generals Grant and Thomas, the Yankees carried the Ridge. Bragg retreated in defeat.

U.S.A.		C.S.A.	
Effectives	56,359	Effectives	46,156
Killed	753	Killed	361
Wounded	4,722	Wounded	2,160
Missing	349	Missing	4,146

Longstreet arrived before Knoxville on November 17, 1863, and Burnside retired into the city. Longstreet attacked Fort Sanders on November 29, but was repelled.

Sherman was sent north to relieve the siege of Knoxville, after the Battle of Chattanooga. Longstreet retreated into Virginia.

General Bragg was replaced by General Joseph Johnston December 1, 1863, as commander of the Army of Tennessee. Bragg was made military adviser to President Davis.

[2] General Joseph E. Johnston was appointed commander of the Army of Tennessee on December 16, 1863.

[3] General Hardee married Mary Foreman Lewis, daughter of a wealthy cotton planter in Marengo County, Alabama. General Cleburne was his best man and Miss Sue Tarleton from Mobile was maid of honor. They fell in love and were later engaged.

[4] Lt. Green Samuels was first captured June 13, 1862, and was exchanged. He was again captured in the Battle of Winchester in September, 1864 and was not released until the end of the war.

[5] Benton Roy, Hardee's A.A.G. married one of Hardee's daughters and settled in Selma, Alabama, after the war.

[6] The Federal Army under Sherman began its spring campaign in Georgia May 4, 1864.

[7] General Joseph Johnston was replaced by General Hood, July 17, 1864. Jefferson Davis wanted to make sure Atlanta would not be lost without a fight. In Johnston's retreat from Chattanooga after assuming command from Bragg, Sherman's army had had over 10,000 casualties. On July 22, 1864, in the Battle of Atlanta, the following casualties were sustained.

Peachtree Creek

U.S.A.		C.S.A.	
Effectives	20,193	Effectives	18,832
Killed & Wounded ..1,600		Killed and	

Battle of Atlanta

U.S.A.		C.S.A.	
Effectives	34,863	Effectives	36,934
Killed	430	Killed and	
Wounded	1,559	wounded	7,000
Missing	1,733	Missing	1,000

Hood pulled back into the fortifications of the city and Atlanta was under siege. On September 1, Hood evacuated Atlanta and Sherman entered.

Hood entered Alabama and went back into northern Georgia to cut Sherman's supplies. Hood then headed his army for Tuscumbia, Alabama, late in October to begin his invasion of Tennessee. Sherman sent a portion of his army to follow Hood, but they were soon recalled and he started his march to the sea from Atlanta, November 16, 1864. Sherman did send General Thomas and the Army of the Cumberland to Nashville to defend that area from Hood's invasion.

[8] Beauregard, who had been commanding the defenses of Charleston, was given the job of protecting southern Virginia and North Carolina in April, 1864. Thus it fell to Beauregard to stop Butler's army on May 16, 1864.

[9] Richard Bayly Buck, wounded at Dinwiddie Court House, was distinguished in the field for gallantry. He was Walter Buck's brother. Walter, as noted earlier, was killed in the Battle of Upperville.

[10] William A. Rust, 3rd Sergeant, Warren Rifles, was wounded at Williamsburg and distinguished on the field for gallantry.

[11] I. A. Buck was wounded in the battle at Jonesboro. General Cleburne sent word to the surgeon, "You must save Buck. He is the best A.A.G. in the army."

[12] General John H. Morgan was killed on September 4, 1864 by a Federal soldier who had deserted from Cleburne's Division.

[13] General Sheridan, U.S.A., followed in the footsteps of his predecessor General Hunter, U.S.A., to make "the Shenandoah Valley a barren waste". Earlier, General Hunter burned the homes of Alexander Hunter, a Virginia state senator and the general's first cousin. Homes of Colonel Edmund Lee and Colonel A. R. Boteler were also fired. After General Early learned of this he decided to "open the eyes of the people of the North to this enormity, by an example in the way of retaliation." On July 29, 1864, he sent his cavalry to Chambersburg, Pennsylvania, to demand $100,000 in gold or $500,000 in greenbacks for the indemnification of the Southern people whose property had been burned by the Yankees and if they did not pay, the town would be burned. On July 30, 1864, Chambersburg was fired. Note the following article was excerpted from the *Confederate Veteran* Magazine, Vol. 34, page 22 and entitled "Famous Letter".

A Famous Letter

[The story, by Thomas J. Arnold, of Hunter as Lincoln's agent, published in the November *Veteran* is a wonderful paper. Few people beyond Virginia have any adequate idea of that monster, Hunter. I have always classed him as a member of the feline species. The hyena of Asia and of Africa has been described as nocturnal and cowardly, feeding mainly on carrion, and even digging up graves, though it also hunts living prey. I am sending you copy of a letter written by Mrs. Edmund I. Lee, of Virginia, to General Hunter on July 20, 1864. Her husband was a cousin of General Robert E. Lee. You will note she refers to Hunter as "hyenalike."

I have preserved the letter for more than fifty years, not only as a part of the history of the country, but because it is a classic. If there is anything superior to it as a rebuke or as a pattern of rhetoric, I have never seen it. It substantiates Mr. Arnold's paper.

James Dinkins, New Orleans.]

General Hunter: Yesterday your underling, Capt. Martindale, of the 1st New York Veteran Cavalry, executed your infamous order and burned my house. You have had the satisfaction ere this of receiving from him the information that your orders were fulfilled to the letter — the dwelling and every outbuilding, seven in number, with their contents, being burned. I, therefore, a helpless woman whom you have cruelly wronged, address you, a major general of the United States army, and demand why this was done? What was my offense?

My husband was absent, an exile. He has never been a politician, or in any way engaged in the struggle now going on, his age preventing. This fact David Strother, your chief of staff, could have told you. The house was built by my father, a revolutionary soldier, who served the whole seven years for your independence. There I was born, there the sacred dead repose; it was my house and my home, and there your niece, who has lived among us through all this horrid war up to the present moment, met with all kindness and hospitality at my hands.

Was it for this that you turned me, my young daughter and little son out upon the world without a shelter? Or was it because my husband is the grandson of the revolutionary patriot and rebel, Richard Henry Lee, and the near kinsman of the noblest of Christian warriors, the greatest of generals, Robert E. Lee? Heaven's blessings be upon his head forever!

You and your government have failed to conquer, subdue, or match him; and disappointed rage and malice find vent upon the helpless and inoffensive.

Hyenalike, you have torn my heart to pieces; for all hallowed memories clustered around that homestead, and demonlike, you have done it without even the pretext of revenge, for I never saw or harmed you. Your office is not to lead, like a brave man and soldier, your men to fight in the ranks of war, but your work has been to separate yourself from all danger; and, with your incendiary band, steal unawares upon helpless women and children, to insult and destroy. Two fair homes did you yesterday ruthlessly lay in ashes, giving not a moment's warning to the startled inmates of your wicked purpose; turning mothers and children out of doors; your very name execrated by your own men for the cruel work you gave them to do.

In the case of Mr. A. R. Boteler, both father and mother were far away. Any heart but that of Captain Martindale (and yours) would have been touched by that little circle, comprising a widowed daughter, just risen from her bed of illness, her little fatherless babes — the oldest not five years old — and her heroic sister. I repeat, any man would have been touched at that sight. But Captain Martindale — one might as well hope to find mercy in the heart of a wolf, bent on its prey to young lambs, as to search for such qualities in his bosom. You have chosen well your man for such deeds; doubtless you will promote him.

A colonel of the Federal army has stated that you deprived forty of your officers of their commands because they refused to carry out your malignant mischief. All honor to their names for this, at least. They are men; they have human hearts and blush for such a commander.

I ask who that does not wish infamy and disgrace attached to him forever would serve under you? Your name will stand on history's page as the hunter of weak women and innocent children; the hunter to destroy defenseless villages and refined and beautiful homes; to torture afresh the agonized hearts of suffering widows; the hunter of Africa's poor sons and daughters to lure them on to ruin and death of soul and body; the hunter with the relentless heart of a wild beast, the face of a field, and the form — of a man. O, earth, behold the monster!

Can I say, "God forgive you?" No prayer can be offered for you. Were it possible for human lips to raise your name heavenward, angels would thrust the foul thing back again and demons claim their own. The curses of thousands, the scorn of the manly and upright, and the hatred of the true and honorable will follow you and yours through all time and brand your name, "Infamy! Infamy!"

Again I demand, why have you burned my house? Answer as you must answer before the searcher of all hearts; why have you added this cruel, wicked deed to your many crimes?
End

[14] Mosby was a thorn in Sheridan's side and prior to the destruction of the Shenandoah by Sheridan, General Grant forwarded Sheridan the following order: "If you can possibly spare a division of cavalry, send them through Loudoun County, to destroy and carry off the crops, animals, Negroes, and all men under fifty years of age capable of bearing arms. In this way, you will get as many of Mosby's men. All male citizens under fifty can fairly be held as prisoners of war, and not as citizen prisoners. If not already soldiers, they will be made so the moment the Rebel army gets hold of them." This order by Grant to Sheridan was followed by another: "The families of most of Mosby's men are known and can be collected. I think they should be taken and kept at Fort McHenry, or some other secure place, as hostages for the good conduct of Mosby's men. When any of Mosby's men are caught, hang them without trial."

On September 22, 1864, approximately 120 of Mosby's men under Sam Chapman attacked a wagon train in the vicinity of Front Royal. To Chapman's surprise the reserve brigade of Merritt's cavalry division was a short distance behind the train. Before the fight could be called off the Confederates were surrounded. The only escape was to fight their way out. In the confusion a Federal lieutenant was ridden over and his body riddled with bullets. There were conflicted stories as to the death of the Federal. The Confederates stated he was killed in the excitement of battle while their smaller force was seeking to escape. The Federals said he was killed after he surrendered and six of Mosby's men captured while attacking the wagon train were ordered by Custer to be executed in retaliation.

On September 23, 1864, four men were shot before the citizens of Front Royal. One, Henry Rhodes, was tied to a horse and dragged through the streets before being shot. His family, hearing of his capture, went to Sheridan and begged for his life, but to no avail. The other two captives were offered freedom if they would disclose Mosby's headquarters. When they refused, they were hanged on a walnut tree and a placard was pinned to their clothing. "Such will be the fate of all of Mosby's men." The following are the names of the executed Confederates.

Lucian Love
Henry C. Rhodes
Thomas E. Anderson
William Thomas Overby
David L. Jones
Mr. Carter (first name unknown)

On November 6, 1864, Colonel Mosby captured twenty-seven men of Custer's command. After drawing lots seven were selected to be hanged for retaliation. Mosby had captured over 700 officers and men between September and November, but had waited patiently to get men of Custer's command. Three Federals were hanged and two shot. Attached to one victim was the following note: "These men have been hung in retaliation for an equal number of Colonel Mosby's men hung by order of General Custer, at Front Royal. Measure for measure."

Mosby then sent a scout to Sheridan's headquarters with this message: "Hereafter any prisoners falling into my hands will be treated with kindness due to their condition unless some new act of barbarity shall compel me reluctantly to adopt a course of policy repulsive to humanity."

This ended the "vendetta" between the two armies.

Aunt Lizzie of Clover Hill died November 15, 1864. It is said she died of shock and distress at seeing her home invaded, pillaged and everything but the dwelling house burned and destroyed. General Custer ordered destruction of the house but the dwelling was saved by the surrender of a small bag of gold, which had been entrusted to the eldest daughter, Julia, for safekeeping. All barns and outhouses were burned and livestock driven off or killed. All food supplies were either taken or destroyed.

[15] Hood crossed into Tennessee and tried to trap General Schofield's 30,000 troops at Spring Hill, but the Federals retreated northward almost through Hood's army. Hood followed and caught Schofield in Franklin, Tennessee on the Harpeth River. The federals threw up fieldworks while they began to cross the river. Hood directed a frontal assault, one of the most dramatic of the war. He was repulsed and Schofield retired to Nashville to rejoin Thomas.

Battle of Franklin

U.S.A.		C.S.A.	
Effectives	27,939	Effectives	26,897
Killed	189	Killed	1,750
Wounded	1,033	Wounded	3,800
Missing	1,104	Missing	702

Six Confederate generals died. One was General Pat Cleburne, upon whose staff Irving Buck had served until the latter was wounded in Jonesboro. Hood pressed on to Nashville with his battered troops and on December 15, 1864, Thomas struck Hood. On the sixteenth Hood's army was in full retreat and was being pursued by General James Harold Wilson's cavalry. General Forrest, C.S.A., fought gallant rear guard actions.

Battle of Nashville

U.S.A.		C.S.A.	
Effectives	49,773	Effectives	23,207
Killed	387	Killed*	
Wounded	2,562	Wounded*	
Missing	112	Missing*	

*No accurate report on Confederate casualties, however approximately 4,462 prisoners were taken by the Federals.

Hood left his beaten command with General Richard Taylor at Tupelo, Mississippi, January 14, 1865.

1865

Americas, Georgia
January 20, 1865

My dear Roy,

I yesterday received a letter from Williams dated Dec 14, which is the first intelligence from him since the battle of Franklin, in which he was wounded, the ball entering near the spinal column and ranging upwards and outward and entering the left arm about the middle from whence it was cut. At the time he wrote he was rapidly recovering at a private house 4 miles from Franklin.

His letter also conveyed to me the particulars of the death of General C — as you will suppose he died at the post of honor and in the thickest of the fight. Poor fellow I mourn his loss — Had become much attached to him but did not know how much I loved him until his death. I have now little inducement to return to the old Division — which Williams writes me is much reduced, and I am satisfied that its glory has departed with its leader.

Wish I could be with Williams during his confinement — I sympathize with him deeply — cut off from home as he is.

Phillips was the only one of our staff wounded. He lost a leg, and I suppose fell into the hands of the Enemy, as he was in a private house in Franklin at last accounts. Palmer of Lenny's staff was wounded and his Aid killed.

Alvin left day before yesterday for Montgomery after remaining three days with me. He was very loth to go — as he made several pleasant lady acquaintances while here.

The atmosphere of the town is very bad on wounds, mine will never get well, at least as long as there are so many bright eyes to give me their sympathy.

I will leave here on Monday week for the army after stopping at Box Spring and remaining a day or two with Alvin will join my command. My wound has not yet healed, but will be well enough by the 1st of Feby to permit me to return to duty. I have now been away for five months during which time, or at least a portion of it I have had a glorious time am now getting tired and will go back to work with pleasure.

My last letter from home was the one you enclosed me, dated Nov 24th.

Write me and direct to the Army. You are now two letters in my debt. Regards to all

Ever your friend
Buck

Americas, Ga
Jan. 22, 1865

My Dear Mother,

I wrote Lucie some three weeks ago, in reply to my birthday letter since which I have had nothing from home but suppose you have written and the letters have gone to the Army. I know of no better way of spending a rainy Sabbath when there is no church than by writing home.

You see that I am still in Americus. It seems impossible to tear myself away from so many attractions. When I found it was out of the question to get home, set about making my time pass as pleasantly as possible and have succeeded beyond my expectations. Have a great many pleasant friends and acquaintances, both male and female. The children all invite me to their candy pullings of which there has not been a few I enjoy it hugely. On two occasions it has rained and the entire party stayed all night and sat up with the girls until sunrise.

One of my particular young lady friends is a Miss Mattie Binns. She is one of the best and most sensible young ladies I have ever known and sings equal to Jenny Lind. We are said to be much alike in appearance. I showed her one of Lucie's letters and from it she seems to have fallen completely in love with Lou — talks of her a great deal, and says I must send her love. Alvin was much pleased with her. She has a younger sister who is much like Nellie the last time I saw her.

The day after New Year a party of us went down to Colonel Farlow plantation where we remained two days. Had a nice time, upon our return, myself, Miss Mattie, her sister Maude, Mrs. Callaway and Miss Holly Farlow (the two last are daughters of Col F) went home with Mrs. Callaway she married since I came here, and is a great friend of mine — lives about sixty miles distant — after spending a week very pleasantly we returned. Two days afterwards Alvin called by on his way from Charleston. Remained with me three days and passed his time most pleasantly. Made several pleasant acquaintances and says he enjoyed himself more than he has before since leaving home. He made a good impression — every one likes him. He went from here to Montgomery where Gen B's Head Quarters are for the present.

Received a letter from Geo Williams written a couple of weeks after the battle of Franklin in which engagement he was wounded. The ball entered near the spinal column and ranging upward and outward and lodging in his left arm near the middle, from whence it had been cut. He was at a private house near Franklin and convalescing. Poor boy I feel so much for him, wish I could have been with him. He came to see me as soon as he was exchanged last Sept. and did much to add to my comfort. He writes me that there is doubt as to Marsh Blakemore's death and a strong probability that he was only captured.

From William's account the fight must have been a terrific one, and as usual our division did the principal part of it. Gen'l. Cleburne had five balls to take effect upon him and Capt Phillips of our staff lost a leg. Geo says he met the General the morning of his death, that he was in the finest spirits and spoke of me in very flattering terms. He had recommended me for promotion before leaving Tuscumbia.[1]

I shall leave here in the course of ten days and after spending a week with Alvin will report to my command. My wound has almost entirely healed and by the 1st of next month I will be fit for duty.

I shall never cease to regret the causes which prevented my spending my long leave at home but I have nearly learned to bear such disappointments apathetically. But I have reason to be very thankful that as I could not get home that I fell into the hands of such kind friends — Mr. & Mrs. Farlow have been to me like parents. Had I have been their son I could not have been treated with more kindness. I trust I may one day have an opportunity to show them—*(Remainder of letter lost)*[2]

---

[1] Irving never received this promotion, but after the war in business in Baltimore he was a Colonel in the Maryland National Guard.

[2] At Appomattox on April 9, 1865, approximately 28,356 men of the proud army of the Confederacy surrendered to Grant's 120,000 troops and were paroled.

Six days later Lincoln died on April 15, 1865. The radicals were now in power. It would be a long reconstruction and this was to leave more scars on the South than war.

Lee's farewell order issued April 10, 1865 reads as follows:

"After four years of arduous service marked by unsurpassed courage and fortitude, the army of Northern Virginia has been compelled to yield to overwhelming numbers and resources.

"I need not tell the brave survivors of so many hard fought battles, who have remained steadfast to the last, that I have consented to this result from no distrust of them; but feeling that valor and devotion could accomplish nothing that could compensate for the loss that must have attended the continuance of the contest, I determined to avoid the useless sacrifice of those whose past services have endeared them to their countrymen.

"By the terms of the agreement, officers and men can return to their homes and remain until exchanged. You will take with you the satisfaction that proceeds from the consciousness of duty faithfully performed; and I earnestly pray that a Merciful God will extend to you His blessing and protection.

"With an unceasing admiration of your constancy and devotion to your Country, and a grateful remembrance of your kind and generous consideration for myself, I bid you all an affectionate farewell."

On April 26, 1865, General Joseph Johnston near Durham Station, North Carolina, surrendered his 37,047 men to Sherman on the same terms Lee had received.

The four years had been costly. The United States dead were 360,222; wounded were 275,175. The Confederate dead were 258,000; wounded unknown. Thus more Americans died than in World War I and II combined and the population at that time was only one-fourth the present population.

Capt. Irving Buck did rejoin the army and was present when General Johnston surrendered to Sherman at Greensboro, North Carolina.

He wrote the following on pages 290-291 in his book *Cleburne and His Command:*

While near East Point a fine-looking young officer, elegantly dressed, was brought in by Cleburne's scouts. He proved to be Lieut. James Coughlan, of the Sixth Kentucky Cavalry, and aide to Gen. Jacob D. Cox (afterwards Secretary of the Interior), commanding a division of the Twenty-third Federal Corps. When mess was ready he was asked to partake of it, such as it was, and treated with every courtesy. The next morning Cleburne learned that after the prisoner had been sent to the provost guard, in the rear, he was robbed of his hat, boots, and blanket. This greatly incensed the General, but being unable to detect the perpetrators or recover the property, he sent the victim an extra hat of his own, and one of the only pair of blankets he owned. This generous act later proved to be "bread cast upon the waters" — if not to Cleburne, at least to one of his military family.*

*Upon the surrender at Greensboro, North Carolina, the writer with several comrades separated from the bulk of the army, moving south, and had to cross the country to our homes in Virginia. We were destitute of money or subsistence. Learning that General Cox was in command, I rode to his quarters, and upon announcing my late position was most courteously received. When I referred to the capture of Lieutenant Coughlan the General said that after exchange the Lieutenant had spoken of the kind treatment received from Cleburne, and he further informed me that the young officer had been killed near the gin house at Franklin, Tennessee; which was close to the spot where Cleburne fell. Upon explaining my needs, General Cox directed his commissary to fill our wagon (we were fortunate enough to have secured one out of the army wreck) with hardtack, bacon, sugar and coffee. This afforded our party good living during the twelve days overland journey to our homes, as the sugar and coffee were current exchange for eggs, milk, and butter from the farm houses we passed.

Post Script

Winchester, Va.
Feb. 20, 1866

My own dear Em:

It has been a long, long time since I wrote to you last; have often thought of you and my dear old uncle whom I so much love and would have written to you long ere this, but didn't know where to direct my letters until I came down here day before yesterday and Alice had just received a letter from you, so I determined to write, believing you would be glad to hear from your Cousin Lucy.[1] Many, many changes have taken place, dear Em, since last we met and some sad ones to me in the loss of dear ones, and the harrowing scenes I have been called to pass through in the last four years. Pa and myself had managed to live rather comfortably until the fall of '64, when Sheridan and his band of robbers came into our once beautiful valley and laid waste the whole county; robbed us of everything we had almost; took every hog, sheep, chicken, turkey, duck, and everything of the kind we had, but one old horse and 3 cows and those I had to beg for as if I were begging for my life; took every ear of corn we had in the world, all our hay and fodder; did not leave us an armful to feed the horse and 3 cows they left. Took one wagon, all the gear, saddles and bridles, and not satisfied with that, they came into the house and took the last piece of meat and the last dust of flour we had in the world — all my preserves, and apple butter that I had worked so hard to get and left us to starve which is what they wanted, for when we would remonstrate with them about it they would curse us, and tell us to starve — that we ought to do it for breaking up the government. For weeks Pa, Welton, Lydia, and myself lived on bread made of horse feed and a little milk, when we could get it, as they milked the cows as often as we did — did not even leave us our vegetables, took all; would search the house sometimes a dozen times a day and take every thing they took a fancy to — scarcely left us bed clothes to cover with. Broke into my wardrobe, trunks and helped themselves to what they pleased. Oh, I can't begin to tell you one half we had to endure. Pa was forced to break up housekeeping as we had nothing to live on. I managed to get a little bread stuff for Pa and Welton. I went out in the spring and took a school. Pa seemed as if he couldn't leave the old Homestead, so he rented the same out to a free negro; he kept his room and Lydia cooked for him and Welton. He lived in that way until after the surrender when Tom and Mr. Adams came home and succeeded in getting provisions and put out a small corn crop. Then I went back home and kept house for them. Took a school at WaterLick but all together it was too much for my strength. My health gave way and I had to give it up in less than 3 months. Brother Charles and family came just before Christmas and he has the farm now and Pa is boarding with them which is fortunate, for us, as we had but little left to keep house on. I have had several letters recently from your Sister Mary. She had heard through

Aunt Lucy how Pa and I had been robbed and sent us a box of clothing, which was most acceptable to us. She has truly cast her bread upon the waters and I trust it may return twofold. I am truly sorry of Cousin Robert's illness, but hope most sincerely he may be restored to his family. I know it is selfish in me, but I could not help feeling sorry to hear that Cousin Gid was married for I had hoped he would make us another visit, but now that he has the cares of a family will have to abandon that hope. Give my love to him for me when you write.

The Presbyterians are carrying on a protracted meeting here. Dr. Stiles of Georgia is officiating. He is a very talented man. All were well when I left home. Brother C had been confined to his room with typhoid fever but is about again. Sister Helen, Alice and all join me in much love to you and Uncle. Give my kindest love to him and ask him to pray for me. Oh what would I give to see him and hear him preach. Direct your letters to Strasburg. We have no P.O. at WaterLick or Buckton. Love to the boys and write to your fond Cousin Lucie. *(Cousin of I.A. Buck)*

Miss Emma Buck, Lauderdale, Mississippi from Miss Lucy C. Buck 2/20/1866[2]

> In the parlor behind the chairs of the company
> Sunday Evening
> February 25, 1866

You don't value friends as I do Scott, else you'd not manifest such indifference to them to those at least who've been truer to you than to themselves.

I go tomorrow quite unexpectedly. 'Twill give thee as little pain to leave feeling there's any misunderstanding between us. I try to do what I think right. If sorrow is committed none regret it more than I.

I only write to say — "forget" that is if you can think of me kindly, otherwise I crave forgiveness.

Kiss your dear Ma and sister for me as I shall not be able to say "goodbye" in person. With all kind wishes most truly your friend

Lucie *(Buck to Scott Roy)*

> March 4, 1866

Dear Benton, *(Roy, in Selma, Alabama)*

I have not had a letter from you since the date of my last — now really two weeks — but will write you a few lines this evening just because I've nothing else to do — that I care much about doing just now. 'Tis just twilight and I am but now returned from a walk down street which I have not enjoyed as much as I would if you had been with me with a Mr. Johnson (a family relation) to Illinois — who expects to remain till June I have not seen her *(Lucy Buck)* for nearly six weeks I have been lame with rheumatism that length of time and have not been ____ in justice to myself to extend my walk further than the post office. She sent me a note which I've half a notion to enclose *(see preceeding letter)* — this I do not exactly understand it perhaps you may — she gave me a scolding the last time I was over there about — I hardly know what to make I have been studying medicine since the first of ____ have been insensible to digest this too. However on account of my rheumatism, I do not find something — a study as I expected. Aaron Brown and William Buck came yesterday to see the baby. Virginia Jackson told me O. that she would like to come but was afraid I'd give her baby to ____ and Susa Brown is in Jefferson teaching school and of course I miss her very much. ____ and Pa have been up to _____ _____ _____ _____ establishment and ____ on very good terms with Lilly and "little ____" and the rest of the ____. Have not made _____ thing out of Jenny Jackson yet — but have a strong notion to lay siege when some of my leisure moments — I'm afraid the post is already occupied by an army in a strong position having this advantage of interior lines in plain English am afraid that rascal Giles Cook is there ahead of me hoping for the best however in all things I remain your affectionate brother

Scott *(Roy)*[3]

The Tapp-Lockhart Company
Wholesale Hats and Caps
1206 Main Street
Columbia, South Carolina
December 21, 1906

My dear Jack,

    Read with greatest interest clipping from "Cosmopolitan" — The wanton and unnecessary butchery at Franklin, has as far as I have read and studied, no parallel in history of the war, for time and numbers embraced — General Forrest pointed out to Hood, as does the author of the article above referred to, that by crossing the Harpeth river, he (Hood) could have turned the Federal left, and without the loss of 100 men accomplished all he did, by the dreadful sacrifice of life, in the course he pursued. The result would have been, a hasty retreat or capture, as the Federals were fighting with a river in their rear — a most dangerous position — Schofield merely halted at Franklin, to gain time in which to allow his troops and trains to close up, after their marvelous escape from capture at Spring Hill, and would have gladly withdrawn to Nashville, so soon as this was accomplished. But Hood, stung by his failure in not having bagged Schofield at Spring Hill, made such rapid pursuit, as to compel the latter to make a stand and fight. Smarting under his too late discovered, inexcusable blunder, Hood in attempting to retrieve his error, did not hesitate as to making a front attack, without artillery, where a dangerless one, on the flank, was plainly practicable. The sickening carnage was the natural result. I have not at hand official records as to losses — below the grade of General officers — but some conception of these may be formed from the fact, that 1 Maj. General and 5 Brigadiers were killed outright — and 7 Generals wounded — a total casualty in this grade of 13 — all within the space of less than two hours. This record cannot be matched at Manassas, Gettysburg or Chickamauga. It has truly been said, that "Franklin was the grave of the Army of Tennessee". Now where does the responsibility rest? I answer: with Hood primarily, and President Davis principally, when he removed their able General and unrivalled strategist, Joe Johnston, and placed the incompetent Hood in Command of the Army — after he had served inconspicuously, as Corp Commander less than six months. Promoting him over such true and tried officers, as Hardee, Stewart, Cheatham, Cleburne and others. The announcement of his appointment to command, caused outspoken expressions of dissatisfaction, almost mutinous from the troops, who were no mean Judges of military ability, but after the appointment was positively made, they loyally gave Hood support, as evidenced by their gallant conduct and losses, before Atlanta, Ezra Church, Jonesboro, Spring Hill, Franklin and Nashville.

When in New Orleans, last spring, I was a guest with General Govan, of George Williams (Govan's, A.A.G.). The General is the sole surviving General officer of Cleburne's division — He is quite infirm and not equal to the labor of writing at length. At the solicitation of George and myself, he made pencil notes of the Tennessee campaign — These I took home and from them, wrote an article, which I submitted to Govan, and it will appear in the "Confederate Veteran" — over his signature. This article will, I think, fully fix the responsibility for the shameful failure of Spring Hill, which had it been the success, easily in the grasp of Hood, Franklin and Nashville battles would not have occurred. Just think, discouraged troops, along the only road of safety open to them, in the face of 40,000 concentrated men, and so close did they defile by, it is said that they "lit their pipes at the Confederate camp files." A strong skirmish line across the pike would have demoralized and thrown them into confusion, retarded and intercepted their retreat, and made them an easy prey with the coming of dawn — But nothing was done, although the Commander of the Army had full knowledge of the existing conditions and was less than a mile away. The Shame of it! My apology for inflicting this long communication upon you, is that I feel strongly upon these subjects, The active participants, and those possessed of facts, are becoming so few, perhaps it is well that one surviving should leave a record. My regret is that time and opportunity have not been mine to go into this and other matters, more fully. For your better understanding, will add, that Columbia — from which the initial move was made, on 27th November, is in round figures, ten or twelve miles from Spring Hill, and latter about same distance from Franklin — and also the same to Nashville — all in a direct northern line. In absence of map, these distances may vary a little, but are approximately correct. Having no time during the day, I've come down to the store to write this, and it is now 10:15 P.M.

It gratifies me beyond expression to learn of your improvement, which I hope and believe will be permanent, but be patient, until this is assured. I told Tapp that I was coming down to write you, and he asked to be most kindly remembered.

With a heart full of love and best wishes for a happy Xmas to all.
Affectionately yours,[4]
Irving

---

[1] A cousin of Lucy R. Buck of Bel Air.

[2] This letter reveals the desperate situation of the Southern people after the war.

[3] Scott Roy married Mattie Cook.

[4] This letter was found among Irving's war letters.

After Appomattox
How One Virginia Family Lived
Through Reconstruction[1]

In April, 1865, Mr. Buck[2] nearing sixty years of age, and living in The Shenandoah Valley, was faced with the problem of how to provide for a large family of dependents, old and young; having a small farm, left bare and desolate by the ravages of war.

With the exception of an enclosure around the yard and garden, there was not left a panel of fencing on the place; the fields having been used as a favorite camping ground by the invading armies, who had speedily destroyed the fences, using the rails for their camp fires, tramping down the growing crops and vegetation; the ground cut up and marred by horses and vehicles and rendered useless for cultivation.

One season, by some means, there was raised a few bushels of corn, which was only saved from robbery and destruction at the hands of marauding soldiers, by borrowing from a neighbour an old, crippled horse, with a dump-cart, hauling to an out building where it was shucked at night, the father, mother and children, boys and girls working by the light of a lantern; the corn was then carried in bags up a ladder and deposited in an attic without door or windows, through a small opening, made by removing a few pieces of the weatherboarding, in the gable end of the house, and the boards then nailed back in place to conceal the prized store of grain from prying eyes, for, upon this small store, the family were dependent for their sustenance.

So desperate was the need of food at one time that they were reduced to the necessity of using the sweepings from the old mill, consisting of grain of various kinds together with corn cobs, which had been ground for horse feed. But for these slender resources, supplemented by what vegetables could be raised in the garden, the matter of near starvation was not remote, for the situation of this family was not different from that of others in the neighbourhood, who were likewise in sore need.

The war being ended, the father had to consider how he was to resume farming operations, with the fields laid waste, all the work animals carried off by the invaders, as well as the former servants, the implements, harness and tools worn out or destroyed, no seed for sowing another crop, the prospect was indeed gloomy, but gradually, by some means, these obstacles were overcome, a start made and the family kept in food and scant clothing; the latter by the women ripping up old garments, turning the material and putting together as best they could. The five small boys had jackets and trousers made of bed ticking, and looked like a flock of small zebras running about the place.

After the surrender of General Johnston, in North Carolina, the two elder sons (who had been in the Confederate army from the beginning of the war) with a group of other soldiers, were given an old army ambulance and two small mules with which to travel back home. These two mules solved the problem of work animals, and for many years, did noble service in helping to make the farm crops and provide the means of a living for the family.

The father and older sons, though all unaccustomed to strenuous labor, went into the fields, and worked together, early and late, even the little eight year old boy was given his tasks, and with the help of the older ones, to keep up and "hoe his own row".

Thus through the years, until old age was upon him, did this father work and plan, living with Spartan like simplicity and rigid economy, but with the consciousness of having succeeded in maintaining his family and holding them in the home until they were old enough to go out into the world and do for themselves.

William R. Buck

----

[1] This article was written by William R. Buck of Bel Air. He was nine years old in 1865.

[2] William Mason Buck, Irving's father.

Other Homes and Occupants Mentioned
in the Front Royal Area
(1861 - 1865)

MOUNTAIN VIEW, located two miles west of Front Royal on the South Fork of the Shenandoah River. Uncle Newton (Dr. Issac Newton Buck, 1801 - 1877) was an uncle of William Mason Buck. His first wife was Susan Taylor. Their children were:

Marcus T. (died Aug. 12, 1862)
Catherine B.
Mary C.

Dr. Buck's second wife was Aunt Jane, (Janet U. Lovell, 1815 - 1893). Their children were:

Sue (Susan R. Buck), 1836 - 1880. (Was engaged to Willie
Richardson who died of wounds, May 29, 1862)
Charlie, (Charles Newton Buck) 1842 - 1925. (Captured in F r o n t
Royal)
Nannie, (Nannie Lovell Buck)
James, (James C. Buck)
Robert, (Robert Buck)
Willie, (Thomas William Buck) 1845 - 1877. (Captured Oct. 1863)

BUCKTON, the home of John Gill Buck and his wife, Eliza McKay Buck, was located near Waterlick, Virginia (between Front Royal and Strasburg). Their children were:

Sandy, (William Alexander) "Most gallant soldier I've ever seen in action,"
(Gen. W.E. Jones)
Meredith
Annice
Elizabeth
Thomas
Samuel Dawson, Capt. C.S.A. "Buck is the bravest man I ever knew," (Gen.
Early)
Mollie
John Gill, Jr. (Born after his father's death)

BLOOMFIELD was located near Berryville in Clarke County, Virginia. It was the home of Aunt Cattie (Catherine Elizabeth Buck, 1805 - 1882) and her husband, John B. Larue. Aunt Cattie, the only sister of William Mason Buck, had no issue, but her husband had several children by a previous marriage.

Aunt Cattie cared for Walker, the son of John Newton Buck. John's wife died in 1859. He was a brother to William Mason Buck.

WILLOW GLEN—The Cloud family home near Front Royal.

HAPPY CREEK—Old Marshall home near Front Royal. Built by James Markham Marshall who married Hester Morris, daughter of Robert Morris.

Hester was the number two female behind Martha Washington in the Colonies. Her father financed the Revolution.

Obituaries

Capt. Irving A. Buck
(From the Reporter, of Front Royal, Va.)

Our community was never more shocked than when Capt. Irving A. Buck died on September 8, 1912. In the full bloom of health, without a moment's warning, the summons came, as he had often expressed the wish that it should, with no lingering nor long suffering. He was in his seventy-second year.

Irving A. Buck's boyhood was spent in his ancestral home, Belair. When the War of the States began, he volunteered in Company B, 17th Virginia Infantry. After serving a few months he was detailed as a clerk in the office of General Beauregard, and from thence was made adjutant general on the staff of Gen. Pat Cleburne. General Cleburne greatly appreciated him and a warm friendship existed between them. He was relied upon in time of danger, and never failed. His career as a soldier was marked by ability and distinguished service. His courage was evinced in most trying ordeals. He was wounded while bearing an important dispatch to the front for General Cleburne in the battle of Jonesboro, Ga., September 1, 1864 (Atlanta).

Succeeding the war, with desolation on every side, Captain Buck was for many years a popular and successful merchant in Baltimore. In later days he moved to Front Royal, Va., the town of his birth, and remained there till the end. He wrote a history entitled "Cleburne and His Men" which was highly regarded both in Europe and America. He was united in marriage with Miss Fannie Ricards of Maryland, in January, 1871; and though no children were born to them, they were through life as young lovers.

Captain Buck had a singularly bright mind. He was ever polite and gentle in his nature, and impressed all who knew him with his own delightful personality. Courageous and firm in his belief of the right, he was charitable to the views of others. He was for several years Commander of William Richardson Camp, U.C.V., and his interest in and brotherly love of his comrades was a distinct characteristic. He was active for the erection of a monument to the Confederate veterans of his native county, and he was proud of the completed work as it stands near the courthouse at Front Royal.

The funeral exercises were conducted by the Camp Chaplain, Dr. J.W. Webster, On September 10. The interment was largely attended. The pallbearers were composed of the officials of the Front Royal National Bank, with which he had been connected for several years. A large number of veterans followed his bier to Prospect Hill Cemetery. He was a prominent Mason, and the Masonic honors were conferred at the grave, after which there was a military salute by Company D. Beautiful flowers covered the grave.

The editor concludes: "We wish we could pay a proper tribute to his unselfish and loyal friendship. He has gone from us and the circle he adorned is broken, but in the heart his memory will ever be green."

(Vol. 20, p. 535. *Confederate Veteran*)

COL. THOMAS B. ROY

Thomas Benton Roy died in Berlin, Germany, on November 20, 1910, aged seventy-two years. He was a native of Warren County, Va. In April, 1861, he enlisted in the Warren Rifles, which was afterwards Company B, 17th Virginia Infantry. At Manassas he was detailed as clerk in General Beauregard's office, and with that officer was transferred to the Western Army in February, 1862. At Shiloh he rode with the staff, though having no commission. Soon after General Hardee applied to Beauregard for a trained adjutant general, and young Roy was recommended and commissioned captain as assistant adjutant general and assigned to General Hardee's staff. His superior ability was immediately recognized, and he was speedily promoted to major and chief of staff. Later he was advanced to lieutenant colonel and then to colonel. Upon General Hood's accession to the command of the army Colonel Roy was offered the position of chief of General Hood's staff with the rank of brigadier general, but Colonel Roy preferred to remain with General Hardee. Upon one occasion he was bearer of important dispatches to the War Department. Arriving in Richmond, he was given an audience with the Chief Executive of the Confederacy, who naturally inquired concerning affairs of the Western Army. Colonel Roy's clear and succinct portrayal and intelligent understanding of the situation so impressed the Confederate President as to receive his commendation.

From a letter of Maj. George A. Williams, of New Orleans, the following is copied: "After the war he went to Selma, Ala., where, while editing the Selma Messenger, he qualified for the bar. He then married Sallie, the second daughter of General Hardee. He became junior partner in the law firm of Brooks, Haralson & Roy, and at once took high rank and became one of the leading lawyers of his State. The late Senator John T. Morgan said: 'I consider him the brightest of the young men at the Alabama bar.' His professional career was cut short on the threshold. A failure in the sense of hearing obliged him to forego his cherished ambition and condemned him to a life of inactivity. For the purpose of educating an adopted daughter, they removed to France and then to Germany, whence they never returned to America. Here was a man whose life was a beautiful outgrowth of our best traditions, a development of the cherished ideals of our fathers. He was a fluent writer, a brilliant conversationalist, and all his expressions were flavored with a chaste, even classic, humor. He was of judicial temperament, of charming personality, altogether an admirable, lovable man, of whom his family and people may well be proud."

Irving A. Buck, of Front Royal, Va., writes: "No braver or more accomplished soldier ever followed the Confederate or any other flag, and in his death has passed one of Warren County's most distinguished sons."

(Vol. 19, p. 81 *Confederate Veteran*)

Capt. George A. Williams

Capt. George A. Williams, Superintendent of the Confederate Home of Louisiana, died at his home in New Orleans, on Sunday, December 29, 1929, at the age of eighty-seven. Attended by his comrades in gray, he was laid to rest with other comrades in the Army of Tennessee tomb in Metairie Cemetery.

Captain Williams for many years was vice president of the Louisiana Division of the Army of Tennessee. He had been a member of the board and Superintendent of the Confederate Home for eleven years, during which time the number of veterans in the Home dwindled from eighty-five to fifteen.

Captain Williams was a native of Front Royal, Va., and there enlisted for the Confederacy, joining Company B, 17th Virginia Regiment, serving for a time as clerk on the staff of General Beauregard, the boy soldier was with the general when he organized the Army of Tennessee. Rising to the rank of captain, he also served as Assistant Adjutant General to Gen. St. John R. Liddell, of Louisiana *(and Gen. Daniel C. Govan)*.

Captain Williams moved to New Orleans in 1869, and in 1874 participated in the famous battle of Canal Street, in which the carpetbaggers were routed.

He became a member of large tobacco and cotton firm of New Orleans, and later founded the wholesale dry goods firm of Williams-Richardson, and still later the Williams Pharmacy. He was at one time a director of the Union Bank and on the board of trade, and president of the freight and transportation bureau.

In 1885, Captain Williams married Miss Heda Kock, of New Orleans, and he is survived by a son and four grandchildren.

Captain Williams was a member of the governing committee of the New Orleans and Pickwick Clubs, also a member of the Boston Club.

(Vol. 38, p. 66. *Confederate Veteran*)

Alvin Duvall Buck

Alvin D. Buck, eldest son of the late Wm. M. Buck of Bel Air was born in Warren County 84 years ago. He was a member of the Warren Rifles, but was detailed at Beauregard's headquarters under Col. Jordan until the end of the war.

After the surrender he moved to Kentucky where he married Miss Rhett Majors returning here later where he made his home for sometime. He then went to Springdale, PA. and lived there until his death which took place on Sunday.

Surviving are four children, Rob't M., Orville M., and Irving A. Buck and Miss Blanche Buck, a sister Miss Laura Buck of Front Royal and a brother Wm. R. Buck of Norfolk.

Mr. Buck was in his earlier years considered an excellent business man, and was especially efficient as a book keeper and accountant. He was of a sociable, kindly disposition and knew how to make and keep friends.

She never married nor did any of her sisters. After the war her father lost, among other things, the ancestral home, "Bel Air", Capon Springs Hotel and Resort, and a block of stores in down town Front Royal.

Lucy moved to a newly built residence in Front Royal which she named "Cozy Corner". It was there she died quietly in 1918.

She kept a diary and the Civil War portion was published under the title, *Sad Earth, Sweet Heaven.*